Using Picture Storybooks to Teach Literary Devices

Recent Titles in Using Picture Books to Teach

Using Picture Storybooks to Teach Literary Devices: Recommended Books for Children and Young Adults
Susan Hall

Using Picture Storybooks to Teach Literary Devices: Recommended Books for Children and Young Adults, Volume 2
Susan Hall

Using Picture Storybooks to Teach Character Education
Susan Hall

Using Picture Storybooks to Teach Literary Devices

Recommended Books for Children and Young Adults

Volume 3

Susan Hall

Using Picture Books to Teach

ORYX PRESS

Westport, Connecticut • London

*The rare Arabian Oryx is believed to have inspired the myth of the unicorn. This desert
antelope became virtually extinct in the early 1960s. At that time several groups of
international conservationists arranged to have nine animals sent to the Phoenix Zoo
to be the nucleus of a captive breeding herd. Today the Oryx population
is over 1,000, and over 500 have been returned to the Middle East.*

Library of Congress Cataloging-in-Publication Data is available.

British Library Cataloguing in Publication Data is available.

Copyright © 2002 by The Oryx Press

ISBN 1–57356–350–1

First published in 2002

Oryx Press, 88 Post Road West, Westport, CT 06881
An imprint of Greenwood Publishing Group, Inc.
www.greenwood.com

Printed in the United States of America

The paper used in this book complies with the
Permanent Paper Standard issued by the National
Information Standards Organization (Z39.48–1984).

10 9 8 7 6 5 4 3 2 1

CONTENTS

❖❖❖❖❖❖❖❖❖❖❖

INTRODUCTION

❖❖❖❖❖❖❖❖❖❖❖

In K–12 language arts programs, among other curriculum objectives, students are expected to develop the ability to read with discriminating appreciation and understanding. They are also expected to be able to organize their thoughts and write clearly with some stylistic awareness. Understanding, recognizing, and applying literary devices is part of this education. To meet curriculum objectives, educators frequently use supplemental materials to enhance textbook content. Although textbooks usually include "suggested resources" in conjunction with specific class assignments, such lists are often dated, and materials are often unavailable.

One dependable teaching resource for teaching literary devices is this book, *Using Picture Storybooks to Teach Literary Devices*. This edition, volume three in the series, is a detailed index to 120 picture storybooks published through the year 2000, which are either in print now or very likely accessible through interlibrary loan. All clearly demonstrate literary devices, such as irony, or metaphor, or tone, and all are published by mainstream book publishers and have received favorable reviews from professional book reviewing journals such as *The Horn Book* and *School Library Journal*. The first of the two books of the series, published in 1990, includes picture storybooks published mainly in the mid- to late 1980s. Volume 2, published in 1994, features books published from 1990 through 1994, as well as many older, still available, picture storybooks considered classics, such as *Angus and the Ducks*, *How the Grinch Stole Christmas*, and *Where the Wild Things Are*.

As in previous volumes, the focus of this index to literary devices is on picture storybooks, that core of a genre the public recognizes simply as a "picture book." Except for blurring "storybook" standards a bit in order to accommodate the occasional Randolph Caldecott Medal winner, all entries in *Using Picture Storybooks to Teach Literary Devices* are truly fictional picture storybooks.

Entries in this book are organized by author name under 41 alphabetically arranged literary devices, from alliteration through understatement, according to the following sample. Starred entries indicate an "all-age" resource. Shown below as a sample of the format used is an entry for a book listed under "Alliteration."

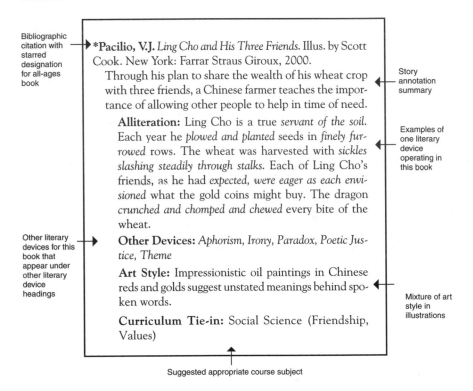

Bibliographic citation with starred designation for all-ages book

Story annotation summary

Examples of one literary device operating in this book

Other literary devices for this book that appear under other literary device headings

Mixture of art style in illustrations

*Pacilio, V.J. *Ling Cho and His Three Friends.* Illus. by Scott Cook. New York: Farrar Straus Giroux, 2000.

Through his plan to share the wealth of his wheat crop with three friends, a Chinese farmer teaches the importance of allowing other people to help in time of need.

Alliteration: Ling Cho is a true *servant of the soil.* Each year he *plowed and planted* seeds in *finely furrowed* rows. The wheat was harvested with *sickles slashing steadily through stalks.* Each of Ling Cho's friends, as he had *expected, were eager as each envisioned* what the gold coins might buy. The dragon *crunched and chomped and chewed* every bite of the wheat.

Other Devices: *Aphorism, Irony, Paradox, Poetic Justice, Theme*

Art Style: Impressionistic oil paintings in Chinese reds and golds suggest unstated meanings behind spoken words.

Curriculum Tie-in: Social Science (Friendship, Values)

Suggested appropriate course subject

TEACHING WITH PICTURE STORYBOOKS

In teaching any skill, moving from simple to complex is one sound method. For language arts educators (of any grade level), abundant examples of good literary models exist in the form of very readily obtainable picture storybooks. Teachers should not underestimate this astonishingly versatile resource to enhance student reading and writing skills. Consider these situations:

- An elementary reading teacher is trying to show students how to recognize simile and metaphor or flashback and foreshadowing.
- A middle school language arts instructor is attempting to instill the concept of atmosphere in the short story.

- A high school literature class needs assistance with ambiguity in character dialogue or with paradox in the plot of a novel.
- A creative writing instructor wants to help students include strong imagery in their work.

Large truths come from small stories. Far from being trivial or trite, picture books can readily supply a sophisticated lesson in understanding satire as well as in recognizing how motif can strengthen a story's message.

Even at the picture storybook level, note the special mirror that satire holds up to life. An eye-opening perspective on our culture's manic pursuit of recreational entertainments is shown for what it is in Russell Hoban's *Trouble on Thunder Mountain* (Orchard Books, 2000). The O'Saurus (as in dino-saurus), family receives a letter from a "developer" regarding their property.

> I am delighted to tell you that Thunder Mountain has been bought by Megafright International. We are going to make it flat and build a hi-tech plastic-mountain theme park on the flat place. We are ready to start work now, so you have twenty-four hours [beginning yesterday] to get out.

A conscious use of literary devices captures the reader's spirit and serves as writing models. Note the uplifting motif represented in the parable about an eagle raised as a chicken in Christopher Gregorowski's retelling of an African tale. In *Fly, Eagle, Fly!* (Simon & Schuster, 2000) children learn they are not bound to a humdrum existence, but are made for something truly glorious. "You belong not to the earth, but to the sky. Fly, Eagle, fly!" is the refrain that finally enables the bird to lean forward and be swept upward into its potential.

No literary genre can so easily instill an awareness of style as can these thirty-two-page wonders. Educators know that powerful language exists in picture books exactly as it can be found in other forms of literature. Perhaps brevity forces authors to choose just the right words.

See this in George Ella Lyon's *One Lucky Girl* (Dorling Kindersley, 2000). In the aftermath of a tornado, a mother suddenly realizes that in the general destruction around her, her baby has been swept away. The author describes her awareness thus: "All the screams nobody had screamed tore out of my mother's mouth."

Regardless of grade level, picture storybooks, under pedagogical direction, help students focus with attention and purpose to recognize an author's tone toward his audience, attitude toward his subject, and overall theme. Short as picture storybooks are, it requires only a single class period to make inference apparent, irony realized, caricature obvious, and allusions recognized, because such devices occur at a level "even a child" can perceive.

A whole genre of fine writing is lost when educators focus only on "grade-level" material. Before introducing Charles Dickens or Mark Twain, or Edgar Allen Poe, see what the quirky mind of David Wisniewski or Anthony Browne has to offer. Study the sociology of Byrd Baylor or Mem Fox. Face the reality issues Eve Bunting highlights. Enjoy the wise slapstick of Brock Cole. Rejoice in Kevin Henkes, the champion of every small person. Surround yourself in the quiet, straight, but great language of Allen Say. And, marvel at the freshness of the enduring contributions of perennial voices like Russell Hoban, William Steig, and James Howe, who can still say it best. Thank goodness there are picture storybook writers who create clearly, succinctly, and even with some stylistic and linguistic brilliance.

Teachers in other disciplines should also use picture storybooks to provide background for character studies, to set the mood for historical topics, to introduce a specific scientific lesson, or even to illustrate human relations issues. And don't forget to share picture storybook art to teach artistic medium and style.

Picture storybooks ought to be part of a student's precollege educational career from beginning to end, and even beyond. Liberal use of picture storybooks throughout the school curriculum will ensure that the wrestling team, the honors physics students, the debater, and the no-nonsense future farmer will not miss the charming vignette about Henry David Thoreau in *Henry Hikes to Fitchburg* by D.B. Johnson (Houghton Mifflin, 2000) even if they never wade through *Walden*. Tim Myers' *Basho and the Fox* (Marshall Cavendish, 2000) might inspire someone to become an aficionado of haiku poetry.

Picture books should not be the exclusive domain of the preschool crowd and those who are hurrying to reach chapter-book status. Give picture storybooks to mature readers, who can truly appreciate their quality. Teach from them, and do it often.

SCOPE

Picture storybooks were deliberately chosen to illustrate literary devices. A picture storybook should not be mistaken for a picture concept book, which might set a rainy afternoon mood, describe a walk on the beach, show what a bird's day is like, define and give examples of geometric shapes, describe occupations that use heavy equipment, or otherwise share any of an endless assortment of quasi-informational topics.

A picture storybook should also not be mistaken for an illustrated storybook. A surfeit of words punctuated with only occasional illustrations at key junctures along the way would suggest an illustrated storybook, even if it has a picture storybook's shape and size. Text and artwork are balanced and work together in a picture storybook in a cooperative way that does not happen in an illustrated storybook.

As opposed to the picture concept book, the short story, or the illustrated storybook, the content of a picture storybook is roughly equal in text and art. The story has a recognizable beginning that sets up a problem to be resolved, a middle that describes means to that end, and a conclusion that resolves the problem. Art is vital to picture storybooks, because it enhances and clarifies the text.

At their best, picture storybooks always mesh visual and auditory components into a complete creative experience. Each supplies its half of the whole. Without one or the other there would not be that interlocking harmony in which the illustrations augment and tell those parts of the story line that the text omits.

This is readily apparent in Marie-Louise Fitzpatrick's simple tale *Lizzy and Skunk* (DK Ink, 2000). Lizzy's hand puppet Skunk becomes lost. The text does not state how this happens, but the reader can see in the illustrations that a cat is carrying the puppet out a window. Later, while passersby are looking up in a tree and seeing Skunk, the reader notices the marauding cat, escaping at the base of the tree.

Art and text also mesh in picture storybooks for more mature readers as in Carmen Agra Deedy's powerful and dignified story of heroic justice, *The Yellow Star: The Legend of King Christian X of Denmark* (Atlanta, Peachtree, 2000). The king devises a plan to thwart the Nazi goal of divisive politics. The author does not describe the plan; she shows it. During his regular morning ride before his subjects in Copenhagen, the king appears wearing a yellow star. The people quietly understand his intent. Soon, everyone in the city is prominently displaying a yellow star on his or her clothing. The message is clear. There are only Danes living in Denmark.

LITERARY FORMS AND LITERARY DEVICES

The distinction between *literary form* and *literary device* is significant. Forms of literature such as the legend or parable or tall tale are excluded as index entries in this book. Devices in literature such as hyperbole or poetic justice or caricature are included as index entries. Form is the whole effect; device is one specific element that adds to the whole effect. Thus, tall tale is a literary form. Within it one might expect to find such specific literary devices as hyperbole or poetic justice or caricature.

Having made this distinction, there is in this index to literary devices one *form* that has been included as a *device*. "Parody" creates an overall effect as a tall tale does, and so it's a literary *form*. But parody that comically imitates a well-known work can also operate as one separate device within a literary piece. For example, among other devices, such as analogy, and stereotype, which are also operating in this book, consider the hilarious parody of the classic detective image in David Wisniewski's *Tough Cookie* (Lothrop, Lee & Shepard, 1999).

> They call me a tough cookie. I guess I am. Came from a regular batch. Lots of dough. Lived the high life. Top of the Jar. Then I hit bottom and stayed here. It was rough. Still is. But you get used to it. Life's still sweet. Just a little stale.

ALL-AGES STORYBOOKS

Many picture storybooks possess universal appeal. Books that speak to all ages were deliberately selected for inclusion in this latest volume of *Using Picture Storybooks to Teach Literary Devices*. Sibling rivalry, childish fears, friendship dilemmas, and other classic "picture book" subjects are not excluded from this compendium. But when they are included, such books offer a writing style and message that set them apart by exhibiting more than a predictable, simple resolution to a baby problem. These books contribute fresh awareness to the world's store of knowledge.

Some picture storybooks take the all-ages characteristic to an added dimension of mature content through choice of subject or treatment of a topic, as in the aforementioned *The Yellow Star*. Denmark was the only European nation to universally reject the Nazi propaganda against Jews. Simple respect for all humanity prevailed, a lesson young and old can appreciate.

Byrd Baylor's *The Table Where Rich People Sit* (Charles Scribner's Sons, 1994) makes nonsense of the prevailing attitude that people need possessions to merit worth. A disgruntled daughter learns to see the true wealth her impoverished family possesses when they sit down to list what they have of value.

And the growing awareness that human beings have not acquitted themselves very well in their treatment of animals, the "lesser" creatures they share earth with, is addressed in a lyrical, highly symbolic story by Laura Berkeley. *The Spirit of the Maasai Man* (Barefoot Books, 2000) could serve as a new paradigm. Maybe future generations will begin to reject dominance as the natural relationship between humans and animals.

Not one book listed in this book is just a plodding story buttressed with grand illustrations to capture a buyer's attention. These books delight with delicious humor and chill with wonderfully expressed truths. They all resonate within the reader's soul. They are "keepers."

In fact, more than one adult is sure to purchase a picture storybook as a gift—for another adult. Kalamazoo, Michigan, public librarian Mary Calletto

Rife said the 2001 Caldecott Medal winner *So You Want to Be President?* will be around for a long time, not only because of the illustrations but also because of the subject matter. "It appeals to everybody." She bought a copy for her twenty-two-year-old grandson, a history buff.

PICTURE STORYBOOK ART STYLES

The complex sophistication of today's book art makes identification of specific art styles and media sometimes difficult for those of us who are not artists. Nevertheless, since art is usually the first thing about a picture book that captures reader (child or adult) attention, and since art contributes so much to the emotional and cognitive impact of a story, some limited reference to general art forms and elements will be included with each entry.

Matching the right style of art to a story's text can mean the difference between a book's being a memorable success or a short-lived failure. David Small's caricature style of cartoon art was especially suited to the 2000 Caldecott winner, Judith St. George's *So You Want to Be President?* (Philomel, 2000), because it offers insights into the lives and careers of various American leaders. Small noted in a *Kalamazoo Gazette* article by James Sanford that this project "gave me a chance to put together the adult and the kid sides of my career." He is also an editorial artist for such publications as the *New Yorker* and the *Atlantic Monthly.*

Cartoon is an art form that produces simple, lively line drawings, colored or not, like those of comic book drawings. The cartoon style is employed to depict both serious and humorous topics. Imaginative, exaggerated features and wonderful detail are possible through this art style.

Collage is the technique of arranging and mounting such diverse materials as fabric, paper, photographs, and paint on a two-dimensional surface in order to create a multitextured scene.

Expressionism exhibits distorted proportions and perspectives. There is exaggeration of natural color, shape, and line to produce a variety of emotional effects such as exuberant joy or somber anxiety. Images may be bold and splashy or free flowing and delicate.

Folk is a term that refers to generally recognized ethnic or cultural influences that adhere to perpetuation of a regional collective awareness. Traditional decorative patterns are employed, which depend not on the particular artist's interpretation but rather on common design elements and common media. This style produces art in which the work of one artist is largely indistinguishable from that of others who choose to depict the same specific society and era. This is true, for example, of Japanese scroll art, which remains distinctly similar through the centuries.

Impressionism emphasizes artistic play with light through color application. Usually figures and objects are depicted in fuzzy outlines rather than in precise detail. Instead of blended strokes, paint is stippled closely in dabs, which depends upon the eye to mix them into a recognizable image. The effect demonstrates the scintillating and changeable quality of light through shadows and fleeting glimpses.

Naïve style is sometimes called "primitive" because of its unsophisticated, childlike, clear outlines that often disregard perspective. Human or animal figures are usually depicted in frontal or profile views with little differentiation in facial detail. Every inch of the page seems filled with simple drawings of extremely detailed intricate scenes. Colors are brilliant rather than a subtle mix of tones that attempt to create shading.

Realism is an attempt to depict figures and objects in close approximation to lifelike color, texture, proportions, and arrangements as perceived in the visible world. This style does not necessarily attempt to produce photographically exact images. Objects are permitted the artist's special vitality of expression.

Surrealism is the deliberate and unexpected combination of incongruous but meticulously rendered, realistic appearing objects assembled in an improbable supernatural atmosphere that defies everyday logic. Impossibly startling, haunting, somewhat repellent imagery is juxtaposed for shock value. The ancient Egyptian sphinx is a sculptural example of surrealistic design.

LITERARY DEVICES

❖❖❖❖❖❖❖❖❖❖❖

LITERARY DEVICES INCLUDED

To broaden the range of teaching opportunities, this third compendium of *Using Picture Storybooks to Teach Literary Devices* includes forty-one devices to emulate as reading and writing models, which adds ten devices to the lists in the first two volumes in the series. Besides the thirty-one used in previous editions, Anachronism, Antihero, Antithesis, Black Humor, Cliché, Connotation, Motif, Oxymoron, Parallelism, and Serendipity are included.

Alliteration	Flash-forward	Parody
Allusion	Foreshadowing	Personification
Ambiguity	Hyperbole	Poetic Justice
Anachronism	Imagery	Point of View
Analogy	Inference	Pun
Antihero	Internal Rhyme	Satire
Antithesis	Irony	Serendipity
Aphorism	Metaphor	Simile
Atmosphere	Motif	Stereotype/Reverse
Black Humor	Onomatopoeia	Stereotype
Caricature	Oxymoron	Symbol
Cliché	Paradox	Theme
Connotation	Parallel Story	Tone
Flashback	Parallelism	Understatement

Definitions for literary devices in this volume have been created with help from J.A. Cuddon's *The Penguin Dictionary of Literary Terms and Literary Theory*, 4th edition, revised by C.E. Preston (Penguin Books) 1999.

ALLITERATION

A repeated consonant sound occurring at the beginning of neighboring words or within words to establish mood.

> Example: To sit in solemn silence in a dull, dark dock,
> In a pestilential prison, with a life-long lock . . .
> W.S. Gilbert, *The Mikado*

Altman, Linda Jacobs. *Amelia's Road.* Illus. by Enrique O. Sanchez. New York: Lee & Low, 1993.

> Tired of moving around so much, Amelia, the daughter of migrant farmworkers, dreams of a stable home.
>> **Alliteration:** Amelia thinks of the migrant cabins as *grim, gray* shanties.
>> **Other Devices:** *Antithesis, Connotation, Serendipity, Simile, Symbol*
>> **Art Style:** Acrylics on canvas in blocky, ethnic folk style depict the farm laborers' nomadic life.
>> **Curriculum Tie-in:** Social Science (Migrant Workers)

Bradbury, Ray. *Switch on the Night.* Illus. by Leo and Diane Dillon. New York: Alfred A. Knopf, 1983.

> A lonely little boy, who is afraid of the dark, is introduced to a whole new world by his new friend, a little girl.
>> **Alliteration:** The child likes *lanterns and lamps, torches and tapers, beacons and bonfires, flashlights and flares.* He won't go outside at night, but inside he can be found in *parlors and pantries, cellars and cupboards, attics and alcoves,* and *hollering in halls.* The child switches off *porch lights, parlor lights, pale lights, pink lights,* and *pantry lights.*
>> **Other Devices:** *Antithesis, Internal Rhyme, Irony, Metaphor, Motif, Paradox, Simile, Symbol*
>> **Art Style:** Surrealistic pastel drawings match the rhythmical text of this slightly magical, slightly scientific, and quite ethereal night world.
>> **Curriculum Tie-in:** Science (Astronomy), Social Science (Fears)

Givens, Terryl. *Dragon Scales and Willow Leaves.* Illus. by Andrew Portwood. New York: G.P. Putnam's Sons, 1997.

Although they are twins, Jonathan and Rachel neither look the same nor see things the same way—especially in the forest.

Alliteration: The children come to a rushing stream, where they hear *sloshing and slapping*. Rachel discovers *boisterous bullfrogs*. Jonathan comes upon a pirate ship, where *bursting bombs* shower them with spray.

Other Devices: *Antithesis, Imagery, Metaphor, Point of View, Simile*

Art Style: Impressionistic watercolor pictures celebrate and exuberantly express the different ways we perceive our surroundings.

Curriculum Tie-in: Social Science (Individuality)

*Gralley, Jean. *Hogula, Dread Pig of Night*. New York: Henry Holt, 1999.

Although he lives high on the hog in his castle on Grimy Pork Chop Hill, Hogula is unhappy because he has no friends—until he meets Elvis Ann, Dread Queen of Kissyface.

Alliteration: Great *sufferin' sausage* links! Hogula realizes, too late, that his new friend, Elvis Ann, may have an even worse character trait than his own. Her lips, like a water *balloon* shot from a *bazooka*, smack kisses around the room. The two must come to an agreement to keep their friendship *perfectly porky*. Together they decide whom to kissyface and whom to *snort* and *send* into a deep, *snoring*, piggie-*snoozie snooze*.

Other Devices: *Allusion, Antihero, Aphorism, Cliché, Foreshadowing, Inference, Irony, Poetic Justice, Pun, Simile, Stereotype, Understatement*

Art Style: Appropriately repulsive expressionistic cartoons in gouache and ink on watercolor paper fit this humorously gentle Dracula-style relationship.

Hesse, Karen. *Come On, Rain!* Illus. by Jon J. Muth. New York: Scholastic Press, 1999.

A young girl eagerly awaits a coming rainstorm to bring relief from the oppressive summer heat.

Alliteration: Mama *lifts* a *listless* vine. It hasn't rained in three weeks. She sags over her *parched plants*. Children don't play out in such heat. Not a *peep* from the girl's *pal* Jackie-Joyce. Then the gray clouds *bunched* and *bulging* appear under a purple sky. The girl *crosses* the *crackling*-dry grass. People are *slick* with *sweat* in the nearly *senseless sizzling* heat. Mama *sinks* onto a kitchen chair and *sweeps* off her hat while *sweat* trickles down her neck. Once it begins, the children *splash* up the block, *squealing* in the *streaming* rain. Everyone dances to the phonograph music that *shimmies* and *sparkles*, and *streaks*. People are *romping* and *reeling* in the moisty green air.

Other Devices: *Foreshadow, Hyperbole, Imagery, Metaphor, Paradox, Simile*

---

*Asterisks are used throughout to indicate all-ages books.

Art Style: Buoyant, ebullient, expressionistic pen/ink watercolors lend emotional credibility to the nervous anxiety of relentless heat accompanied by worrisome drought and the tremendous sense of relief that accompanies a thorough, nourishing rain.

Curriculum Tie-in: Science (Meteorology)

Johnston, Tony. *Alice Nizzy Nazzy, the Witch of Santa Fe.* Illus. by Tomie dePaola. New York: G.P. Putanm's Sons, 1995.

When Manuela's sheep are stolen, she has to go to Alice Nizzy Nazzy's talking roadrunner-footed adobe house and try to get the witch to give the flock back.

Alliteration: The adobe hut sat on *sizzling sand* surrounded by a *prickly pear* fence. Draped over the witch's shoulder was a *huge horned* lizard. The sly *crone croaked* her replies to Manuela. In anger, the witch called her own pet lizard a *bloated bag* of scales. Desperate to find a special flower that would keep her young, the witch flew off in a huge mortar over *mountains* and *mesas*. Thunder *clapped* and *clashed*. The witch cackled a cackle that could *gouge* out *gorges*. The sheep were *baa-ing* and *bleating* and *bumping* around. Manuela *happily herded* them home.

Other Devices: *Connotation, Foreshadowing, Hyperbole, Internal Rhyme, Motif, Poetic Justice, Simile*

Art Style: Bright pastel and acrylic cartoons illustrate the western folk motif in this good vs. bad character tale.

Curriculum Tie-in: Geography (New Mexico), Literature (Fairy Tales—America), Social Science (Values)

Laden, Nina. *Roberto the Insect Architect.* San Francisco: Chronicle Books, 2000.

Roberto the architect, who also happens to be a termite, sets off to the city to find success.

Alliteration: "Like most termites, he *melted* over *maple*, and *pined* for *pine*. Oak was *okay*, too." He went to the "*busy, buzzing* hive of the *big* city." After he built them new homes, the roaches remarked, "You won't find us *sleeping* in *salads* anymore." Later his *bug buddies* threw him a *big bash*.

Other Devices: *Allusion, Antithesis, Cliché, Parallelism, Pun*

Art Style: Astoundingly detailed mixed-media collage of paper, wood, blueprints, and gouache paint creatively brings this carefully crafted, witty text to life.

Curriculum Tie-in: Social Science (Values)

Lowell, Susan. *Cindy Ellen: A Wild Western Cinderella.* Illus. by Jane Manning. New York: Joanna Cotler Books (HarperCollins), 2000.

Cindy Ellen loses one of her diamond spurs at the square dance in this retelling of a classic fairy tale.

Alliteration: Cindy Ellen irons her stepsisters' *frilly* shirts and *frizzes* their hair for them. Her fairy godmother tells her to get some *gumption* and *gravel* in her *gizzard* to fight for her rights. The *rich rancher's* son wears the *biggest belt buckle* you ever saw. Cindy Ellen's *bronc* has a *bellyful* of *bedsprings*. At the stroke of midnight she has to leave because her fine duds have *shriveled* into *sorry* rags again.

Other Devices: *Aphorism, Foreshadowing, Internal Rhyme, Parallelism, Parody, Simile, Tone*

Art Style: Action-packed expressionistic acrylic cartoons hilariously support the story's western flavor.

Curriculum Tie-in: Social Science (Self-esteem)

Mahy, Margaret. *Simply Delicious.* Illus. by Jonathan Allen. New York: Orchard Books, 1999.

A resourceful father engages in all kinds of acrobatic moves to keep an assortment of jungle creatures from getting the double-dip, chocolate-chip-and-cherry ice cream cone he is taking home to his son.

Alliteration: Mr. Minky must *baffle the butterflies, taunt the toucan, muddle the monkey,* and *trick the tiger* to keep the ice cream safe. This is not easy. The *butterflies fluttered.* The *toucan tweedled.* The *spider monkey swooped.* Mr. Minkey *bounced, balanced and biked* home with the ice cream.

Other Devices: *Foreshadowing, Hyperbole, Internal Rhyme, Poetic Justice, Simile, Understatement*

Art Style: Lively line and gouache cartoons in lush jungle colors satisfyingly follow the father's adventures as he delivers his son an appreciated treat.

Curriculum Tie-in: Literature (Cumulative Tale)

*Myers, Christopher. *Black Cat.* New York: Scholastic Press, 1999.

Black Cat ambles on an eye-opening journey of exploring feelings about identity, beauty, and home.

Alliteration: On Black Cat's poetic journey, he can be found on rooftops *seeking sun-soaked spots.* He *leaps* onto *ledges.* He can sit on sills, *balanced* like *bottles* left on a wall.

Other Devices: *Imagery, Internal Rhyme, Metaphor, Simile*

Art Style: Bold combinations of collage, ink and gouache with striking perspectives lend an intensity to the peculiarities of metropolitan life.

Curriculum Tie-in: Art (Media and Techniques)

*Pacilio, V.J. *Ling Cho and His Three Friends.* Illus. by Scott Cook. New York: Farrar Straus Giroux, 2000.

Through his plan to share the wealth of his wheat crop with three friends, a Chinese farmer teaches the importance of allowing other people to help in time of need.

Alliteration: Ling Cho is a true *servant of the soil.* Each year he *plowed and planted* seeds in *finely furrowed* rows. The wheat was harvested with *sickles slashing steadily through stalks.* Each of Ling Cho's friends, as he had *expected,* *were eager as each envisioned* what the gold coins might buy. The dragon *crunched and chomped and chewed* every bite of the wheat.

Other Devices: *Aphorism, Irony, Paradox, Poetic Justice, Theme*

Art Style: Impressionistic oil paintings in Chinese reds and golds suggest unstated meanings behind spoken words.

Curriculum Tie-in: Social Science (Friendship, Values)

Pawagi, Manijusha. *The Girl Who Hated Books.* Illus. by Leanne Franson. Hillsboro, OR: Beyond Words, 1998.

Although she lives in a house full of avid readers, Meena hates books—until she discovers the magic inside them.

Alliteration: The books that Meena hates are in *dressers* and *drawers* and *desks,* in *closets* and *cupboards* and *chests.* When a pile of books tumbles to the floor, out comes *princes* and *princesses, fairies* and *frogs.* There are *elephants, emperors, emus,* and *elves.* Monkeys tear down the *curtains* and use them as *capes.*

Other Devices: *Allusion, Antithesis, Foreshadowing, Hyperbole, Inference, Internal Rhyme, Pun, Tone*

Art Style: Pen/ink watercolor expressionistic cartoons emphasize emotion and background action that complement the text.

Ruurs, Margriet. *Emma and the Coyote.* Illus. by Barbara Spurll. New York: Stoddart Kids, 1999.

Emma thinks chickens are smarter than coyotes, and she struts boldly where no chicken should go to prove it.

Alliteration: Out in the garden, Emma *ran* around *radishes* and *munched* on *marigolds* and picked *bugs* off *beets.* In the pig pen she *wrestled with worms* and *picked* at *potato peels.*

Other Devices: *Foreshadowing, Imagery, Inference, Irony, Motif, Parallelism, Serendipity, Simile*

Art Style: Bright, primary-color acrylic paintings expressionistically follow the fortunes of Emma and the barnyard animals.

Curriculum Tie-in: Social Science (Self-Esteem)

Steig, William. *Wizzil.* Illus. by Quentin Blake. New York: Farrar Straus Giroux, 2000.

A bored witch causes trouble when she decides to take revenge on an old man, but her mischief leads to a happy ending.

Alliteration: The story begins, *"Wizzil* the *witch* was *busy biting* her nails." Her parrot, Beatrice, suggests something to alleviate her boredom. "Now, go make *somebody suffer!"* She points toward *Frimp Farm,* where a *Frimpy family* lives. Wizzil checks them out. She finds old DeWitt *snoozing and snoring* with a flyswatter in his fist. He'd *swing* and he'd *swat,* and he'd hear the *swatter swoosh.* Missing a fly would make *DeWitt dippy.* The witch turns herself into a glove and becomes a *happy harpy* on *his hand*. Eventually DeWitt, who *witnessed* the *weird* things happening, figures the cause is related to the glove he'd found, and *wrenched* it from his *wrist*. The glove lands in a stream and turns back into the *hateful hag*. Disliking water, she has never washed any part of herself except her two *horrid hands*. Later, after the witch's personality change, Beatrice's parrot resigns herself to living with these *humdrum humans*: "It'll be a *whole* new *hayride*."

Other Devices: *Ambiguity, Connotation, Foreshadowing, Internal Rhyme, Irony, Serendipity, Tone*

Art Style: Delightfully awful watercolor cartoons capture the personalities and behaviors of the rotten witch and the hillbilly family she pesters.

Curriculum Tie-in: Social Science (Love)

Waite, Judy. *Mouse, Look Out!* Illus. by Norma Burgin. New York: Dutton Children's Books (Penguin Putnam), 1998.

Inside an old, abandoned house a mouse searches for a safe place to hide from a cat.

Alliteration: When the wind comes calling, it *bangs*, and *bashes*. The hallway is *dusty*, *damp*, and *dark*. *Cobweb curtains* pull apart. The tattered carpet is *frayed* and *faded*. The kitchen is *grubby*, *grim*, and *gray*. The *wind wailes* through and around the *piles* of *pots*. The little mouse goes *scrabbling* and *scratching* and *struggling* up the stairs. A bed is *jumbled* up with *junk*.

Other Devices: *Atmosphere, Internal Rhyme, Metaphor, Poetic Justice, Simile*

Art Style: Realistic acrylic paint with shadowy hues is a perfect complement to the pleasingly ominous, gently scary text.

Zagwÿn, Deborah. *Apple Batter.* Berkeley, CA: Tricycle Press, 1999.

Because of their persistence, Delmore succeeds in learning to hit a baseball and his mother Loretta succeeds in growing apples.

Alliteration: As his skills gradually improve, *Daring Delmore clouts* the balls *closer* and *closer* to Loretta's orchard.

Other Devices: *Analogy, Antithesis, Foreshadowing, Inference, Irony, Parallelism, Pun, Simile*

Art Style: Expressionistic watercolor cartoons compare the changing fortunes of mother and son as they struggle toward their respective goals.

Curriculum Tie-in: Athletics (Baseball), Science (Apple Production)

ALLUSION

A brief, casual reference that calls forth within the reader an appropriate association to a presumably familiar person, historical event, place, literary work, or object.

Examples: having the patience of Job (biblical character)
met his Waterloo (historical site: Napolean's defeat)
Black Monday (event: stock market collapse in 1929)
sour grapes (Aesop fable)

Ernst, Lisa Campbell. *Goldilocks Returns.* New York: Simon & Schuster Books for Young Readers, 2000.

Fifty years after Goldilocks first met the three bears, she returns to fix up their cottage and soothe her guilty conscience.

Allusion: Her hobby as a child was to snoop in houses where no one was at home—until, of course, "all that dreadful trouble with the bears." She returns to dump their porridge and replace the cooked cereal with Rutabaga Breakfast Bars and Tart-N-Tasty Celery Juice, so they won't have to "eat their nasty tasting stuff anymore." She takes the broken baby chair that has been turned into a rocking horse and cobbles it back into a chair. She "fixes those other ghastly chairs." She "adjusted the stuffings" in the bears' beds. She even naps on the smaller bed, just as the long-ago story of her adventures describes.

Other Devices: *Antihero, Connotation, Flash-forward, Inference, Irony, Parallelism, Tone, Understatement*

Art Style: Large, bulky cartoons emulate the story's original atmosphere, intended for young listeners, while the language and picture complexity expand the interest level for more savvy audiences.

Fearnley, Jan. *Mr. Wolf's Pancakes.* Waukesha, WI: Little Tiger Press, 1999.

When Mr. Wolf seeks help from his neighbors about how to make pancakes, he is rudely rebuffed and must rely upon his own efforts.

Allusion: Mr. Wolf's experiences are similar to those of the fairy tale "Little Red Hen." Nobody helps him, and in the end he eats, all by himself, all the pancakes, among other things. His neighbors turn out to be familiar storybook characters. There are Chicken Little, Wee Willy Winkle, the Gingerbread Man, Little Red Riding Hood, the Three Little Pigs, and, for good measure, Old Mother Hubbard, who runs the general store. Close observation of the art reveals such humorous tid-bits as a wanted poster regarding a lost sheep and whom to contact for a reward if found—L. Bo Peep, of course.

Other Devices: *Antihero, Black Humor, Irony, Poetic Justice, Stereotype*

Art Style: Detailed cartoons in pen/ink, watercolor drawings virtually cover the pages not only with the story in progress but also with humorous nods to many Mother Goose rhymes and fairy tale personalities.

Curriculum Tie-in: Social Science (Conduct and Behavior)

*Gralley, Jean. *Hogula, Dread Pig of Night.* New York: Henry Holt, 1999.

Although he lives high on the hog in his castle on Grimy Pork Chop Hill, Hogula is unhappy because he has no friends—until he meets Elvis Ann, Dread Queen of Kissyface.

Allusion: Hogula's castle, like his character, is reminiscent of the legend of Dracula, friend to bats and fond of the necks of his victims. (Hogula snorts on his victim's necks, sending them into sleeping swoons.) When Elvis Ann, who is determined to make the acquaintance of Hogula, goes from house to house, trying to find the owner of the shoe he leaves behind at the mall, there is similarity to the Prince's quest for the girl who fits the glass slipper in the story of Cinderella. There is also a suggestion of the wicked witch in *The Wizard of Oz* when Hogula says to his bats, "Dance, my pretties." Hogula's two companions, Chad and Igoretta, would be right at home in a Frankenstein story. Hogula discovers going to the mall is great fun, for he has chosen October 31. He finds that he fits right in with all the weird costumes he sees, which he finds perfectly ordinary.

Other Devices: *Alliteration, Antihero, Aphorism, Cliché, Foreshadowing, Inference, Irony, Poetic Justice, Pun, Simile, Stereotype, Understatement*

Art Style: Appropriately repulsive expressionistic cartoons in gouache and ink on watercolor paper fit this humorously gentle Dracula-style relationship.

Curriculum Tie-in: Social Science (Friendship)

*Hamanaka, Sheila. *Peace Crane.* New York: Morrow Junior Books, 1995.

After learning about the Peace Crane created by Sadako, a survivor of the bombing of Hiroshima, a young African-American girl wishes it would carry her away from the violence of her own world.

Allusion: The young narrator says, "When the sun fell on Hiroshima, you rose like a phoenix from the fire." The crane arose from atomic destruction like the mythical Arabian phoenix, which is said to live a number of years, at the end of which it makes a nest of spices, flaps its wings to set fire to the pile, and burns itself to ashes. From the ashes it comes forth as new life. The crane, a symbol for renewal and long life, became the focus of hope for a devastated Japan after World War II. The American child has adapted the crane as a symbol of peace and hope in her crime-filled neighborhood.

Other Devices: *Antithesis, Flash-forward, Imagery, Pun, Simile, Symbol*

Art Style: Luminous, expressionistic oil paintings on canvas celebrate the spirit of the Peace Crane's hope for a troubled world.

Curriculum Tie-in: History (War and Peace—Japan and America)

Howe, James. *Horace and Morris but Mostly Dolores.* Illus. by Amy Walrod. New York: Atheneum Books for Young Readers (Simon & Schuster), 1999.

Three mice friends learn that the best clubs include everyone.

> **Allusion:** The three friends love adventure. They sail the "seven sewers" (seven seas). They climb "Mount Ever-Rust" (Mount Everest). They "dared to go where no mouse had gone before," which alludes to the popular television science fiction series *Star Trek*.
> **Other Devices:** *Internal Rhyme, Parallelism, Pun, Stereotype, Theme*
> **Art Style:** Acrylics and collage cartoons, occasionally aided by additional funny aside notes, humorously provide a lesson in social interaction.
> **Curriculum Tie-in:** Social Science (Gender Equality)

*Johnson, D.B. *Henry Hikes to Fitchburg.* Boston: Houghton Mifflin, 2000.

While his friend works hard to earn train fare to Fitchburg, young Henry Thoreau walks the thirty miles through woods and fields, enjoying nature.

> **Allusion:** In the mid-1800s in New England, when this incident occurred, the author contrasts Henry's day on the road with his friend's day, which is spent here and there earning his train fare. The friend fills Mrs. *Alcott*'s kitchen wood box and weeds Mr. *Hawthorne*'s garden and moves bookcases in Mr. *Emerson*'s study. He even cleans out Mrs. *Thoreau*'s chicken house. These names figured prominently in that time of American history.
> **Other Devices:** *Irony, Paradox, Theme, Understatement*
> **Art Style:** Colored pencil and acrylic paint in stylishly simple, expressionistic designs contrast interesting visual perspectives and provide period detail.
> **Curriculum Tie-in:** Literature (Henry David Thoreau), Philosophy (Quality of Life)

*Kaplan, Howard. *Waiting to Sing.* Illus. by Hervé Blondon. New York: DK Ink, 2000.

A family, who loves music and spends many hours at the piano, is devastated by the death of the mother, but those still living find consolation in the beautiful music that remains.

> **Allusion:** When life is still pleasantly normal, the boy speaks of harvesting clams on the beach. "If it was small enough to pass through a metal ring you had to throw it back." Later, in a haunting, terse revelation of his mother's death, the boy says, "I loved her by heart, but one late summer evening she passed through the ring of the world and died." In both instances, there is loss. The clam cannot be kept as food; the mother cannot be kept as a loving member of the family. Continuing with beach images, he says he "missed the blue beach glass of her eyes." He had earlier enjoyed collecting such glass during walks along the sand—"blue was my favorite." His family's favorite piano piece is Beethoven's *Für Elise*. It has always been in the boy's life. As the healing begins, this song is the first one the boy's father is able to play again, and becomes the symbol of their

mutual recovery. When the boy hears the familiar opening notes, E and D, "it had such a pull on me, it made me think of the bread dropped in a fairy tale when you're finally ready to turn around and leave the woods." As in *Hansel and Gretel*, he will follow the notes as a road to recovery from his grief. Before becoming a competent piano player, the boy had observed that the difficult notes "looked like a thousand birds had landed in front of us." At the end of the story, when he, like his sister before him, is ready to perform *Für Elise* at his first recital, he harks back to his first impressions, noting that, "when I opened the sheet music, my thousand birds were waiting to sing."

Other Devices: *Antithesis, Aphorism, Atmosphere, Foreshadowing, Imagery, Inference, Metaphor, Parallelism, Simile, Symbol*

Art Style: Full-page sepia tone pastel cartoon drawings expressionistically evoke a fragile emotional period in the life of a family coping with wrenching loss.

Curriculum Tie-in: Music (Piano), Social Science (Death, Family Relationships, Feelings)

Krensky, Stephen. *The Youngest Fairy Godmother Ever.* Illus. by Diana Cain Bluthenthal. New York: Simon & Schuster Books for Young Readers, 2000.

Mavis tries to pursue her goal of playing fairy godmother and granting wishes to those around her, but she finds the process trickier than she thought.

Allusion: On career day at school, most kids see so many interesting job possibilities, they can't decide what they like best. Cindy "felt like she had too many jobs already." When the class pet mouse gets out of its cage and creates havoc trying to escape, Cindy helps Mavis clean up. "I do a lot of cleaning up at home," she says. Later, when the discussion turns to Halloween costumes, Cindy says she doesn't have one. Her stepsisters will be wearing the new outfits. Mavis, the would-be fairy godmother, has a modern Cinderella story before her wand.

Other Devices: *Irony, Understatement*

Art Style: A mix of ink and paint produces lively cartoons that complement the wry humor in this funny tale of determination to succeed.

Curriculum Tie-in: Social Science (Values)

Laden, Nina. *Roberto the Insect Architect.* San Francisco: Chronicle Books, 2000.

Roberto the architect, who also happens to be a termite, sets off to the city to find success.

Allusion: Roberto goes on a train to "Bug Central Station" in the city to begin his destiny. He can't find work with any of the big-name architects like "Hank Floyd Mite" or "Fleas Van Der Rohe" or "Antonia Gaudi." So he decides to build homes, anonymously, for those in need, like the ladybug

with a problem: "My house is on fire and my children are gone!" The home he built for "Tudor" the house fly resembles a fine English mansion. Soon he is in demand. "Barbara Waterbugs" wants an exclusive interview. "Robin Leech" promises to make him rich and famous. "Seven Shieldbug" wants the movie rights. "Diane Spider" searches the World Wide Web for the scoop. The "Insect Inquirer" offers a reward to the first bug that brings him to light.
Other Devices: *Alliteration, Antithesis, Cliché, Parallelism, Pun*
Art Style: Astoundingly detailed mixed-media collage of paper, wood, blueprints, and gouache paint creatively brings this carefully crafted, witty text to life.
Curriculum Tie-in: Social Science (Values)

McNaughton, Colin. *Yum!* New York: Harcourt Brace, 1998.
Preston Pig suggests that Mr. Wolf get a job so he can buy what he wants to eat, but as he considers different lines of work, Mr. Wolf has a one-track mind.
Allusion: As Mr. Wolf contemplates being an astronaut, he pictures himself sitting at the controls of a space ship and thinks, "Beam me up, Scotty!" an allusion to the television series *Star Trek*.
Other Devices: *Ambiguity, Pun, Satire, Tone, Understatement*
Art Style: Detailed cartoons and humorous sidebars add to the impish joy of this wolf and pig encounter.
Curriculum Tie-in: Social Science (Values)

*Meddaugh, Susan. *Hog-Eye.* New York: Walter Lorraine Books (Houghton Mifflin), 1995.
A young pig uses her ability to read to outwit a wolf that intends to eat her.
Allusion: The piglet casts a "hog-eye" (evil eye) on the wolf. Sure enough, when she finishes reciting her spell, the wolf begins to feel a dreadful itch and cannot stop scratching. Of course, she has taken precaution that her magic spell will be a success. She has conned him into rolling around and rubbing himself with "green threeleaf" (i.e., poison ivy).
Other Devices: *Antithesis, Flashback, Foreshadowing, Hyperbole, Inference, Irony, Understatement*
Art Style: Split page watercolor cartoons tell the "true story" of a schoolchild, who dislikes her daily bus ride.
Curriculum Tie-in: Literature (Tall Tale)

Modarressi, Mitra. *Yard Sale.* New York: DK Pub., 2000.
When Mr. Flotsam has a yard sale in the quiet town of Spudville, his neighbors are first upset, then delighted by their purchases.
Allusion: Each of the mundane sale items proves to possess capabilities beyond their expectations. For example, there is a phone that connects the listener to the dearly departed. One of the townspeople finds himself

talking "with a singer named Elvis." The two enjoy a "rocking version of 'Blue Suede Shoes' together." Later, that same phone rings with "Amelia Earhart" on the line. A certain Mr. "Rotelli" tries out his purchase, a pasta maker that eventually enables him to go into a new business—his Ristorante Rotelli. Miss "Milton" becomes an overnight success as an author when her typewriter zips off page after page of its own writing.

Other Devices: *Antithesis, Connotation, Hyperbole, Inference, Paradox, Serendipity, Understatement*

Art Style: Lively full page watercolor naïve art accompanies an understated text.

**Nolen, Jerdine. *Big Jabe.* Illus. by Kadir Nelson. New York: Lothrop, Lee & Shepard, 2000.*

Momma Mary tells stories about a special young man who does wondrous things, especially for the slaves on the Plenty Plantation.

Allusion: "Addy saw something bobbing in the water. It was a wicker basket, and something was inside it." Just when the American southern slaves need help most, their Moses comes to save them like the ancient Hebrew slaves in Egypt were saved from a harsh pharaoh. This little child, too, grows up to serve the downtrodden as he performs miracles on their behalf. Later, in the fashion of John Henry, work around the plantation seems to get done in half the time, due to his superhuman strength.

Other Devices: *Anachronism, Antithesis, Flashback, Flash-forward, Foreshadowing, Hyperbole, Imagery, Inference, Parallelism, Simile, Symbol, Understatement*

Art Style: Strong, detailed pen/ink, watercolor and gouache drawings provide wonderful expressionistic period ambience to this folk tale.

Curriculum Tie-in: History (Slavery—America), Literature (Tall Tale)

Pawagi, Manjusha. *The Girl Who Hated Books.* Illus. by Leanne Franson. Hillsboro, OR: Beyond Words, 1998.

Although she lives in a house full of avid readers, Meena hates books—until she discovers the magic inside them.

Allusion: Meena attempts to climb a pile of books to rescue her cat. It topples over, and creatures fall from the pages. There are combinations of animals that allude to particular familiar stories, such as a wolf and three pigs. There is a troll on a log and a nervous white rabbit with a hat. There is allusion to details in the Humpty Dumpty tale. He "went flying and then broke in half," just as he does when he falls in the famous Mother Goose rhyme. And, finally, there is one rabbit "in a little blue coat" that is, of course, Beatrix Potter's Peter.

Other Devices: *Alliteration, Antithesis, Foreshadowing, Hyperbole, Inference, Internal Rhyme, Pun, Tone*

Art Style: Pen/ink watercolor expressionistic cartoons emphasize emotion and background action.

AMBIGUITY

A verbal nuance that simultaneously gives room for alternative interpretations of the same word or statement.

Example: In the Bible at Luke 2:49, the child Jesus chastises his parents when they believe he is lost and then find him in the temple with teachers. He asks them, "Did you not know I must be about my Father's business?" They are confused; his "father" is a carpenter.

Alexander, Lloyd. *The House Gobbaleen.* Illus. by Diane Goode. New York: Dutton Children's Books (Penguin Books), 1995.

Unhappy over what he considers his bad luck, Tooley ignores his cat's warnings and invites a greedy little man into his home in the mistaken hope of improving his fortunes.

Ambiguity: Tooley wants so much for the "Friendly Folk" to help him change his luck that he is willing to believe that the first creature who comes along will help him. "I can just feel the luck stirring already," he enthuses. "Stir, is it?" says the little man. "Stir me some porridge, and put a nice lump of butter in it." Later, Tooley hints about receiving a "pot of gold." The little man declares, "Pot of stew!" These two are clearly not connecting in their purposes. When Tooley's cat begins a brainwashing program to pry the little nuisance from their home, he deliberately befuddles the fellow about whether a Gobbaleen has invaded the house. The cat appears to agree with the little man's protestations against such a being as a Gobbaleen. "There's no such thing as a Gobbaleen. You said so yourself." The worried little man squints shrewdly at the cat. "Unless there is and you'd have me think there isn't," he says. "Unless there isn't and I'd have you think there is," replied the cat, who continues, "There might be a Gobbaleen I didn't want you to know about. But in that case, I might say there was and have you think there wasn't. Unless, of course, there was one. But there's none at all, as I've been telling you."

Other Devices: *Foreshadowing, Hyperbole, Inference, Irony, Simile, Theme, Tone, Understatement*

Art Style: Humorous gouache and watercolor cartoons illustrate this modern folktale.

Curriculum Tie-in: Social Science (Values)

Bunting, Eve. *Can You Do This, Old Badger?* Illus. by Le Uyen Pham. New York: Harcourt, 1999.

Although Old Badger cannot do some things as easily as he used to, he can still teach Little Badger the many things he knows about finding good things to eat and staying safe and happy.

Ambiguity: After a busy day of learning important things, Little Badger has been told by Old Badger that someday he, too, will be an old badger and "You will teach a little badger what you know. That's the way it was planned." Little Badger asks if the young one he'll care for will "love me as much as I love you." Old Badger assures him he will. "That's part of the plan, too." Then, Old Badger tells him, "Now it's nap time." Little Badger asks, "Is that another part of the plan?" Old Badger replies, "It's another part of my plan." Wordplay with *plan* is used to good effect.

Other Devices: *Foreshadowing, Theme*

Art Style: Detailed, expressionistic gouache on watercolor paper lovingly shows this special age/youth relationship.

Curriculum Tie-in: Social Science (Intergenerational Relationships)

*Bunting, Eve. *The Memory String.* Illus. by Ted Rand. New York: Clarion Books (Houghton Mifflin), 2000.

While still grieving for her mother and unable to accept her stepmother, a girl clings to the memories represented by forty-three buttons on a string.

Ambiguity: It gets dark before the family finds the one remaining button from the string that the cat broke. After Laura goes to bed, her father and stepmother go out into the yard to hunt one more time. Laura's stepmother, Jane, finally finds the lost button. Her father tells Jane to give it to her at breakfast the next morning, but Jane says, "I don't think so. She won't like it that I'm the one who found it. Let's just leave it on the porch. Like a gift from a good fairy." Laura overhears this exchange. The next morning she of course knows the button is awaiting her. She picks it up and engages in a special exchange with her stepmother. "A good fairy must have brought it," she says. Laura now knows what a "good fairy" her stepmother really is, and she means to express her appreciation of the woman when she says so. Her stepmother assumes she is probably only speaking traditionally, as a little girl would in the usual concept of the "good fairy," who pays a child a mysterious nighttime visit.

Other Devices: *Antithesis, Aphorism, Foreshadowing, Imagery, Inference, Parallelism, Simile*

Art Style: Shadowy, impressionistic watercolor paintings detail the emotional changes the child experiences as she feels both separation from and reconnection to her family.

Curriculum Tie-in: Social Science (Family Relationships, Grief)

Dahan, André. *Squiggle's Tale*. San Francisco: Chronicle, 2000.

Squiggle sends a letter assuring his parents that he is being a good pig while visiting his cousins in Paris, but the pictures tell another story.

Ambiguity: The kids are having a fun time at the park, though they do miss some of the reality around them. They find ponies and climb on, not realizing that there is a fee for this pleasure. "A man with a cap came chasing after us shouting, 'the money, the money!' I looked down but I didn't see any money."

Other Devices: *Understatement*

Art Style: Impressionistic pastels and pencil serve nicely to reveal the truth of Squiggle's Parisian adventures.

*Hayes, Joe. *A Spoon for Every Bite*. Illus. by Rebecca Lear. New York: Orchard Books, 1996.

A poor husband and wife ask their rich neighbor to be godfather to their child, and once they are compadres, prey upon his pride and extravagance to trick him out of his fortune.

Ambiguity: The term "compadre" in this story serves the meaning of both "godfather" and "friend." And, in this instance, "compadre" has something of an adversarial connotation. The poor "friend" consciously tries to use the powerful, rich friend's greed to bring about his ruin. The rich man is asked to be compadre (godfather) to the poor couple's baby. After baptism the neighbors become compadres (friends). Now that the rich man is their compadre (godfather and friend), the young couple invite him to supper. At this meal the young couple become insulted when the insensitive rich man laughs because they have only three spoons. He brags that he could use a different spoon every day of the year. To get back at him, they tell him they have a friend who uses a different spoon for every bite of food he eats. The rich man does not wish to be bested, so he foolishly embarks on a path to personal ruin. He throws away all his spoons after eating one bite, and eventually must sell his assets to keep replacing spoons. Too late he discovers it is impossible to sustain such a lifestyle, and finally, after exhausting his resources, accuses the young couple of lying to him. No one can use a new spoon for every bite. They prove they are not lying by taking him to the friend who uses a new spoon for every bite. The friend "broke off a piece of tortilla and scooped up some beans. The beans and the spoon disappeared into his mouth." He'll never use that spoon again.

Other Devices: *Antihero, Antithesis, Foreshadowing, Hyperbole, Motif, Poetic Justice*

Art Style: Realistic pastel drawings depict the striking differences in circumstances between the compadres and their different emotional responses to these circumstances.

Curriculum Tie-in: History (American Southwest), Literature (Folktales—Hispanic), Social Science (Values)

Lawson, Julie. *Emma and the Silk Train.* Illus. by Paul Mombourquette. Buffalo, NY: Kids Can Press, 1997.

After seeing the beautiful silk blouse her mother made, Emma dreams of having a piece of silk for herself, so when the opportunity arises, she determinedly pursues it.

Ambiguity: When Emma's rescue is completed, and she and the silk have been fished out of the fast-moving river, Emma asks her mother, "Will it be all right?" Her mother, who has just finished admonishing her for putting her life at risk to acquire a piece of silk from the train wreck, replies, "Now that you're safe and sound? Of course." But Emma was not talking about her own safety. She was referring to the cloth. "I meant"—Then, her mother satisfies her real concern. "And the silk will be grand, you'll see."

Other Devices: *Foreshadowing, Imagery, Inference, Parallelism, Simile*

Art Style: Lush, impressionistic oil paintings capture the time and adventure of the silk train era.

Curriculum Tie-in: History (Railroads—Silk)

Lyon, George Ella. *One Lucky Girl.* Illus. by Irene Trivas. New York: Dorling Kindersley, 2000.

Even though their trailer is destroyed by a tornado, a young boy's family is grateful because they find his baby sister alive.

Ambiguity: When the danger is past and the family is reunited, the boy remembers the loss of their home. "Where are we going to live?" he asks. His father, with one arm around his wife and daughter, and the other around his son, replies, "Together." The boy is thinking about the physical problem of a place to live; the father can only think about the fact that having his family together is all that matters.

Other Devices: *Antithesis, Foreshadowing, Imagery, Inference, Metaphor, Parallelism, Simile*

Art Style: Smudgy pastel illustrations impressionistically assist the story line through use of both dark and bright colors.

Curriculum Tie-in: Science (Tornadoes), Social Science (Family Relationships)

McKissack, Patricia. *The Honest to Goodness Truth.* Illus. by Giselle Potter. New York: Atheneum Books for Young Readers (Simon & Schuster), 2000.

After promising never to lie, Libby learns it's not always necessary to blurt out the whole truth either.

Ambiguity: Having had some unpleasant experiences telling her friends the truth lately, Libby tries to clear up her confusion by asking Miss

Tusselbury, "Can the truth be wrong?" Miss Tusselbury answers, "Oh no. The Truth is never wrong. Always, always tell the truth!" This causes a "smile of relief" to light up Libby's face. She feels correct in proceeding to tell Miss Tusselbury that her garden looks like a jungle. Suddenly, Miss Tusselbury becomes angry. If telling the truth is always right, why does it seem to be wrong? Apparently, Libby's truth and Miss Tusselbury's conception of truth are not quite the same.

Other Devices: *Antithesis, Aphorism, Foreshadowing, Paradox, Simile, Understatement*

Art Style: Pencil, ink, gouache and watercolor are combined in a luxuriant, expressionistic, naïve style in this tale of honesty.

Curriculum Tie-in: Social Science (Values)

McNaughton, Colin. *Yum!* New York: Harcourt Brace, 1998.

Preston Pig suggests that Mr. Wolf get a job so he can buy what he wants to eat, but as he considers different lines of work, Mr. Wolf has a one-track mind.

Ambiguity: When Preston suggests that Mr. Wolf could become a soccer player, Mr. Wolf imagines kicking a pig to "soften him up." Mr. Wolf likes the idea of becoming an astronaut, too. He sees his spaceship heading to giant pig planets. As a teacher of piglets, Mr. Wolf imagines the lunch menu. Preston suggests pilot; Mr. Wolf thinks pig "pie in the sky" as he imagines an aerial battle in which his plane chases a pig in another plane. And so it goes. Every job Preston suggests becomes, in Mr. Wolf's mind, a good way to access pigs, his favorite food. There is no meeting of minds here.

Other Devices: *Allusion, Pun, Satire, Tone, Understatement*

Art Style: Detailed cartoons and humorous asides add to the impish joy of this wolf and pig encounter.

Curriculum Tie-in: Social Science (Values)

Meggs, Libby Phillips. *Go Home! The True Story of James the Cat.* Morton Grove, IL: Albert Whitman, 2000.

A homeless cat spends several seasons trying to survive the elements until at last a suburban family adopts him.

Ambiguity: When James is taken to the veterinarian after being attacked by a dog, the doctor comments, "He's lucky you found him." He means the cat could have died from his injuries if left unattended. The woman, however, has a different take on who's "lucky." She says, "I have a feeling we are the lucky ones." She is recognizing in this loving animal the potential for a wonderful household companion.

Other Devices: *Antithesis, Connotation, Inference, Metaphor, Point of View, Simile*

Art Style: Realistic pastel illustrations follow James's admittance into a family that provides what has been missing in his life for a long time.
Curriculum Tie-in: Social Science (Animal Companions)

*Myers, Tim. *Basho and the Fox.* Illus. by Oki S. Han. New York: Marshall Cavendish, 2000.

A Japanese poet is challenged by a fox to create his best haiku.
Ambiguity: The foxes ask Basho for "one good haiku." They give him three chances. "We only ask for one, and it needn't be great—only good." They have in mind only one concept that will be acceptable; the haiku must say something about foxes. Basho doesn't know this. He smiles happily to himself. "One good haiku—that would be easy!" He has written many excellent haiku examples upon a wide range of topics. But can he please the foxes, not knowing what constitutes their concept of "good" poetry?
Other Devices: *Aphorism, Antithesis, Imagery, Irony, Motif, Parallelism, Theme*
Art Style: Mischievous watercolor folk paintings convey the Eastern sensibility of feudal Japan.
Curriculum Tie-in: History (Japan), Social Science (Self-esteem)

*Say, Allen. *The Sign Painter.* Boston: Walter Lorraine Books (Houghton Mifflin), 2000.

An assignment to paint a large billboard in the desert changes the life of an aspiring artist.
Ambiguity: The man and the boy have differing attitudes about their labor. The man paints to fulfill a job; the boy paints to express his skills. When their task is finished, the man looks back at one empty billboard frame following a storm that has broken out the billboard panels, leaving the frame open to the sky. A cloud floats by. "There it goes, just passing by, like you and me." The boy echoes the phrase to himself later, when he decides to strike out on his own to pursue his own dream. "And as the last bus came around the corner he said softly to the empty street, 'Just passing by . . . .'" The two have used the same words, but they mean separate realities. The man is just passing by to the next lucrative job; the boy is passing by on the way to his artistic destiny.
Other Devices: *Antithesis, Imagery, Inference, Point of View, Theme, Tone*
Art Style: Magnificent realistic acrylic paintings unfold the contrasts in this provocative story about personal choices between security and dreams.
Curriculum Tie-in: Philosophy (Quality of Life)

Steig, William. *Wizzil.* Illus. by Quentin Blake. New York: Farrar Straus Giroux, 2000.

A bored witch causes trouble when she decides to take revenge on an old man, but her mischief leads to a happy ending.

Ambiguity: DeWitt Frimp interprets the glove he finds as a good thing. "It's your lucky day!" he says to himself as he traipses home, unknowingly, with a "happy harpy on his hand." The witch, resolved on revenge, has turned herself into a glove. She, too, is pleased with herself as she thinks ahead to the trouble she is planning. For entirely different reasons the two are both looking forward to the glove's potential.

Other Devices: *Alliteration, Connotation, Foreshadowing, Internal Rhyme, Irony, Serendipity, Tone*

Art Style: Delightfully awful watercolor cartoons capture the personalities and behaviors of the rotten witch and the hillbilly family she pesters.

Curriculum Tie-in: Social Science (Love)

Strete, Craig Kee. *The Lost Boy and the Monster.* Illus. by Steve Johnson and Lou Fancher. New York: G.P. Putnam's Sons (Penguin Books for Young Readers), 1999.

With the help of a rattlesnake and a scorpion, a lost boy gains two names and defeats the horrible foot-eating monster.

Ambiguity: Stuck and tangled by the monster, the lost boy doesn't recognize that the one pulling him up into the tree is not a benefactor. He calls out, "Could you please help me get free?" The monster replies, "I'd be happy to help you out of that rope." The boy expects freedom; the monster expects lunch. The boy thanks the monster "for saving me." The monster says he deserves a reward for saving the boy, and asks, "How about a nice lunch?" The boy says he'd be glad to provide lunch, but he doesn't have any food with him. "Oh yes you do. You're standing on them!" says the monster, who plans to cook and eat the boy's feet.

Other Devices: *Connotation, Internal Rhyme, Motif, Poetic Justice, Simile, Theme, Tone*

Art Style: Textured paste, oil paint, potato stamping, and scratching tools create expressionistic paintings in brown and yellow tones reminiscent of American Indian art.

Curriculum Tie-in: Art (American Indian), Literature (Folktales— American Indian)

ANACHRONISM

Something inappropriately placed outside its proper time in history.

Example: the clock in *Julius Caesar*

Johnson, Angela. *Down the Winding Road.* Illus. by Shane Evans. New York: DK Ink, 2000.

> The annual summer visit to the country home of the Old Ones, the uncles and aunts who raised Daddy, brings joy and good times.
>
> > **Anachronism:** Nothing changes with the Old Ones or where they live. The world around them has changed, but they go on with their same lifestyle. Every year the boy's family eagerly leaves the city behind and steps back into the same world Daddy lived in as a child. The Old Ones are there waiting "all in a row, looking just alike," all seven of them. These enduring folk, Daddy's people, "have been the Old Ones since he could remember, and since I can remember, too," says the young narrator. They always serve food, tell family stories that they all know by heart, and always take a walk through the grassy woods to the pond.
> >
> > **Other Devices:** *Atmosphere, Inference, Irony*
> >
> > **Art Style:** In expressionistic pen/ink drawings and oil paintings, the gentle, loving life of a caring family is made believable.
> >
> > **Curriculum Tie-in:** Social Science (Family Relationships)

*Nolen, Jerdine. *Big Jabe.* Illus. by Kadir Nelson. New York: Lothrop, Lee & Shepard, 2000.

> Momma Mary tells stories about a special young man who does wondrous things, especially for the slaves on the Plenty Plantation.
>
> > **Anachronism:** "Jabe opened his little-boy mouth and laughed a big man-sized laugh." As a promise of things to come, this child performs his first miracle at the site at which he was discovered when he calls fish from the river to jump into Addy's empty wagon.
> >
> > **Other Devices:** *Allusion, Antithesis, Flashback, Flash-forward, Foreshadowing, Hyperbole, Imagery, Inference, Parallelism, Simile, Symbol, Understatement*
> >
> > **Art Style:** Strong, detailed pen/ink, watercolor, and gouache drawings provide wonderful expressionistic period ambience to this folktale.
> >
> > **Curriculum Tie-in:** History (Slavery—America), Literature (Tall Tale)

*Yaccarino, Dan. *Deep in the Jungle.* New York: Anne Schwartz Book from Atheneum Books for Young Readers (Simon & Schuster), 2000.

> After being tricked into joining the circus, an arrogant lion escapes and returns to the jungle, where he lives peacefully with the animals he used to terrorize.
>
> > **Anachronism:** One day the monkeys "were picking bananas for the almighty king," the lion. This carnivore would not be eating bananas.
> >
> > **Other Devices:** *Antihero, Antithesis, Black Humor, Foreshadowing, Irony, Motif, Parallelism, Poetic Justice, Pun, Tone*
> >
> > **Art Style:** Expressionistic, gouache naïve cartoons against white backgrounds, reminiscent of the "Curious George" series, accent the droll language in this lesson in humility.
> >
> > **Curriculum Tie-in:** Literature (Parable), Social Science (Values)

ANALOGY

For purposes of illustrative example, the likening of one thing to another on the basis of some similarity between the two.

> Example: 'Tis with our judgments as our watches,
>   None go just alike,
>   Yet each believes his own.
>   Alexander Pope, *An Essay on Criticism*

*Gregorowski, Christopher. *Fly, Eagle, Fly! An African Tale.* Illus. by Niki Daly. New York: Margaret K. McElderry Books (Simon & Schuster), 2000.
    A farmer finds an eagle and raises it to behave like a chicken, until a friend helps the eagle learn its rightful place in the sky.
        Analogy: An eagle chick is trained early by a farmer to live the life of a village chicken. It learns to walk, talk, eat, and think like a chicken. First attempts by the visiting friend to reintroduce the bird to its life in the sky are laughable in their failure. Placed on the top of the thatch on a village hut, the eagle ignominiously slides down the roof "and sailed in among the chickens." But when the determined visitor introduces the grown eagle to its mountain habitat early one morning as the sun is rising, the eagle, without really moving, feels the updraft of a wind "more powerful than any man or bird." It leans forward and is effortlessly swept upward into the brightness of the new day, "never again to live among the chickens." Children, too, must strain to rise to their potential, to gaze at the rising sun, lift off, and soar above their humdrum existence. They are destined for freedom, goodness, and love.
        Other Devices: *Antithesis, Foreshadowing, Imagery, Motif, Parallelism*
        Art Style: Expressionistic watercolor line washes in brown and blue tones satisfyingly re-create the ambience of an African village.
        Curriculum Tie-in: Literature (Parable)

*Wisniewski, David. *Golem.* New York: Clarion Books (Houghton Mifflin), 1996 (Caldecott-1997)
    A saintly rabbi miraculously brings to life a clay giant who helps him watch over the Jews of sixteenth-century Prague.
        Analogy: The rabbi chants a spell and the words soar aloft to unleash the power of Life itself. "As lightning strikes iron and flashes to earth, so the infinite energy of creation blazed through the rabbi into the coarse clay," turning it into a live man.
        Other Devices: *Atmosphere, Foreshadowing, Imagery, Inference, Irony, Motif, Paradox, Simile*

Art Style: Paper cut in expressionistic collage produces a powerful physical and emotional effect for this cautionary tale.

Curriculum Tie-in: Literature (Legend), Social Science (Values)

*Wisniewski, David. *Tough Cookie*. New York: Lothrop, Lee and Shepard (William Morrow), 1999.

When his friend Chips is snatched and chewed, Tough Cookie sets out to stop Fingers.

Analogy: In this wonderfully inventive story, life in the cookie jar is compared to life in a large city. There's the "Upjar" neighborhood of "just-baked and best-quality store-bought citizens." The "Midjar" level is the major business, cultural, and government centers. The "Els" connect the two levels. Below them are the shops, services, schools, and apartment buildings in the "Downjar" level. Below them all is "Bottom of the Jar." Visitors to this area should travel in groups. The "crumbs" live there. The Jar Transit Authority reminds you to carry your ID card and sell-by date with you at all times. Freshness determines your level within the Jar. It's the law! When your sell-by date expires, you should report to the nearest processing center for clearance to the next level down. Those assigned to the Bottom of the Jar no longer need report to a processing center. Crumbs won't be issued ID cards and must remain at the Bottom of the Jar. The story's narrator is like the classic Sergeant Friday detective. He speaks in short, terse statements. "The bottom's loaded with nice folks. Some call them crumbs. I call them friends. I like helping them out. Anybody makes trouble, I step in. That's my job. I'm a tough cookie." There is the obligatory dame, "Pecan Sandy." She's a "classy blond. Store-bought. Easy on the eyes." And, she proves smart, too. In the end, the city takes care of its own.

Other Devices: *Parody, Pun, Satire, Simile, Stereotype, Theme*

Art Style: Complex cut paper illustrations in an expressionistic collage work amazingly well to support this munchable mystery.

Curriculum Tie-in: Social Science (Friendship)

Zagwÿn, Deborah. *Apple Batter*. Berkeley, CA: Tricycle Press, 1999.

Because of their persistence, Delmore succeeds in learning to hit a baseball and his mother, Loretta, succeeds in growing apples.

Analogy: To emphasize their separate interests and their mutual regard for each other, the author uses apple language to describe how the mother feels about her son: "A mere sprout. Well rooted. The apple of my eye." The son uses baseball language to express his affection for his mother: "I love you more than my glove."

Other Devices: *Alliteration, Antithesis, Foreshadowing, Inference, Irony, Parallelism, Pun, Simile*

Art Style: Expressionistic watercolor cartoons compare the changing fortunes of mother and son as they struggle toward their respective goals.
Curriculum Tie-in: Athletics (Baseball), Science (Apple Production)

ANTIHERO

A type of protagonist lacking traditional heroic qualities such as courage or fortitude, but is a rather incompetent, unlucky, clumsy, buffoonish, comic, or even antisocial figure, who rejects conventional value expectations and accepts the status of outcast.

Example: Arthur Miller's Willy Loman in *Death of a Salesman* or J.D.
          Salinger's Holden Caufield in *Catcher in the Rye* or maybe Lewis
          Carroll's Alice of *Alice in Wonderland*

*Armstrong, Jennifer. *Pierre's Dream.* Illus. by Susan Gaber. New York: Dial (Penguin Putnam), 1999.

Thinking he is dreaming, Pierre, a lazy, foolish man, shows no fear as he performs many amazing and dangerous circus acts.

Antihero: Pierre "had no job, no interest, and no hobby besides sitting under the olive trees in the afternoon, thinking of dinner." But, when he awakes from a nap, a circus surrounds him. He decides this bustling village that had not been there before, must be the product of a realistic dream. A dream is not real. Pierre confronts a lion; in a dream there is no need for fear. He walks and does tricks on a tightrope, and many other circus acts. He is not surprised that the people of his town are at the evening performance. They would, of course, be in his dream. He amazes everyone with his fearlessness and abilities. After a busy performance, he returns to rest under the tree again. The circus has moved on when he wakens. He is the same lazy Pierre, except there really is more to think about than just his dinner. A dainty parasol with a slip of paper pinned to the frill is next to him on the ground. The message says, "Au revoir, Pierre." Pierre smiles and then begins to laugh. Even a lazy, foolish man can sometimes surprise himself with bursts of extraordinary achievement.

Other Devices: *Foreshadowing, Inferences, Irony, Theme*
Art Style: Ethereal, expressionistic acrylic paintings alternate between stunning perspectives and large close-ups.
Curriculum Tie-in: Social Science (Values)

*Baylor, Byrd. *The Table Where Rich People Sit.* Illus. by Peter Parnall. New York: Charles Scribner's Sons, 1994.

A girl discovers that her impoverished family is rich in things that matter in life, especially being outdoors and experiencing nature.

Antihero: The girl says her parents are inadequate. She tells them they "should both get better jobs so we could buy a lot of nice new things," and, "It would help if you both had a little more ambition." They insist the "only jobs worth having are jobs outdoors." They "want cliffs or canyons or desert or mountains around them wherever they work. They even want a good view of the sky." They always work together. Their table is "made out of lumber somebody else threw away." Clearly, "You can tell it didn't come from a furniture store." She thinks her parents' favorite thing, panning for gold, is "just an excuse to camp in some beautiful wild place again." They could "make more money working in a building somewhere in town." They don't care that she "looks worse than anyone in school." She concludes about her parents: "Sometimes I think that I'm the only one in my whole family who is really sensible." What kind of parents would give birth to their daughter in a mountain cabin at sunrise just because they wanted her first sight at eight minutes of age to be that "most magical place, the most beautiful mountain they ever climbed?" And they do this with their second child. Their son's first sight is an ocean that touches jungle with a "certain kind of purple-blue night sky and the exact green waves" they like.

Other Devices: *Aphorism, Foreshadowing, Irony, Paradox*

Art Style: Sweeping pen/ink and watercolor on white spaces flow majestically in expressionistic celebration of nature.

Curriculum Tie-in: Geography (American Southwest), Literature (Parable)

Ernst, Lisa Campbell. *Goldilocks Returns.* New York: Simon & Schuster Books for Young Readers, 2000.

Fifty years after Goldilocks first met the three bears, she returns to fix up their cottage and soothe her guilty conscience.

Antihero: The bears are shocked at the tacky and distasteful things the mature, but still offensive, Goldilocks has done to their home. In a tardy effort to make amends, she blithely goes about wreaking havoc again, replacing food they like with her choices, decorating the place according to her taste, and adjusting their furnishings as she prefers them. "Now, don't thank me. I know you're terribly grateful! But after all, I was the one who caused the trouble to begin with—of course I've more than made up for *that.*"

Other Devices: *Allusion, Connotation, Flash-forward, Inference, Irony, Parallelism, Tone, Understatement*

Art Style: Large, bulky cartoons emulate the story's original atmosphere intended for young listeners while the language and picture complexity expand the interest level for more savvy audiences.

Fearnley, Jan. *Mr. Wolf's Pancakes.* Waukesha, WI: Little Tiger Press, 1999.
> When Mr. Wolf seeks help from his neighbors about how to make pancakes, he is rudely rebuffed and must rely upon his own efforts.
>
> > **Antihero:** What kind of protagonist is this central character? Mr. Wolf politely asks for help in reading the recipe, writing his shopping list, counting his money, carrying home his groceries, and cooking his pancakes. He offers to share his pancakes if his neighbors will help him. Everyone rudely refuses. Mr. Wolf works very hard and manages to do all these tasks by himself. Then his impudent neighbors have the audacity to demand some of the pancakes he has made. There is nothing for the put-upon Mr. Wolf to do but to invite them in, since they won't leave. They dash for the kitchen, pushing him aside. But once they are in, there is the wolf-thing. "Snippity! Snappity! Mr. Wolf gobbled them up."
> >
> > **Other Devices:** *Allusion, Black Humor, Irony, Poetic Justice, Stereotype*
> >
> > **Art Style:** Detailed cartoons in pen/ink and watercolor drawings virtually cover the pages not only with the story in progress but also with humorous nods to many Mother Goose rhymes and fairy tale personalities.
> >
> > **Curriculum Tie-in:** Social Science (Conduct and Behavior)

*Gralley, Jean. *Hogula, Dread Pig of Night.* New York: Henry Holt, 1999.
> Although he lives high on the hog in his castle on Grimy Pork Chop Hill, Hogula is unhappy because he has no friends—until me meets Elvis Ann, Dread Queen of Kissyface.
>
> > **Antihero:** Hogula's reputation precedes him. His housekeeper warns him, "Remember one thing, mahster: you moost be back by bedtime, before you turn into your usual monstrous, snorting self!" He heads out to the mall to make a friend. When the mall closes at bedtime, the shoppers yawn and stream out the double doors. Hogula is left alone and friendless. "His face burned pinker. His tail curled tighter. No more Mr. Nice Hog! No more trying to make friends! Making friends was too hard! From now on he would roam the world as the one, true thing he was: the awful, snortful, fangful and friendless Hogula, Dread Pig of Night."
> >
> > **Other Devices:** *Alliteration, Allusion, Aphorism, Cliché, Foreshadowing, Inference, Irony, Poetic Justice, Pun, Simile, Stereotype, Understatement*
> >
> > **Art Style:** Appropriately repulsive expressionistic cartoons in gouache and ink on watercolor paper fit this humorously gentle Dracula-style relationship.
> >
> > **Curriculum Tie-in:** Social Science (Friendship)

*Hayes, Joe. *A Spoon for Every Bite.* Illus. by Rebecca Lear. New York: Orchard Books, 1996.
> A poor husband and wife ask their rich neighbor to be godfather to their child, and once they are compadres, prey upon his pride and extravagance to trick him out of his fortune.

Antihero: The poor husband and wife opportunistically count on the rich man's arrogance when they set his ruin in motion. They know he will not be able to resist trying to match the challenge they have so deliberately set him up to lose. The rich man boasts that he can use a different spoon every day of the year. The poor couple knows that by telling him there is someone able to use a different spoon for every single bite he eats, the rich man will feel obligated to prove than he can do this, too. The rich man orders his servant to get rid of each used spoon. The poor man "laughs to himself. This was just the kind of thing he and his wife had hoped would happen." Then he asks the servant, "And what does your master tell you to do with the spoons you're ordered to get rid of?" The servant replies, "Give them to my compadres. They have only three spoons!" But not for long. Soon a huge mound of spoons piles up outside the poor couple's shack. When these silver spoons are sold, the poor couple will no longer be poor. There are no heroes in this tale, just an arrogant snob and self-serving, conniving peasants.

Other Devices: *Ambiguity, Antithesis, Foreshadowing, Hyperbole, Motif, Poetic Justice*

Art Style: Realistic pastel drawings contrast the striking differences in lifestyles between the compadres and their emotional responses to their circumstances.

Curriculum Tie-in: History (American Southwest), Literature (Folktales—Hispanic), Social Science (Values)

Nickle, John. *The Ant Bully.* New York: Scholastic Press, 1999.

Lucas learns a lesson about bullying from the ants he has been tormenting.

Antihero: When a larger neighbor boy sprays Lucas with a water hose, he takes out his frustration by spraying a colony of small ants with his squirt gun. When they've had enough, they show him the error of his ways. They reduce him to their size and sentence him to hard labor. Surprisingly, he acquits himself well as he gathers food, defends against wasps and spiders, and tends to the queen's needs. He even bravely puts his life on the line for his fellow ants and wins the queen's respect. He earns his freedom and their unexpected support just when he needs it most in his own troubles with the neighbor boy.

Other Devices: *Antithesis, Foreshadowing, Inference, Personification, Poetic Justice, Point of View*

Art Style: Expressionistic acrylic cartoons skillfully play with perspective as the boy and the ants view the same environment.

Curriculum Tie-in: Social Science (Bullies, Values)

*Yaccarino, Dan. *Deep in the Jungle.* New York: Anne Schwartz Book from Atheneum Books for Young Readers (Simon & Schuster), 2000.

After being tricked into joining the circus, an arrogant lion escapes and returns to the jungle where he lives peacefully with the animals he used to terrorize.

Antihero: The lion "was king of this jungle and he made sure everyone knew it." The animals "couldn't stand him one bit." He rules by fear. "I'm afraid I must eat you if you don't obey me." When a strange man promises to make him a circus star, "the animals were more than happy to be rid of him." After gaining a perspective on his own value, the lion returns a better jungle neighbor and defender of his fellow creatures.

Other Devices: *Anachronism, Antithesis, Black Humor, Foreshadowing, Irony, Motif, Parallelism, Poetic Justice, Pun, Tone*

Art Style: Expressionistic, gouache naïve cartoons against white backgrounds, reminiscent of the "Curious George" series, accent the droll language in this lesson in humility.

Curriculum Tie-in: Literature (Parable), Social Science (Values)

ANTITHESIS

A balanced grammatical placement of sharply opposing thoughts, usually in two phrases, clauses, or sentences to heighten their effect by contrast.

Example: You are going; I am staying.

Altman, Linda Jacobs. *Amelia's Road.* Illus. by Enrique O. Sanchez. New York: Lee & Low, 1993.

Tired of moving around so much, Amelia, the daughter of migrant farm workers, dreams of a stable home.

Antithesis: Following the harvesting of crops meant she had little time to develop relationships. "Amelia spent six weeks at Fillmore Elementary School, and not even the teacher had bothered to learn her name. This year, the teacher bothered."

Other Devices: *Alliteration, Connotation, Serendipity, Simile, Symbol*

Art Style: Acrylics on canvas in blocky, ethnic folk style depict the classic farm workers' nomadic life.

Curriculum Tie-in: Social Science (Migrant Workers)

Bradbury, Ray. *Switch on the Night.* Illus. by Leo and Diane Dillon. New York: Alfred A. Knopf, 1983.

A lonely little boy, who is afraid of the dark, is introduced to a whole new world by his new friend, a little girl.

Antithesis: "He liked only the sun. The yellow sun. He didn't like the Night." He met a girl named Dark. "She had dark hair and dark eyes, and

wore a dark dress and dark shoes. But her face was as white as the moon. And the light in her eyes shone like white stars."
Other Devices: *Alliteration, Internal Rhyme, Irony, Metaphor, Motif, Paradox, Simile, Symbol*
Art Style: Surrealistic pastel drawings match the rhythmical text of this slightly magical, slightly scientific, and quite ethereal night world.
Curriculum Tie-in: Science (Astronomy), Social Science (Fears)

***Bunting, Eve.** *The Memory String.* Illus. by Ted Rand. New York: Clarion Books (Houghton Mifflin), 2000.
While still grieving for her mother and unable to accept her stepmother, a girl clings to the memories represented by forty-three buttons on a string.
Antithesis: The young girl feels left out of the happiness her father has found in his remarriage. "They seemed so happy. It hurt to hear them happy like that." She tries to make the cat sit still as she recites the memories each button on the string represents. But, she realizes the cat's patience is fast ending as she condenses the litany. "Get to the good parts, she thought. Forget the cousins. Get to Mom." The frustrated cat leaps, and the button string breaks. Everyone joins in an early evening hunt for the scattered buttons. "Jane's voice was soft, as Mom's would have been. But this wasn't Mom. Mom had died three years ago. This was Jane."
Other Devices: *Ambiguity, Aphorism, Foreshadowing, Imagery, Inference, Parallelism, Simile*
Art Style: Shadowy, impressionistic watercolor paintings detail the emotional changes the child experiences as she feels both separation and reconnection to her family.
Curriculum Tie-in: Social Science (Family Relationships, Grief)

***Bunting, Eve.** *Swan in Love.* Illus. by Jo Ellen McAllister Stammen. New York: Atheneum Books for Young Readers (Simon & Schuster), 2000.
Despite ridicule of the other animals, Swan persists in his adoration of a swan-shaped boat named Dora.
Antithesis: "On the lake was a boat shaped like a swan. Her name, DORA, was printed in black on her sparkling paint. Swan loved her." So begins this haunting tale of the essence of love. The other swans think his devotion to the boat makes them look stupid. "Swan knew. He knew that it didn't matter." As winter approaches, some Canada geese try to persuade him to leave his vigil beside the boat. They tell him, "Winter is long, and you will be alone." As time passes, the boat owner eventually decides Dora is too old to repair. He tells Swan, "Our Dora's finished. And you don't look so good yourself." The boat and the swan come to their earthly end. They float away together through time. "But she wasn't Dora though he knew she was. And he wasn't Swan though he knew he was."

Other Devices: *Aphorism, Foreshadowing, Imagery, Inference, Simile, Theme*
Art Style: Pastel expressionistic illustrations shimmer with grace as they illuminate the story of transforming love.
Curriculum Tie-in: Social Science (Love)

*Deedy, Carmen Agra. *The Yellow Star: The Legend of King Christian X of Denmark.* Illus. by Henri Sorensen. Atlanta: Peachtree, 2000.
King Christian must abide by Nazi orders regarding the wearing of the identifying yellow star, but he must also protect all the Danes from harm.
Antithesis: A Nazi officer asks King Christian who has taken down the Nazi flag from the palace. "I sent a soldier to remove it," replies the king. "Well, tomorrow another will fly in its place," the officer boasts. "Then tomorrow I will send another soldier to remove it," counters the king. "And I will have that man shot," threatens the Nazi. "Then be prepared to shoot the king—for I will be that soldier," King Christian says.
Other Devices: *Aphorism, Atmosphere, Foreshadowing, Inference, Irony, Paradox, Parallelism, Pun, Simile, Symbol, Theme*
Art Style: Impressionistic oil paintings accompany the spare, terse text in this vignette showing the political reality of the Danes' circumstances during a very somber period of history.
Curriculum Tie-in: History (World War II—Nazi Occupation—Denmark), Literature (Legend), Social Science (Values)

Dengler, Marianna. *Fiddlin' Sam.* Illus. by Sibyl Graber Gerig. Flagstaff, AZ: Rising Moon (Northland), 1999.
Wandering through the Ozarks and bringing joy to people with his music, Fiddlin' Sam seeks the right person to take up his fiddle and carry on the practice.
Antithesis: After fiddling for his supper, Sam was treated to plates heaped with golden brown hush puppies and fragrant possum stew or cornbread and kidney beans with apple pie. "Only the best for the fiddler would do." During the fever he experienced after his snakebite, "Sometimes he seemed to be walking through fragrant pines, light as air and feeling fine. Other times he'd be crawling down a burning road, parched with thirst, the fiddle dragging along behind." Later, Sam hopes the young stranger he meets will be the one to carry on the tradition. First efforts produce squeaks and squawks. "You'll get the hang of it," Sam tells him. "Naw, it's a mean old thing," the boy responds. Yet the boy certainly appreciates Sam's skills. "You've a mighty fine gift," he tells Sam. "Tain't a gift. It's a loan," Sam responds.
Other Devices: *Atmosphere, Foreshadowing, Internal Rhyme, Parallelism, Serendipity*

Art Style: Exuberant realistic and expressionistic watercolors in bright yellows, pinks, and blues faithfully express the emotional and physical details of this musician's life.

Curriculum Tie-in: Social Science (Missouri Ozarks)

*Dengler, Marianna. The Worry Stone. Illus. by Sibyl Graber Gerig. Flagstaff, AZ: Rising Moon (Northland), 1996.

When a small, serious boy joins Amanda on the park bench, she remembers that once she was small and serious, too, but she had Grandfather—and his wonderful stories.

Antithesis: The old woman walks daily to a nearby park and sits on a bench where she can see children at play. Hers are "grown and gone, scattered to the winds." "When she counts the years, she knows she is old. So she doesn't count, and she doesn't look around." The woman recalls the death of her grandfather, when she was a young girl. "She did not cry. She only walked out on the veranda and sat in Grandfather's chair." As a girl, the old woman had found comfort in the worry stone. She wants the boy to experience this same comfort. She describes the worry stone to the skeptical child. "The boy watches. Then he looks away." He tells her, "I don't believe it." She replies, "It works for me." Though her persistence prevails, the boy is a hard sell as she tries to reach him. He even drops the worry stone on the ground through disinterest. The woman feels defeated. "She looks away, too sad to stay longer but too tired to start home."

Other Devices: *Flashback, Foreshadowing, Inference, Parallel Story, Parallelism*

Art Style: Bold realistic watercolor paintings expressionistically maintain focus on the threads of this woman's past and present.

Curriculum Tie-in: History (Chumash Indians), Social Science (Grandparents, Intergenerational Relationships)

Dörrie, Doris. *Lottie's Princess Dress.* Illus. by Julia Kaergel. New York: Dial (Penguin Putnam), 1998.

Lottie and her mother disagree about suitable schoolday attire but resolve the matter agreeably, to the surprise of all.

Antithesis: There is much abrupt opposing thought between these two characters. Lottie "looked at the red sweater. It was too red. She looked at the blue skirt. It was too blue. Then she saw her princess dress. It was glittery gold and it was perfect!" Lottie says, "Today is a glittery gold day." Mother replies, "Today is a freezing cold day." When mother's patience has come to an end, she yells at Lottie. Lottie says, "You looked like a dragon. I am glad I remembered that princesses are not afraid of dragons." Mother replies, "And I'm sorry I forgot that tantrums don't work, for me or for you!" When Lottie's mother gives in and lets Lottie wear her princess dress, Lottie says, "I will polish my crown." "How about brushing your teeth instead?" her mother says.

Other Devices: *Paradox, Theme, Understatement*

Art Style: Spare lines, bright colors of chalk pastels, and accent gold foil complement this expressionistic, naïve rendering of an emotional confrontation.

Curriculum Tie-in: Social Science (Conflict Resolution)

Givens, Terryl. *Dragon Scales and Willow Leaves.* Illus. by Andrew Portwood. New York: G.P. Putnam's Sons, 1997.

Although they are twins, Jonathan and Rachel neither look the same nor see things the same way—especially in the forest.

Antithesis: Jonathan's imagination tinges his view of life. A weeping willow tree becomes a dragon to fight. Rachel's love of nature enables her to appreciate the tree's rustle and shimmer as leaves come floating down in the breeze. "Jonathan went into the woods to hunt for buried treasure, and Rachel went to look for robins' nests."

Other Devices: *Alliteration, Imagery, Metaphor, Point of View, Simile*

Art Style: Impressionistic watercolor pictures expressionistically celebrate the different ways we perceive our surroundings.

Curriculum Tie-in: Social Science (Individuality)

*Gregorowski, Christopher. *Fly, Eagle, Fly! An African Tale.* Illus. by Niki Daly. New York: Margaret K. McElderry Books (Simon & Schuster), 2000.

A farmer finds an eagle and raises it to behave like a chicken, until a friend helps the eagle learn its rightful place in the sky.

Antithesis: The farmer says, "The eagle is the king of the birds. We shall train it to be a chicken." When a friend drops in for a visit, he sees the bird among the chickens. "That's not a chicken. It's an eagle!" The friend decides to prove that the eagle can rise to its natural abilities. They bring the bird to the mountain and climb up, carrying it. The friend "looked down the cliff and saw the ground thousands of feet below. They were very near the top." The friend talks to the eagle. "You belong to the sky, not to the earth." Feeling an updraft, the bird leans forward and is swept upward, "lost to sight in the brightness of the rising sun, never again to live among the chickens."

Other Devices: *Analogy, Foreshadowing, Imagery, Motif, Parallelism*

Art Style: Expressionistic watercolor line washes in brown and blue tones satisfyingly re-create the ambience of an African village.

Curriculum Tie-in: Literature (Parable)

*Hamanaka, Sheila. *Peace Crane.* New York: Morrow Junior Books, 1995.

After learning about the Peace Crane created by Sadako, a survivor of the bombing of Hiroshima, a young African-American girl wishes it would carry her away from the violence of her own world.

Antithesis: The paper cranes are "each one a tiny wish for life, each one a wish for peace." The souls of those killed in the bomb went soaring up, "high above the heat, high above the cries of war." The American child worries about her future "when the sun falls in the city, when I hear shooting on my street." In her dream "I wanted to take you home with me, I wanted you to stay." She realizes the Peace Crane belongs to the world. "Your home is in my heart, your home is with the homeless." There is hope in the goodness of people. "We have new hearts, we have new eyes to see you with." She wishes for "a world without borders, a world without guns."
Other Devices: *Allusion, Flash-forward, Imagery, Pun, Simile, Symbol*
Art Style: Luminous, expressionistic oil paintings on canvas celebrate the spirit of the Peace Crane's hope for a troubled world.
Curriculum Tie-in: History (War and Peace—Japan and America)

Harris, Jim. *The Three Little Dinosaurs.* Gretna, LA: Pelican Publishing, 1999.
Three young dinosaurs set out on their own, only to be hassled by a Tyrannosaurus rex who gets a big surprise in the end.
Antithesis: The first little dinosaur isn't into home construction. He throws together a house of dried grass and sits down to enjoy his video games. He hears a heavy thump, thump, thump coming up to his house. "Maybe it's the pizza deliveryman! It wasn't the pizza deliveryman—it was the Tyrannosaurus rex."
Other Devices: *Foreshadowing, Inference, Parody, Poetic Justice, Tone*
Art Style: Lush, detailed acrylic expressionistic paintings provide satisfyingly humorous perspectives and points of view of aggressor and victim.

*Hayes, Joe. *A Spoon for Every Bite.* Illus. by Rebecca Lear. New York: Orchard Books, 1996.
A poor husband and wife ask their rich neighbor to be godfather to their child, and once they are compadres, prey upon his pride and extravagance to trick him out of his fortune.
Antithesis: "A long time ago there was a poor couple who lived in a small, tumbledown house. They were so poor that they owned only two spoons— one for the husband and one for the wife." This half of the story characterization is contrasted to its opposite. "Their neighbor, on the other hand, was very rich. His house was big and elegant and filled with fine furniture. He was very proud of his wealth and his possessions, and he lived in an extravagant way."
Other Devices: *Ambiguity, Antihero, Foreshadowing, Hyperbole, Motif, Poetic Justice*
Art Style: Realistic pastel drawings contrast the striking differences in circumstances between the compadres, and their emotional responses to these circumstances.

Curriculum Tie-in: History (American Southwest), Literature (Folktales—Hispanic), Social Science (Values)

Henkes, Kevin. *Wemberly Worried.* New York: Greenwillow Books (HarperCollins), 2000.

A mouse named Wemberly, who worries about everything, finds that she has a whole list of things to worry about when she faces the first day of nursery school.

Antithesis: "'Don't worry,' said her mother. 'Don't worry,' said her father. But Wemberly worried."

Other Devices: *Cliché, Irony, Parallelism, Pun*

Art Style: Watercolor and pen/ink cartoons with sidebar comments delightfully enhance the rhythmic text.

Curriculum Tie-in: Social Science (Fears)

Hopkinson, Deborah. *A Band of Angels: A Story Inspired by the Jubilee Singers.* Illus. by Raúl Colón. New York: Atheneum Books for Young Readers (Simon & Schuster), 1999.

The daughter of a slave forms a gospel singing group and goes on tour to raise money to save Fisk University.

Antithesis: "There were few people singing the old songs, and some were even being forgotten." "They reminded people of their pain, of the hard days of slavery. But they were about hope, too." "Sometimes songs arise from happiness, sometimes from sorrow." "Night after night Ella would put on her one fine dress, her face hopeful. But night after night she would look out to see just a few people in a dark, empty hall." "We haven't been able to raise even five hundred dollars—and our school needs five thousand."

Other Devices: *Foreshadowing, Irony, Simile*

Art Style: Watercolor/pencil expressionistic muted lines, and shades of brown, yellow and greens with scratch lines, illustrate the contrasts of loss and hope in this grand success story.

Curriculum Tie-in: History (Black Culture)

Hutchins, Hazel. *One Duck.* Illus. by Ruth Ohi. New York: Annick (Firefly Books), 1999.

A mother duck defends her nest of eggs from a marauding crow and a farmer's tractor and cultivator.

Antithesis: On the one hand, the duck "feels the pull of the eggs beneath her," but she also "feels the danger moving down upon her" from the tractor and cultivator. There is "no way to save the eggs no way but to save herself." When she flies off the nest, the farmer knows she has left eggs in the path of his machinery. "He shakes his head at the foolishness of ducks." Then he checks the sky to note the progress of an approaching storm. He "shakes his head at the foolishness of farmers."

Other Devices: *Atmosphere, Imagery, Inference, Onomatopoeia, Parallelism, Tone*

Art Style: Expressionistic pen/ink watercolor drawings sensitively complement the lyrical text of this common farming drama.

Curriculum Tie-in: Science (Agriculture, Animal Behavior)

Jones, Joy. *Tambourine Moon.* Illus. by Terry Widener. New York: Simon & Schuster Books for Young Readers, 1999.

Noni is afraid as she and her granddaddy walk home, until he tells her how he met her Grandma Ismay one dark night in Alabama, and how the big yellow moon came to light up the sky.

Antithesis: "The Angel Voices from over to the AME church—they were pretty good, and the Gospelettes, they were the best. But the Star Fire Choir—they couldn't carry a tune in a bucket." "We even sang songs together—Ismay with her pretty voice, me with my voice like a rusty nail."

Other Devices: *Hyperbole, Imagery, Personification, Simile*

Art Style: Acrylic art in expressionistic, ethnic folk design employs both sharp angles and puffy rounded curves.

Curriculum Tie-in: History (Black Culture), Social Science (Grandparents)

Kajikawa, Kimiko. *Yoshi's Feast.* Illus. by Yumi Heo. New York: DK Ink, 2000.

When Yoshi's neighbor, Sabu, the eel broiler, attempts to charge him for the delicious-smelling aromas he has been enjoying, Yoshi hatches a plan to enrich them both.

Antithesis: Yoshi and his neighbor have a difference of opinion. "'The eel broiler should share leftovers with his neighbor,' muttered Yoshi." "'The fan maker should buy eels from his neighbor,' grumbled Sabu."

Other Devices: *Aphorism, Foreshadowing, Inference, Onomatopoeia, Parallelism, Poetic Justice*

Art Style: Oil, pencil, and paper collage folk art come together in satisfyingly expressionistic design to transmit the flavor of this ethnic quarrel.

Curriculum Tie-in: Literature (Folktales—Japan)

*Kaplan, Howard. *Waiting to Sing.* Illus. by Hervé Blondon. New York: DK Ink, 2000.

A family, who loves music and spends many hours at the piano, is devastated by the death of the mother, but those still living find consolation in the beautiful music that remains.

Antithesis: After the father and son are alone, eventually they mutually turn to the piano for solace, sitting side by side on the bench. "We didn't say anything. We didn't have to. We let the piano speak for us. It was our way of crying, the way it had once been our way of laughing."

Other Devices: *Allusion, Aphorism, Atmosphere, Foreshadowing, Imagery, Inference, Metaphor, Parallelism, Simile, Symbol*
Art Style: Full-page sepia-tone pastel cartoon drawings expressionistically evoke a fragile emotional period in the life of a family coping with wrenching loss.
Curriculum Tie-in: Music (Piano), Social Science (Death, Family Relationships, Feelings)

Kitamura, Satoshi. *Me and My Cat?* New York: Farrar Straus Giroux, 2000.
A young boy spends an unusual day after awakening to find that he and his cat have switched bodies.
Antithesis: The day begins as always. Nicholas' mother must drag him out of bed, and says he'll be late for school. He thinks, "It must be Mom. It must be morning again."
Other Devices: *Inference, Irony, Parallelism, Point of View, Understatement*
Art Style: Busy, hilarious acrylic cartoons detail a boy's thoughts in a cat's body as he watches a cat's activities in his boy's body.
Curriculum Tie-in: Social Science (Animal Companions, Values)

Kurtz, Jane. *River Friendly, River Wild.* Illus. by Neil Brennan. New York: Simon & Schuster Books for Young Readers, 2000.
A family experiences a renewed appreciation for home and community after they are evacuated during a spring flood and then return to survey the damage.
Antithesis: In this emotionally charged depiction of a life-altering event, poetic language and special effects, such as the balance of sharply opposing thoughts, are abundant. First, the setting is identified as a community with a river bordering it. The narrator says, "That was us.—That was the river." When the flood becomes imminent, she says, "Most things you lie awake and worry about don't happen.—This one does." They must hurry to save their lives, and the cat must be left behind. "I cry over Kiwi.—Max kisses Kiwi. I blow kisses to Kiwi.—Max cries over Kiwi." They rush "away from the river—away from our home." On TV at the shelter where they must stay, in fear of what they will discover when they return home, they watch a fire sweeping their downtown. "The sky turns red.—The sky turns black." They watch people navigating the river-streets any way they can. "They wade.—They rumble in Humvees.—They ripple through the streets in boats, ducking under power lines." Earlier, during the winter, cars leaped from behind giant snowbanks, "making brakes slam—making hearts thud." When they return to the city, the snow is gone, but snowbanks of garbage and sandbags line every street, again "making brakes slam—making hearts hollow." "Every pile is someone's story.—Every story is sad." As people return to their property, they step with caution, because "The steps could be crumbles. The floors could be buckled. The stairs could be slick. The windows could be broken, and snakes could be inside." "My toes wince on

the icy floor and I wish for the wood-burning stove." Later, during clean-up, "My feet shiver in the big gray boots—My hands shiver in the yellow rubber gloves." News of the tragedy spreads nationally. "Kids I never met made pictures of my school.—Someday, I'll do the same for someone else." Anger at losses: "I'm mad at this doll because she was upstairs, so she's fine and my favorite doll wasn't, so she isn't." In final assessment: "The flood didn't get the tree, but the new dike will."

Other Devices: *Aphorism, Atmosphere, Imagery, Metaphor, Onomatopoeia, Simile*

Art Style: Oil glaze of brown paint overlaid by thin layers of color in different areas and additional glazes for depth create fuzzy, impressionistic scenes that reflect the essence of this emotional experience.

Curriculum Tie-in: Geography (Flood—Grand Forks, North Dakota)

Laden, Nina. *Roberto the Insect Architect.* San Francisco: Chronicle Books, 2000.
Roberto the architect, who also happens to be a termite, sets off to the city to find success.

Antithesis: Whoever heard of a termite who wanted to be an architect? "You should be a chef," his friends advise. "Roberto didn't want to cook. He wanted to build." Roberto needed to find a place to begin his development project. "He finally found an abandoned, run-down block of crumbling buildings. It was a total mess. There were piles of old wood and garbage everywhere. It was just what he was looking for." He had a dream. "Roberto wished he could do something for others, but what could one termite do? 'A lot of damage,' Fleas Van Der Rohe had told him."

Other Devices: *Alliteration, Allusion, Cliché, Parallelism, Pun*

Art Style: Astoundingly detailed mixed-media collage of paper, wood, blueprints, and gouache paint creatively brings to life this carefully crafted, witty text.

Curriculum Tie-in: Social Science (Values)

Lorbiecki, Marybeth. *Just One Flick of a Finger.* Illus. by David Diaz. New York: Dial (Penguin Putnam), 1996.
A young boy takes a gun to school to scare off the bully who has been tormenting him, and the gun is accidentally fired during a scuffle.

Antithesis: Prison is described as a place where "most don't survive"; "they just shrivel up inside." The boy has access to a gun. "He kept it in a box, but I could trip the lock." When he shows it to his friend, the friend says, "I thought you were somebody." Then he walks away.

Other Devices: *Foreshadowing, Inference, Internal Rhyme, Metaphor, Pun, Simile, Theme*

Art Style: Acrylics, watercolor, and digitally manipulated photographic backgrounds blend to create powerful, stylized, expressionistic heavy-lined comic book images that evoke danger and tension.

Curriculum Tie-in: Social Science (Bullies and School Violence)

Lyon, George Ella. *One Lucky Girl.* Illus. by Irene Trivas. New York: DK Pub., 2000.
> Even though their trailer is destroyed by a tornado, a young boy's family is grateful because they find his baby sister alive.
>> **Antithesis:** "The Pooles' trailer lay on its side; the Higgins' was upside down. It took a minute to realize ours was gone." It took a bit of time to assess the damage. "Mom's cheek was cut. I still had the glove on my hand."
>> **Other Devices:** *Ambiguity, Foreshadowing, Imagery, Inference, Metaphor, Parallelism, Simile*
>> **Art Style:** Smudgy pastel illustrations impressionistically assist the story line through use of both dark and bright colors.
>> **Curriculum Tie-in:** Science (Tornadoes), Social Science (Family Relationships)

McKissack, Patricia. *The Honest to Goodness Truth.* Illus. by Giselle Potter. New York: Atheneum Books for Young Readers (Simon & Schuster), 2000.
> After promising never to lie, Libby learns it's not always necessary to blurt out the whole truth.
>> **Antithesis:** When Libby is surprised that her friend took offense about the hole she pointed out in her sock, she says, "It was the truth." Her friend responds, "It was plain mean!"
>> **Other Devices:** *Ambiguity, Aphorism, Foreshadowing, Paradox, Simile, Understatement*
>> **Art Style:** Pencil, ink, gouache, and watercolor give a luxuriant, expressionistic naïve style to this tale of honesty.
>> **Curriculum Tie-in:** Social Science (Values—Honesty; Friendship)

Martin, Jacqueline Briggs. *Snowflake Bentley.* Illus. by Mary Azarian. Boston: Houghton Mifflin, 1998 (Caldecott—1999).
> This is a biography of a self-taught scientist who photographed thousands of individual snowflakes in order to study their unique formation.
>> **Antithesis:** "He expected to find whole flakes that were the same. But he never did." "His first pictures were failures—no better than shadows. Yet he would not quit." "Snow is as common as dirt. We don't need pictures." "While other farmers sat by the fire or rode to town with horse and sleigh, Willie studied snowstorms." "Some winters he was able to make only a few dozen good pictures. Some winters he made hundreds." "The little farmer came to be known as the world's expert on snow. But he never grew rich."
>> **Other Devices:** *Imagery, Parallelism, Simile*
>> **Art Style:** Woodcuts with hand-tinted watercolors serve this nineteenth-century tale well.
>> **Curriculum Tie-in:** Science (Meteorology, Photography)

*Meddaugh, Susan. *Hog-Eye.* New York: Walter Lorraine Books (Houghton Mifflin), 1995.

A young pig uses her ability to read to outwit a wolf that intends to eat her.

Antithesis: The little pig got on the wrong school bus and asked to be let out. "The bus driver let me off at the side of the road. I had no idea where I was." She looks at a road sign. "If I followed the road, it would take a long time to get home. If I followed the path through the forest, I could be home before dark."

Other Devices: *Allusion, Flashback, Foreshadowing, Hyperbole, Inference, Irony, Understatement*

Art Style: Split-page watercolor cartoons tell the "true story" of a schoolchild who dislikes her daily bus ride.

Curriculum Tie-in: Literature (Tall Tale)

Meggs, Libby Phillips. *Go Home! The True Story of James the Cat.* Morton Grove, IL: Albert Whitman, 2000.

A homeless cat spends several seasons trying to survive the elements until at last a suburban family adopts him.

Antithesis: "In earlier days he had been a strong and swift hunter. These days, he looked for leftover food by the back doors of houses where other cats lived."

Other Devices: *Ambiguity, Connotation, Inference, Metaphor, Point of View, Simile*

Art Style: Realistic pastel illustrations follow James's admittance into a family that provides what has been missing in his life for a long time.

Curriculum Tie-in: Social Science (Animal Companions)

Mochizuki, Ken. *Passage to Freedom: The Sugihara Story.* Illus. by Dom Lee. Afterword by Hiroki Sugihara. New York: Lee & Low, 1997.

Following refusal by the Japanese government to issue visas to Jewish refugees from Poland, Consul Sugihara and his family make a crucial decision that saved thousands of lives.

Antithesis: As the family ponders what it should do, the narrator says: "Exhausted from the day's excitement, I slept soundly. But it was one of the worst nights of my father's life." The contrast is between the child's innocence and the heavy burden of the knowing adult. A decision to help the refugees could put the family in danger, but not to help could mean all the refugees would die. Later, the father says to his wife, "I have to do something. I may have to disobey my government, but if I don't I will be disobeying God." The consul will choose a higher authority than his country's government. The consul's children and the refugees' children take the opportunity to play together with the narrator's toy car. "They pushed as we rode, and they rode as we pushed." They "did not speak the

same language, but that didn't stop us." There is a universality in the
behavior of the children that defies circumstances. Years later, reflecting
on that time of his life, the narrator states, "Back then, I did not fully
understand what the three of them had done, or why it was so important.
I do now."

Other Devices: *Aphorism, Foreshadowing, Point of View, Theme*

Art Style: The stark fear of survival is shown in realistic, photograph-like,
sepia-tone oil paint and pencil over scratched beeswax paper. Emotionally
charged, unrelenting shades of brown shadowing focus on the grim refugee
predicament—their barely contained explosive violence—and the terrible
decision facing the diplomat.

Curriculum Tie-in: History (World War II)

Modarressi, Mitra. *Yard Sale.* New York: DK Pub., 2000.

When Mr. Flotsam has a yard sale in the quiet town of Spudville, his neighbors
are first upset, then delighted by their purchases.

Antithesis: When Miss Milton complains about her clattering typewriter
keeping her awake all night, one neighbor sympathizes, "How annoying."
Another remarks, "How interesting!" He had begun to read the pages.
Mrs. Applebee warns her neighbors not to answer the phone that is ringing
off the hook. "We should get rid of it," someone says. "Let's answer it!"
someone else says. Mrs. Frumkin says of her music box, "It's out of control."
A neighbor says, "It's a party!" The noodles at Mr. Rotelli's home are waist
deep. "Appalling!" says Miss Milton. "Delicious!" said Nellie Crumb.

Other Devices: *Allusion, Connotation, Hyperbole, Inference, Paradox,
Serendipity, Understatement*

Art Style: Lively, full-page watercolor naïve art accompanies an understated
text.

*Morrison, Toni, with Slade Morrison. *The Big Box.* Illus. by Giselle Potter. New
York: Hyperion, 1999.

To make three unique youngsters conform to their rules, grown-ups create a
world inside a box, including treats and simulated nature, but all the kids really
want is the freedom to be themselves.

Antithesis: A confused child can't understand why the adults find her
unacceptable. "I don't mean to be rude: I want to be nice." This fine, big,
brown box "has carpets and curtains and beanbag chairs. And the door has
three big locks." "It's pretty inside and the windows are wide—with shutters
to keep out the day." The children "have swings and slides and custom-
made beds—and the doors open only one way."

Other Devices: *Inference, Internal Rhyme, Irony, Oxymoron, Satire, Theme*

Art Style: Naïve watercolors show the contrast between the real joy
expressed naturally by the children in their simple outdoor amusements
and the cloying dissatisfaction with adult-provided commercial rubbish.

Curriculum Tie-in: Social Science (Values)

*Myers, Tim. *Basho and the Fox.* Illus. by Oki S. Han. New York: Marshall Cavendish, 2000.

A Japanese poet is challenged by a fox to create his best haiku.

Antithesis: The fox is contemptuous of human poetry and poets. "We've given you our left-over poems—and you think they're masterpieces! I'll eat these cherries whenever I feel like it." The fox, however, is intrigued with Basho's claim that he is not an ordinary poet. The fox tells him, "We agree to let you have all the cherries of this tree—but only if you can write us one good haiku." When the fox hears Basho's first poem, he tells him he has a long way to go before he can call himself a poet. "Meet me at the next full moon—if you have something better." Eventually, Basho accidentally stumbles upon a poem pleasing to the foxes. He learns that "the foxes of Fukagawa were not such great poets as they thought they were. But he shared the late summer cherries with them anyway."

Other Devices: *Ambiguity, Aphorism, Imagery, Irony, Motif, Parallelism, Theme*

Art Style: Mischievous watercolor folk paintings convey the Eastern sensibility of feudal Japan.

Curriculum Tie-in: History (Japan), Social Science (Self-esteem)

Nickle, John. *The Ant Bully.* New York: Scholastic Press, 1999.

Lucas learns a lesson about bullying by the ants he has been tormenting.

Antithesis: "Sid the neighborhood bully was especially mean to him. So Lucas bullied the ants."

Other Devices: *Antihero, Foreshadowing, Inference, Personification, Poetic Justice, Point of View*

Art Style: Expressionistic acrylic cartoons skillfully play with perspective as both the boy and the ants view the environment.

Curriculum Tie-in: Social Science (Bullies, Values)

*Nolen, Jerdine. *Big Jabe.* Illus. by Kadir Nelson. New York: Lothrop, Lee & Shepard, 2000.

Momma Mary tells stories about a special young man who does wondrous things, especially for the slaves on the Plenty Plantation.

Antithesis: When Addy was a house slave on Simon Plenty's plantation, "she had to clean out the Big House. What she loved to clean out was the river." "Not a single person, in the Big House or the Quarters, knew that a new day had dawned. Everyone slept late." The twister "tore the roof clean off the barn; not a shingle was left behind." Though the overseer "could find no fault with the roof, and he didn't dare find fault with Jabe, he could let loose on Jubal—and he did." Where were the disappearing slaves? "Maybe Moses come in the night…," said Mazey. "Jabe took them to that pear tree," Addy whispered.

Other Devices: *Allusion, Anachronism, Flashback, Flash-forward, Foreshadowing, Hyperbole, Imagery, Inference, Parallelism, Simile, Symbol, Understatement*

Art Style: Strong detailed pen/ink, watercolor, and gouache drawings provide expressionistic period ambience to this folktale.

Curriculum Tie-in: History (Slavery—America), Literature (Tall Tale)

O'Malley, Kevin. *Bud.* New York: Walker & Company, 2000.

The orderly Sweet-Williams are dismayed at their son's fondness for the messy pastime of gardening.

Antithesis: Bud's habits are in direct contradiction to those of his family. The son loves dirt. "He'd jump in it, roll in it, and plant things in it. The very proper, very sensible Sweet-Williams were stunned." They did appreciate nature. But "it was just so disorderly, and that would never do." Said Bud's father, "Order marches with weighty and measured strides. Disorder is always in a hurry."

Other Devices: *Aphorism, Foreshadowing, Inference, Irony, Pun, Theme, Understatement*

Art Style: Large, expressive gouache cartoons lovingly follow the development of tolerance, respect, and appreciation for a beloved child's radical approach to life.

Curriculum Tie-in: Science (Gardening), Social Science (Family Relationships, Values)

Pawagi, Manjusha. *The Girl Who Hated Books.* Illus. by Leanne Franson. Hillsboro, OR: Beyond Words, 1998.

Although she lives in a house full of avid readers, Meena hates books—until she discovers the magic inside them.

Antithesis: Meena "hated to read, and she hated books." Books in this house are "not just on bookshelves and bedside tables where books usually are, but in all sorts of places where books usually aren't." When her cat, Max, is missing, "she found more books, but she didn't find Max." When the creatures tumble out of a fallen pile of books in the dining room, a sobbing wolf does not know where he belongs. "He wailed and blew his nose on the table cloth." To return all the book characters to their own stories, "One by one she began reading all her books. And one by one the creatures found out where they belonged."

Other Devices: *Alliteration, Allusion, Foreshadowing, Hyperbole, Inference, Internal Rhyme, Pun, Tone*

Art Style: Pen/ink watercolor expressionistic cartoons emphasize emotion and background action.

*Say, Allen. *The Sign Painter.* Boston: Walter Lorraine Books (Houghton Mifflin), 2000.

An assignment to paint a large billboard in the desert changes the life of an aspiring artist.

Antithesis: As the sign painter and the boy he hires work day after day through the defined layout of 12 billboards, the boy comments, "I keep wondering, who'll know the difference if I put mountains in the background, even just a cloud?" The man replies, "Son, when someone pays you to paint a woman, will you give him a landscape?" The boy would like to add his artistic expression to their monotonous work; the man is satisfied with commissions and doesn't ask questions about the job.

Other Devices: *Ambiguity, Imagery, Inference, Point of View, Theme, Tone*

Art Style: Magnificent realistic acrylic paintings unfold the contrasts in this provocative story about personal choices between security and dreams.

Curriculum Tie-in: Philosophy (Quality of Life)

*St. George, Judith. So You Want to Be President? Illus. by David Small. New York: Philomel (Penguin Putnam Books for Young Readers), 2000 (Caldecott—2000).

The text is a lively assortment of facts about the qualifications and characteristics of U.S. presidents from George Washington to Bill Clinton.

Antithesis: From the first line—"There are good things about being President and there are bad things about being President," the style of writing incorporates many antithetical comments. As a child George Bush didn't care for a particular vegetable. "When George Bush grew up, he became President. That was the end of the broccoli!" "Abraham Lincoln was the tallest—six feet four inches. James Madison was the smallest—five feet four inches and only one hundred pounds." William McKinley was so nice that he tried to stop a mob from attacking the man who had just shot him. Benjamin Harrison was so cold that one senator said talking to Harrison was "like talking to a hitching post."

Other Devices: *Atmosphere, Caricature, Parallelism, Tone*

Art Style: In the cherished tradition of political commentary, foibles, quirks, and humanity are illustrated in hilarious cartoons.

Curriculum Tie-in: History (American Presidents)

*Wilkon, Piotr. Rosie the Cool Cat. Illus. by Jozef Wilkon. New York: Viking (Penguin Books), 1989.

Casper and Carolina are proud of their jet-black fur and despair trying to cope with their orange kitten, who likes to play with mice and sleep in the doghouse.

Antithesis: Rosie does not fit in with the family's way of living. "She did just what she liked to do, and she did everything differently from her sisters and brothers." She became quite difficult. "She would not drink milk. She only wanted tea." Her relationship with rodents bothers her parents. "Instead of catching mice with her brothers and sisters, Rosie played and danced with them." Her attitude toward the dog is unacceptable. "Rosie decided not to sleep in the basket with her sisters and brothers. She slept outside with Punk the dog."

Other Devices: *Foreshadowing, Inference, Irony, Poetic Justice, Satire, Stereotype, Symbol*

Art Style: Pastel and colored pencil expressionistic cartoons capture the family pride in its unique sameness as well as its sense of puzzlement in the jolting difference of the odd one.

Curriculum Tie-in: Social Science (Family Relationships, Individuality, Values)

*Yaccarino, Dan. *Deep in the Jungle.* New York: Anne Schwartz Book from Atheneum Books for Young Readers (Simon & Schuster), 2000.

After being tricked into joining the circus, an arrogant lion escapes and returns to the jungle, where he lives peacefully with the animals he used to terrorize.

Antithesis: "The leopards brought him food, the gorillas brushed his mane, and the elephants gave him shade. The animals couldn't stand him one bit."

Other Devices: *Anachronism, Antihero, Black Humor, Foreshadowing, Irony, Motif, Parallelism, Poetic Justice, Pun, Tone*

Art Style: Expressionistic gouache naïve cartoons against white backgrounds, reminiscent of the "Curious George" series, accent the droll language in this lesson in humility.

Curriculum Tie-in: Literature (Parable), Social Science (Values)

Zagwÿn, Deborah. *Apple Batter.* Berkeley, CA: Tricycle Press, 1999.

Because of their persistence, Delmore succeeds in learning to hit a baseball and his mother, Loretta, succeeds in growing apples.

Antithesis: In describing his skills: "Throwing and catching were Delmore's thing. Batting was another matter." "He felt himself useful with a glove and useless with a bat."

Other Devices: *Alliteration, Analogy, Foreshadowing, Inference, Irony, Parallelism, Pun, Simile*

Art Style: Expressionistic watercolor cartoons compare the changing fortunes of mother and son as they struggle toward their respective goals.

Curriculum Tie-in: Athletics (Baseball), Science (Apple Production)

APHORISM

A short, pointed statement expressing a wise, clever, general truth. A maxim, proverb, adage, epigram, or saying, sometimes with a new twist.

Example: It takes a village to raise a child.

Battle-Lavert, Gwendolyn. *The Music in Derrick's Heart.* Illus. by Colin Bootman. New York: Holiday House, 2000.

> Uncle Booker T., who makes magic by playing harmonica music from his heart, spends the summer teaching Derrick how to play.
>
> > **Aphorism:** Uncle Booker T. tells Derrick, "Summer ain't as long as it seems." They mustn't waste time. There are lessons to learn. But Derrick wants instant skills. Uncle Booker T. tells him to slow down. "Tadpoles don't turn into frogs overnight." When Derrick finally learns to play from his heart, the old man tells him to keep the harmonica alive when he's gone. "Sometimes you got to pass along the things you love."
> >
> > **Other Devices:** *Atmosphere, Inference, Simile, Tone*
> >
> > **Art Style:** Expressionistic oil paintings show an appreciation of small town African-American music played from the heart.
> >
> > **Curriculum Tie-in:** Social Science (Ethnicity—African-American)

*Baylor, Byrd. *The Table Where Rich People Sit.* Illus. by Peter Parnall. New York: Charles Scribner's Sons, 1994.

> A girl discovers that her impoverished family is rich in things that matter in life, especially being outdoors and experiencing nature.
>
> > **Aphorism:** In a homemade truism, the mother in this untraditional approach to family life declares, "If all the rulers of the world could get together at a friendly wooden table in somebody's kitchen, they would solve their arguments in half the time." The father adds, "It wouldn't hurt to have a lot of cookies piled up on a nice blue plate that everyone could reach without asking."
> >
> > **Other Devices:** *Antihero, Foreshadowing, Irony, Paradox*
> >
> > **Art Style:** Sweeping pen/ink watercolor on white spaces flows majestically in expressionistic celebration of nature.
> >
> > **Curriculum Tie-in:** Geography (American Southwest), Literature (Parable)

*Bunting, Eve. *The Memory String.* Illus. by Ted Rand. New York: Clarion Books (Houghton Mifflin), 2000.

> While still grieving for her mother and unable to accept her stepmother, a girl clings to the memories represented by forty-three buttons on a string.
>
> > **Aphorism:** Laura secretly listens as her stepmother discusses with her father the missing button from the memory string. She says each button is a true moment. "Laura would rather have that button missing than have a replacement." "It's like a mother. No substitute allowed."
> >
> > **Other Devices:** *Ambiguity, Antithesis, Foreshadowing, Imagery, Inference, Parallelism, Simile*
> >
> > **Art Style:** Shadowy, impressionistic watercolor paintings detail the emotional changes this child experiences as she feels both separation and reconnection to her family.
> >
> > **Curriculum Tie-in:** Social Science (Family Relationships, Grief)

*Bunting, Eve. *Swan in Love.* Illus. by Jo Ellen McAllister Stammen. New York: Atheneum Books for Young Readers (Simon & Schuster), 2000.

Despite ridicule of the other animals, Swan persists in his adoration for a swan-shaped boat named Dora.

Aphorism: Swan's life illustrates the truth of love. "Difference makes no difference to love." "Love is never wrong." "Love isn't always wise." "Love makes magic."

Other Devices: *Antithesis, Foreshadowing, Imagery, Inference, Simile, Theme*

Art Style: Pastel expressionistic illustrations shimmer with grace as they illuminate the story of transforming love.

Curriculum Tie-in: Social Science (Love)

*Cole, Brock. *Buttons.* New York: Farrar Straus Giroux, 2000.

When their father eats so much that he pops the buttons off his britches, each of his three daughters tries a different plan to find replacements.

Aphorism: The youngest daughter's plan is to run about in a meadow with her shoes off and holding out her apron to catch any buttons falling from the sky. No buttons fall into her apron. Still, she keeps trying. "For isn't it written somewhere that if at first you don't succeed, try, try again?" A clever young cowherd enjoys watching her. He advises her to look the next morning for falling buttons under a large, dense tree. He sees to it that some fall into her apron, and she is most grateful. How can she settle such a large debt? She is willing to give him everything she possesses, but it couldn't possibly be enough. He suggests, "Perhaps we should get married. For it is often said that between a husband and wife there can be no debts, but they must share all and all together."

Other Devices: *Inference, Irony, Pun, Tone*

Art Style: Pen/ink and watercolor humorous cartoons complement this lighthearted spoof on courtship and family duty.

Curriculum Tie-in: Literature (Fairy Tale)

*Deedy, Carmen Agra. *The Yellow Star: The Legend of King Christian X of Denmark.* Illus. by Henri Sorensen. Atlanta: Peachtree, 2000.

King Christian must abide by Nazi orders regarding the wearing of the identifying yellow star, but he must also protect all the Danes from harm.

Aphorism: A stranger in Denmark is astonished that the king rides without a bodyguard. A Dane explains, "A king so loved needs no bodyguard." A beloved political figure has no need to fear the public.

Other Devices: *Antithesis, Atmosphere, Foreshadowing, Inference, Irony, Paradox, Parallelism, Pun, Simile, Symbol, Theme*

Art Style: Impressionistic oil paintings accompany the spare, terse text in this vignette showing the political reality of the Danes' circumstances during a very somber period of history.

Curriculum Tie-in: History (World War II—Nazi Occupation—Denmark), Literature (Legend), Social Science (Values)

*Gralley, Jean. *Hogula, Dread Pig of Night.* New York: Henry Holt, 1999.

Although he lives high on the hog in his castle on Grimy Pork Chop Hill, Hogula is unhappy because he has no friends—until he meets Elvis Ann, Dread Queen of Kissyface.

Aphorism: Hogula realizes he is powerless before Elvis Ann's charms. They are a perfect match, made-for-each-other friends. "In friendship, sometimes you have to give a little to get a lot back." Hogula likes to hang around with the bats, upside down. The illustration shows that Elvis Ann has accepted this practice and is hanging with her knees over the bar, along with Hogula and all the castle bats.

Other Devices: *Alliteration, Allusion, Antihero, Cliché, Foreshadowing, Inference, Irony, Poetic Justice, Pun, Simile, Stereotype, Understatment*

Art Style: Appropriately repulsive, expressionistic cartoons of gouache and ink on watercolor paper develop the characters of this humorously gentle Dracula-style relationship.

Curriculum Tie-in: Social Science (Friendship)

Hoban, Russell. *Trouble on Thunder Mountain.* Illus. by Quentin Blake. New York: Orchard Books (Grolier), 2000.

When Megafright International flattens their beautiful mountain to put up a hi-tech plastic theme park, the O'Saurus family uses faith and lots of Monsta-Gloo to put things right.

Aphorism: The dinosaur family and their mountain friends bring back the chunks of their former home in a pickup truck. Jim O'Saurus, the son, remarks how hard the work is. "Sometimes there is no easy way," Dad replies as they restore their home little by little.

Other Devices: *Connotation, Foreshadowing, Hyperbole, Irony, Poetic Justice, Satire, Understatement*

Art Style: Humorous pen/ink watercolor cartoons spiritedly produce a funny tribute to old-fashioned ingenuity and to nature.

Curriculum Tie-in: Science (Ecology)

Kajikawa, Kimiko. *Yoshi's Feast.* Illus. by Yumi Heo. New York: DK Ink, 2000.

When Yoshi's neighbor, Sabu, the eel broiler, attempts to charge him for the delicious-smelling aromas he has been enjoying, Yoshi hatches a plan to enrich them both.

Aphorism: Yoshi thinks he is satisfied eating rice and simply smelling the eels, but when confronted with a debt that he must find a way to pay, he discovers that he is wrong. "Neighbor, you get what you pay for," Sabu warns him. Since Yoshi won't pay for the aroma of broiling eel, he is assailed by the aroma of stinky fish. Mutual cooperation is more satisfying. Yoshi brings customers to Sabu, and Sabu shares his eels with Yoshi. "Sniffing broiled eels by myself is nowhere near as good as eating them with a friend," he concludes.

Other Devices: *Antithesis, Foreshadowing, Inference, Onomatopoeia, Parallelism, Poetic Justice*
Art Style: Oil, pencil, and paper collage come together in a satisfyingly expressionistic design to transmit the flavor of this ethnic quarrel.
Curriculum Tie-in: Literature (Folktales—Japan)

*Kaplan, Howard. *Waiting to Sing.* Illus. by Hervé Blondon. New York: DK Ink, 2000.

A family who loves music, and spends many hours at the piano, is devastated by the death of the mother, but those still living find consolation in the beautiful music that remains.

Aphorism: The young narrator notes that the apartments in his building each exhibit their own kind of sound. "Every house was a story waiting to be heard." Later, after suffering the loss of his mother and feeling isolated in his grief, he and his father find each other again by returning to the source of their life's pleasure, the household piano. "Sometimes I think the greatest distance to be traveled is that between two beating hearts."
Other Devices: *Allusion, Antithesis, Atmosphere, Foreshadowing, Imagery, Inference, Metaphor, Parallelism, Simile, Symbol*
Art Style: Full-page, sepia-tone pastel cartoon drawings expressionistically evoke a fragile emotional period in the life of a family coping with restructuring itself after the wrenching loss of one of its members.
Curriculum Tie-in: Music (Piano), Social Science (Death, Family Relationships, Feelings)

Kurtz, Jane. *River Friendly, River Wild.* Illus. by Neil Brennan. New York: Simon & Schuster Books for Young Readers, 2000.

A family experiences a renewed appreciation for home and community after they are evacuated during a spring flood and then return to survey the damage.

Aphorism: Much later, when people have returned to a semblance of their original lives, they reflect on their experience of loss and come to understand that "some memories live in things"—in old clothes and photographs, drawings, and trees. Some of those memories will have to be let go. It's time to make new memories.
Other Devices: *Antithesis, Atmosphere, Imagery, Metaphor, Onomatopoeia, Simile*
Art Style: Oil glaze of brown paint overlaid by thin layers of color in different areas and additional glazes for depth create fuzzy, impressionistic scenes that suggest the essence of this emotionally wrenching natural disaster.
Curriculum Tie-in: Geography (Flood—Grand Forks, North Dakota)

Lowell, Susan. *Cindy Ellen: A Wild Western Cinderella.* Illus. by Jane Manning. New York: Joanna Cotler Books (HarperCollins), 2000.

Cindy Ellen loses one of her diamond spurs at the square dance in the retelling of this classic fairy tale.

Aphorism: Cindy Ellen's fairy godmother offers her words of wisdom when she helps her prepare for social occasions. "Remember, Miss Cindy, pretty is as pretty does." "Magic is plumb worthless without gumption." Other devices: *Alliteration, Foreshadowing, Internal Rhyme, Parallelism, Parody, Simile, Tone*

Art Style: Action-packed expressionistic acrylic cartoons hilariously support the story's western flavor.

Curriculum Tie-in: Social Science (Self-esteem)

Lowell, Susan. *Little Red Cowboy Hat.* Illus. by Randy Cecil. New York: Henry Holt, 1997.

Little Red rides her pony, Buck, to Grandma's ranch with a jar of cactus jelly in the saddlebag.

Aphorism: After successfully dealing with the wolf threat, Grandma and Little Red take a break to eat a bread and cactus jelly sandwich. They ruminate over their experience. "Now, Red, have you learned your lesson?" Grandma asks. "Yep. A girl's gotta stick up for herself," Little Red replies.

Other Devices: *Atmosphere, Caricature, Hyperbole, Inference, Onomatopoeia, Parody, Simile, Stereotype, Tone*

Art Style: Gouache cartoons in expressionistic naïve style humorously match this unique geographical version of a familiar fairy tale.

McKissack, Patricia. *The Honest to Goodness Truth.* Illus. by Giselle Potter. New York: Atheneum Books for Young Readers (Simon & Schuster), 2000.

After promising never to lie, Libby learns it's not always necessary to blurt out the whole truth.

Aphorism: When she straightens out her views about telling the truth, Libby finds it necessary to apologize to the people who were the recipients of her harsh version of the honest truth. One of them is Miss Tusselbury, who puts the matter in perspective. "The truth is often hard to chew. But if it is sweetened with love, then it is a little easier to swallow."

Other Devices: *Ambiguity, Antithesis, Foreshadowing, Paradox, Simile, Understatement*

Art Style: Pencil, ink, gouache, and watercolor render a luxuriant, expressionistic, naïve style to this tale of honesty.

Curriculum Tie-in: Social Science (Friendship, Honesty, Values)

*Martin, Nora. *The Stone Dancers.* Illus. by Jill Kastner. New York: Atheneum Books for Young Readers (Simon & Schuster), 1995.

A young girl uses an old legend about stone dancers to teach her mountain village a lesson in hospitality and sharing.

Aphorism: The village was founded by folks who were misfits in their society. Many years later the descendants have forgotten their heritage until strangers come seeking a safe place to live. This new family is a bit frightening because they are dirty and look nothing like the villagers. Then the villagers realize that "they are strangers until they live here and then they are our neighbors. And we must always care for our neighbors."
Other Devices: *Imagery, Inference, Irony, Metaphor, Parallel Story, Simile*
Art Style: Impressionistic oil paintings show the interplay of light and shadow, melding the real with the enchanted in this nineteenth-century French peasant village.
Curriculum Tie-in: History (Nineteenth-Century France), Literature (Legends), Social Science (Values)

Mochizuki, Ken. *Passage to Freedom: The Sugihara Story.* Illus. by Dom Lee. Afterword by Hiroki Sugihara. New York: Lee & Low, 1997.
Following refusal by the Japanese government to issue visas to Jewish refugees from Poland, Consul Sugihara and his family make a crucial decision that saved thousands of lives.
Aphorism: The first sentence says, "The eyes tell everything about a person." And the eyes of those beseeching help from the young narrator's diplomat father cannot be denied. He risks his career and his family when he disobeys his government and issues visas to the people trying to escape Hitler during World War II.
Other Devices: *Antithesis, Foreshadowing, Point of View, Theme*
Art Style: The stark fear of survival is shown in the realistic, photograph-like, sepia-tone, oil paint and pencil over scratched beeswax paper. Emotionally charged, unrelenting shades of brown shadowing focus on the grim refugee predicament—their barely contained explosive violence—and the terrible decision facing the diplomat.
Curriculum Tie-in: History (World War II)

*Myers, Tim. *Basho and the Fox.* Illus. by Oki S. Han. New York: Marshall Cavendish, 2000.
A Japanese poet is challenged by a fox to create his best haiku.
Aphorism: Basho is appalled that his best poems seem not good enough for the foxes. He begins to doubt his own abilities. Then when he dashes off an average poem, which has a fox as its subject, he is astonished to find himself lavished with praise. He learns the foxes are not such great poets as they thought they were. A poem should be written for its own sake.
Other Devices: *Ambiguity, Antithesis, Imagery, Irony, Motif, Parallelism, Theme*
Art Style: Mischievous watercolor folk paintings convey the Eastern sensibility of feudal Japan.
Curriculum Tie-in: History (Japan), Social Science (Self-esteem)

O'Malley, Kevin. *Bud.* New York: Walker & Company, 2000.

The orderly Sweet-Williams are dismayed at their son's fondness for the messy pastime of gardening.

Aphorism: Bud's parents are ruled by strict adherence to accepted norms. "Cleanliness is next to godliness." And "Order marches with weighty and measured strides. Disorder is always in a hurry." Bud teaches them some moderation in their code of life. "Hard work is easy to take…when you finish with chocolate cake!"

Other Devices: *Antithesis, Foreshadowing, Inference, Irony, Pun, Theme, Understatement*

Art Style: Large, expressive gouache cartoons lovingly follow the development of tolerance, respect, and appreciation for a beloved child's unconventional approach to life.

Curriculum Tie-in: Science (Gardening), Social Science (Family Relationships, Values)

*Pacilio, V.J. *Ling Cho and His Three Friends.* Illus. by Scott Cook. New York: Farrar Straus Giroux, 2000.

Through his plan to share the wealth of his wheat crop with three friends, a Chinese farmer teaches the importance of allowing other people to help in time of need.

Aphorism: "A man who will allow his friends to help in time of need is— more than even he who gives—a valued friend, indeed." The measure of a family's wealth is that family's health.

Other Devices: *Alliteration, Irony, Paradox, Poetic Justice, Theme*

Art Style: Impressionistic oil paintings in Chinese reds and golds suggest unstated meanings behind spoken words.

Curriculum Tie-in: Social Science (Friendship, Values)

ATMOSPHERE

General mood developed through descriptions of setting and details about how things look, sound, feel, taste, and smell in order to create an emotional climate that establishes a reader's expectations and attitudes.

Example: A boring afternoon suddenly promises something of interest: "So she was considering in her own mind (as well as she could, for the hot day made her feel very sleepy and stupid), whether the pleasure of making a daisy-chain would be worth the trouble of getting up and picking the daisies, when suddenly a White Rabbit with pink eyes ran close by her."

Lewis Carroll, *Alice's Adventures in Wonderland*

Battle-Lavert, Gwendolyn. *The Music in Derrick's Heart.* Illus. by Colin Bootman. New York: Holiday House, 2000.

Uncle Booker T., who makes magic by playing his harmonica music from his heart, spends the summer teaching Derrick how to play.

Atmosphere: Derrick looks forward to his summer lessons as they go around town making music. "Uncle Booker T. played gold and silver notes." They sat on Big Mama's front porch. "She always had a big platter of homemade teacakes and a pitcher of squeezed lemonade." The summer days got hotter. "If there was a breeze, the big pecan trees in the yard surely blocked it." They visited Aunt Agnes on her wash day. "The white sheets on her clothesline snapped and popped in the noonday sun." They are joined by an impromptu marching band. There's "tall Jimmy, skinny Larry, and the twins, Kevin and Ken." "Aunt Fannie Mae trailed behind them, holding baby LaToya on her left hip and a picnic basket over her right arm." In the evening "neighbors sat on their porches gossiping, swatting mosquitoes, and listening as Derrick practiced."

Other Devices: *Aphorism, Inference, Simile, Tone*

Art Style: Expressionistic oil paintings show an appreciation of rural small-town African-American music played from the heart.

Curriculum Tie-in: Social Science (Ethnicity—African-American)

*Burleigh, Robert. *Edna.* Illus. by Joanna Yardley. New York: Orchard Books, 2000.

Carefree meanderings during her time in New York City give Edna St. Vincent Millay grist for a famous poem she later pens.

Atmosphere: This is a time in her life when Edna is "living in the world's greatest city, being young, and caring for nothing but to be alive here and now." All things seem possible. "The Great War is ending, women are getting the vote, and it's a new America." Her delight cannot be dimmed by poverty. "We don't have much money, my friends and I. I help pay the rent by acting in small plays and selling my poems to newspapers and magazines—when I can. It's spring here and I'm happy."

Other Devices: *Foreshadowing, Imagery, Parallelism, Simile*

Art Style: Expressionistic watercolors in vivid hues help recreate the marvelous feelings of expectation and freedom experienced by youthful artists in a city of promise that welcomes their enthusiasm.

Curriculum Tie-in: Literature (Biography—Poets)

*Deedy, Carmen Agra. *The Yellow Star: The Legend of King Christian X of Denmark.* Illus. by Henri Sorensen. Atlanta: Peachtree, 2000.

King Christian must abide by Nazi orders regarding the wearing of the identifying yellow star, but he must also protect all the Danes from harm.

Atmosphere: War in Europe is likened to a fierce storm, which even good King Christian was powerless to stop. Soon Nazi soldiers gather in dark clouds at the Danish border. Their arrival in Copenhagen brings food shortages, curfews, and a new flag. The terrible news about Jews being required to wear the yellow star at all times makes the people of Denmark frightened. They've heard "terrible stories."

Other Devices: *Antithesis, Aphorism, Foreshadowing, Inference, Irony, Paradox, Parallelism, Pun, Simile, Symbol, Theme*

Art Style: Impressionistic oil paintings accompany the spare, terse text in this vignette showing the political reality of the Danes' circumstances during a very somber period of history.

Curriculum Tie-in: History (World War II—Nazi Occupation— Denmark), Literature (Legend), Social Science (Values)

Dengler, Marianna. *Fiddlin' Sam.* Illus. by Sibyl Graber Gerig. Flagstaff, AZ: Rising Moon, (Northland), 1999.

Wandering through the Ozarks and bringing joy to people with his music, Fiddlin' Sam seeks the right person to take up his fiddle and carry on the practice.

Atmosphere: As Sam walks the Ozark Mountains, it's sometimes "hotter'n blazes." He thinks how good it would feel "to dunk his feet in a nice cool crick." When bitten by a snake, he notes, "I'm a goner. Sure as shootin'." When the boy first tries to play the fiddle, "the consarned thing wouldn't stay in his hands." Later, he, too, can make the fiddle sing. While folks sit at his feet, "the single thread of the fiddle tune reaches up and up, mingles with the wind in the pines and meanders on to the sky."

Other Devices: *Antithesis, Foreshadowing, Inference, Internal Rhyme, Parallelism, Serendipity*

Art Style: Exuberant realistic and expressionistic watercolors in shades of bright yellow, pink, and blue faithfully reveal the emotional and physical details of this musician's life.

Curriculum Tie-in: Social Science (Missouri Ozarks)

DePaola, Tomie. *The Art Lesson.* New York: G.P. Putnam's Sons, 1989.

Having learned to be creative in drawing pictures at home, young Tommy is dismayed when he goes to school and finds the art lessons there much more regimented.

Atmosphere: To the preschool-aged Tommy, school means art lessons! After looking forward with great expectations, reality falls short. First, there are no art lessons at all in kindergarten! "Oh, you won't have your art lessons until next year." Though students do get to paint, "the paint was awful and the paper got all wrinkly." Paint is made by mixing powder and water. "The paint didn't stick to the paper very well and it cracked." On windy days, "the paint blew right off the paper" when Tommy carried his picture home. In first grade, "you only get one piece" of paper. Tommy looks forward to using his new box of sixty-four Crayola crayons. But,

again, reality dampens his hopes. Each child must "use the same crayons.
SCHOOL CRAYONS." There are only eight colors. And, since they are
school property, students must not "break them, peel off the paper, or wear
down the points." Tommy can't imagine how he can practice his drawing
under such restrictions. But, worst of all, when the real art lesson begins,
he is asked to COPY what the teacher draws. "This was supposed to be a
real art lesson." "He folded his arms and just sat there." "Now what's the
matter?" asks his classroom teacher. Thank goodness, his art teacher thinks
of a suitable compromise that allows Tommy to express his individuality.
Other Devices: *Flash-forward, Inference, Irony, Parallelism, Serendipity,
Theme*
Art Style: Blocky pastel cartoons follow the fortunes of a budding young
artist in a conformist world.
Curriculum Tie-in: Social Science (Individuality)

Glass, Andrew. *Bewildered for Three Days: As to Why Daniel Boone Never Wore His
Coonskin Cap.* New York: Holiday House, 2000.
   With the help of what he learned from a Delaware Indian boy and an
accommodating mother raccoon, young Daniel Boone escapes danger when
a bear steals his coonskin cap.
   Atmosphere: In his old age Boone has his portrait painted. He puts on the
worn buckskin britches he used to wear when he "ventured into the dark
Allegheny Mountains to explore the howling wilderness of Kentucky."
Then he begins his story for the benefit of the painter. Bands of Cherokee
"crossed the distant blue mountains to raid scattered cabins at the edge of
the wilderness." When the Delawares come on the day they are at work
in their hardscrabble field, "warriors burst through the trees, shrieking and
waving hatchets. Folks screamed and snatched up little children. Women
lifted their long skirts and sprinted for the log cabins." But the Delawares
turned out to be friendly. Boone's sister and he "made some room for Little
Beaver. We sat together by the hearth, shoulder to shoulder, listening to
an old trapper's stories." Due to his Indian friend's influence, he "took to
dressing in skins and stuck feathers into the old trapper's coonskin cap.
We played at painting ourselves for war and throwing the heavy hatchet."
Later, the young Boone encounters a bear as he "fell asleep in a mossy
glade. I awoke to a malodorous sniffling and snorting. A warm black nose
glistened over me." Next he encounters enemy Indians. "A way off the
braves commenced to whoop and holler. I broke for the woods. But the
braves chased me through the flapping turkeys, right to the edge of a sheer
rock cliff. It fell some sixty feet to a rushing stream. Arrows whizzed by."
Other Devices: *Flashback, Foreshadowing, Motif, Point of View, Tone,
Understatement*

Art Style: Impressionistic colored pencil and oil pastel humorously accompany this frontier yarn of a great adventurer told in a blend of humility and exaggeration.
Curriculum Tie-in: History (Biography—Daniel Boone), Literature (Tall Tale)

Hest, Amy. *Mabel Dancing.* Illus. by Christine Davenier. Cambridge, MA: Candlewick Press, 2000.

Mabel doesn't want to go to sleep while Mama and Papa are having a dance party downstairs.

Atmosphere: The irresistible rhythm of dance and the magical beauty of swishing, swirling gowns, bright shoes, and formal bow ties are described in words of sound and movement: "Shall we dance . . . shall we dance . . . shall we dance?" "one, two, three—one, two three," "shhh, two, three—shhh, two, three," "spin, two, three—spin, two, three," and in words of visual delight: "twirled and jumped in the bright party light," "blanket blew up like a yellow cape in the wind making swirls," "floating through the rooms," "spinning past the guests."
Other Devices: *Foreshadowing, Imagery, Parallelism*
Art Style: Airy, expressionistic watercolor washes and ink line drawings capture the contrast of bright excitement and action downstairs with gloomy loneliness and boring isolation upstairs.
Curriculum Tie-in: Social Science (Values)

Hutchins, Hazel. *One Duck.* Illus. by Ruth Ohi. New York: Annick (Firefly Books), 1999.

A mother duck works to defend her nest of eggs from a marauding crow and a farmer's cultivator.

Atmosphere: There is tension between the time constraints the farmer is facing and the time constraints the duck is facing. The farmer must hurry to finish cultivating the field before the rain comes. The duck has just a little more time before the ducklings hatch. She finishes feeding at a lake and "settles down upon them knowing it is almost time and waits." Meanwhile the farmer sees "one small cloud on the horizon" and thinks about the day. "Cultivator to hook up and pull onto the stubble field to till the soil for the wheat he'll plant and tend and sell to feed and clothe his family four children still asleep upstairs." He "turns the soil the first row of a pattern leading ever inward towards . . . . One Duck on twelve eggs." A crow distracts her, but the duck stays. The tractor continues to make passes around the field. The crow flees, but the duck sits, "a single thought is clamoring—danger."
Other Devices: *Antithesis, Imagery, Inference, Onomatopoeia, Parallelism, Tone*

Art Style: Expressionistic pen/ink watercolor drawings sensitively complement the lyrical text of this common farming drama.

Curriculum Tie-in: Science (Agriculture, Animal Behavior)

Johnson, Angela. *Down the Winding Road.* Illus. by Shane Evans. New York: DK Ink, 2000.

The annual summer visit to the country home of the Old Ones, the uncles and aunts who raised Daddy, brings joy and good times.

Atmosphere: "We take the winding road every year. Past the city, way past all the people" to visit the Old Ones. They "laugh with us, the sounds echoing down the road." They all go "on a long walk through the grassy woods that stretch along the winding road." They reminisce how sad it was "when they cut down the old-growth trees around here to put up more highway." Soon they are at the lake the Old Ones swam in when they were young—"and sit beside now that they are old." The old tire swing still hangs out on a willow over the lake. The Old Ones "stand at the shore clapping, laughing, and yelling" as the children swing out over the water. "There's nothing like flying." The children let loose and drop into the water as the "lake glimmers beside the winding road." The sameness and serenity of this place spark appreciation in the souls of these city kids. They care not half as much for their convenient streets as they do for this winding road, which is clearly as aged as the Old Ones.

Other Devices: *Anachronism, Inference, Irony*

Art Style: In expressionistic pen/ink drawings and oil paintings, the gentle, loving life of a caring family is made enviously believable.

Curriculum Tie-in: Social Science (Family Relationships)

Johnson, Paul Brett. *Bearhide and Crow.* New York: Holiday House, 2000.

After Sam tricks Amos into swapping a prize-winning gourd for a smelly old bearhide, Amos decides to give Sam a taste of his own medicine by negotiating an even more worthless trade.

Atmosphere: This tale of swapping is set in the Appalachian country. Amos is "a swapping fool." If "it wasn't a button for a bucket lid, it was a hat for a horseshoe. And, if it wasn't a hat for a horseshoe, it was a jackknife for a jimmy-diddle." Amos soon realizes he has been tricked. He "figured anything he got from the likes of Sam Hankins wouldn't be worth chicken teeth." In his payback scheme, Amos tells Sam, "This ain't no ordinary crow; I split its tongue and learnt it to talk." Appalachian lore holds that if a crow's tongue is split, it can be taught human speech. Amos does manage to best Sam in a swap, but "that wasn't the end of it, though, not hardly." In the end, Amos has made enough on his deals to go to the city to buy his wife "a whole poke full of pretties."

Other Devices: *Poetic Justice, Serendipity*

Art Style: Pencil sketches and painted acrylic cartoons humorously illustrate the changing fortunes and effects of greed upon these mountain swappers.

*Kaplan, Howard. *Waiting to Sing*. Illus. by Hervé Blondon. New York: DK Ink, 2000.

A family who loves music and spends many hours at the piano is devastated by the death of the mother, but those still living find consolation in the beautiful music that remains.

Atmosphere: The family is joyful and close. "I'd come home [from school], run up the four flights of stairs to my apartment, and the music would greet me halfway, even before I came breathless to our red door." Friends would come over. "My father played songs he made up that made people laugh." Even if the boy was in bed before guests left, his father would come later to "fill my favorite green glass with water, and hold it for me while I sat up in bed and took a few sips." After his mother dies, "I tried to play the piano, but it wasn't the same. Everything went quiet for a time. We closed the piano. It seemed even the G-clef lamp ran out of light." Grief paralyzes them. "My father and I didn't say much to each other. He stayed in his room and I stayed in mine. He stopped making up songs, and none of my parents' friends came over to laugh anymore. No more birds landed on the piano." Later, they find each other as a family again when the father tentatively turns to the piano, playing two notes of a recognized and beloved favorite song. "I walked from my bedroom to the piano bench, as if holding on to the music for balance, and sat by my father's side." They find no need to speak. They play the piano instead. As the boy turns on the piano lamp in the dark living room, "the light seemed to remember us."

Other Devices: *Allusion, Antithesis, Aphorism, Foreshadowing, Imagery, Inference, Metaphor, Parallelism, Simile, Symbol*

Art Style: Full-page, sepia-tone pastel cartoon drawings expressionistically evoke a fragile emotional period in the life of a family coping with restructuring itself after the wrenching loss of one of its members.

Curriculum Tie-in: Music (Piano), Social Science (Death, Family Relationships, Feelings)

Kimmel, Eric A. *Grizz!* Illus. by Andrew Glass. New York: Holiday House, 2000.

Cowboy Lucky Doolin makes a deal with the Devil, agreeing not to wash, shave, or change his clothes for seven years, thus earning a fortune and the hand of his true love.

Atmosphere: This comedy western has the typical poor but noble cowboy, the rich and disdainful ranch owner father, and the lovely, desirable ranch owner's daughter. Then there are the minor characters: the opportunists. The lawyer who buys the right to marry the daughter, and the slick stranger who expects to take advantage of the innocent cowboy. "Shelby weren't raised to be no cowboy's wife," says the interfering ranch owner. So the cowboy is sent on his way. His naivete brings him in contact with a smooth-talking stranger. A deal is struck. "Within a year, Lucky Doolin was the richest man in the West. Everything he touched turned to money." "Back in those days, lots of folks tended toward the wild and wooly, so Lucky didn't attract too much attention." Hard times hit the ranch owner. There is only one way to save the ranch. Lawyer Parmelee Jones points out to the lovely Shelby, "You ain't got no choice. It's me or nothin'. Make up your mind, darlin'. Time's a wastin'." The noble cowboy steps in. His basic goodness enables him to prevail, because his motives are pure. Everyone gets their just deserts, as is only right and expected in a good western soap opera.

Other Devices: *Hyperbole, Inference, Motif, Poetic Justice, Simile, Understatement*

Art Style: Oil sticks and water color dust create exaggerated cartoons that complement this version of a soul-selling wager folktale.

Curriculum Tie-in: Literature (Folktale—United States)

Kurtz, Jane. *River Friendly, River Wild.* Illus. by Neil Brennan. New York: Simon & Schuster Books for Young Readers, 2000.

A family experiences a renewed appreciation for home and community after they are evacuated during a spring flood and then return to survey the damage.

Atmosphere: This poetic diary of a traumatic flooding experience is enhanced by vignettes expressing anxiety, fear, devastation, anger, and hope. It has language such as "Sometimes, full of spring rain, it crawled up her yard, leaving chunks of trees that we made into pirate ships." And "Everybody's bagging sand. Piling the bags on top of the dikes. One, lift, two, swing, three, catch, four, toss." And "We grab our bags. Rush, rush, everybody out." "Through the midnight streets out of the silent city away from the river away from our home." And "How can things burn when they're sitting in water?" "On TV the walls fall down again and again and again and again." And "Snowbanks of garbage and sandbags line every street." "Every pile is someone's story." And "My dad lifts a box and turns it over. Water and paper dolls gush out. The paper dolls saw it all. I wish they could tell me what happened to my cat. And "I don't love the smell of the river water anymore." And "I'm mad at these books because they used to look like books and now they're gooshy, soggy, slimy, lumps that no one will ever want to read." And "A squirrel runs by the ash tree that Max planted in fourth grade. It's popping with buds. The flood didn't get the tree, but the new dike will." And "Time to start over—someplace else. This was one terrific neighborhood."

Other Devices: *Antithesis, Aphorism, Imagery, Metaphor, Onomatopoeia, Simile*
Art Style: Oil glaze of brown paint overlaid by thin layers of color in different areas and additional glazes for depth, create fuzzy, impressionistic scenes that reflect the essence of this emotional experience.
Curriculum Tie-in: Geography (Flood—Grand Forks, North Dakota)

Lowell, Susan. *Little Red Cowboy Hat.* Illus. by Randy Cecil. New York: Henry Holt, 1997.
Little Red rides her pony, Buck, to Grandma's ranch with a jar of cactus jelly in the saddlebag and learns how to fend for herself.
Atmosphere: After saddling her buckskin pony and putting on her cowboy hat, Little Red rode off for her grandmother's ranch several miles away. She went down into a deep canyon where her pony's feet struck sparks from the rocks. She rode up onto a wide mesa where gold poppies and blue lupines blossomed in the grass. And she watched out for rattlesnakes. At the ranch she heard nothing except the windmill creaking. Grandma was usually outside doctoring a cow or mixing cement.
Other Devices: *Aphorism, Caricature, Hyperbole, Inference, Onomatopoeia, Parody, Simile, Stereotype, Tone*
Art Style: Gouache cartoons in expressionistic naïve style humorously match this unique geographical take on a familiar fairy tale.

*St. George, Judith. *So You Want to Be President?* Illus. by David Small. New York: Philomel (Penguin Putnam Books for Young Readers), 2000 (Caldecott—2000).
These comments are a lively assortment of facts about the qualifications and characteristics of U.S. presidents from George Washington to Bill Clinton.
Atmosphere: Facts meant to amuse and surprise are selected for inclusion. "When he (Andrew Jackson) ran for President, his opponents printed a list of his duels, fights, shootings, and brawls. Fourteen in all!" "Andrew Johnson once served his guests turtle soup, oysters, fish, beef, turkey, mutton chops, chicken, mushrooms, string beans, partridges, duck, pudding, jellies, and lots of wine. All at one dinner!" "Someone once threw a cabbage at William Howard Taft. He quipped, 'I see that one of my adversaries has lost his head.'" "Someone once called Lincoln two-faced. 'If I am two-faced, would I wear the face that I have now?' Lincoln asked." He wasn't much of a dancer either. "Miss Todd, I should like to dance with you the worst way," he told his future wife. Miss Todd later told a friend, "He certainly did."
Other Devices: *Antithesis, Caricature, Parallelism, Tone*
Art Style: In the cherished tradition of political commentary, foibles, quirks, and humanity are illustrated in hilarious cartoons.
Curriculum Tie-in: History (American Presidents)

Turner, Ann. *Drummer Boy: Marching to the Civil War*. Illus. by Mark Hess. New York: HarperCollins, 1998.

> A thirteen-year-old soldier, coming of age during the American Civil War, beats his drum to raise tunes and spirits, and muffle the sounds of the dying.
>
> > **Atmosphere:** With terse, haunting text, the story conveys the randomness of fate and the bleak futility of war. "It started when I saw Mr. Lincoln on his way to Washington. Sometimes you take to a person, the way a horse snuffs up the smell of someone. I knew I had to go to war somehow, though I wasn't old enough to fight." He describes his first battle experience as being too afraid to run. "The air whizzing with bullets, the screams of the shot horses, cannonballs pounding the earth, the men falling like grain cut down." In due time he says, "The worst thing is, I am beginning to forget their faces, the boys I knew. So at night before battle, I go round a few campfires to fix their faces in my mind, the boys who might be gone by next day."
> >
> > **Other Devices:** *Imagery, Point of View, Simile*
> >
> > **Art Style:** Stunningly realistic paintings bring to life what it must have been like to be a very young soldier in an uncommon situation.
> >
> > **Curriculum Tie-in:** History (Civil War)

Waite, Judy. *Mouse, Look Out!* Illus. by Norma Burgin. New York: Dutton Children's Books (Penguin Putnam), 1998.

> Inside an old, abandoned house a mouse searches for a safe place to hide from a cat.
>
> > **Atmosphere:** An air of mystery and danger is engendered by language such as "silent as the sunset, a shadow came creeping." This shadowy presence comes "prowling down the tangled path" to the house. Wind "came calling." It "pounded, banged, and bashed" through the battered door "no one knocked on." It "wailed through" the empty house, causing "cobweb curtains" to pull apart. The "shadow came lurking" down the hallway, only a few steps behind the mouse, approaching relentlessly closer. Soon it is "slinking up behind," and now it is lunging.
> >
> > **Other Devices:** *Alliteration, Internal Rhyme, Metaphor, Poetic Justice, Simile*
> >
> > **Art Style:** Realistic acrylic paintings in detailed perspective are a perfect complement to the pleasingly ominous, gently scary text.

White, Linda Arms. *Comes a Wind*. Illus. by Tom Curry. New York: DK Pub., 2000.

> While visiting their mother's ranch, two brothers who constantly try to best each other swap tall tales about big winds, and are surprised by the fiercest wind they have ever seen.
>
> > **Atmosphere:** This is the land of squeaking windmills. Cowboys with "spit-shined, high-heeled, pointy-toed boots" propped up on porch rails outdo each other telling tall tales. They drive "racehorse-sleek" midnight black

pickups or "longhorned, rooster red pickups" with genuine steerhide interiors. They shuffle and shamble when they walk, and wear ten- or fifteen-gallon hats. They live in places called "Lariat County," "Muleskin Knob," and "Rattlesnake Hill." City parks contain Texas Ranger statues. Native plants are prickly pears, sagebrush, and mesquite trees.

Other Devices: *Foreshadowing, Hyperbole, Inference, Parallelism, Simile*
Art Style: Acrylic paintings in expressionistic, naïve perspectives illustrate the peculiar and humorous effects of the forces of wind and imagination.
Curriculum Tie-in: Literature (Tall Tales)

*__Wisniewski, David.__ *Golem.* New York: Clarion Books (Houghton Mifflin), 1996 (Caldecott—1997).

A saintly rabbi miraculously brings to life a clay giant who helps him watch over the Jews of sixteenth-century Prague.

Atmosphere: "Within the beautiful city of Prague, fierce hatreds have raged for a thousand years. In the year 1580, the Jews of Prague were bearing the ignorant fury of others. Enemies had accused them of mixing the blood of Christian children with the flour and water of matzoh, the unleavened Passover bread. This 'Blood Lie' incited angry mobs to great cruelty against the Jews." "When darkness fell, the three men left the ghetto through a secret opening in the wall. They hurried along the forbidden avenues of Prague to the cold clay banks of the river Vltava. Itzak and Yakov began to dig." The clay man performs his duties, but when the time comes for him to return to earth, he wishes, instead, to live. "Golem staggered and fell to his knees. 'Oh, Father!' he pleaded. 'Do not do this to me.' Even as he lifted his mighty hands, they were dissolving. 'Please!' Golem cried. 'Please let me live! I did all that you asked of me! Life is so . . . precious . . . to me!' With that, he collapsed into clay." "Perhaps, when the desperate need for justice is united with holy purpose, Golem will come to life once more."
Other Devices: *Analogy, Foreshadowing, Imagery, Inference, Irony, Motif, Paradox, Simile*
Art Style: Paper cut in sophisticated expressionistic collage produces a powerful physical and emotional effect for this cautionary tale.
Curriculum Tie-in: Literature (Legend), Social Science (Values)

BLACK HUMOR

Grotesque, grim, gruesome, or horrifying elements irreverently juxtaposed with humorous or farcical ones for shock value, sometimes called gallows humor when the topic is joking about death.

Example: "The worms go in; the worms go out . . . " in reference to the
decay of a body. Or "It took a licking and is still ticking" in
reference to a functioning watch on a severed arm.

Fearnley, Jan. *Mr. Wolf's Pancakes.* Waukesha, WI: Little Tiger Press, 1999.
When Mr. Wolf seeks help from his neighbors about how to make pancakes,
he is rudely rebuffed and must rely upon his own efforts.

Black Humor: After refusing to lend a hand, the neighbors are only too
willing to share the finished pancakes. They push into his house and tell
Mr. Wolf they won't go away until he gives them some. Mr. Wolf thinks
"very hard for a moment. There was only one decent thing to do." He sighs
and tells them, "Oh, very well then, you better come in." Too bad for
them. He follows them to his kitchen, and when they are all in . . . he
gobbles them up. "That was the end of his unhelpful neighbors!" Then he
ate the whole pile of pancakes, too, all by himself. "Well, there was nobody
else around."

Other Devices: *Allusion, Antihero, Irony, Poetic Justice, Stereotype*

Art Style: Detailed cartoons in pen/ink and watercolor drawings virtually
cover the pages not only with the story in progress but also with humorous
nods to many Mother Goose rhymes and fairy-tale personalities.

Curriculum Tie-in: Social Science (Conduct and Behavior)

Johnson, Paul Brett. *Old Dry Frye: A Deliciously Funny Tall Tale.* New York: Scholastic Press, 1999.
A humorous retelling of an Appalachian folktale about a preacher who chokes
on a chicken bone.

Black Humor: When Old Dry Frye gets a chicken bone caught in his
throat, he falls to the floor of the home where he has chosen to partake of
his Sunday chicken dinner. The family can only think, "We got to get shed
of him," or everyone will think they killed him. They take him up the road
to "a poor widder woman's hen house. And that's where they left him."
Her rooster alerts her to the intruder. She comes wielding a frying pan and
"walloped Old Dry Frye." He "teetered a second and then just plopped
over." When she sees whom she's hit, she thinks she's killed him and
"heaped him in a wheelbarrow and lit out down the hill." The wheelbarrow
hits a rock in the road and bounces Old Dry Frye out and flings him up in
a tree. Two brothers mistake him for a possum that evening and decide to
have some possum stew for supper. They chuck a rock at him. He falls out
of the tree. They see their mistake. They put him into a feed sack and
throw him into a creek. "That would be the end of Old Dry Frye, and
nobody would be the wiser." It's not the end. The mayhem continues until
Old Dry Frye finally gets the last laugh on his community.

Other Devices: *Cliché, Hyperbole, Inference, Poetic Justice, Serendipity, Tone,
Understatement*

Art Style: Ebullient acrylic cartoons share the fortunes and misfortunes of the self-serving characters in this raucous Appalachian romp.
Curriculum Tie-in: Literature (Tall Tales), Social Science (Appalachian Culture)

*Yaccarino, Dan. *Deep in the Jungle.* New York: Anne Schwartz book from Atheneum books for Young Readers (Simon & Schuster), 2000.

After being tricked into joining the circus, an arrogant lion escapes and returns to the jungle, where he lives peacefully with the animals he used to terrorize.

Black Humor: Says the lion to his fellow jungle creatures, "I'm afraid I must eat you if you don't obey me." When a man from the circus visits the jungle looking for new acts, the lion leaps on him. "I am the king of this jungle! Now prepare to be eaten!" The lion doesn't find circus life to his liking. So when the man cracks the whip one time too often, the lion says, "I'm afraid I must eat you up. Jungle law, you know." And "he swallowed the man, one gulp, right down." Then he goes back to the jungle because he's had a "bellyful of show business." He sees another man trying to take away other jungle creatures. The lion steps in, pretending to show him a trick that he can do. "So the man stuck his head right in the lion's mouth, and, well, you can figure out the rest."

Other Devices: *Anachronism, Antihero, Antithesis, Foreshadowing, Irony, Motif, Parallelism, Poetic Justice, Pun, Tone*

Art Style: Expressionistic, naïve gouache cartoons against white backgrounds, reminiscent of the "Curious George" series, accent the droll language in this lesson in humility.

Curriculum Tie-in: Literature (Parable), Social Science (Values)

CARICATURE

Ludicrous exaggeration of distinguishing features for humorous effect.

Example: "Droll little mouth drawn up like a bow," "His belly, it shook like a bowl full of jelly," describes jolly old St. Nicholas from Clement Moore's poem *'Twas the Night Before Christmas.*

Lowell, Susan. *Little Red Cowboy Hat.* Illus. by Randy Cecil. New York: Henry Holt, 1997.

Little Red rides her pony, Buck, to Grandma's ranch with a jar of cactus jelly in the saddlebag.

Caricature: This wolf has the hint of masher about him. "What's your name, honey?" he asks. A "creepy feeling ran up her backbone." He "came closer than she liked." He asks, "Where are you going, sugar? Why not take a little ride with me?" Later, when she remarks about his features

while he's in bed, wearing Grandma's clothes, he makes amorous allusions to food, such as "Quiet, you delicious morsel." He calls her "dumpling," "sweetie," "honey bun," and "angel pie." But Grandma comes to the rescue. "Get your paws off her, you varmint." As the wolf tries to escape, he trips over his nightgown and gets stuck in the window. "His tail waved helplessly behind him." Grandma chases him with her shotgun, saying, "You'd look mighty good as a rug." Grandma is outraged, "Breaking into my house! Wearing my clothes! Getting fleas in my bed! Messing with my granddaughter!"
Other Devices: *Aphorism, Atmosphere, Hyperbole, Inference, Onomatopoeia, Parody, Simile, Stereotype, Tone*
Art Style: Gouache cartoons in expressionistic naïve style humorously match this unique geographical take on a familiar fairy tale.

St. George, Judith. *So You Want to Be President?* Illus. by David Small. New York: Philomel (Penguin Putnam Books for Young Readers), 2000 (Caldecott—2000).
This is a lively assortment of facts about the qualifications and characteristics of U.S. presidents from George Washington to Bill Clinton.
Caricature: "William McKinley wore a frock coat, vest, pin-striped trousers, stiff white shirt, black satin tie, gloves, a top hat, and a red carnation in his buttonhole every day!" "Some Presidents threw money around and some were penny pinchers. James Monroe ordered French silverware, china, candlesticks, chandeliers, clocks, mirrors, vases, rugs, draperies, and furniture for the White House. Ninety-three crates in all! William Harrison was thrifty. He walked to market every morning with a basket over his arm." Despite lack of military prowess men became president. "In his very first battle, Franklin Pierce's horse bucked, he was thrown against his saddle and fainted, his horse fell, broke its leg, and Pierce hurt his knee." Almost any job can lead to the White House. "Harry Truman owned a men's shop. Andrew Johnson was a tailor. Ronald Reagan was a movie actor. Ulysses Grant raced his rig through the streets of Washington and was arrested for speeding."
Other Devices: *Antithesis, Atmosphere, Parallelism, Tone*
Art Style: In the cherished tradition of political commentary, foibles, quirks, and humanity are illustrated in these hilarious cartoons.
Curriculum Tie-in: History (American Presidents)

CLICHÉ

Overused expressions that have lost their original vitality.

Example: "busy as bees," "working like dogs," "stub of a pencil," "filthy
lucre"

Garland, Michael. *Dinner at Magritte's.* New York: Dutton (Penguin), 1995.
Young Pierre spends the day with surrealist artists René Magritte and Salvador
Dali.
Cliché: Pierre's parents are boring. They sit knitting and reading the
newspaper "as still as stone" when the neighbors promise a much more
interesting day. He visits the Magrittes and enjoys himself. They all dash
for the house when it starts to rain "cats and dogs."
Other Devices: *Foreshadowing, Inference*
Art Style: Predictable routine is contrasted with surrealistic surprises as
a young boy finds entertainment away from his boring family.
Curriculum Tie-in: Art (Biography)

*Gralley, Jean. *Hogula, Dread Pig of Night.* New York: Henry Holt, 1999.
Although he lives high on the hog in his castle on Grimy Pork Chop Hill,
Hogula is unhappy because he has no friends—until he meets Elvis Ann,
Dread Queen of Kissyface.
Cliché: Things were "high on the hog" where Hogula lived. His companions
were two "faithful servants."
Other Devices: *Alliterations, Allusion, Antihero, Aphorism, Foreshadowing,
Inference, Irony, Poetic Justice, Pun, Simile, Stereotype, Understatment*
Art Style: Appropriately repulsive gouache and ink on watercolor paper,
expressionistic cartoons develop the characters of this humorously gentle
Dracula-style relationship.
Curriculum Tie-in: Social Science (Friendship)

Henkes, Kevin. *Wemberly Worried.* New York: Greenwillow Books (HarperCollins),
2000.
A mouse named Wemberly, who worries about everything, finds that she has
a whole list of things to worry about when she faces the first day of nursery
school.
Cliché: Wemberly's grandmother says the household has too much worry.
She wears a shirt with "Go with the Flow" printed on it. She points to a
sampler on the wall that says "Take it as it Comes."
Other Devices: *Antithesis, Irony, Parallelism, Pun*
Art Style: Watercolor and black pen/ink cartoons with sidebar comments
delightfully enhance the rhythmic text.
Curriculum Tie-in: Social Science (Fears)

Johnson, Paul Brett. *Old Dry Frye: A Deliciously Funny Tall Tale.* New York: Scholastic Press, 1999.
A humorous retelling of an Appalachian folktale about a preacher who chokes
on a chicken bone.

Cliché: On the day he partakes of a chicken dinner at the home of a family whom he has joined, uninvited, he gobbles so fast he chokes on a bone and dies right there on the spot. "Dead as a doornail. Dead as a bucket lid."
Other Devices: *Black Humor, Hyperbole, Inference, Poetic Justice, Serendipity, Tone, Understatement*
Art Style: Ebullient acrylic cartoons depict the fortunes and misfortunes of the self-serving characters in this raucous Appalachian romp.
Curriculum Tie-in: Literature (Tall Tales), Social Science (Appalachian Culture)

Laden, Nina. *Roberto the Insect Architect.* San Francisco: Chronicle Books, 2000. Roberto the architect, who also happens to be a termite, sets off to the city to find success.

Cliché: Roberto's mother chastises him for playing with his food. "Don't you know there are termites starving in Antarctica?" He goes to the city, where you can "build your dreams." He finds "hope doesn't come cheap." But, he determines, "I'll show them all." He "came up with a plan." Soon he is building extraordinary homes, each one "a work of art." He becomes "the talk of the town." Parents now admonish their children to "be creative" like Roberto.
Other Devices: *Alliteration, Allusion, Antithesis, Parallelism, Pun*
Art Style: Astoundingly detailed mixed media collage of paper, wood, blueprints, and gouache paint creatively brings to life this carefully crafted, witty text.
Curriculum Tie-in: Social Science (Values)

Littlesugar, Amy. *Tree of Hope.* Illus. by Floyd Cooper. New York: Philomel (Penguin Putnam), 1999.
Florrie's daddy used to be a stage actor in Harlem before the Depression forced the Lafayette Theater to close, but he gets a chance to act again when Orson Welles reopens the theater to stage an all-black version of Macbeth.

Cliché: When her daddy tells her how much he loved acting, her mama has no time for this kind of daydream. She remarks, "We ain't got but two dimes to rub together." Her daddy takes a job in an all-night bakery and comes home "bone tired." On the night of the performance, Harlem is "a sea of people." The stage is "bathed in silver light" and the Lafayette Theater was a "glittering palace."
Other Devices: *Flashback, Foreshadowing, Inference, Paradox, Serendipity, Simile, Stereotype/Reverse Stereotype, Symbol*
Art Style: Rich, gauzy, oilwash impressionistic paintings suggest not only happier memories of when times were more prosperous, but also the temporary bleakness of the Depression and emerging hope for a better future.
Curriculum Tie-in: History (Black Culture—Depression)

CONNOTATION

Implications or suggestions evoked by word choice.

Example: "Statesman" vs. "Politician"

Alderson, Brian. *The Tale of the Turnip.* Illus. by Fritz Wegner. Cambridge, MA: Candlewick Press, 1999.

A humble farmer's garden produce pleases the king, who handsomely rewards his efforts, but an arrogant squire gets more than he bargained for when he attempts to claim a similar reward.

Connotation: The humble farmer lives in a "ramshackle" cottage. The arrogant squire lives in a "swanky" house. The king recognizes the gift he receives from the farmer as "the most champion" turnip he ever saw. The squire is outraged that the "old codger" received a carload of gold for a "miserable" turnip. In response to the squire's gift, the king notes it is the most "gussied-up" horse he ever saw.

Other Devices: *Hyperbole, Motif, Poetic Justice, Satire, Tone*

Art Style: Humorously detailed watercolor and ink cartoons delight the visual sense and the sense of justice.

Curriculum Tie-in: History (Nineteenth-Century England), Literature (Folktales—England)

Altman, Linda Jacobs. *Amelia's Road.* Illus. by Enrique O. Sanchez. New York: Lee & Low, 1993.

Tired of moving around so much, Amelia, the daughter of migrant farmworkers, dreams of a stable home.

Connotation: When her father got out the road map, Amelia started to cry. She hated roads. They led to strange places and to nowhere at all. They went to farms where workers labored long, cheerless days. "Roads never went where you wanted them to go." Amelia wanted a permanent home. It would have a fine old shade tree growing in the yard. "She would live there forever." Roads meant constant moving.

Other Devices: *Alliteration, Antithesis, Serendipity, Simile, Symbol*

Art Style: Acrylics on canvas in blocky, ethnic folk style depict the classic farm laborers' nomadic life.

Curriculum Tie-in: Social Science (Migrant Workers)

Baker, Jeannie. *The Hidden Forest.* New York: Greenwillow Books (HarperCollins), 2000.

When a friend helps him retrieve the fish trap he lost while trying to fish off the coast of eastern Tasmania, Ben comes to see the giant kelp forest he has feared in a new light.

Connotation: When the dinghy flips from under him, Ben tumbles into the sea. He feels "slimy" kelp slide over him. He senses "dark movement." He panics as kelp "clings" to his oars and won't let him go. Later, his friend takes him on an exploration trip underwater. When the kelp touches him, it now feels like "velvet swirling against his skin." He even holds on to a piece of bull kelp and "rides with it." The presence that he earlier felt nearby is a whale. It watches him and "glides gently by." It has a "dark, gleaming shape."

Other Devices: *Imagery, Inference, Simile*

Art Style: Photographed collages of natural materials such as pressed seaweeds, sponges, and sand re-create the multidimensional, enchanting world of ocean life.

Curriculum Tie-in: Science (Ocean Ecology)

*Browne, Anthony. *Voices in the Park.* New York: DK Pub., 1998.

Lives briefly intertwine when two youngsters meet in the park.

Connotation: The mother describes her dog as a "pedigree Labrador." And she is displeased that it runs off with another park dog, which she immediately labels a "scruffy mongrel." She's also displeased that her son has found a playmate, "a rough-looking child." Her son describes this stranger as "nice" and her pet as a "very friendly dog." The playmate describes "Charlie" as "okay" and the Labrador as a "nice dog," because it plays with her dog, but the angry woman she finds to be a "silly twit." The girl's father barely notices either the children or the dogs, because he is so wrapped up in searching the job want ads in his newspaper. He does admire his dog. "I wish I had half the energy he's got." But he misses noticing the new friend his daughter made as well as the bossy woman sharing the park bench with him.

Other Devices: *Foreshadowing, Inference, Point of View*

Art Style: The story moves from one voice to another. Each character's perspective is reflected in the shifting landscape and seasons through acrylic surrealistic paintings that match the bossy woman, the sad man, the lonely boy and the cheerful girl.

Curriculum Tie-in: Social Science (Feelings)

Ernst, Lisa Campbell. *Goldilocks Returns.* New York: Simon & Schuster Books for Young Readers, 2000.

Fifty years after Goldilocks first met the three bears, she returns to fix up their cottage and soothe her guilty conscience.

Connotation: Goldi (name now shortened) returns to put things right after her brief destructive venture as a child. She does her best, but her efforts are not appreciated. Clearly, as an adult, her tastes have not improved. She hangs "hoity-toity" drapes and covers all the furniture with "shiny plastic covers." She works over the bear family's chairs so that Papa

Bear falls uncomfortably into his "now-poofy" chair. The bears move awkwardly about in their "fancy-shmancy" house.

Other Devices: *Allusion, Antihero, Flash-forward, Inference, Irony, Parallelism, Tone, Understatement*

Art Style: Large, bulky cartoons emulate the story's original atmosphere intended for young listeners, while the language and picture complexity expand the interest level for more savvy audiences.

Hoban, Russell. *Trouble on Thunder Mountain.* Illus. by Quentin Blake. New York: Orchard Books (Grolier), 2000.

When Megafright International flattens their beautiful mountain to put up a hi-tech plastic theme park, the O'Saurus family uses faith and lots of Monsta-Gloo to put things right.

Connotation: Names clue the reader to the author's positive and negative attitudes toward persons, places, and things in this story. A happy dinosaur (the "O'Saurus") family encounters "J.M. Flatbrain," the president of "Megafright International." A certain "A. Worser" gives the family the deed to their new home, a garbage dump. The train through "Megafright Mountain" goes to "Endsville." It's going to take "Monsta-Gloo" to restore their mountain. The family believes a real mountain of dirt and "interactive ants" and "creepy-crawlies" is superior to a plastic, clean, tidy, substitute mountain where no ants come to the picnic. Tourists apparently agree. They find the Tunnel of Terror in the plastic mountain boring. Mr. Flatbrain becomes "megafrightened" and has to run away to a town where nobody knows him.

Other Devices: *Aphorism, Foreshadowing, Hyperbole, Irony, Poetic Justice, Satire, Understatement*

Art Style: Humorous pen/ink watercolor cartoons spiritedly produce a funny tribute to old-fashioned ingenuity and to nature.

Curriculum Tie-in: Science (Ecology)

Johnston, Tony. *Alice Nizzy Nazzy, the Witch of Santa Fe.* Illus. by Tomie dePaola. New York: G.P. Putnam's Sons, 1995.

When Manuela's sheep are stolen, she has to go to Alice Nizzy Nazzy's talking roadrunner-footed adobe house and try to get the witch to give the flock back.

Connotation: Manuela peeks over the fence to see if her sheep are there. The fence (made of prickly pear plants) rudely tells her to go away in a "prickly voice." Likewise, when the roadrunner-footed adobe house tells her to go away, it "squawked a fowl voice." In both circumstances, Manuela, though "scared out of her wits," replies with politeness. "What a beautiful talking fence!" "What a wonderful talking house!" The effect is positive and immediate. The fence is so pleased, it opens itself up. The house is so pleased, it opens its door.

Other Devices: *Alliteration, Foreshadowing, Hyperbole, Internal Rhyme, Motif, Poetic Justice, Simile*
Art Style: Bright pastel and acrylic folk cartoons illustrate the western lifestyle in this good vs. bad character tale.
Curriculum Tie-in: Geography (New Mexico), Literature (Fairytales—America), Social Science (Values)

Meggs, Libby Phillips. *Go Home! The True Story of James the Cat.* Morton Grove, IL: Albert Whitman, 2000.
A homeless cat spends several seasons trying to survive the elements until at last a suburban family adopts him.
Connotation: James has been on his own a long time. When he makes overtures to a family, he is told, "You need to Go Home now." Then the woman squirts him with a hose. He stumbles away in confusion. He does not know "where 'Home' was." Later, at the veterinarian's clinic, the doctor says, "He should become a 'House Cat.'" He wonders what that is. At home the family cuddles him, gives him a soft blanket, some toys, and lets him sleep with them at night. Now he knows what "My Home" is.
Other Devices: *Ambiguity, Antithesis, Inference, Metaphor, Point of View, Simile*
Art Style: Realistic pastel illustrations follow James' admittance into a family that provides what has been missing in his life for a long time.
Curriculum Tie-in: Social Science (Animal Companions)

Modarressi, Mitra. *Yard Sale.* New York: DK Pub., 2000.
When Mr. Flotsam has a yard sale in the quiet town of Spudville, his neighbors are first upset, then delighted by their purchases.
Connotation: This is a story with truth in names. Mr. Flotsam, of course, has the yard sale, because he has a collection of odds and ends for sale. The town has a mundane name, Spudville, because it is quiet and "nothing strange ever happened." The Frumkins purchase a music box that gives their predictable life a new focus on fun and dancing. Common, comfortable Mrs. Applebee has to rename herself Madame Olga when her phone can mysteriously contact the spirits of the dead. Who but someone named Rotelli would purchase a pasta maker and open a thriving spaghetti house?
Other Devices: *Allusion, Antithesis, Hyperbole, Inference, Paradox, Serendipity, Understatement*
Art Style: Lively, full-page watercolor naïve art accompanies an understated text.

Steig, William. *Wizzil.* Illus. by Quentin Blake. New York: Farrar Straus Giroux, 2000.
A bored witch causes trouble when she decides to take revenge on an old man, but her mischief leads to a happy ending.

Connotation: As the witch lies in wait for DeWitt to pass by, she positions herself near the Frimp mailbox, "skulking" in the bushes. DeWitt is unaware of her presence as she first turns herself into a fly and "sallied" down his nose. He swishes the swatter, missing the witch by "only a hair." That upsets her. He "darn near did me in!" She vows revenge and turns herself into a glove. He is delighted with the glove he finds and happily "traipsed" home with it. Soon, though, trouble begins. He can't hit flies accurately. Wizzil jerks his arm "a tad" to this side or that . . . "no soap." Eventually, DeWitt recognizes weird things have happened since he put on the glove. The glove, he decides, has to be the "culprit."

Other Devices: *Alliteration, Ambiguity, Foreshadowing, Internal Rhyme, Irony, Serendipity, Tone*

Art Style: Delightfully awful watercolor cartoons capture the personalities and behaviors of the rotten witch and the hillbilly family she pesters.

Curriculum Tie-in: Social Science (Love)

Strete, Craig Kee. *The Lost Boy and the Monster.* Illus. by Steve Johnson and Lou Fancher. New York: G.P. Putnam's Sons (Penguin Books for Young Readers), 1999.

With the help of a rattlesnake and a scorpion, a lost boy gains two names and defeats the horrible foot-eating monster.

Connotation: The monster keeps a long, sticky rope hanging down from his tree in order to trap unsuspecting children, who get tangled in its loops. "When that happened, the monster did not call it an accident, he called it lunch." He likes to eat children's feet.

Other Devices: *Ambiguity, Internal Rhyme, Motif, Poetic Justice, Simile, Theme, Tone*

Art Style: Textured paste, oil paint, potato stamping, and scratching tools create expressionistic paintings in brown and yellow tones reminiscent of American Indian folk art.

Curriculum Tie-in: Art (American Indian), Literature (Folktales—American Indian)

*Turner, Ann. *Red Flower Goes West.* Illus. by Dennis Nolan. New York: Hyperion Books for Children, 1999.

As they journey west, a family nurtures the red flower they have carried with them from their old home.

Connotation: After traveling many weeks, the family comes to the Sierra—the "last thing" that stands in the way of their new home. They are terrified to see those mountains "knifing" the sky. This barrier seems insurmountable. Eventually, they reach their destination beyond the mountains. Pa "pursed" his lips but agrees to journey on until the family finds a "green meadow." Ma and the children do not wish to settle for a mining camp. They prefer a more peaceful and private spot to make their new permanent home. Pa may wish to object but wisely does not.

Other Devices: *Inference, Metaphor, Parallelism, Simile, Symbol*
Art Style: Soft crayon and pastel realistic drawings, mostly in shades of gray, depict a stern pioneer experience accented by the bright red beacon of the family's talisman.
Curriculum Tie-in: History (Westward Expansion)

FLASHBACK

Interruption of present action to insert an incident that took place at an earlier time for the purpose of giving the reader information to make the present situation understandable or to account for a character's current motivation.

Example: Orson Welles employed this device in the opening scene of the classic movie *Citizen Kane*. A rich man on his deathbed is holding a snow-scene water-filled ball which he drops as he utters the enigmatic "Rosebud." The rest of the movie is a flashback to the dead man's life and a search for the meaning of his last words.

*Dengler, Marianna. *The Worry Stone.* Illus. by Sibyl Graber Gerig. Flagstaff, AZ: Rising Moon (Northland), 1996.
When a small, serious boy joins Amanda on the park bench, she remembers that once she was small and serious, too, but she had Grandfather—and his wonderful stories.
Flashback: As she sits on the park bench watching the sad child and wishing she could do something for him, an old woman recalls her own childhood experiences, feeling that no one had much time for her. "She remembers it now as if it were yesterday." The story switches to her youth, when she lived in a large family on a sprawling Spanish hacienda surrounded by rolling hills and rich pasturelands.
Other Devices: *Antithesis, Foreshadowing, Inference, Parallel Story, Parallelism*
Art Style: Appealing realistic watercolor paintings expressionistically maintain focus on the separate threads of this woman's past and present.
Curriculum Tie-in: Social Science (Intergenerational Relationships)

Glass, Andrew. *Bewildered for Three Days: As to Why Daniel Boone Never Wore His Coonskin Cap.* New York: Holiday House, 2000.
With the help of what he learned from a Delaware Indian boy and an accommodating mother raccoon, young Daniel Boone escapes danger when a bear steals his coonskin cap.
Flashback: In 1818, when Daniel Boone is in his eighties, he poses for a portrait, wearing his old worn buckskin britches. The painter wonders

why he is not wearing his legendary coonskin cap. He proceeds to explain why through a "solemn debt of gratitude" he stopped wearing the cap while still a boy. As an adult he wore a "wide-brimmed hat near as tall as this tale I'll tell ye to pass the time." So Boone begins the story of why the legend about the cap is untrue. "From the day I took my first step, I had the itching foot and was apt to wander off."

Other Devices: *Atmosphere, Foreshadowing, Motif, Point of View, Tone, Understatement*

Art Style: Impressionistic colored pencil and oil pastel humorously accompany this frontier yarn of a great adventurer told in a curious blend of humility and exaggeration.

Curriculum Tie-in: History (Biography—Daniel Boone), Literature (Tall Tale)

Littlesugar, Amy. *Tree of Hope.* Illus. by Floyd Cooper. New York: Philomel (Penguin Putnam), 1999.

Florrie's daddy used to be a stage actor in Harlem before the Depression forced the Lafayette Theater to close, but he gets a chance to act again when Orson Welles reopens the theater to stage an all-black version of Macbeth.

Flashback: Daddy "met Mama at the Lafayette. He'd landed a bit part in a new play. Every night he'd get the chance to stand on that big stage and face the lights." For awhile, he talks about the pretty young woman who handed him up a red, red rose. But then the Depression hit. And that is the world of Florrie and her family now.

Other Devices: *Cliché, Foreshadowing, Inference, Paradox, Serendipity, Simile, Stereotype/Reverse Stereotype, Symbol*

Art Style: Rich oil wash impressionistic paintings suggest not only happier memories in the past when times were more prosperous, but also the bleakness of the current Depression and emerging hope for a better future.

Curriculum Tie-in: History (Black Culture—Depression)

*Meddaugh, Susan. *Hog-Eye.* New York: Walter Lorraine Books (Houghton Mifflin), 1995.

A young pig uses her ability to read to outwit a wolf that intends to eat her.

Flashback: "Yesterday my whole family met me at the door. They wanted to know why I didn't go to school. So I told them the true story." Then she proceeds to spin a slightly improbable story of her capture by a wolf and, by means of her sharp wits, her subsequent escape.

Other Devices: *Allusion, Antithesis, Foreshadowing, Hyperbole, Inference, Irony, Understatement*

Art Style: Split-page watercolor cartoons tell the "true story" of a schoolchild who dislikes her daily bus ride.

Curriculum Tie-in: Literature (Tall Tale)

*Nolen, Jerdine. *Big Jabe*. Illus. by Kadir Nelson. New York: Lothrop, Lee & Shepard, 2000.

> Momma Mary tells stories about a special young man who does wondrous things, especially for the slaves on the Plenty Plantation.
>
> **Flashback:** A woman brings a little boy to an old pear tree now too old to bear fruit. "Poppa Jabe planted it there in slavery times." She then begins to tell a long-long-time-ago story, "about how freedom came to the slaves on the Plenty Plantation."
>
> **Other Devices:** *Allusion, Anachronism, Antithesis, Flash-Forward, Foreshadowing, Hyperbole, Imagery, Inference, Parallelism, Simile, Symbol, Understatement*
>
> **Art Style:** Strong, detailed pen/ink, watercolor, and gouache drawings provide wonderful expressionistic period ambience to this folktale.
>
> **Curriculum Tie-in:** History (Slavery—America), Literature (Tall Tale)

FLASH-FORWARD

A sudden jump forward in time from chronologically narrated events to a later time that shows the aftermath of the present events.

> Example: Martha angrily threw the toy locomotive, and although it missed her brother Albert, a tiny piece of mama's precious mantel clock disappeared. One dainty leg was gone. The clock listed clumsily.
>
> Martha tenderly touched the rough place where the missing leg had been. Carefully rewrapping the clock in its tissue, she laid it back into the old trunk as her grandchildren slammed the kitchen door. Someday she would share her memories with them.

DePaola, Tomie. *The Art Lesson*. New York: G.P. Putnam's Sons, 1989.

> Having learned to be creative in drawing pictures at home, young Tommy is dismayed when he goes to school and finds the art lessons there much more regimented.
>
> **Flash-forward:** His art teacher asks Tommy if he would be willing to follow the class lesson and then, "if there's any time left, I'll give you another piece of paper and you can do your own picture with your own crayons." He tells her he'll try. He did then. And he still does now. There is a grownup Tommy sitting at his painting desk, still drawing and painting in his special creative style.
>
> **Other Devices:** *Atmosphere, Inference, Irony, Parallelism, Serendipity, Theme*
>
> **Art Style:** Blocky pastel cartoons follow the fortunes and budding development of a young artist in a conformist world.
>
> **Curriculum Tie-in:** Social Science (Individuality)

Ernst, Lisa Campbell. *Goldilocks Returns.* New York: Simon & Schuster Books for Young Readers, 2000.

> Fifty years after Goldilocks first met the three bears, she returns to fix up their cottage and soothe her guilty conscience.
>
> > **Flash-forward:** "As a child she was known as Goldilocks, and she was very naughty indeed." So opens the sequel, showing a child running away from the bears' cottage following her exposure as the culprit who wrecked their home. The next page begins, "Then Goldilocks grew up, and the older she got, the worse she felt about her horrid behavior." She is shown as a mature-looking woman with her bright hair "pinned up so no one would recognize her." She is now running a lock and key shop "to help people protect themselves against snoops."
> >
> > **Other Devices:** *Allusion, Antihero, Connotation, Inference, Irony, Parallelism, Tone, Understatement*
> >
> > **Art Style:** Large, bulky cartoons emulate the story's original atmosphere, intended for young listeners, while the language and picture complexity expand the interest level for more savvy audiences.

*Hamanaka, Sheila. *Peace Crane.* New York: Morrow Junior Books, 1995.

> After learning about the Peace Crane created by Sadako, a survivor of the bombing of Hiroshima, a young African-American girl wishes it would carry her away from the violence of her own world.
>
> > **Flash-forward:** The narrator begins with a brief review of the event that brought about the legend of Sadako, who hoped that folding a thousand paper cranes would save her from the deadly radiation illness she contracted from the atomic bombing of her city during World War II. A "quarter million souls went soaring up, high above the heat, high above the cries of war." She says, "Like a phoenix from the fire" they "flew toward heaven in a flock." Then, in the present time, the narrator wonders whether anybody would care if she folded a thousand paper cranes, "each one a tiny wish for life, each one a wish for peace." Do the souls of those who fall victim to city crime fly to heaven? "Have a quarter million gone?" Is she next?
> >
> > **Other Devices:** *Allusion, Antithesis, Imagery, Pun, Simile, Symbol*
> >
> > **Art Style:** Luminous, expressionistic oil paintings on canvas celebrate the spirit of the Peace Crane's hope for a troubled world.
> >
> > **Curriculum Tie in:** History (War and Peace   Japan and America)

*Nolen, Jerdine. *Big Jabe.* Illus. by Kadir Nelson. New York: Lothrop, Lee & Shepard, 2000.

> Momma Mary tells stories about a special young man who does wondrous things, especially for the slaves on the Plenty Plantation.
>
> > **Flash-forward:** When the story is finished, Momma Mary says, "Jabe moved on, though he turned up at difference times in difference places

throughout the South. And everywhere he did, burdens were lifted." The little boy listening to the story of Jabe says, "Momma Mary tells me all the stories, but the most wonderful, she says, happened right here at our old pear tree."

Other Devices: *Allusion, Anachronism, Antithesis, Flashback, Foreshadowing, Hyperbole, Imagery, Inference, Parallelism, Simile, Symbol, Understatement*

Art Style: Strong, detailed pen/ink, watercolor, and gouache drawings provide wonderful expressionistic period ambience to this folk tale.

Curriculum Tie-in: History (Slavery—America), Literature (Tall Tale)

FORESHADOWING

Builds suspense and adds plot plausibility by providing clues ahead of time to events that will occur later in the narrative.

> Example: Toad has just witnessed his first motorcar. He is transfixed. "All those wasted years that lie behind me, I never knew, never even dreamt! But now—but now that I know, now that I fully realize! O what a flowery track lies spread before me, henceforth!"
>
> Kenneth Grahame, *The Wind in the Willows.*

Alexander, Lloyd. *The House Gobbaleen.* Illus. by Diane Goode. New York: Dutton Children's Books (Penguin Books), 1995.

Unhappy over what he considers his bad luck, Tooley ignores his cat's warnings and invites a greedy little man into his home, in the mistaken hope of improving his fortunes.

Foreshadowing: The little man warns, "Do you ask me in? For I've got to tell you this, Tooley: Once in, never out; and once out, never back."

Other Devices: *Ambiguity, Hyperbole, Inference, Irony, Simile, Theme, Tone, Understatement*

Art Style: Humorous gouache and watercolor cartoons illustrate this modern folktale.

Curriculum Tie-in: Literature (Folktale), Social Science (Values)

*Armstrong, Jennifer. *Pierre's Dream.* Illus. by Susan Gaber. New York: Dial (Penguin Putnam), 1999.

Thinking he is dreaming, Pierre, a lazy, foolish, man, shows no fear as he performs many amazing and dangerous circus acts.

Foreshadowing: While Pierre's predictable, if aimless, existence continues during one last nap under the olive trees, a large semi truck with a bright, fluttering flag atop the cab can be seen coming toward the meadow. A hint of a caged vehicle behind the semi promises animals. When the startled

Pierre awakens to a "bustling village that had not been there before," he has "a wonderful sense of accomplishment." He believes all that he surveys is part of a marvelous dream. And he is "very pleased with himself." There seems an air of change about this lazy fellow.

Other Devices: *Antihero, Inference, Irony, Theme*

Art Style: Ethereal, expressionistic acrylic paintings alternate between stunning perspectives and large close-ups.

Curriculum Tie-in: Social Science (Values)

Aylesworth, Jim. *The Full Belly Bowl.* Illus. by Wendy Anderson Halpern. New York: Atheneum Books for Young Readers (Simon & Schuster), 1999.

In return for the kindness he showed a wee small man, a very old man is given a magical bowl that causes problems when it's not used properly.

Foreshadowing: As the story commences, mention is made of Angelina, a white cat with black patches. "The very old man thought that she was just about the sweetest cat in the whole world." She is all he has. A time comes when he has much more, and the potential for very much more. But, by book's end, all that is left to him are several more 'Angelinas,' and "in truth, he loved them all. To him, they were just about the sweetest cats in the whole world!" The full belly bowl must be turned upside down after use, or anything in it that is taken out will keep multiplying in the bowl. "In the days before the bowl, Angelina had kept the house free of mice, but now, with so much other food around, she "hadn't taken as much interest in them." And worst of all, "one of the mice, a great big one, thought he smelled something good to eat in the full belly bowl and started climbing up the very old man's chair, which was right next to the table." Clearly, there will be trouble with mice, since, unfortunately, the old man "had forgotten to put the bowl away."

Other Devices: *Irony*

Art Style: Pen/ink intricate, cartoon-style colored pencil drawings are delicate, beautifully whimsical bordered details, perfect for a gentle cautionary folktale.

Curriculum Tie-in: Social Science (Values)

*Baylor, Byrd. *The Table Where Rich People Sit.* Illus. by Peter Parnall. New York: Charles Scribner's Sons, 1994.

A girl discovers that her impoverished family is rich in things that matter in life, especially being outdoors and experiencing nature.

Foreshadowing: As the girl calls for the family meeting, she intends to make her parents admit how poor they are, so that they will change their way of life. She wants a fiscal accounting. Her father suggests, "Let's make a list of the money we earn in a year." The girl asks, "How much is that?" Then her mother says, "Not so fast. We have a lot of things to think about before we add them up." This is a hint that Mountain Girl has a lesson in values coming.

Other Devices: *Antihero, Aphorism, Irony, Paradox*
Art Style: Sweeping pen/ink watercolors on white spaces flow majestically in expressionistic celebration of nature.
Curriculum Tie-in: Geography (American Southwest), Literature (Parable)

*Browne, Anthony.** *Voices in the Park.* New York: DK Pub., 1998.
   Lives briefly intertwine when two youngsters meet in the park.
   Foreshadowing: A rigid routine is followed. The mother tells the boy that it's time for his and the dog's walk to the park. They go to a park bench. She orders him to sit, and promptly forgets him as she muses about what to prepare for dinner. He obediently sits. The art shows a hint of a bright sweatshirt and pants and a foot that doesn't touch the ground. Young Charles is intently watching this person, just out of view, who is also sitting on the bench. Perhaps, like his dog racing around happily with a playmate, he, too, will have fun at the park today.
   Other Devices: *Connotation, Inference, Point of View*
   Art Style: The story moves from one voice to another. Each character's perspective is reflected in the shifting landscape and seasons with bright acrylic surrealistic paintings that match the bossy woman, the sad man, the lonely boy, and the cheerful girl.
   Curriculum Tie-in: Social Science (Feelings)

Bunting, Eve.** *Can You Do This, Old Badger?* Illus. by Le Uyen Pham. New York: Harcourt, 1999.
   Although Old Badger cannot do some things as easily as he used to, he can still teach Little Badger the many things he knows about finding good things to eat and staying safe and happy.
   Foreshadowing: As the two walk along, Little Badger jumps and rolls and climbs trees. Old Badger doesn't do those things very often. But he tells Little Badger that when he does climb, he climbs backward because it's easier. Little Badger remarks, "That's good to know." Then he says how sad it is that "you are old now and can't do many things." That's when Old Badger proceeds to tell him many useful things. "There are some things I can't do now." But there are "lots of things I can teach you." Little Badger learns where tasty earthworms are, where to find honey and how to get it, how to clean mud out from between toes, and even how to fish.
   Other Devices: *Ambiguity, Theme*
   Art Style: Detailed, expressionistic gouache on watercolor paper lovingly shows this special age/youth relationship.
   Curriculum Tie-in: Social Science (Intergenerational Relationships)

*Bunting, Eve.** *The Memory String.* Illus. by Ted Rand. New York: Clarion Books (Houghton Mifflin), 2000.

While still grieving for her mother and unable to accept her stepmother, a girl clings to the memories represented by forty-three buttons on a string.

Foreshadowing: The cat in this story is a barometer for future events. Laura holds the increasingly unhappy animal tightly as she relates a litany of memories associated with each button on the string, as though they were prayer beads. "'Yowww!' Whiskers Warned." When he breaks for his freedom, as he is bound to do, there will be trouble.

Other Devices: *Ambiguity, Antithesis, Aphorism, Imagery, Inference, Parallelism, Simile*

Art Style: Shadowy, impressionistic watercolor paintings detail the emotional changes the child experiences as she feels both separation and reconnection to her family.

Curriculum Tie-in: Social Science (Family Relationships, Grief)

*Bunting, Eve. *Swan in Love.* Illus. by Jo Ellen McAllister Stammen. New York: Atheneum Books for Young Readers (Simon & Schuster), 2000.

Despite ridicule of the other animals, Swan persists in his adoration for a swan-shaped boat named Dora.

Foreshadowing: Swan is happy merely to be near his Dora. But, "winters did seem longer and colder every year. He was stiffer than he'd once been. Slower." There is a hint that this relationship is coming to a close. In the spring the boat owner notices what bad shape the old boat is in. "Swan's heart beat thick in his breast. Dora!" He senses her end, though he tries to forestall it. The man tells him, "Our Dora's finished." And then he tells him that he doesn't look so good himself. When the man leaves, Swan listens to the silence of their lake. "Finished!" He drifts through "waves of time" and hears a voice tell him, as "comforting as that hand that had once stroked his feathers," "Love makes magic." Perhaps there is yet something more for this devoted swan and the object of his love.

Other Devices: *Antithesis, Aphorism, Imagery, Inference, Simile, Theme*

Art Style: Resplendent pastel expressionistic illustrations shimmer with grace as they illuminate the story of transforming love.

Curriculum Tie-in: Social Science (Love)

*Burleigh, Robert. *Edna.* Illus. by Joanna Yardley. New York: Orchard Books, 2000.

Carefree meanderings during her time in New York City give Edna St. Vincent Millay grist for a famous poem she later pens.

Foreshadowing: The poet's dedication to her craft is already evident early in her efforts. She mentions going to "a basement place where I sometimes sip tea and write all afternoon." And during parties where her friends huddle around the fireplace and read their work to each other, they laugh when she waves her hands about as she reads. "But they stop laughing and listen when they hear my poems." Already the power of her words commands attention.

Other Devices: *Atmosphere, Imagery, Parallelism, Simile*
Art Style: Expressionistic watercolors in vivid hues help recreate the marvelous feelings of expectation and freedom experienced by youthful artists in a city of promise that welcomes their enthusiasm.
Curriculum Tie-in: Literature (Biography—Poets)

*Deedy, Carmen Agra. *The Yellow Star: The Legend of King Christian X of Denmark.* Illus. by Henri Sorensen. Atlanta: Peachtree, 2000.

King Christian must abide by Nazi orders regarding the wearing of the identifying yellow star, but he must also protect all the Danes from harm.

Foreshadowing: The Danes say they will all stand together in defense of their king. "Little did the Danes know how much they would need their wise king in the dark days to come." They obtain a small success when the king confronts the Nazi flag over the palace and secures its removal. "Yet it was only a small victory; the king and his people's greatest test was still to come."
Other Devices: *Antithesis, Aphorism, Atmosphere, Inference, Irony, Paradox, Parallelism, Pun, Simile, Symbol, Theme*
Art Style: Impressionistic oil paintings accompany the spare terse text in this vignette showing the political reality of the Danes' circumstances during a very somber historical period.
Curriculum Tie-in: History (World War II—Nazi Occupation—Denmark), Literature (Legend), Social Science (Values)

Dengler, Marianna. *Fiddlin' Sam.* Illus. by Sibyl Graber Gerig. Flagstaff, AZ: Rising Moon (Northland), 1999.

Wandering through the Ozarks and bringing joy to people with his music, Fiddlin' Sam seeks the right person to take up his fiddle and carry on the practice.

Foreshadowing: In his old age, Sam fears he will not find someone to pass along his gift of fiddling. "That's when a boy came trudging along, dragging his feet." The boy looks vaguely familiar. Years ago another youth with similar red hair and freckles saved his life after a rattlesnake bit him. Sam had hoped to teach him to fiddle, but that youth "only listened, tapping his toe in time to the music." He had "a feel for the land." Now, Sam is eager to learn more about this boy, who is, like him, a restless wanderer. Sam learns the boy had hoped to find something better away from home. "Now I gotta go back and tell him I ain't found it." Without a word, Sam takes out his fiddle and begins to play. He must hurry if he is to fulfill his task. "If only I have time," he thinks. The boy is a willing player, and the two work together on the boy's playing. Then, after playing the best ever, "the boy looked down. His eyes filled with tears. The old fiddler could no longer hear him."

Other Devices: *Antithesis, Atmosphere, Inference, Internal Rhyme, Parallelism, Serendipity*
Art Style: Exuberant, realistic, and expressionistic watercolors in shades of bright yellow, pink, and blue faithfully reveal the emotional and physical details of this musician's life.
Curriculum Tie-in: Social Science (Missouri Ozarks)

*Dengler, Marianna. *The Worry Stone.* Illus. by Sibyl Graber Gerig. Flagstaff, AZ: Rising Moon (Northland), 1996.
When a small, serious boy joins Amanda on the park bench, she remembers that once she was small and serious too, but she had Grandfather—and his wonderful stories.
Foreshadowing: The old woman tries some of the tactics that her grandfather used on her to make her feel special. As she hints at a story, "the boy moves toward her on the bench, 'Did he have any other stories?'" he asks. She replies, "Many stories. Wonderful stories." The two begin their relationship.
Other Devices: *Antithesis, Flashback, Inference, Parallel Story, Parallelism*
Art Style: Appealing, realistic watercolor paintings expressionistically maintain focus on the separate threads of this woman's past and present.
Curriculum Tie-in: History (Chumash Indians), Social Science (Grandparents, Intergenerational Relationships)

Fox, Mem. *Harriet, You'll Drive Me Wild.* Illus. by Marla Frazee. New York: Harcourt, 2000.
When a young girl has a series of mishaps at home one Saturday, her mother tries not to lose her temper—and does not quite succeed.
Foreshadowing: The story opens with "Harriet Harris was a pesky child. She didn't mean to be. She just was." The stage is set for irritating behavior. During nap time, "There was a terrible silence" in Harriet's room. Her mother is on instant alert.
Other Devices: *Inference, Understatement*
Art Style: Pencil and transparent drawing ink cartoons wonderfully augment the spare text in this timeless story of childhood exuberance and parental restraint.
Curriculum Tie-in: Social Science (Family Relationships)

Garland, Michael. *Dinner at Magritte's.* New York: Dutton (Penguin), 1995.
Young Pierre spends the day with surrealist artists René Magritte and Salvador Dali.
Foreshadowing: Pierre goes on weekends with his parents to their cottage in the country to escape the heat of summertime in Paris. It is cool and quiet. "A little too quiet, Pierre thought." There is nothing for a child to play with. He is drawn to the interesting next-door neighbors, though his

parents think they are strange. Laughter and music come from their house. "I think I'll go next door," Pierre announces. René Magritte is an artist. A fun afternoon is ahead.

Other Devices: *Cliché, Inference*

Art Style: Normal routine is contrasted with surrealistic surprises as a young boy finds entertainment away from his boring family.

Curriculum Tie-in: Art (Biography)

Gibbons, Faye. *Mama and Me and the Model T.* Illus. by Ted Rand. New York: Morrow, 1999.

When Mr. Long says any man can drive a car, Mama gets behind the wheel to show women can drive, too.

Foreshadowing: Everyone is present when Mr. Long leaves for town. The wild ride begins when Mr. Long says, "Mandy, girl, I'll be bringing a surprise when I come home today." He winks at the narrator. Something is going to affect the whole family, especially Mandy, who will become involved in a way that none of the other four Searcy and the seven Long kids will be.

Other Devices: *Hyperbole, Imagery, Inference, Onomatopoeia, Parallelism, Stereotype, Understatement*

Art Style: Expressionistic watercolors exuberantly dramatize the mysterious intricacies of mastering the wondrous but tricky skills of automobile driving.

Glass, Andrew. *Bewildered for Three Days: As to Why Daniel Boone Never Wore His Coonskin Cap.* New York: Holiday House, 2000.

With the help of what he learned from a Delaware Indian boy and an accommodating mother raccoon, young Daniel Boone escapes danger when a bear steals his coonskin cap.

Foreshadowing: Before details unfold, Boone warns that he may be about to embellish the truth. "I was wearing a wide-brimmed hat near as tall as this tale I'll tell ye to pass the time." In a prophetic nod to the future, an Indian plants the notion in young Boone of becoming a leader into unexplored Kentucky wilderness. "An entire people might cross together, but they would need a guide with the heart of a brave to lead them." Then, as the time approaches for the Indian child and the white child to part company and begin their respective destinies, Boone's father unwittingly predicts a distant future of strife between the red and white cultures. "The Delaware live in the forest and love the savage wilderness as their mother. When we ask them to honor our fences, it is an unreasonable thing we ask. I fear there is no way to share a land so differently understood." His first serious scrape with enemy Indians is followed by his distraction with a bear. Daniel loses his cap to the bear, who is "easy enough to follow. Crows announce his passing from the treetops, all the way to a high meadow where a commotion of wild turkeys makes the hill seem about to up and fly away. I never even saw the braves until they saw me."

Other Devices: *Atmosphere, Flashback, Motif, Point of View, Tone, Understatement*
Art Style: Impressionistic colored pencil and oil pastel humorously accompany this frontier yarn of a great adventurer told in a curious blend of humility and exaggeration.
Curriculum Tie-in: History (Biography—Daniel Boone), Literature (Tall Tale)

*Gralley, Jean. *Hogula, Dread Pig of Night.* New York: Henry Holt, 1999.
Although he lives high on the hog in his castle on Grimy Pork Chop Hill, Hogula is unhappy because he has no friends—until he meets Elvis Ann, Dread Queen of Kissyface.
Foreshadowing: Hogula drew attention to himself at the mall, hoping to make a friend. He hung from the second-level balcony. People dropped their bags and cheered. But, then the clock struck quarter to bedtime and "all the shoppers yawned and streamed out the double doors. In no time at all, Hogula was alone." He'd shown off for an entire evening and hadn't made a single, solitary friend. How will Hogula react?
Other Devices: *Alliteration, Allusion, Antihero, Aphorism, Cliché, Inference, Irony, Poetic Justice, Pun, Simile, Stereotype, Understatement*
Art Style: Appropriately repulsive gouache and ink on watercolor paper, expressionistic cartoons develop the characters of this humorously gentle Dracula-style relationship.
Curriculum Tie-in: Social Science (Friendship)

*Gregorowski, Christopher. *Fly, Eagle, Fly! An African Tale.* Illus. by Niki Daly. New York: Margaret K. McElderry Books (Simon & Schuster), 2000.
A farmer finds an eagle and raises it to behave like a chicken, until a friend helps the eagle learn its rightful place in the sky.
Foreshadowing: When first attempts to reintroduce the eagle to the sky fail, the determined visitor thinks of another approach. He gets the farmer up before dawn, and they take the bird up on the mountain. "Hurry," the visitor urges, "or the dawn will arrive before we do!" He has something in mind to help the eagle recognize where its true destiny lies.
Other Devices: *Analogy, Antithesis, Imagery, Motif, Parallelism*
Art Style: Expressionistic watercolor line washes in brown and blue tones satisfyingly re-create the ambience of an African village.
Curriculum Tie-in: Literature (Parable)

Harris, Jim. *The Three Little Dinosaurs.* Gretna, LA: Pelican Publishing, 1999.
Three young dinosaurs set out on their own, only to be hassled by a Tyrannosaurus rex, who gets a big surprise in the end.
Foreshadowing: When the rex is foiled in his attempt to get the three little dinos inside their stone house, he sits down to think of a way to get at them. The art shows the reader that the little dinosaurs' house is at the

base of a mountain upon which a very large rock balances. Sooner or later Tyrannosaurus rex will think of dislodging the stone and allowing nature to take its course. When at last he does figure out what to do, it is years later. He is able to smash the house, but he can't find the little dinosaurs. As he looks around, he finds himself "eye-to-eye with . . . a rather round belly!" The little dinos have grown up. The position of the aggressor is changing.

Other Devices: *Antithesis, Inference, Parody, Poetic Justice, Tone*

Art Style: Lush, detailed acrylic expressionistic paintings provide satisfyingly humorous perspective and point of view between aggressor and victim.

*Hayes, Joe. *A Spoon for Every Bite.* Illus. by Rebecca Lear. New York: Orchard Books, 1996.

A poor husband and wife ask their rich neighbor to be godfather to their child, and once they are compadres, prey upon his pride and extravagance to trick him out of his fortune.

Foreshadowing: The wife suggests to her husband that they invite their rich neighbor to be godfather to their baby. She goes on to convince her skeptical husband. "He might accept. Maybe somehow it will change our luck." And, indeed, in a year's time their roles are reversed. The rich man has lost his wealth, and the poor couple has gained it.

Other Devices: *Ambiguity, Antihero, Antithesis, Hyperbole, Motif, Poetic Justice*

Art Style: Realistic pastel drawings contrast the striking differences in circumstances between the compadres, and their varied emotional responses to these circumstances.

Curriculum Tie-in: History (American Southwest), Literature (Folktales—Hispanic), Social Science (Values)

Hesse, Karen. *Come On, Rain!* Illus. by Jon J. Muth. New York: Scholastic Press, 1999.

A young girl eagerly awaits a coming rainstorm to bring relief from the oppressive summer heat.

Foreshadowing: People "squint into the endless heat." Will it ever rain? Way off in the distance "I see it coming, clouds rolling in, gray clouds, bunched and bulging under a purple sky." Finally, there is a hint that relief is on the way. "A creeper of hope circles 'round my bones."

Other Devices: *Alliteration, Hyperbole, Imagery, Metaphor, Paradox, Simile*

Art Style: Buoyant, ebullient expressionistic pen/ink watercolors lend emotional credence to the nervous anxiety of relentless heat accompanied by worrisome drought, and the tremendous sense of relief that accompanies a thorough, nourishing rain.

Curriculum Tie-in: Science (Meteorology)

Hest, Amy. *Mabel Dancing.* Illus. by Christine Davenier. Cambridge, MA: Candlewick Press, 2000.

> Mabel doesn't want to go to sleep while Mama and Papa are having a dance party downstairs.
>
> > **Foreshadowing:** As Mabel watches her parents prepare for the downstairs party, she begins to think, "I can dance." The more she hears the enticing music and watches the swirling ball gowns from her vantage point on the stairs, the more she knows she can. "Watch me!" she tells her dog. And off she goes to join the excitement.
> >
> > **Other Devices:** *Atmosphere, Imagery, Parallelism*
> >
> > **Art Style:** Airy, expressionistic watercolor washes and ink line drawings capture the contrast of bright excitement and action downstairs with gloomy loneliness and boring isolation upstairs.
> >
> > **Curriculum Tie-in:** Social Science (Values)

Hoban, Russell. *Trouble on Thunder Mountain.* Illus. by Quentin Blake. New York: Orchard Books (Grolier), 2000.

> When Megafright International flattens their beautiful mountain to put up a hi-tech plastic theme park, the O'Saurus family uses faith and lots of Monsta-Gloo to put things right.
>
> > **Foreshadowing:** The family quickly gathers together their belongings to leave. "Have you packed the Monsta-Gloo?" Mom says to Dad. Their mountain home is going to be blasted to ground level, but Mom is thinking ahead. Later, when they hear the first big bang and see the top of Thunder Mountain go up into the air, Mom says, "I have an idea. But we will need a little faith and a lot of Monsta-Gloo for it to work." The family watches to see where the mountain chunks are hauled. Then Mom says, "Do you know what I have in mind?" Later, when the robot-monster foreman lifts the privacy curtain to see what might be happening, "Dad was waiting for it with a screwdriver and a wrench." Thereafter, the monster-robot sounds like Dad.
> >
> > **Other Devices:** *Aphorism, Connotation, Hyperbole, Irony, Poetic Justice, Satire, Understatement*
> >
> > **Art Style:** Humorous pen/ink watercolor cartoons spiritedly produce a funny tribute to old-fashioned ingenuity and to nature.
> >
> > **Curriculum Tie-in:** Science (Ecology)

Hopkinson, Deborah. *A Band of Angels: A Story Inspired by the Jubilee Singers.* Illus. by Raúl Colón. New York: Atheneum Books for Young Readers (Simon & Schuster), 1999.

> The daughter of a slave forms a gospel singing group and goes on tour to raise money to save Fisk University.
>
> > **Foreshadowing:** Young Ella is so eager and excited to be going to a school just for freed slaves, she fails to notice details about the school site. "When

its shabby wooden buildings appear before her, she's not even disappointed. She's too excited to be going to school at last." Later in the story, these buildings become unfit to use. However, raising money to restore them eventually results in Ella becoming a famous member of a singing troop of national fame.

Other Devices: *Antithesis, Irony, Simile*

Art Style: Watercolor/pencil expressionistic muted lines and shades of brown, yellow, and green overlaid with scratch lines illustrate the contrasts of loss and hope in this grand success story.

Curriculum Tie-in: History (Black Culture)

Johnston, Tony. *Alice Nizzy Nazzy, the Witch of Santa Fe.* Illus. by Tomie dePaola. New York: G.P. Putnam's Sons, 1995.

When Manuela's sheep are stolen, she has to go to Alice Nizzy Nazzy's talking roadrunner-footed adobe house and try to get the witch to give the flock back.

Foreshadowing: When the house opens up to her, Manuela does not see her sheep, but she does see "dirty pillows everywhere." She confronts the witch, who is "sly as can be." The old crone tells her, "No sheep here. Just some dirty old pillows." What are so many woolly pillows doing in the home of a witch—who can cast spells, changing one thing into something else?

Other Devices: *Alliteration, Connotation, Hyperbole, Internal Rhyme, Motif, Poetic Justice, Simile*

Art Style: Bright pastel and acrylic folk cartoons illustrate the western lifestyle in this good vs. bad character tale.

Curriculum Tie-in: Geography (New Mexico), Literature (Fairytales— America), Social Science (Values)

Kajikawa, Kimiko. *Yoshi's Feast.* Illus. by Yumi Heo. New York: DK Ink, 2000.

When Yoshi's neighbor, Sabu, the eel broiler, attempts to charge him for the delicious-smelling aromas he has been enjoying, Yoshi hatches a plan to enrich them both.

Foreshadowing: Neighbor Sabu has not had many customers to buy his broiled eels. His hibachi is difficult to find on a small street on the outskirts of the city. When Yoshi performs a wild dance with his moneybox to pay for smelling Sabu's broiled eels, "A few people heard the jingling coins and gathered to watch. They clapped and cheered. More and more people came . . . . " Perhaps the dancing will have something to do with bringing paying customers to buy Sabu's excellent food.

Other Devices: *Antithesis, Aphorism, Inference, Onomatopoeia, Parallelism, Poetic Justice*

Art Style: Oil, pencil, and paper collage folk art come together in a satisfyingly expressionistic design to transmit the flavor of this ethnic quarrel.

Curriculum Tie-in: Literature (Folktales—Japan)

*Kaplan, Howard. *Waiting to Sing.* Illus. by Hervé Blondon. New York: DK Ink, 2000.

A family who loves music and spends many hours at the piano is devastated by the death of the mother, but those still living find consolation in the beautiful music that remains.

Foreshadowing: The reader's pleasure in this family's tender closeness is suddenly threatened as the young narrator describes his mother's habit of standing nearby when he practices his piano pieces. She "was always on the lookout for wrong notes, even when she wasn't feeling well herself."

Other Devices: *Allusion, Antithesis, Aphorism, Atmosphere, Imagery, Inference, Metaphor, Parallelism, Simile, Symbol*

Art Style: Full-page sepia-tone pastel cartoon drawings expressionistically evoke a fragile emotional period in the life of a family coping with restructuring itself after the wrenching loss of one of its members.

Curriculum Tie-in: Music (Piano), Social Science (Death, Family Relationships, Feelings)

Kirkpatrick, Katherine. *Redcoats and Petticoats.* Illus. by Ronald Himler. New York: Holiday House, 1999.

Members of a family in the village of Setauket on Long Island are displaced by the Redcoats and serve as spies for the Revolutionary Army of George Washington.

Foreshadowing: In the first paragraph the setting of war is outlined. The church has been made into a fort. "The worst was soon to come." Political alliances are also quickly delineated. Mother's parents urge her to remain "loyal to our king." Mother replies, "I'm sorry, but I have my principles."

Other Devices: *Inference*

Art Style: Impressionistic pen/ink watercolors illustrate the essence of the relationship between two political views. Bright red both ties together and contrasts the patriots and the loyalists.

Curriculum Tie-in: History (Revolutionary War)

Krudop, Walter Lyon. *The Man Who Caught Fish.* New York: Farrar Straus Giroux, 2000.

A stranger magically catches fish and hands them out to villagers one at a time, but the king will not be content until he receives a whole basket of fish.

Foreshadowing: This man may be more than he appears, for when the king orders his royal guards to use the man's magic pole to catch a basketful of fish, "even the strongest guard could not pull the pole from the stranger's hand." Later, when the king disguises himself as a rag-clad commoner to try to get a basketful of fish, one after the other, and holds out his hand to the stranger, "instead of pulling up a fish, the stranger did something that confused even the king. He handed him the pole." What is the significance of so easily passing off the pole that previously could not be pulled from the stranger's hand?

Other Devices: *Poetic Justice, Theme*

Art Style: Exquisite impressionistic folk paintings bring to life a culture of long ago.

Curriculum Tie-in: History (Thailand), Literature (Folktales—Thailand)

Krudop, Walter Lyon. *Something Is Growing.* New York: Atheneum Books for Young Readers (Simon & Schuster), 1995.

When Peter plants a seed near a city street, things quickly change.

Foreshadowing: In the midst of a city, where nothing grows, Peter has found a small patch of dirt by a street. He plants a seed, waters it carefully, and talks to it every day. He tells it, "You're going to grow." While he is busy doing this, "Nobody noticed him." What has he started by this simple act?

Other Devices: *Satire*

Art Style: Impressionistic acrylic paintings soften the truly shocking effects of plant life gone lushly abundant.

Curriculum Tie-in: Science (Ecology)

Kurtz, Jane. *Faraway Home.* Illus. by E.B. Lewis. New York: Gulliver Books (Harcourt), 2000.

Desta's father, who needs to return briefly to his Ethiopian homeland, describes what it was like for him to grow up there.

Foreshadowing: People do not wear shoes; there are hippos and crocodiles and a cold whooshing wind. "She shivers to think of the hyenas' cry." "Your home is too wild," Desta tells her father. She fears he will not come back. But as she thinks about the face of her grandmother in the locket she wears, she sees "sadness glimmering in those eyes." And during school she looks up flamingos and "almost hears the sound of a haunting lullaby somewhere at the edge of the classroom." Walking home after school, she takes off her shoes, "feeling the sun under her feet where it has soaked into the ground." As she talks with him later, she says, "I think you miss your home a lot." Little by little, Desta is adjusting her thoughts to her father's visit to his homeland. She will come to terms with his absence and will understand his need to go.

Other Devices: *Imagery, Metaphor, Simile*

Art Style: Pen line drawings and watercolor expressionistic art capture the poignant reality immigrants face when they leave a beloved homeland for a new home.

Curriculum Tie-in: Geography (Ethiopia), Social Science (Ethiopian Immigrants)

Lawson, Julie. *Emma and the Silk Train.* Illus. by Paul Mombourquette. Buffalo, NY: Kids Can Press, 1997.

After seeing the beautiful silk blouse her mother made, Emma dreams of having a piece of silk for herself, and when the opportunity arises, determinedly pursues it.

Foreshadowing: Emma is bedazzled with silk. But the silk trains never slow down as they cross the country west to east to the fashion houses. They set speed records. There is enough silk left over from her mother's blouse for her to have a hair ribbon. "But from that moment on, Emma longed for a silk blouse of her own." She is single-minded. This will bear on the story's plot. Later, when she is stranded on a small island in the river that has washed her downstream, she fears no one will find her. Then she thinks about the train tracks going along the shore. "Tracks! The thought of them gave Emma an idea." She will use their presence to help her get rescued.

Other Devices: *Ambiguity, Imagery, Inference, Parallelism, Simile*

Art Style: Lush impressionistic oil painting capture the time and adventure of the silk train era.

Curriculum Tie-in: History (Railroads—Silk)

Littlesugar, Amy. *Tree of Hope.* Illus. by Floyd Cooper. New York: Philomel (Penguin Putnam), 1999.

Florrie's daddy used to be a stage actor in Harlem before the Depression forced the Lafayette Theater to close, but he gets a chance to act again when Orson Welles reopens the theater to stage an all-black version of *Macbeth.*

Foreshadowing: In the "golden days" before the Depression hit Harlem, her daddy enjoyed acting. He tells her how "one night, a pretty young woman handed him up a red, red rose" as a token of her appreciation for his performance. Later they married. Then, the reality of earning a living embittered Mama, who had no time for such daydreams. Yet, when the director Orson Welles comes to the old Lafayette to produce a black version of *Macbeth,* Florrie's daddy is part of the cast. After the night's production, her mama "did something Florrie'd never forget. She reached inside her coat and took out a rose. A red, red rose." Then, just as in the old days, the golden days, she smiles back at Daddy and hands him the rose.

Other Devices: *Cliché, Flashback, Inference, Paradox, Serendipity, Simile, Stereotype/Reverse Stereotype, Symbol*

Art Style: Rich, oil wash impressionistic paintings suggest not only happier memories the past when times were more prosperous, but also the temporary bleakness of the current Depression and emerging hope for a better future.

Curriculum Tie-in: History (Black Culture—Depression)

Lorbiecki, Marybeth. *Just One Flick of a Finger.* Illus. by David Diaz. New York: Dial (Penguin Putnam), 1996.

> A young boy takes a gun to school to scare off the bully who has been tormenting him, and the gun is accidentally fired during the scuffle.
>
> > **Foreshadowing:** The boy and his best friend, Sherms, decide to stick together to stay out of everyone's way. "Couldn't be done." Trouble will find them. Later, during a school incident, the bully flashes his right hand toward his pocket, but a teacher comes upon the scene yelling, "What're you boys doing?" The bully "just smiled, like ice sliced thin, and we backed away." That smile seems to promise there is surely more trouble to come between the bully and his victim. The boy makes a blood brother pact with his friend to stick together. "Still, I got to thinking how I'd like a gun—." If he follows through, someone is bound to be hurt.
> >
> > **Other Devices:** *Antithesis, Inference, Internal Rhyme, Metaphor, Pun, Simile, Theme*
> >
> > **Art Style:** Acrylics, watercolor, and digitally manipulated photographic backgrounds blend to create powerful stylized, expressionistic heavy-lined comic book images that evoke danger and tension.
> >
> > **Curriculum Tie-in:** Social Science (Bullies and School Violence)

Lowell, Susan. *Cindy Ellen: A Wild Western Cinderella.* Illus. by Jane Manning. New York: Joanna Cotler Books (HarperCollins), 2000.

> Cindy Ellen loses one of her diamond spurs at the square dance in the retelling of this classic fairy tale.
>
> > **Foreshadowing:** The stepsisters do not recognize Cindy Ellen as the champion cowgirl at the rodeo. They tell her that, "ol' Joe Prince is eating his heart out" over her. Cindy Ellen replies with a daredevil grin that she bets that cowgirl comes to the square dance tomorrow night. When the sisters strut off to the dance, they leave Cindy Ellen all alone. "But not for long."
> >
> > **Other Devices:** *Alliteration, Aphorism, Internal Rhyme, Parallelism, Parody, Simile, Tone*
> >
> > **Art Style:** Action-packed expressionistic acrylic cartoons hilariously support the story's western flavor.
> >
> > **Curriculum Tie-in:** Social Science (Self-esteem)

Lyon, George Ella. *One Lucky Girl.* Illus. by Irene Trivas. New York: DK Pub., 2000.

> Even though their trailer is destroyed by a tornado, a young boy's family is grateful because they find his baby sister alive.
>
> > **Foreshadowing:** "No matter how bright the sun, how high the ball, I was there to catch it. Hawkeye, Dad called me." His good vision will be helpful later when the family searches for the baby. "Sky looks funny," the boy says. This portends the coming tornado. The boy runs toward the training track. "I thought I saw something."

Other Devices: *Ambiguity, Antithesis, Imagery, Inference, Metaphor, Parallelism, Simile*
Art Style: Smudgy pastel illustrations impressionistically assist the story line through use of both dark and bright colors.
Curriculum Tie-in: Science (Tornadoes), Social Science (Family Relationships)

McKissack, Patricia. *The Honest to Goodness Truth.* Illus. by Giselle Potter. New York: Atheneum Books for Young Readers (Simon & Schuster), 2000.
After promising never to lie, Libby learns it's not always necessary to blurt out the whole truth.
Foreshadowing: Libby feels so bad about her lie to Mama that she decides "from now on, only the truth." Determined to be honest, "Libby started her truth-telling come Sunday morning." The world can't take too much truth. Libby is headed for trouble.
Other Devices: *Ambiguity, Antithesis, Aphorism, Paradox, Simile, Understatement*
Art Style: Pencil, ink, gouache, and watercolor in a luxuriant, expressionistic naïve style illustrate this tale of honesty.
Curriculum Tie-in: Social Science (Friendship, Values—Honesty)

Mahy, Margaret. *Simply Delicious.* Illus. by Jonathan Allen. New York: Orchard Books, 1999.
A resourceful father engages in all kinds of acrobatic moves to keep an assortment of jungle creatures from getting the double-dip chocolate-chip-and-cherry ice cream cone he is taking home to his son.
Foreshadowing: When the frustrated jungle animals realize they have missed having the ice cream cone, and that they are hungry, they look at each other. The crocodile licks his lips looking at the tiger, who licks his lips looking at the spider money, who licks his lips looking at the toucan, who clicks his beak looking at the butterflies. "Simply delicious!" they all cry, and begin chasing each other.
Other Devices: *Alliteration, Hyperbole, Internal Rhyme, Poetic Justice, Simile, Understatement*
Art Style: Lively line and gouache cartoons in lush jungle colors satisfyingly follow the father's adventures as he delivers his son an appreciated treat.
Curriculum Tie-in: Literature (Cumulative Tale)

*Meddaugh, Susan. *Hog-Eye.* New York: Walter Lorraine Books (Houghton Mifflin), 1995.
A young pig uses her ability to read to outwit a wolf that intends to eat her.
Foreshadowing: "I don't like school bus 37. So yesterday I took my time getting to the corner. . . ." As the little pig relates her adventures, she shocks her family by telling how she took a shortcut through the forest. "Wolves, Poison Ivy," say her siblings, as they think about possible troubles

she may encounter and, in fact, does encounter. She tries to outwit the wolf, who has caught her, by telling him which garden to raid to get the right ingredients for the soup he intends to put her into. Her brother remarks, "Did you tell him about the traps?" The wolf is going to face problems at that garden.

Other Devices: *Allusion, Antithesis, Flashback, Hyperbole, Inference, Irony, Understatement*

Art Style: Split-page watercolor cartoons tell the "true story" of a schoolchild who dislikes her daily bus ride.

Curriculum Tie-in: Literature (Tall Tale)

Mochizuki, Ken. *Passage to Freedom: The Sugihara Story.* Illus. by Dom Lee. Afterword by Hiroki Sugihara. New York: Lee & Low, 1997.

Following refusal by the Japanese government to issue visas to Jewish refugees from Poland, Consul Sugihara and his family make a crucial decision that saved thousands of lives.

Foreshadowing: On the first page the narrator sets up the plight of the Jewish refugees. Young Hiroki Sugihara and his father are in a store and watch as a Jewish child can't buy what he wants. The father gives the child some of his money. It is the beginning of a need displayed by supplicants that the father has power to ameliorate. As the diplomat's little boy plays with toy German soldiers, tanks, and planes, "Little did we know that the real soldiers were coming our way." The peaceful mornings in a city where "houses and churches around us were hundreds of years old," and where birds sing in the trees and play is uninterrupted in "a huge park near our home," will soon change to a desperate race to preserve life.

Other Devices: *Antithesis, Aphorism, Point of View, Theme*

Art Style: The stark fear of survival is shown in the realistic, photograph-like, sepia-tone oil paint and pencil over scratched beeswax paper. Emotionally charged, unrelenting shades of brown shadowing focus on the grim refugee predicament—their barely contained explosive violence, and the terrible decision facing the diplomat.

Curriculum Tie-in: History (World War II)

Nickle, John. *The Ant Bully.* New York: Scholastic Press, 1999.

Lucas learns a lesson about bullying from the ants he has been tormenting.

Foreshadowing: Lucas sprays the ants with his squirt gun. "But the ants didn't like to get wet and soon they had had enough." Lucas is about to receive retribution.

Other Devices: *Antihero, Antithesis, Inference, Personification, Poetic Justice, Point of View*

Art Style: Expressionistic acrylic cartoons skillfully play with perspective as the boy and the ants view the same environment.

Curriculum Tie-in: Social Science (Bullies, Values)

*Nolen, Jerdine. *Big Jabe.* Illus. by Kadir Nelson. New York: Lothrop, Lee & Shepard, 2000.

Momma Mary tells stories about a special young man who does wondrous things, especially for the slaves on the Plenty Plantation.

Foreshadowing: When Addy finds the mysterious child in a wicker basket in the stream where she is fishing, he presents her with a pear. After Addy eats it, the child plants the pear seeds. "They want to grow," he says. From night to night the tree changes from a sprout to sapling to young tree full of white blossoms. Soon it bears luscious pears. "And there, shining between them, the North Star sparkled overhead." This portends the tree's mysterious role in the Plenty Plantation's slaves' disappearance to freedom in the north.

Other Devices: *Allusion, Anachronism, Antithesis, Flashback, Flash-forward, Hyperbole, Imagery, Inference, Parallelism, Simile, Symbol, Understatement*

Art Style: Strong, detailed pen/ink, watercolor, and gouache drawings provide wonderful expressionistic period ambience to this folktale.

Curriculum Tie-in: History (Slavery—America), Literature (Tall Tale)

O'Malley, Kevin. *Bud.* New York: Walker & Company, 2000.

The orderly Sweet-Williams are dismayed at their son's fondness for the messy pastime of gardening.

Foreshadowing: His parents try to direct their son's gardening tendencies by buying him a pail, shovel, and cute little gardening outfit. But soon they are laughing nervously as he waters the expensive silk flower arrangement and prunes the plastic ficus tree. Where will these gardening tendencies take him? When grandfather visits, Bud's parents fearfully keep curtains drawn so Bud's garden is out of sight. All goes well until the night of the storm and its effect on Bud's efforts.

Other Devices: *Antithesis, Aphorism, Inference, Irony, Pun, Theme, Understatement*

Art Style: Large, expressive gouache cartoons lovingly follow the development of tolerance, respect, and appreciation for a beloved child's unconventional approach to life.

Curriculum Tie-in: Science (Gardening), Social Science (Family Relationships, Values)

Pawagi, Manjusha. *The Girl Who Hated Books.* Illus. by Leanne Franson. Hillsboro, OR: Beyond Words, 1998.

Although she lives in a house full of avid readers, Meena hates books—until she discovers the magic inside them.

Foreshadowing: The later problem of toppled books is suggested first by a particular habit of Max, the cat. He dislikes books because of a tail injury he received as a kitten when an atlas fell on him. Since then he has tried "to stay on top of the books rather than below them." It is because he was on the very top of a book pile that Meena tried to climb the books to rescue him and they all fell down, spilling out the book characters.

Other Devices: *Alliteration, Allusion, Antithesis, Hyperbole, Inference, Internal Rhyme, Pun, Tone*

Art Style: Pen/ink watercolor expressionistic cartoons emphasize emotion and background action.

Ruurs, Margriet. *Emma and the Coyote.* Illus. by Barbara Spurll. New York: Stoddart Kids, 1999.

Emma thinks chickens are smarter than coyotes, and she struts boldly where no chicken should go to prove it.

Foreshadowing: Emma has had some good fortune with her efforts to get rid of the coyote. But luck can't last forever. She flutters up into the magnolia tree to watch the coyote trap. "She sat there waiting on a swaying branch . . . . Emma teetered back and forth, trying to hold onto her branch." If she falls, the coyote awaits underneath.

Other Devices: *Alliteration, Imagery, Inference, Irony, Motif, Parallelism, Serendipity, Simile*

Art Style: Bright primary color paintings expressionistically follow the fortunes of Emma and the barnyard animals.

Curriculum Tie-in: Social Science (Self-esteem)

Sierra, Judy. *The Gift of the Crocodile: A Cinderella Story.* Illus. by Reynold Ruffins. New York: Simon and Schuster Books for Young Readers, 2000.

Damura, a child of the Spice Islands, escapes her cruel stepmother and stepsister and marries a handsome prince with the help of Grandmother Crocodile.

Foreshadowing: Before she dies, Damura's mother reminds her to "respect all wild creatures, for they would help and comfort her." It turns out to be the wildest of all of them who brings good fortune her way. Later, after the night of the palace dance, during which Damura has dropped one of the golden slippers Grandmother Crocodile had given to her, Damura apologizes for having lost it. "You needn't be sorry. That one slipper will make you a princess," the knowing benefactor tells her.

Other Devices: *Irony, Motif, Poetic Justice, Pun*

Art Style: Folk images painted in bright acrylics portray this Indonesian version of an international folktale.

Curriculum Tie-in: Literature (Folktales)

Steig, William. *Wizzil.* Illus. by Quentin Blake. New York: Farrar Straus Giroux, 2000.

A bored witch causes trouble when she decides to take revenge on an old man, but her mischief leads to a happy ending.

Foreshadowing: Weird things have happened since he put on the glove he found. In frustration, DeWitt throws it into the water under a bridge.

He watches it turn into a repulsive witch. But he can't bear to see a fellow creature drowning, so he dives in and tows her ashore. Suddenly, before his eyes, "he was startled to see that this witch, instead of looking sinister, was blushing. And smiling with gratitude into his wide-open eyes." This is a light-bulb moment. Their relationship is headed for an abrupt change.
Other Devices: *Alliteration, Ambiguity, Connotation, Internal Rhyme, Irony, Serendipity, Tone*
Art Style: Delightfully awful watercolor cartoons capture the personalities and behaviors of the rotten witch and the hillbilly family she pesters.
Curriculum Tie-in: Social Science (Love)

Turner, Ann. *Secrets from the Dollhouse.* Illus. by Raúl Colón. New York: HarperCollins, 2000.
The life of a family of dolls and their servants living in a dollhouse in a young girl's room is told from the perspective of Emma, oldest of the doll children.
Foreshadowing: Several things concern the narrating doll. "Cat is too lazy to hunt mice. Sometimes Cat comes so close his breath steams up the window. I do not trust him." This menacing creature is likely to figure in the story. But the bold mice are mentioned often. "One even bit Baby's hat, and Baby screamed. I rocked and tilted until I fell on that mouse and frightened him away!" These mice are much too present. Also, Emma "would like to have an adventure." She is not sure what that is, but "Papa says it is excitement and not being safe." The reader wonders what kind of action will occur and how it might threaten the doll character.
Other Devices: *Imagery, Metaphor, Personification, Point of View, Simile*
Art Style: Stiff 1920s folk images in scratched line pastels capture the whimsy of a toy world.

Wallace, Karen. *Scarlette Beane.* Illus. by Jon Berkeley. New York: Dial Books for Young Readers (Penguin Putnam), 2000.
When family members give five-year-old Scarlette a garden, she succeeds in growing gigantic vegetables and creating something wonderful.
Foreshadowing: This gardening family knows it has a special child when they look upon their new baby daughter. She not only has the proverbial green thumb; the ends of all her fingers are green. They predict she will do "something wonderful."
Other Devices: *Hyperbole, Pun, Simile*
Art Style: Bright primary colors and muted shadowy hues combine in expressionistic acrylic paintings on textured paper to illustrate a fantastic world of prodigious vegetable growth.
Curriculum Tie-in: Literature (Tall Tales)

White, Linda Arms. *Comes a Wind.* Illus. by Tom Curry. New York: DK Pub., 2000.

While visiting their mother's ranch, two brothers who constantly try to best each other, swap tall tales about big winds and are surprised by the fiercest wind they have ever seen.

Foreshadowing: The boys have always been rivals. "Mama had hoped it would stop when Clement and Clyde became grown-ups, but things only got worse." How will this affect the birthday visit? They each wish her Happy Birthday, but they do so "glaring at each other." While the two wait on the porch for Mama to bring them lemonade, they engage in tall tales and watch a fierce wind become stronger by the minute. Mama is unaware of the growing problem. She comes to the screen door carrying cake. "No, Mama, don't—" they shout in warning. What will happen when she and her big skirts step out into the wind?

Other Devices: *Atmosphere, Hyperbole, Inference, Parallelism, Simile*

Art Style: Painted acrylics in expressionistic naïve perspectives illustrate the peculiar and humorous effects of the forces of wind and imagination.

Curriculum Tie-in: Literature (Tall Tales)

*Wilkon, Piotr. Rosie the Cool Cat. Illus. by Jozef Wilkon. New York: Viking (Penguin Books), 1989.

Casper and Carolina are proud of their jet-black fur and despair of trying to cope with their orange kitten, who likes to play with mice and sleep in the doghouse.

Foreshadowing: The perfect couple live in a beautiful house on the top of Black Hill. In every room are pictures of family members, going way back. Each has the lovely signature black fur. The two are looking forward to having their own kittens. When the moment comes, Casper is delighted to see four beautiful black kittens. "This is the most wonderful day of my life!" he says. His wife, Carolina, remarks, "I am not sure about that. There is still one more kitten."

Other Devices: *Antithesis, Inference, Irony, Poetic Justice, Satire, Stereotype, Symbol*

Art Style: Pastel and colored pencil expressionistic cartoons capture the family pride in its uniqueness as well as its sense of puzzlement in the jolting difference of the odd one.

Curriculum Tie-in: Social Science (Family Relationships, Individuality, Values)

*Wisniewski, David. Golem. New York: Clarion Books (Houghton Mifflin), 1996 (Caldecott—1997).

A saintly rabbi miraculously brings to life a clay giant who helps him watch over the Jews of sixteenth-century Prague.

Foreshadowing: At the moment the clay giant awakens to life, he presages the effect his existence will have upon history. " 'Father,' his great voice rumbled, 'was this wise to do?' "

Other Devices: *Analogy, Atmosphere, Imagery, Inference, Irony, Motif, Paradox, Simile*
Art Style: Paper cut in sophisticated, expressionistic collage produces a powerful physical and emotional effect on this cautionary tale.
Curriculum Tie-in: Literature (Legend), Social Science (Values)

*Yaccarino, Dan. *Deep in the Jungle.* New York: Anne Schwartz Book from Atheneum Books for Young Readers (Simon & Schuster), 2000.

After being tricked into joining the circus, an arrogant lion escapes and returns to the jungle, where he lives peacefully with the animals he used to terrorize.
Foreshadowing: The lion has learned from his short stint as a circus performer that he prefers his former jungle life. He returns to discover his fellow jungle creatures are being loaded up to be taken away. He's ready for the next smooth talker who asks him whether he can perform any tricks. He willingly shows off his famous man's-head-in-the-lion's-mouth trick . . . .
Other Devices: *Anachronism, Antihero, Antithesis, Black Humor, Irony, Motif, Parallelism, Poetic Justice, Pun, Tone*
Art Style: Expressionistic gouache naïve cartoons against white backgrounds, reminiscent of the "Curious George" series, accent the droll language in this lesson in humility.
Curriculum Tie-in: Literature (Parable), Social Science (Values)

Zagwÿn, Deborah. *Apple Batter.* Berkeley, CA: Tricycle Press, 1999.

Because of their persistence, Delmore succeeds in learning to hit a baseball and his mother, Loretta, succeeds in growing apples.
Foreshadowing: Early on, there is ample warning that Delmore's aim is inaccurate. "Delmore had hit a lot of things but never a fair ball." As his swing begins to improve, he starts to get hits. Balls are getting "closer and closer to Loretta's orchard." As more time passes, the single apple remaining on one of her trees has grown to "the size of a baseball now." While Delmore focuses on the pale ball atop the pipe, he swings in the direction "of the last thing he'd looked at—Loretta's prized apple. He never expected them to meet."
Other Devices: *Alliteration, Analogy, Antithesis, Inference, Irony, Parallelism, Pun, Simile*
Art Style: Expressionistic watercolor cartoons compare the changing fortunes of mother and son as they struggle toward their respective goals.
Curriculum Tie-in: Athletics (Baseball), Science (Apple Production)

HYPERBOLE

Emphasis achieved by deliberate exaggeration.

Example: I'm so hungry I could eat a horse. They were packed in the
subway like sardines. I wouldn't give him the time of day.

Alderson, Brian. *The Tale of the Turnip.* Illus. by Fritz Wegner. Cambridge, MA:
Candlewick Press, 1999.

A humble farmer's garden produce pleases the king, who handsomely rewards
his efforts, but an arrogant squire gets more than he bargained for when he
attempts to claim a similar reward.

Hyperbole: The jealous squire notes that he has a stable full of horses out
there, "and any one of 'em's worth a thousand turnips." Still, the turnip
that the humble farmer brings to the king is a bit out of the ordinary. It
takes a "block and tackle" to heave it up out of the ground onto a wagon.
In biblical similarity to the parable of the Widow's Mite, the king receives
the squire's offering of a fine horse and considers the source. He tells the
squire, who is expecting a fine reward for his gift, that "not even the crown
jewels are a fit reward" for a horse like that. But perhaps a champion turnip
would be appropriate payback!

Other Devices: *Connotation, Motif, Poetic Justice, Satire, Tone*

Art Style: Humorously detailed watercolor and ink cartoons delight the
visual sense and the sense of justice.

Curriculum Tie-in: History (Nineteenth-Century England), Literature
(Folktales—England)

Alexander, Lloyd. *The House Gobbaleen.* Illus. by Diane Goode. New York: Dutton
Children's Books (Penguin Books), 1995.

Unhappy over what he considers his bad luck, Tooley ignores his cat's warnings
and invites a greedy little man into his home in the mistaken hope of improving
his fortunes.

Hyperbole: When they've had enough of their guest, they set about making
his stay uncomfortable. The cat hides inside the food pot and bursts out,
"bristling until he looked three times his size," moving through the air like
a "bolt of yellow lightning." The little man can't get away fast enough. He
loses his footing and pitches to the floor, "so round and fat on Tooley's
hospitality that he could not pick himself up again." He begins rolling, and
"without slackening speed, the whirling figure shot across the threshold."
He keeps rolling "through the dooryard, over the field, and down the hill
until he vanished from sight."

Other Devices: *Ambiguity, Foreshadowing, Inference, Irony, Simile, Theme,
Tone, Understatement*

Art Style: Humorous gouache and watercolor cartoons illustrate this
modern folktale.

Curriculum Tie-in: Literature (Folktale), Social Science (Values)

Gibbons, Faye. *Mama and Me and the Model T.* Illus. by Ted Rand. New York: Morrow, 1999.

When Mr. Long says any man can drive a car, Mama gets behind the wheel to show women can drive, too.

> **Hyperbole:** When the new car arrives, it's time for a ride. All fourteen pile in. "We were sitting on legs and standing on toes, poking elbows in ribs and noses in hair." Mama takes a turn for herself at the wheel. "The car leaped forward, dragging the clothesline behind. We tore across the yard, cutting through a flower bed and bouncing over the woodpile. We bobbed across a stump and ran over a crape myrtle bush. Mama flattened a pine sapling before tearing through the pasture fence and shimmying over a hill."
>
> **Other Devices:** *Foreshadowing, Imagery, Inference, Onomatopoeia, Parallelism, Stereotype, Understatement*
>
> **Art Style:** Expressionistic watercolors exuberantly dramatize the mysterious intricacies of mastering the wondrous but tricky skills of automobile driving.
>
> **Curriculum Tie-in:** Social Science (Family Relationships)

*Hayes, Joe. *A Spoon for Every Bite.* Illus. by Rebecca Lear. New York: Orchard Books, 1996.

A poor husband and wife ask their rich neighbor to be godfather to their child, and once they are compadres, prey upon his pride and extravagance to trick him out of his fortune.

> **Hyperbole:** The rich man makes a social gaffe when he laughs at the efforts made by the young couple to offer him hospitality. They had only two spoons and tell him that when they were finally able to buy a third spoon, they invited him to supper. He denigrates their generosity and boasts, "I have so many spoons in my house I could use a different one each day of the year if I wished to." This insult is hurled back by the wife, who responds that she has a friend who "uses a different spoon for every bite he eats. He never uses the same spoon twice."
>
> **Other Devices:** *Ambiguity, Antihero, Antithesis, Foreshadowing, Motif, Poetic Justice*
>
> **Art Style:** Realistic pastel drawings contrast the striking differences in circumstances between the compadres, and their varied emotional responses to these circumstances.
>
> **Curriculum Tie-in:** History (American Southwest), Literature (Folktales—Hispanic), Social Science (Values)

Hesse, Karen. *Come On, Rain!* Illus. by Jon J. Muth. New York: Scholastic Press, 1999.

A young girl eagerly awaits a coming rainstorm to bring relief from the oppressive summer heat.

> **Hyperbole:** The girl would like to put on her bathing suit; she's hot. The mother understands how dangerous that could be under such a hot sun.

She tells the girl, "You'll burn all day out in this sun." She may be exaggerating to make her point. Heat wavers off tar patches "in the broiling alleyway." Maybe the street isn't broiling, but the effect is clear. There is such relief when the rain comes that people say, "The rain has made us new." Perhaps the sense of refreshing moisture has done wonders for folks' spirits as they "gulp down rain" in mouths open wide.

Other Devices: *Alliteration, Foreshadowing, Imagery, Metaphor, Paradox, Simile*

Art Style: Buoyant, ebullient, expressionistic pen/ink watercolors lend emotional credibility to the nervous anxiety of relentless heat accompanied by worrisome drought, and the tremendous sense of relief that accompanies a thorough, nourishing rain.

Curriculum Tie-in: Science (Meteorology)

Hoban, Russell. *Trouble on Thunder Mountain.* Illus. by Quentin Blake. New York: Orchard Books (Grolier), 2000.

When Megafright International flattens their beautiful mountain to put up a hi-tech plastic theme park, the O'Saurus family uses faith and lots of Monsta-Gloo to put things right.

Hyperbole: The dinosaur family watches where the developers haul the chunks of their mountain, which are being blasted off. Then "they loaded all the pieces of the top of Thunder Mountain into the pickup truck. When they got back, they stuck them together with Monsta-Gloo." They hide their progress behind a privacy curtain. "Everybody got busy with needle and thread, and they made a great big curtain. Then they made a frame to hang it on." Behind the curtain they glue together their original dirt mountain. "They put wheels under it and moved it next to Megafright Mountain. Among the O'Sauruses' friends are "four hundred mole technicians and two or three thousand ants." A tunnel is made through the mountain and train tracks are installed. Then, they take apart the plastic mountain and haul it on the train through the tunnel to Endsville and dump it off. This is all accomplished the day before the big plastic mountain is to open to tourists.

Other Devices: *Aphorism, Connotation, Foreshadowing, Irony, Poetic Justice, Satire, Understatement*

Art Style: Humorous pen/ink watercolor cartoons spiritedly produce a funny tribute to old-fashioned ingenuity and to nature.

Curriculum Tie-in: Science (Ecology)

Johnson, Paul Brett. *Old Dry Frye: A Deliciously Funny Tall Tale.* New York: Scholastic Press, 1999.

A humorous retelling of an Appalachian folktale about a preacher who chokes on a chicken bone.

Hyperbole: Old Dry Frye is "the chicken-eatingest sermonizer that ever laid fire to a pulpit." He turns up at mealtime wherever fried chicken is being served. Once he gobbles so fast that he chokes on a bone and "died right there on the spot." So begins the saga of "getting shed of him." He is taken to a neighbor's chicken house and left there. He is heaped into a wheelbarrow, carted off, and bounced into a tree. He is stuffed into a feed sack and dropped in a creek. He is hung up in a smoke house. He is set atop a mean-spirited horse. And, in the end, he still manages to show up wherever fried chicken is being served.

Other Devices: *Black Humor, Cliché, Inference, Poetic Justice, Serendipity, Tone, Understatement*

Art Style: Ebullient acrylic cartoons share the fortunes and misfortunes of the self-serving characters in this raucous Appalachian romp.

Curriculum Tie-in: Literature (Tall Tales), Social Science (Appalachian Culture)

Johnston, Tony. *Alice Nizzy Nazzy, the Witch of Santa Fe.* Illus. by Tomie dePaola. New York: G.P. Putnam's Sons, 1995.

When Manuela's sheep are stolen, she has to go to Alice Nizzy Nazzy's talking roadrunner-footed adobe house and try to get the witch to give the flock back.

Hyperbole: This witch "cackled a cackle that could wear down cliffs." When she finds the black cactus flower she desired, "instantly thunder clapped and clashed. Lightning slashed the sky. And all weathers happened at once."

Other Devices: *Alliteration, Connotation, Foreshadowing, Internal Rhyme, Motif, Poetic Justice, Simile*

Art Style: Bright pastel and acrylic folk cartoons illustrate the western lifestyle in this good vs. bad character tale.

Curriculum Tie-in: Geography (New Mexico), Literature (Fairytales—America), Social Science (Values)

Jones, Joy. *Tambourine Moon.* Illus. by Terry Widener. New York: Simon & Schuster Books for Young Readers, 1999.

Noni is afraid as she and her granddaddy walk home, until he tells her how he met her Grandma Ismay one dark night in Alabama, and how the big yellow moon came to light up the sky.

Hyperbole: They called themselves the Star Fire Choir. And "even barking dogs sounded better." When granddaddy walked home alone in the dark, he was so scared his arm shook the tambourine. It "jumped right out of my hand! It shot itself up higher, higher, higher till it settled in the sky" and "hung there, glowing and pouring light all over the night."

Other Devices: *Antithesis, Imagery, Personification, Simile*

Art Style: Acrylic art in expressionistic, ethnic folk designs employs both sharp angles and puffy, rounded curves.

Curriculum Tie-in: Social Science (Ethnicity—African-American, Grandparents)

Kimmel, Eric A. *Grizz!* Illus. by Andrew Glass. New York: Holiday House, 2000. Cowboy Lucky Doolin makes a deal with the Devil, agreeing not to wash, shave, or change his clothes for seven years, thus earning a fortune and the hand of his true love.

Hyperbole: As the years passed, Lucky kept his end of the bargain. "His hair looked like a buzzard's nest." "His smell could make a buzzard weep. He could empty out a town by walking into it. Dogs barked. Children screamed. Horses pulled up their hitching posts and galloped away." "He resembled a haystack on legs and smelled like something that should have been buried." "The only time water touched his skin was when it rained." But Lucky became rich. It was a good thing, because the Rocking M Ranch had come upon hard times. "The ranch house had burned down, the cattle died, rustlers ran off the horses." "I got enough money to pay that mortgage a hundred times over," said Lucky when he learned of Shelby's dire straits.

Other Devices: *Atmosphere, Inference, Motif, Poetic Justice, Simile, Understatement*

Art Style: Oil sticks and watercolor dust create exaggerated cartoons that complement this version of a classic soul-selling wager folktale.

Curriculum Tie-in: Literature (Folktales—America)

Lowell, Susan. *Little Red Cowboy Hat.* Illus. by Randy Cecil. New York: Henry Holt, 1997.

Little Red rides her pony, Buck, to Grandma's ranch with a jar of cactus jelly in the saddlebag.

Hyperbole: Regarding the wolf, Grandma minces no words about how she feels. "That yellow-bellied, snake-blooded, skunk-eyed, rancid son of a parallelogram! Together grandmother and granddaughter light out after the fleeing wolf. "Take that, you low-life lobo!" shouts Grandma, as she fires off a shotgun round. She has grievances to settle. The wolf has broken into her house, is wearing her clothes, is getting fleas in her bed, and, most unspeakable, is messing with her granddaughter.

Other Devices: *Aphorism, Atmosphere, Caricature, Inference, Onomatopoeia, Parody, Simile, Stereotype, Tone*

Art Style: Gouache cartoons in expressionistic naïve style humorously match this unique geographical take on a familiar fairy tale.

Lum, Kate. *What! Cried Granny: An Almost Bedtime Story.* Illus. by Adrian Johnson. New York: Dial (Penguin Putnam), 1998.

Granny can do whatever it takes to make Patrick's first sleepover a success.

Hyperbole: Granny points out that it will be dark soon. It's time for Patrick, "dear boy," to get ready for bed. He points out that he has no bed here. "WHAT?" Granny exclaims. She goes out to her yard, chops down a tree, takes it to her workroom, opens her toolbox, and makes Patrick a fine bed. Then she paints it "a restful shade of blue," puts a "comfy red mattress on it," and takes it to the bedroom. He is told to climb into it and lay his head on the pillow and "sail off to dreamland." Patrick points out that he has no pillow. Granny sets off to the hen house for a big batch of feathers. When the pillow is in place, she tells him to "tuck the blanket under your chin, and I'll kiss you good night." He has no blanket either. Off Granny goes to the hills, where "a flock of fat sheep were snoozing." She shears their wool, spins it into yarn, and knits a fuzzy blanket, after which she dyes it the "prettiest shade of twilight purple." The next thing missing is a teddy bear to hug. The energetic, resourceful Granny tears down the living room curtains, cuts, sews, stuffs, adds button eyes and a red ribbon. By the time the bear is tucked in Patrick's arms—it's morning. Patrick has managed not to have to go to bed. And Granny—she's feeling somewhat tired, no doubt.

Other Devices: *Inference*

Art Style: Bright acrylic expressionistic cartoons illustrate Granny's increasingly jaundiced view of this stalling child's bedtime tactics.

Curriculum Tie-in: Social Science (Grandparents)

Mahy, Margaret. *Simply Delicious.* Illus. by Jonathan Allen. New York: Orchard Books, 1999.

A resourceful father engages in all kinds of acrobatic moves to keep an assortment of jungle creatures from getting the double-dip, chocolate-chip-and-cherry ice cream cone he is taking home to his son.

Hyperbole: To dodge the animals following him, Mr. Minky, riding his bicycle, "tossed the ice cream high into the air. As it came down, he cleverly caught it on his toe, kicked it up into the air again, caught it on his elbow, flicked it high, tilted his head back, then caught it once more— this time, on his nose!" Finally close to his home, "at long last he burst out of the jungle, shot up his home-made ramp, and, flying through the air across the back fence, glided gracefully into his own back garden."

Other Devices: *Alliteration, Foreshadowing, Internal Rhyme, Poetic Justice, Simile, Understatement*

Art Style: Lively line and gouache cartoons in lush jungle colors satisfyingly follow the father's adventures as he delivers his son an appreciated treat.

Curriculum Tie-in: Literature (Cumulative Tale)

*Meddaugh, Susan. *Hog-Eye.* New York: Walter Lorraine Books (Houghton Mifflin), 1995.

A young pig uses her ability to read to outwit a wolf that intends to eat her.

Hyperbole: The young pig misses her school bus and proceeds to explain how the rest of her day went. She tells her family she took a shortcut into the woods and was captured by a wolf. Then she uses her reading ability to con the wolf into going after soup ingredients that result in his getting caught in a garden trap, falling over a steep cliff and a tall waterfall, and rolling around in a bed of poison ivy. She puts a "hog-eye" magic spell on him, and he begs her to make the itching stop. He releases her and even receives a nice apology. The next morning on the school bus, she is telling the kids her story again. "Wolves to the left of me . . . wolves to the right . . . ."

Other Devices: *Allusion, Antithesis, Flashback, Foreshadowing, Inference, Irony, Understatement*

Art Style: Split-page watercolor cartoons tell the "true story" of a schoolchild who dislikes her daily bus ride.

Curriculum Tie-in: Literature (Tall Tale)

Modarressi, Mitra. *Yard Sale.* New York: DK Pub., 2000.

When Mr. Flotsam has a yard sale in the quiet town of Spudville, his neighbors are first upset, then delighted by their purchases.

Hyperbole: The typewriter "zipped off page after page of its own writing." When Mr. Twitchett planted some of the seeds he had bought, "he instantly found himself surrounded by a garden of monstrous proportions." Children found a delightful jungle gym. Mr. Rotelli's pasta maker quickly produced a room full of spaghetti. The "noodles were waist deep," and the entire town agreed it was the best-tasting spaghetti they had ever eaten. The music box kept everyone dancing at the best party they'd been to in years. And, the special phone would let folks visit with the dear departed. "I can finally get my great-great-great-aunt Sylvia's recipe for carrot cake."

Other Devices: *Allusion, Antithesis, Connotation, Inference, Paradox, Serendipity, Understatement*

Art Style: Lively, full-page watercolor naïve art accompanies an understated text.

*Nolen, Jerdine. *Big Jabe.* Illus. by Kadir Nelson. New York: Lothrop, Lee & Shepard, 2000.

Momma Mary tells stories about a special young man who does wondrous things, especially for the slaves on the Plenty Plantation.

Hyperbole: In this typical tall tale, the main character accomplishes great feats. The child calls forth fish. "Suddenly the earth began to tremble, the river began to roil, and the air was filled with fish—jumping, hopping, flying right into Addy's wagon." Other marvelous things occur. "Cotton plumped up so quick, it seemed to blossom overnight. Cornstalks looked to scrape the sky, yielding foot-long ears of sweet, sweet corn. Chicks hatched by the dozen. New foals were ready to saddle break at six months. Speckled cows spotted the fields and gave enough milk to fill a river. Sheep produced enough wool in one shearing to knit a blanket big enough to cover the entire farm."

Other Devices: *Allusion, Anachronism, Antithesis, Flashback, Flash-forward, Foreshadowing, Imagery, Inference, Parallelism, Simile, Symbol, Understatement*
Art Style: Strong, detailed pen/ink, watercolor, and gouache drawings provide wonderful expressionistic period ambience to this folktale.
Curriculum Tie-in: History (Slavery—America), Literature (Tall Tale)

Osborne, Mary Pope. *Kate and the Beanstalk.* Illus. by Giselle Potter. New York: Atheneum Books for Young Readers (Simon & Schuster), 2000.
In this version of the classic tale, a girl climbs to the top of a giant beanstalk, where she uses her quick wit to outsmart a giant and make her and her mother's fortune.
Hyperbole: A giant woman at the top of the beanstalk complains to Kate that her husband "makes me cook from the cock's crow to the owl's hoot." When the giant thinks he can smell an Englishwoman, the wife replies, "You only smell the wagonload of bacon I fried for your breakfast." Another time she tells him, "You only smell the mountain of hash I made for your breakfast." And a third time she says, "You only smell the sea of fish soup I made for your breakfast." When the giant is no longer a threat, the grateful woman makes a biscuit for Kate and her mother "as big as a cow."
Other Devices: *Inference, Motif, Poetic Justice, Simile, Stereotype/Reverse Stereotype*
Art Style: Naïve drawings in pencil, ink, gouache, and watercolor expressionistically tell the familiar tale of the thieving giant and the rescue of stolen treasure.
Curriculum Tie-in: Literature (Folktale), Social Science (Values)

Pawagi, Manijusha. *The Girl Who Hated Books.* Illus. by Leanne Franson. Hillsboro, OR: Beyond Words, 1998.
Although she lives in a house full of avid readers, Meena hates books—until she discovers the magic inside them.
Hyperbole: Books in this story are everywhere. They are "crammed in the fireplace." Books are "in the bathtub and behind the dryer." Meena must climb on a "stack of encyclopedias so she could reach the cereal." And she must move "a pile of magazines to get the milk" in the fridge. She must "take books out of the sink to brush her teeth." In the dining room is the tallest stack of books in the house, from floor to ceiling. These are her books, bought for her by her parents in hopes she would read them. She begins climbing them to rescue her cat at the top. "At first it was easy because the picture books had hard covers, and she felt as if she were climbing stairs. But when she reached the paperbacks her foot slipped on a book of poetry." When the heap falls, "people and animals started falling out of the pages and tumbling to the ground." Soon "the elephant was balancing on a coffee table juggling the good china plates." Rabbits "were nibbling on the table legs."

Other Devices: *Alliteration, Allusion, Antithesis, Foreshadowing, Inference, Internal Rhyme, Pun, Tone*
Art Style: Pen/ink watercolor expressionistic cartoons emphasize emotion and background action.

Wallace, Karen. *Scarlette Beane.* Illus. by Jon Berkeley. New York: Dial Books for Young Readers (Penguin Putnam), 2000.

When family members give five-year-old Scarlette a garden, she succeeds in growing gigantic vegetables and creating something wonderful.

Hyperbole: Scarlette's seeds turn into carrots as "huge as tree trunks," onions as "big as hot-air balloons," and parsley as "thick as a jungle." It takes bulldozers to dig up the carrots. Forklifts have to carry the onions. Parsley is cut with chain saws. Soup has to be made in a concrete mixer.
Other Devices: *Foreshadowing, Pun, Simile*
Art Style: Bright primary colors and muted shadowy hues combine in expressionistic acrylic paintings on textured paper to illustrate a fantastic world of prodigious vegetable growth.
Curriculum Tie-in: Literature (Tall Tales)

White, Linda Arms. *Comes a Wind.* Illus. by Tom Curry. New York: DK Pub., 2000.

While visiting their mother's ranch, two brothers who constantly try to best each other swap tall tales about big winds, and are surprised by the fiercest wind they have ever seen.

Hyperbole: There is exaggeration in the boys' stories and in the day's events. When their mother notes, "Looks like it comes a wind," the boys launch into tales of one outlandish windy experience after the other, each trying to best the other's story. One of them says, "One day it was so windy it plucked every last feather off my chickens. Shamed 'em so, Mimi had to knit 'em little woollies to wear till their feathers grew back." That prompts the other to recall that "One day it was so windy, it whooshed through the high school marching band, caught the bell of my boy's tuba, and screwed him twelve feet into the ground." So goes the one-upmanship between the two while a real wind gains strength. It "yanked the buttons from Clement's shirt." It "snatched Clyde's words out of his mouth." They both have to "grab hold of the porch rail to keep from blowing straight to Kansas." Chickens whirl by, "beaks, wings, feathers, and all." The outhouse, a whole herd of longhorns, a red barn with kittens still in the loft, and twenty miles of barbed-wire fence come through the air. A hay baler bales mile after mile of prickly pears, sagebrush, and mesquite trees as it flies by. Mama's skirt billows out and lifts her up, snagging her atop the barn on the rickety weather vane.
Other Devices: *Atmosphere, Foreshadowing, Inference, Parallelism, Simile*

Art Style: Painted acrylics in expressionistic naïve perspectives illustrate the peculiar and humorous effects of the forces of wind and imagination.
Curriculum Tie-in: Literature (Tall Tales)

IMAGERY

Mental pictures summoned through language that appeals to the senses.

Example: A car in *Wind in the Willows* is passing. "The 'poop-poop' rang with a brazen shout in their ears, they had a moment's glimpse of an interior of glittering plate-glass and rich morocco, and the magnificent motor-car, immense, breath-snatching, passionate, with its pilot tense and hugging his wheel, possessed all earth and air for the fraction of a second, flung an enveloping cloud of dust that blinded and enwrapped them utterly, and then dwindled to a speck in the far distance, changed back into a droning bee once more."

Baker, Jeannie. *The Hidden Forest.* New York: Greenwillow Books (HarperCollins), 2000.
When a friend helps him retrieve the fish trap he lost while trying to fish off the coast of eastern Tasmania, Ben comes to see the giant kelp forest he had feared in a new light.
Imagery: "Gigantic golden trees of kelp reach toward the sun. Shafts of sunlight shimmer in their branches." He "parts some kelp to reveal rock alive with all kinds of strangely beautiful textures." Ben and his friend see a whale and "catch glimpses of its dark, gleaming shape rolling and sliding against the kelp as it passes on around the bay."
Other Devices: *Connotation, Inference, Simile*
Art Style: Photographed collages are constructions of natural materials such as pressed seaweeds, sponges, and sand in multidimensional effect to create the enchanting world of ocean life.
Curriculum Tie-in: Science (Ocean Ecology)

*Berkeley, Laura. *The Spirit of the Maasai Man.* New York: Barefoot Books, 2000.
Locked inside their cages, the zoo animals have given up hope until the spirit of the Maasai Man hums his haunting songs of their homeland.
Imagery: When the Maasai Man sings, the trapped animals suddenly remember their natural environment and the role they had in that world. "The elephant smelled storm clouds in the air. Silently, she followed the echoes of her herd as it traced its sacred rain-paths across the African plains." The lion is able to sit high on his rocky throne, seeing "through

hooded eyelids, as his kingdom shimmered in the heat of the sun." The
tiger "weaved sinewed pathways through her jungle realm in the warmth
of the Indian night." The spirit of the wolf "ran fast into the cold embrace
of a lonely wilderness." High in mountain forests "dark, misty forms gathered
around the spirit of the gorilla." The python "felt coolness of the rain forest
moist against its skin." The polar bear "could see the Arctic brightness
and, standing high, touched the frozen landscape with a longing paw."
The eagle followed the Maasai song to "heights of a mountain ledge and
the blueness of the sky unfurled his giant wings."
Other Devices: *Symbol, Theme, Tone*
Art Style: Realistic acrylic and crayon drawings touchingly illuminate the
plight of captive wild animals in expressionistic settings.
Curriculum tie-In: Geography (Animal Habitats), Science (Zoos)

*Bunting, Eve. *The Memory String.* Illus. by Ted Rand. New York: Clarion Books
(Houghton Mifflin), 2000.
   While still grieving for her mother and unable to accept her stepmother, a girl
clings to the memories represented by forty-three buttons on a string.
      Imagery: "Jane stopped and pushed her hair away from her face. She wore
      an old paint-stained shirt and skinny-leg jeans." "The buttons strung on
      the string shone and silvered, patterned with oak-leaf shadows." "She
      watched the white circles of the flashlights, the dark figures of Jane and
      Dad crawling through the grass. She could smell the fresh paint. The
      crickets had stopped singing to listen."
      Other Devices: *Ambiguity, Antithesis, Aphorism, Foreshadowing, Inference,
      Parallelism, Simile*
      Art Style: Shadowy, impressionistic watercolor paintings detail the
      emotional changes the child experiences as she feels both separation and
      reconnection to her family.
      Curriculum Tie-in: Social Science (Family Relationships, Grief)

*Burleigh, Robert. *Edna.* Illus. by Joanna Yardley. New York: Orchard Books,
2000.
   Carefree meanderings during her time in New York City give Edna St. Vincent
Millay grist for a famous poem she later pens.
      Imagery: Everything about the city seems enchanting. "I can see the far-
      off tall buildings, the laundry flapping on nearby roofs, and down below,
      the hurdy-gurdy man playing his organ and kids zipping by on roller skates."
      She and her friends take "long walks over the Brooklyn Bridge, and feel the
      wind on our faces. We ride the open, upper deck of a bus down Fifth
      Avenue, looking up at the big-windowed buildings and down at the
      policemen on their horses." It is possible to take a ferryboat at night from
      the tip of Manhattan to Staten Island. "The ride made me feel peaceful.
      I watched the white foam billow in the boat's wake. I leaned out and

listened to the buoy bells—gong, gong, gong, gong—in the watery dark."
From the grassy hills of Staten Island "we gazed out on the distant, blinking
lights—hundreds and hundreds of them—from the windows of New York's
giant skyscrapers." At the same time "far down in the darkness, we could
hear the ghostly whistles and lonely horns of the boats and ships in the
harbor."

Other Devices: *Atmosphere, Foreshadowing, Parallelism, Simile*

Art Style: Expressionistic watercolors in vivid hues help recreate the
marvelous feelings of expectation and freedom experienced by youthful
artists in a city of promise that welcomes their enthusiasm.

Curriculum Tie-in: Literature (Biography—Poets)

*Bunting, Eve. *Swan in Love.* Illus. by Jo Ellen McAllister Stammen. New York:
Atheneum Books for Young Readers (Simon & Schuster), 2000.

Despite ridicule of the other animals, Swan persists in his adoration for a swan-
shaped boat named Dora.

Imagery: On the boat Dora's name was printed "in black on her sparkling
paint." The other swans "muttered" their criticism of Swan. The fish
"laughed their silvery laughs" as they made fun of him. The frogs who lived
in the "thin lake reeds" croaked their accusations. Even the opossum, who
"tiptoed down to drink the lake water," gently told him he would be wiser
to give his love to another swan. But Swan was "happy there with only the
floating moon between them." In winter the "lake clinked with floating
ice." He "lay, day and night, on the frosted grass beside her." In time the
boat developed cracks, and her "white gleam had turned to the gray of lake
pebbles." In winter, "the voice spoke to him through the pale sunshine or
starlit wind." The man came in spring. "His great rubber boots squelched
mud." When the man left, "Swan hunched over next to Dora, listening as
the man's truck roared away, listening to the silence of their lake."

Other Devices: *Antithesis, Aphorism, Foreshadowing, Inference, Simile, Theme*

Art Style: Resplendent pastel expressionistic illustrations shimmer with
grace as they illuminate the story of transforming love.

Curriculum Tie-in: Social Science (Love)

Gibbons, Faye. *Mama and Me and the Model T.* Illus. by Ted Rand. New York:
Morrow, 1999.

When Mr. Long says any man can drive a car, Mama gets behind the wheel
to show women can drive, too.

Imagery: Only one thing makes such a rackety-put-pow sound. "Sure
enough down the road came a Model T, chugging along the pasture fence,
scaring the mules and the cows. It lurched into the ward, burping and
hissing, and came to a stop with a honk on the horn." Soon all the family
wants a ride. "We bounced and jiggled down to the spring. We rattled by
our cotton fields. We joggled around the barn and splashed through the
creek."

Other Devices: *Foreshadowing, Hyperbole, Inference, Onomatopoeia, Parallelism, Stereotype, Understatement*
Art Style: Expressionistic watercolors exuberantly dramatize the mysterious intricacies of mastering the wondrous but tricky skills of automobile driving.
Curriculum Tie-in: Social Science (Family Relationships)

Givens, Terryl. *Dragon Scales and Willow Leaves.* Illus. by Andrew Portwood. New York: G.P. Putnam's Sons, 1997.
    Although they are twins, Jonathan and Rachel neither look the same nor see things the same way—especially in the forest.
    Imagery: Rachel discovers "boisterous bullfrogs, splashing their noisy way from rock to rock." Jonathan interprets the sloshing and slapping of bullfrogs as the firing of pirates. "The ground shuddered with the roar of cannons, and the bursting bombs showered them with spray." Rachel sees "countless rows of corn, with their ripe ears and golden tassels bending and nodding in the breeze." Jonathan sees Vikings, the mightiest of warriors, "so stunned that they froze in terror," while he and Rachel passed safely through.
    Other Devices: *Alliteration, Antithesis, Metaphor, Point of View, Simile*
    Art Style: Impressionistic watercolor pictures expressionistically celebrate the separate ways we perceive our surroundings.
    Curriculum Tie-in: Social Science (Individuality)

*Gregorowski, Christopher. *Fly, Eagle, Fly! An African Tale.* Illus. by Niki Daly. New York: Margaret K. McElderry Books (Simon & Schuster), 2000.
    A farmer finds an eagle and raises it to behave like a chicken, until a friend helps the eagle learn its rightful place in the sky.
    Imagery: "He wandered over the hillside and through the dark and tangled forests where everything began, then out again along the muddy cattle tracks." He "searched in the long thatch grass, taller than his own head. He climbed the slopes of the high mountain with its rocky cliffs rising to the sky." "The first light crept into the sky as they began to climb the mountain. Below them they could see the river snaking like a long, thin ribbon through the golden grasslands, the forest, and the veld, stretching down toward the sea. The wispy clouds in the sky were pink at first and then began to shimmer with a golden brilliance." The "sun's first rays shot out over the mountain, and suddenly the world was ablaze with light." The "great bird stretched out its wings to greet the sun and feel the life-giving warmth on its feathers." Its "legs leaned forward as its claws clutched the rock."
    Other Devices: *Analogy, Antithesis, Foreshadowing, Motif, Parallelism*
    Art Style: Expressionistic watercolor line washes in brown and blue tones satisfyingly re-create the ambience of an African village.
    Curriculum Tie-in: Literature (Parable)

*Hamanaka, Sheila. *Peace Crane.* New York: Morrow Junior Books, 1995.

After learning about the Peace Crane created by Sadako, a survivor of the bombing of Hiroshima, a young African-American girl wishes it would carry her away from the violence of her own world.

Imagery: The girl dreams that the Peace Crane has come for her. Together they "flew past golden mountains, red rivers, forests green." They see "trees that have lived for a thousand years" and listen "to lullabies sung by whales till our troubles disappeared." She reaches toward the stars "in a rainbow cloud of paper cranes."

Other Devices: *Allusion, Antithesis, Flash-forward, Pun, Simile, Symbol*

Art Style: Luminous, expressionistic oil paintings on canvas celebrate the spirit of the Peace Crane's hope for a troubled world.

Curriculum Tie-in: History (War and Peace—Japan and America)

Hesse, Karen. *Come On, Rain!* Illus. by Jon J. Muth. New York: Scholastic Press, 1999.

A young girl eagerly awaits a coming rainstorm to bring relief from the oppressive summer heat.

Imagery: Her mother tends "beds of drooping lupines." A phonograph plays in "the dim, stuffy cave of her room." Mama presses "the ice-chilled glass against her skin" as "sweat trickles down her neck and wets the front of her dress and under her arms." As the rain gets closer, "a breeze blows the thin curtains into the kitchen, then sucks them back against the screen again." "All the insects have gone still. Trees sway under a swollen sky, the wind grows bold and bolder." Then "the air cools and the clouds burst." The mothers "skim off their hose, tossing streamers of stockings over their shoulders." Following the rain, "everywhere, everyone, everything is misty limbs, springing back to life."

Other Devices: *Alliteration, Foreshadowing, Hyperbole, Metaphor, Paradox, Simile*

Art Style: Buoyant, ebullient, expressionistic pen/ink watercolors lend emotional credibility to the nervous anxiety of relentless heat accompanied by worrisome drought and the tremendous sense of relief that accompanies a thorough, nourishing rain.

Curriculum Tie-in: Science (Meteorology)

Hest, Amy. *Mabel Dancing.* Illus. by Christine Davenier. Cambridge, MA: Candlewick Press, 2000.

Mabel doesn't want to go to sleep while Mama and Papa are having a dance party downstairs.

Imagery: On this magical night the "curtain blew and Mama's gown did, too." The music downstairs "had a way of floating up the stairs." There are "papas in bow ties" and "mamas in swirling gowns." Alluringly, "the swirling had a way of swooshing up the stairs." Mabel's "blanket blew up like a yellow cape in the wind making swirls." Soon she is "spinning past the guests" as they all "danced away in the velvet light." Later, after her brief time in the limelight, she is able to "snuggle way down deep in the big blue bed" while downstairs the music plays on.

Other Devices: *Atmosphere, Foreshadowing, Parallelism*

Art Style: Airy, expressionistic watercolor washes and ink line drawings capture the contrast of bright excitement and action downstairs with gloomy loneliness and boring isolation upstairs.

Curriculum Tie-in: Social Science (Family Relationships, Values)

Hutchins, Hazel. *One Duck.* Illus. by Ruth Ohi. Annick (Firefly Books), 1999.
A mother duck works to defend her nest of eggs from a marauding crow and a farmer's cultivator.

Imagery: "Hidden perfectly in a hollow of ground down-lined, down-covered, still warm one nest with twelve olive eggs." "Slowly, steadily, the cultivator cuts and lifts and turns the soil the first row of a pattern leading ever inward . . . . " A crow "alights before her, taunts and teases, scolds and flaps, torments her any way he can, tries to lure her from the nest so he can eat the eggs." The tractor makes a fourth pass, "closest of all is a sudden wall of loudness, fumes and rolling dust that sends the crow fleeing." Still the duck sits "though somewhere in her duck-brain a single thought is clamoring—danger." When the farmer realizes the problem, he "reaches down with big hands careful not to touch the eggs, feels the earth cool on the backs of his hands, feels the warmth of life within his cupped palms, lifts the down tangle." The crow returns to the unguarded nest. "Drops on bent, black wings to glorious feast."

Other Devices: *Antithesis, Atmosphere, Inference, Onomatopoeia, Parallelism, Tone*

Art Style: Expressionistic pen/ink watercolor drawings sensitively complement the lyrical text of this common farming drama.

Curriculum Tie-in: Science (Agriculture, Animal Behavior)

Jones, Joy. *Tambourine Moon.* Illus. by Terry Widener. New York: Simon & Schuster Books for Young Readers, 1999.
Noni is afraid as she and her granddaddy walk home, until he tells her how he met her Grandma Ismay one dark night in Alabama, and how the big yellow moon came to light up the sky.

Imagery: "That's an Alabama moon—round and deep and low in the trees." Ismay's voice "rippled over the trees, floated through the branches and made that empty night sparkle." "Out in the open field, you can see so many stars in the sky all at once that it's like someone done overturned a bucket of cream and flung it up so high it stuck to the ceiling of heaven." "As soon as that woman stepped outside, the clouds rolled back and the night took on a glow." She is the lady "with that mellow night-magic voice." When Grandma Ismay sings, it fills your ears the way a starry night fills the sky." "That big, yellow tambourine just hung there, glowing and pouring light all over the night."

Other Devices: *Antithesis, Hyperbole, Personification, Simile*

Art Style: Acrylic art in expressionistic, ethnic folk designs employs both sharp angles and puffy rounded curves.

Curriculum Tie-in: Social Science (Ethnicity—African-American, Grandparents)

*Kaplan, Howard. *Waiting to Sing.* Illus. by Hervé Blondon. New York: DK Ink, 2000.

A family who loves music and spends many hours at the piano is devastated by the death of the mother, but those still living find consolation in the beautiful music that remains.

Imagery: The boy's father would bring him a glass of water to sip as he was tucked into bed for the night. "The glass stayed on the windowsill collecting moonlight till morning." The lamp over the piano is "shaped like a G-clef, and it poured a fountain of light over our hands." He believes the "keys on the right, with their light sound glassily ringing out, were filled with happiness. And on the left, those deep, dark notes felt the way I did when I had a bad day at school or felt sad for no reason at all." He thinks the piano "was revealing its true heart to me." In Beethoven's *Für Elise* he counts notes. "There were notes everywhere, peeking over and under the margins I was used to." He turns out all the lights except the piano lamp and "practiced under its generous white moon." "Mother loved everything about the sea: how it changed colors in the shifting light and left the taste of salt on our skin. The tide made our footprints disappear behind us." When she dies, he notices the "sparrows were leaving the September trees, looking for a home elsewhere. The cool, gray sky looked the way I felt inside."

Other Devices: *Allusion, Antithesis, Aphorism, Atmosphere, Foreshadowing, Inference, Metaphor, Parallelism, Simile, Symbol*

Art Style: Full-page sepia-tone pastel cartoon drawings expressionistically evoke a fragile emotional period in the life of a family coping with restructuring itself after the wrenching loss of one of its members.

Curriculum Tie-in: Music (Piano), Social Science (Death, Family Relationships, Feelings)

Kurtz, Jane. *Faraway Home.* Illus. by E.B. Lewis. New York: Gulliver Books (Harcourt), 2000.

Desta's father, who needs to return briefly to his Ethiopian homeland, describes what it was like for him to grow up there.

Imagery: Her father asks her to close her eyes to "see green-gray mountains" and to think about a "thick cloud of fog crawling up the valley and the

lonely sound of cowbells in the hills." Outside his home are "silver blue
leaves of eucalyptus trees." "Hippos yawn from muddy pools and crocodiles
arch their backs above the river water." He hears "hyena's strange coughing
cry close by." "Shepherds pipe songs of longing in the hills, and thousand
of flamingos flap." On his way to school, her father "sometimes couldn't
wait for lunch but chewed out the sweet juices" of a "stick of purple
sugarcane" as he walked "with mud squeezing up between his toes." He
admits, "My stomach is always hungry to go home."
Other Devices: *Foreshadowing, Metaphor, Simile*
Art Style: Pen lines and expressionistic watercolor art capture the poignant
reality immigrants face when they leave a beloved homeland for a new
country.
Curriculum Tie-in: Geography (Ethiopia), Social Science (Immigration—
Ethiopia)

Kurtz, Jane. *River Friendly, River Wild.* Illus. by Neil Brennan. New York: Simon &
Schuster Books for Young Readers, 2000.
A family experiences a renewed appreciation for home and community after
they are evacuated during a spring flood and then return to survey the damage.
Imagery: Before the flood, the narrator loves "the wet, muddy smell of the
summer river." They live where "ice slicks tree branches" in winter and
"drips from telephone wires." People watch over the dikes for "cracks that
could sprout and let river trickle through." When the air-raid sirens sound,
"parents pop up from everywhere" to collect children from school. In their
shelter the narrator misses "that motor-stomach Kiwi cat." Back inside
their damaged house, they try to stay warm in their sleeping bags and miss
the wood-burning stove "downstairs with curls of mud and orange rust."
The box of Christmas ornaments must be dumped into the black plastic
bag that goes to the curbside. Mother's "eyes are fat with tears." All is lost
except three glass angels, "survivors of the flood—like us." Special
machinery is needed for cleanup. "A square machine with a wide, wide
mouth moves crablike down the street to pick up freezers and stoves." "A
big machine with a looong neck lumbers and swings, nudges a pile of
garbage into the street and picks it up in its teeth." The water-soaked
books are "gooshy, soggy, slimy lumps that no one will ever want to read."
But, next Christmas, for sure, "the three flood angels will shimmer and
glimmer and shine again on our Christmas tree, wherever in the whole
world we are."
Other Devices: *Antithesis, Aphorism, Atmosphere, Metaphor, Onomatopoeia,
Simile*
Art Style: Oil glaze of brown paint overlaid by thin layers of color in
different areas and additional glazes for depth create fuzzy, impressionistic

scenes that reflect the essence of this emotionally wrenching natural disaster.

Curriculum Tie-in: Geography (Flood—Grand Forks, North Dakota)

Lawson, Julie. *Emma and the Silk Train.* Illus. by Paul Mombourquette. Buffalo, NY: Kids Can Press, 1997.

After seeing the beautiful silk blouse her mother made, Emma dreams of having a piece of silk for herself, and when the opportunity arises, determinedly pursues it.

Imagery: Children are drawn by "the wail of the whistle, the billowing smoke and the rhythm of wheels rolling over the rails." Emma's search for a bolt of cloth that escaped the silk train wreck pays off. "The current caught the color and unfolded it into one long rippling stream. It looked red, until the sunlight touched it. Then it shimmered gold." As she wades into the river after it, "The water licked at the hem of her skirt and swirled around her knees." As she waits for rescue, "in the distance she heard a low shaky rumble that swelled to a locomotive roar. A train burst around the curve." But it doesn't stop. The "train thundered past, vanishing in a cloud of flying cinders." "A circle of light burst through the darkness. The whistle wailed as the train roared past the station."

Other Devices: *Ambiguity, Foreshadowing, Inference, Parallelism, Simile*

Art Style: Lush, impressionistic oil paintings capture the time and adventure of the silk train era.

Curriculum Tie-in: History (Railroads—Silk)

Lyon, George Ella. *One Lucky Girl.* Illus. by Irene Trivas. New York: DK Pub., 2000.

Even though their trailer is destroyed by a tornado, a young boy's family is grateful because they find his baby sister alive.

Imagery: "Becky's baby summer, we lived in a trailer at the racetrack." "Right then it got sick quiet—no breeze, no bird cry." After the tornado hits, "All the screams nobody had screamed tore out of my mother's mouth." "Parts of our trailer made a line across the field." The boy hardly dares hope he is seeing what he thinks he has found. "It looked like—I got through the fence and was running, gulping air—it couldn't be, but it looked like—a dream, the best you could ever have, the one where you find your treasure."

Other Devices: *Ambiguity, Antithesis, Foreshadowing, Inference, Metaphor, Parallelism, Simile*

Art Style: Smudgy pastel illustrations impressionistically assist the story line through use of both dark and bright colors.

Curriculum Tie-in: Science (Tornadoes), Social Science (Family Relationships)

Martin, Jacqueline Briggs. *Snowflake Bentley.* Illus. by Mary Azarian. Boston: Houghton Mifflin, 1998 (Caldecott—1999).

This is a biography of a self-taught scientist who photographed thousands of individual snowflakes in order to study their unique formations.

> **Imagery:** "In the days when farmers worked with ox and sled and cut the dark with lantern light, there lived a boy who loved snow more than anything else in the world." "He watched snowflakes fall on his mittens, on the dried grass of Vermont farm fields, on the dark metal handle of the barn door." "In the summer his nieces and nephews rubbed coat hangers with sticky pitch from spruce trees. Then Willie could use them to pick up spider webs jeweled with water drops and take their pictures."
>
> **Other Devices:** *Antithesis, Parallelism, Simile*
>
> **Art Style:** Woodcuts with hand-tinted watercolors serve this nineteenth-century period folk art well.
>
> **Curriculum Tie-in:** Science (Meteorology, Photography)

*Martin, Nora. *The Stone Dancers.* Illus. by Jill Kastner. New York: Atheneum Books for Young Readers (Simon & Schuster), 1995.

A young girl uses an old legend about stone dancers to teach her mountain village a lesson in hospitality and sharing.

> **Imagery:** "High on a mountain near where the wind and the stars collide lie the ruins of an ancient castle, left long ago to crumble away stone by stone." Stones on the mountaintop appear to come to life in the form of the old king and his subjects. "In the howling storms of winter, the dancers move with huge bursts of hard rock muscles, leaping and turning, lifting one another against the flashing sky. Their great weight crashes like thunder, shaking the mountain each time their feet strike the ground." Anise watches until "the light fades or the shadows lengthen and the dancers slip away into the distance of dreams."
>
> **Other Devices:** *Aphorism, Inference, Irony, Metaphor, Parallel Story, Simile*
>
> **Art Style:** Impressionistic oil paintings show the interplay of light and shadow, melding the real with the enchanted in this nineteenth-century French peasant village.
>
> **Curriculum Tie-in:** History (Nineteenth-Century France), Literature (Legends), Social Science (Values)

*Myers, Christopher. *Black Cat.* New York: Scholastic Press, 1999.

Black Cat ambles on an eye-opening journey of exploring feelings about identity, beauty, and home.

> **Imagery:** Black Cat is described as "cousin to the concrete creeping down our city streets." He ducks under the "red circling of sirens cutting through the night." He passes "Sunday night families spilling from blue neon churches." He leaves "paw prints and chalk flowers on concrete sidewalks." He throws "shadows and tags on graffiti covered walls." He slam-dunks

himself "through a thick orange halo." He watches children "screaming in playground cages." He tiptoes across the "click-clacking glow of bodega lights."

Other Devices: *Alliteration, Internal Rhyme, Metaphor, Simile*

Art Style: Bold combination of collage, ink, and gouache with striking perspectives lends an intensity to the peculiarities of metro life.

Curriculum Tie-in: Art (Medium and Technique)

*Myers, Tim. *Basho and the Fox.* Illus. by Oki S. Han. New York: Marshall Cavendish, 2000.

A Japanese poet is challenged by a fox to create his best haiku.

Imagery: Basho spends his winter "struggling to stay warm on his thin sleeping mat" and "felt his mouth watering at the thought of late-summer cherries." He meets the fox "that spring, when the cherry tree by the river hung thick with glowing white blossoms." When the fox finishes hearing one of Basho's poems, "there was no sound except the burbling of the river over its stones." On another occasion, Basho finds the fox waiting, "the red of its fur pale in the moonlight."

Other Devices: *Ambiguity, Antithesis, Aphorism, Irony, Motif, Parallelism, Theme*

Art Style: Mischievous watercolor folk paintings convey the Eastern sensibility of feudal Japan.

Curriculum Tie-in: History (Japan), Social Science (Self-esteem)

*Nolen, Jerdine. *Big Jabe.* Illus. by Kadir Nelson. New York: Lothrop, Lee & Shepard, 2000.

Momma Mary tells stories about a special young man who does wondrous things, especially for the slaves on the Plenty Plantation.

Imagery: "On days when the wind blows in whispers that only bees can hear," the time is right for stories about the wonderful things that happened on the Plenty Plantation. The pear tree quickly becomes "a young tree full of pretty white blossoms to decorate Addy's hair."

Other Devices: *Allusion, Anachronism, Antithesis, Flashback, Flash-forward, Foreshadowing, Hyperbole, Inference, Parallelism, Simile, Symbol, Understatement*

Art Style: Strong, detailed pen/ink, watercolor, and gouache drawings provide wonderful expressionistic period ambience to this folktale.

Curriculum Tie-in: History (Slavery—America), Literature (Tall Tale)

Preston, Tim. *The Lonely Scarecrow.* Illus. by Maggie Kneen. New York: Dutton Children's Books (Penguin Books), 1999.

A lonely scarecrow with a scary face has trouble making friends with the animals who surround him, until a heavy snowfall transforms him into a jolly snowman.

Imagery: "Under a sky the color of cornflowers" stood a scarecrow. As the wheat field grew taller, the scarecrow became "marooned in his golden sea." The snow "slipped off the scarecrow's shoulders and dripped from the brim of his hat."

Other Devices: *Inference, Metaphor, Paradox, Parallelism, Theme*

Art Style: Lavishly embossed, finely detailed, watercolor and acrylic cartoons fondly render scenes of glorious seasonal changes.

Curriculum Tie-in: Social Science (Friendship), Science (Seasons)

Ruurs, Margriet. *Emma and the Coyote.* Illus. by Barbara Spurll. New York: Stoddart Kids, 1999.

Emma thinks chickens are smarter than coyotes, and she struts boldly where no chicken should go to prove it.

Imagery: While Emma and the chickens are sitting on their nests in the coop, the "rooster kept watch over ten dandelion chicks" out in the barnyard. The life of a chicken is spent pleasantly "scuttling in the garden," and "gobbling up some corn" in the pigpen, and dreaming on "the lower limbs of the magnolia tree." But "she lost her balance, and a huge, feathery, flapping, clucking, magnolia blossom tumbled out of the tree."

Other Devices: *Alliteration, Foreshadowing, Inference, Irony, Motif, Parallelism, Serendipity, Simile*

Art Style: Bright primary color paintings expressionistically follow the fortunes of Emma and the barnyard animals.

Curriculum Tie-in: Social Science (Self-esteem)

*Say, Allen. *The Sign Painter.* Boston: Walter Lorraine Books (Houghton Mifflin), 2000.

An assignment to paint a large billboard in the desert changes the life of an aspiring artist.

Imagery: When the author describes what the man and boy find in the middle of the desert, he uses this language: "An immense curtain hung in the sky, and under that a cluster of houses nested on a rock as if floating on a cloud." The two go closer. "They peered into gaping windows of empty houses with not a single piece of furniture inside. The only sound came from their footsteps."

Other Devices: *Ambiguity, Antithesis, Inference, Point of View, Theme, Tone*

Art Style: Magnificent realistic acrylic paintings unfold the contrasts between security and dreams in this provocative story about personal choices.

Curriculum Tie-in: Philosophy (Quality of Life)

Turner, Ann. *Drummer Boy: Marching to the Civil War.* Illus. by Mark Hess. New York: HarperCollins, 1998.

A thirteen-year-old soldier, coming of age during the American Civil War, beats his drum to raise tunes and spirits, and muffle the sounds of the dying.

Imagery: The boy can't stand how "they'd got those slaves all locked up in little houses with nary a floor in them or breathing space." The enemy "spread out below" and moves "like a herd of beasts, with the dust smoking up." After he holds the hand of a dying soldier, he remarks, "I always feel his fingers on mine, how hot and dry they were, how they grabbed mine and crushed them until his eyes stopped seeing." He tries to remember each soldier. "Sam with the hay-colored hair, Jeff with an almost mustache, and Abraham all the way from Maine, who could spit tobacco four feet to one side."

Other Devices: *Atmosphere, Point of View, Simile*

Art Style: Stunningly realistic paintings bring to life what it must have been like to be a very young soldier in an uncommon situation.

Curriculum Tie-in: History (Civil War)

Turner, Ann. *Secrets from the Dollhouse.* Illus. by Raúl Colón. New York: HarperCollins, 2000.

The life of a family of dolls and their servants living in a dollhouse in a young girl's room is told from the perspective of Emma, oldest of the doll children.

Imagery: Emma describes life in her world. "Mama has round red cheeks and a lemon yellow dress that swoops with lace." When she asks the butler if he's ever had an adventure, he replies, "I went for a ride on Boy's bicycle. The world hurt my ears, and the road made me dizzy." Mice make bold through the dollhouse. They "scamper in our kitchen, putting twitchy paws on lids and pans." Emma finally realizes her dream to go outside and notes that a "snake stared with eyes of glitter." When Cat threatenes at the door, "Papa knocked four splinters from the wall for spears." At Christmastime the doll family sit at the table piled high with "bright red lobster, plum puddings, and mounded potatoes."

Other Devices: *Foreshadowing, Metaphor, Personification, Point of View, Simile*

Art Style: Stiff 1920s folk images in scratch-lined pastels capture the whimsy of a toy world.

*Wisniewski, David. *Golem.* New York: Clarion Books (Houghton Mifflin), 1996 (Caldecott—1997).

A saintly rabbi miraculously brings to life a clay giant who helps him watch over the Jews of sixteenth-century Prague.

Imagery: "Staggering, the rabbi lifted his arms higher and uttered the Holy Name. Howling wind and torrential rain lashed down. Writhing columns of steam shrieked from the figure." "The smallest thing—the scent of a rose, the flight of a pigeon—filled him with wonder." "With a hail of bricks and curses, the mob arrived and stormed the gates. The massive doors swayed but held. A jeering cry went up. A battering ram had arrived. At each blow, wood splintered. Hinges wailed in protest. Still Golem stood . . . taller, much taller. Rabbi Loew could see him grow. Then the gates came crashing down. The mob poured into the ghetto. The first wave of attackers screamed in terror when they saw Golem looming above them. With the back of his hand, he swept them aside. Golem took hold of the battering ram and, snapping it in two, raked great furrows in the crowd."

Other Devices: *Analogy, Atmosphere, Foreshadowing, Inference, Irony, Motif, Paradox, Simile*

Art Style: Paper cut in sophisticated, expressionistic collage produces a powerful physical and emotional effect for this cautionary tale.

Curriculum Tie-in: Literature (Legend), Social Science (Values)

INFERENCE

Without direct comment, an author's clues enable a reader to form reasonable conclusions about characters or events.

Example: The poet feels rejected and bereft.
      Tonight in this town
   Where I was born, my only
      Friends are the crickets.

                                                         Anon.

Alexander, Lloyd. *The House Gobbaleen.* Illus. by Diane Goode. New York: Dutton Children's Books (Penguin Books), 1995.

Unhappy over what he considers his bad luck, Tooley ignores his cat's warnings and invites a greedy little man into his home in the mistaken hope of improving his fortunes.

Inference: To remove the entrenched little man, the cat has Tooley bring in a wheelbarrow full of brambles, a moldy cabbage, a bottle of vinegar, and the biggest pot he can find. Once the idea of a Gobbaleen is implanted in the little man's mind, he hasn't a moment's peace. He can't get a night's sleep, because "there was something sharp as brambles jabbing and pinching, scratching and tweaking at me every time I moved." He gets no pleasure from his pipe. "This tobacco might as well be moldy cabbage!" The pot of cider doesn't taste right. "Sour as vinegar! That's the Gobbaleen's doing," concludes the little man. And, as for his nightly meal, a large pot is brought to the table, but when the lid comes off, "It's himself!" squeals the little man. "The Gobbaleen!" A streak of yellow lightning shoots out, yowling at the top of its voice and bristling three times its size. By this time, the frenzied little man doesn't even recognize the cat as himself.

Other Devices: *Ambiguity, Foreshadowing, Hyperbole, Irony, Simile, Theme, Tone, Understatement*

Art Style: Humorous gouache and watercolor cartoons illustrate this modern folktale.

Curriculum Tie-in: Literature (Folktale), Social Science (Values)

*Armstrong, Jennifer. *Pierre's Dream.* Illus. by Susan Gaber. New York: Dial (Penguin Putnam), 1999.

Thinking he is dreaming, Pierre, a lazy, foolish, man, shows no fear as he performs many amazing and dangerous circus acts.

Inference: The community knows him to be a foolish, lazy man, but, the traveling circus members don't. They see him do marvelous things. They vote to make him their ringmaster for the evening's performance. Such confidence rubs off on him. When he sees the people of his town out in the audience, he remarks, "Tonight they shall see they are wrong" about him. Like Dumbo the baby elephant, which holds a "magic" feather to enable him to fly, Pierre believes anything is possible in a dream. He becomes an excellent circus performer, a one-man show. When it's all over and he awakens in the field under his tree, he sees evidence that he had not been dreaming after all. He begins to smile, then laugh. "He had much more to think of than just his dinner." Perhaps he wonders what else a lazy, foolish man might be capable of accomplishing.

Other Devices: *Antihero, Foreshadowing, Irony, Theme*

Art Style: Ethereal, expressionistic acrylic paintings alternate between stunning perspectives and large close-ups.

Curriculum Tie-in: Social Science (Self-esteem, Values)

Baker, Jeannie. *The Hidden Forest.* New York: Greenwillow Books (Harper Collins), 2000.

When a friend helps him retrieve the fish trap he lost while trying to fish off the coast of eastern Tasmania, Ben comes to see the giant kelp forest where he lost his fish trap in a new light.

Inference: Ben is intent upon fishing "down in the dark, tangled world of the weed," where he knows big and small fish are. He finds the marine environment slightly frightening and lacks an ecological focus on the big picture, showing his lack of understanding and appreciation by behaving with disrespect toward the marine world he abuses. When he pulls up his fish trap time after time, he catches only minnows. "Ben empties them out in disgust to let them die." Later, a friend helps him see things differently. Now, when he pulls up his basket, "he sees how wonderful these creatures are here in their mysterious, hidden world. He feels this is where they belong." He empties the basket, setting them free to swim away.

Other Devices: *Connotation, Imagery, Simile*
Art Style: Collage photographs are constructions of natural materials such as pressed seaweeds, sponges, and sand in multidimensional effect to create the enchanting world of ocean life.
Curriculum Tie-in: Science (Ocean Ecology)

Battle-Lavert, Gwendolyn. *The Music in Derrick's Heart.* Illus. by Colin Bootman. New York: Holiday House, 2000.
Uncle Booker T., who makes magic by playing his harmonica music from his heart, spends the summer teaching Derrick how to play.
Inference: Not until one day Uncle Booker T. doesn't show up at Derrick's house does Derrick finally learn to play music from his heart. It is the day a "cool breeze sent the leaves flying around him. Derrick waited and waited." He finds his friend on his front porch, a wool sweater on his thin body. The change in weather has brought "old Arthur" to his door. "He's all in my hands. No music today." Derrick knows how to make Uncle Booker T. feel better even if arthritis is hurting his hands. "With a deep breath, he started playing notes. Ever so quietly, ever so slowly. Then fast and faster." When he finishes, "Uncle Booker T. wiped tears from his eyes. 'All right! Yes, indeed! Yes, indeed!'"
Other Devices: *Aphorism, Atmosphere, Simile, Tone*
Art Style: Expressionistic oil paintings show an appreciation of rural small town African-American music played from the heart.
Curriculum Tie-in: Social Science (Ethnicity—African-American)

*Browne, Anthony. *Voices in the Park.* New York: DK Pub., 1998.
Lives briefly intertwine when two youngsters meet in the park.
Inference: The bossy woman takes Victoria, "our pedigree Labrador," and Charles, "our son," for a walk. The son clearly does not rate as much respect as does the family dog. The woman commands her son in much the same fashion as most people do their dogs. "'Sit,' I said to Charles. 'Here.'" Later, when she finds Charles playing with another child, she orders him to "come here. At once!" Then she calls her dog. "And come here please, Victoria." She actually speaks with more courtesy to the dog than to her son. The boy seems to be an obligation in her day's routine. Just as she is planning the evening meal, she looks around and sees that Charles has disappeared. Her calls are loud and immediate, because "You get some frightful types in the park these days! I called his name for what seemed like ages." The boy, meanwhile, is glad to have someone to play with even if, "unfortunately," she is a girl. He finds her surprisingly good on the slide. "She went really fast. I was amazed." The girl finds the boy "okay," though she "thought he was kind of a wimp at first" for sitting beside his mother on the park bench. She notes that "he didn't say much, but later on he was more friendly." The boy knows how ephemeral his fun is. "My mother

caught us talking together, and I had to go home." He hopes "maybe Smudge will be there next time" he gets to the park. The girl is impressed that he picked a flower and gave it to her. She notices, when his mom calls him to go that "he looked sad." Her kind nature is expressed when she "put the flower in some water and made Dad a nice cup of cocoa."

Other Devices: *Connotation, Foreshadowing, Point of View*

Art Style: The story moves from one voice to another. Each character's perspective is reflected in the shifting landscape and seasons with bright acrylic surrealistic paintings that match the bossy woman, the sad man, the lonely boy, and the cheerful girl.

Curriculum Tie-in: Social Science (Feelings)

*Bunting, Eve. *The Memory String.* Illus. by Ted Rand. New York: Clarion Books (Houghton Mifflin), 2000.

While still grieving for her mother and unable to accept her stepmother, a girl clings to the memories represented by forty-three buttons on a string.

Inference: Laura shakes her head when her stepmother Jane asks her if she wants lemonade. Instead, she opens the red velvet box that holds her memory button string. "Jane dipped her brush in the paint and went back to work. Her shoulders were stiff." (Jane has been hurt by Laura's rejection.) Laura "told Whiskers in a loud voice" about each button on her string. (Jane cannot help but hear her excluding recitation.) "Be quiet," Laura tells her squirming cat. "I can't talk about my memory string to myself, can I? You have to stay here." (Laura wants to make sure Jane hears how important her memories before Jane came on the scene are.) But when the cat leaps to freedom, causing the memory string to break, it is Jane who understands the impact of the accident. Laura overhears her father suggesting they substitute another button for the missing one. "How can you think of such a thing?" Jane asks. "Those are true moments on that string. You can't cheat Laura like that." "Laura heard the chokiness in Jane's voice. She felt choked up herself. So much to think about. So much." At this moment, Laura begins to accept her stepmother. After the missing button is found and accepted, Laura "noticed that the buttons on Jane's painting shirt were a deep, dark green. Pretty! Maybe one day she'd ask Jane for one to put on the memory string." (Jane is now part of her beloved family, too.)

Other Devices: *Ambiguity, Antithesis, Aphorism, Foreshadowing, Imagery, Parallelism, Simile*

Art Style: Shadowy, impressionistic watercolor paintings detail the emotional changes the child experiences as she feels both separation and reconnection to her family.

Curriculum Tie-in: Social Science (Family Relationships, Grief)

*Bunting, Eve. *Swan in Love.* Illus. by Jo Ellen McAllister Stammen. New York: Atheneum Books for Young Readers (Simon & Schuster), 2000.

Despite ridicule of the other animals, Swan persists in his adoration for a swan-shaped boat named Dora.

> **Inference:** Among the voices, yet separate from them, was another that did not criticize Swan. "Don't ever stop loving," this voice said. It seemed to come "from the sky, or the lake, or the air itself. The voice was a friend." In the winter, "the voice spoke to him through the pale sunshine or starlit wind. Faithful Swan, you have found the answer." And, finally, when the end of his time on earth comes, "he heard the voice, soft and comforting as that hand that had once stroked his feathers. 'Love makes magic,' it said." The Creator had been with Swan on earth, and now would bring Swan to his dearest reward.
>
> **Other Devices:** *Antithesis, Aphorism, Foreshadowing, Imagery, Simile, Theme*
>
> **Art Style:** Resplendent pastel expressionistic illustrations shimmer with grace as they illuminate the story of transforming love.
>
> **Curriculum Tie-in:** Social Science (Love)

Camp, Lindsay. *Why?* Illus. by Tony Ross. New York: G.P. Putnam's Sons (Penguin Putnam Books for Young Readers), 1998.

Lily's constant "why" questions drive her father crazy until one day he discovers that questioning the way things are, can be a very good thing.

> **Inference:** Lily's habit of asking "why" has just caused the enemy aliens from space to pause and reflect on the reason they destroy planets. "We realize destroying planets hasn't done us much good. It just makes everybody hate us. We're going home to Tharg to think it over." Lily is "just about to say something." Her father's hand clamps over her mouth before her "Wh" can turn into "Why." There is certainly no advantage in encouraging the Thargon's leader to reflect upon why they have decided to take their spaceship home, after all, and not destroy earth.
>
> **Other Devices:** *Irony, Paradox, Serendipity, Understatement*
>
> **Art Style:** Colored pencil cartoons illustrate the repetitious, rapid-fire questions from Lily and the answers she receives that make up Lily's day and the day of those who suffer her presence.
>
> **Curriculum Tie-in:** Social Science (Family Relationships)

*Cole, Brock. *Buttons.* New York: Farrar Straus Giroux, 2000.

When their father eats so much that he pops the buttons off his britches, each of his three daughters tries a different plan to find replacements.

> **Inference:** The cowherd, who is quite smitten with the youngest daughter, tells her he can help in her efforts to replace her father's britches buttons. As he advises her, she holds out her apron under a large and dense oak tree the next morning. "And what do you think?" "A set of used trouser buttons" falls out of the leaves for her. Later, at their marriage celebration, the

groom's "trousers are tied up with a bit of string." His trouser buttons are missing, but she doesn't care. "It's a small fault and seems to run in the family."

Other Devices: *Aphorism, Irony, Pun, Tone*

Art Style: Pen/ink and watercolor humorous cartoons complement this lighthearted spoof on courtship and family duty.

Curriculum Tie-in: Literature (Fairy Tale)

Cowley, Joy. *The Video Shop Sparrow.* Illus. by Gavin Bishop. Honesdale, PA: Boyds Mills Press, 1999.

When George and Garry try to return a video, they find the shop closed. Trapped inside is a sparrow, which they try to rescue.

Inference: When the mayor, busy with a press conference, discovers what the boys want, "she smiled a big warm smile." She immediately recognizes how this problem can be turned into a positive public relations story for her. Though she has the connections to enable the trapped bird to be released, her motives are somewhat suspect, especially when a photo of the rescue appears in the next day's paper along with the caption "The Champion of Sparrows and Children." The boys are simply grateful for her help. "She's a very nice lady." Their father reads more into her actions, "And very smart," he observes.

Other Devices: *Satire, Theme, Tone*

Art Style: Pen/ink line watercolor cartoons show the innocent intentions of the children in contrast to the distinctly uninterested attitude of the adults, except where self-serving advantage may be gained.

Curriculum Tie-in: Social Science (Values)

*Cronin, Doreen. *Click, Clack, Moo Cows That Type.* Illus. by Betsy Lewin. New York: Simon & Schuster, 2000.

Farmer Brown's cows find a typewriter in the barn and start making demands that result in their going on strike when he refuses to give them what they want.

Inference: Messages between Farmer Brown and the striking cows are carried by the "neutral" ducks. It doesn't take the ducks long to figure out how the game of negotiation is played. The final message from the cows to the farmer is a compromise. The typewriter will be given to Farmer Brown in exchange for electric blankets. Farmer Brown agrees and provides the blankets. But the typewriter is not returned. The ducks are now typing messages to Farmer Brown. They find their pond rather dull. They would like a diving board. The final picture shows the ducks diving off such a board into their pond.

Other Devices: *Irony, Symbol*

Art Style: Lampblack watercolor overlaid by watercolor washes creates simple cartoons with striking perspectives that illustrate the developing

agreements finally reached.
Curriculum Tie-in: Economics (Unions)

Deedy, Carmen Agra. The Yellow Star: The Legend of King Christian X of Denmark. Illus. by Henri Sorensen. Atlanta: Peachtree, 2000.
King Christian must abide by Nazi orders regarding the wearing of the identifying yellow star, but he must also protect all the Danes from harm.

Inference: King Christian faces down the Nazis concerning the flying of the German flag. The Nazi officer says he will kill the next Danish soldier who tries to remove the Nazi flag over the palace. King Christian replies that the officer should "be prepared to shoot the king—for I will be that soldier." "The Nazi flag did not fly from the palace again." Then a directive requires Jews to wear a yellow star. The king is seen wearing such a star the following day, during his usual riding tour of the city. "As they watched him pass, the subjects of King Christian understood what they should do." All the Danes will be wearing the yellow star. "And, once again, in the country of Denmark, there were only Danes." Jew and Gentiles alike are citizens, without separate distinction.

Other Devices: *Antithesis, Aphorism, Atmosphere, Foreshadowing, Irony, Paradox, Parallelism, Pun, Simile, Symbol, Theme*

Art Style: Impressionistic oil paintings accompany the spare terse text in this vignette showing the political reality of the Danes' circumstances during a very somber historical period.

Curriculum Tie-in: History (World War II—Nazi Occupation—Denmark), Literature (Legend), Social Science (Values)

Dengler, Marianna. *Fiddlin' Sam.* Illus. by Sibyl Graber Gerig. Flagstaff, AZ: Rising Moon (Northland), 1999.
Wandering through the Ozarks and bringing joy to people with his music, Fiddlin' Sam seeks the right person to take up his fiddle and carry on the practice.

Inference: Sam wakes up after a snake bite and finds himself resting under a pine tree, with a nearby creek gurgling. He is stunned to find himself alive. "How'd I get here?" he asks the youth beside him. "You ain't heavy, and it ain't far," the boy replies. The fiddler is hopeful this young man will be the one who will carry on fiddling. "But the boy only listened, tapping his toe in time to the music." He has "a feel for the land." This boy is not the one to carry on with the fiddle. As the years progress, "more and more he was sleeping in soft beds folks offered him" instead of out under the stars, as the fiddler used to prefer. Finally Sam meets another young boy with just the right degree of restlessness. As he listens to the boy tell how he is hoping for a better life and must now return home to admit defeat, Sam sees an opportunity. "Without a word, he took out his fiddle and began to play." Finally, this boy shows the right kind of interest.

Other Devices: *Antithesis, Atmosphere, Foreshadowing, Internal Rhyme, Parallelism, Serendipity*

Art Style: Exuberant, realistic, expressionistic watercolors in shades of bright yellow, pink, and blue faithfully reveal the emotional and physical details of this musician's life.

Curriculum Tie-in: Social Science (Missouri Ozarks)

*Dengler, Marianna. *The Worry Stone.* Illus. by Sibyl Graber Gerig. Flagstaff, AZ: Rising Moon (Northland), 1996.

When a small, serious boy joins Amanda on the park bench, she remembers that once she was small and serious, too, but she had Grandfather—and his wonderful stories.

Inference: The old woman tries to draw out the boy by the storytelling methods employed by her own grandfather when she was a child. But this boy has not grown up with the tradition. She lures him by telling him she has something to show him. When he sees a rock in her hand, he is disappointed. Instead of guessing what the rock might mean, he bluntly asks her what it is. "Now it's her turn to be disappointed, but, of course, he doesn't know how to play the game." She must work harder. Soon, she is getting a better response from him. "Where did it come from?" he questions. That gives her an opening. "Well now, a long, long time ago, there was an Indian maiden named Tokatu . . . ." She has the boy's attention at last.

Other Devices: *Antithesis, Flashback, Foreshadowing, Parallel Story, Parallelism*

Art Style: Appealing, realistic watercolor paintings expressionistically maintain focus on the separate threads of this woman's past and present.

Curriculum Tie-in: History (Chumash Indians), Social Science (Grandparents, Intergenerational Relationships)

DePaola, Tomie. *The Art Lesson.* New York: G.P. Putnam's Sons, 1989.

Having learned to be creative in drawing pictures at home, young Tommy is dismayed when he goes to school and finds the art lesson there much more regimented.

Inference: Though his family is supportive of his artistic development, there are limits. They will display his pictures on the refrigerator, at the barber shop, framed on grandma's table, on the wall on his side of his room. "Once Tommy took a flashlight and a pencil under the covers and drew pictures on his sheets." His mom's reaction is definite. "No more drawing on the sheets, Tommy." When the family builds a new house, before the Sheetrock is painted, Tommy "drew beautiful pictures all over the unfinished walls." But when the painters came, his dad said, "That's it, Tommy. No more drawing on the walls." The young artist must learn there are limits to his free expression.

Other Devices: *Atmosphere, Flash-forward, Irony, Parallelism, Serendipity, Theme*

Art Style: Blocky pastel cartoons follow the fortunes and budding development of a young artist in a conformist world.

Curriculum Tie-in: Social Science (Individuality)

Ernst, Lisa Campbell. *Goldilocks Returns.* New York: Simon & Schuster Books for Young Readers, 2000.

Fifty years after Goldilocks first met the three bears, she returns to fix up their cottage and soothe her guilty conscience.

Inference: Goldi may be trying to make amends for her earlier intrusion into the bears' lives, but her efforts are doomed to unsuccessful conclusions. "She threw away any food she thought was unhealthy or didn't like herself." She decides to "fix those ghastly chairs" of yesteryear. Her own tacky tastes are expressed in the "Ravishing Roses" perfume she sprays and in her décor preference, "bouquets of plastic flowers" for a back-to-nature look. She lacks finesse as well as good taste. "The Rutabaga Breakfast Bars are fat free, so you might even be able to lose that extra weight there," she chuckles as she taps Papa Bear in the stomach. After she leaves, the bear family can't get comfortable in their chairs or their beds. And they don't like their breakfast the next morning. They take a walk to get away from the house and spot a "mischievous looking little girl, skipping along the path that led straight to their cottage." Not again! They think how she might eat their food, mess up the fancy decorations, break the chairs . . . . Suddenly they smile and continue on their walk.

Other Devices: *Allusion, Antihero, Connotation, Flash-forward, Irony, Parallelism, Tone, Understatement*

Art Style: Large, bulky cartoons mirror the story's original atmosphere intended for young listeners, while the language and picture complexity expand the interest level for more savvy audiences.

Fox, Mem. *Harriet, You'll Drive Me Wild.* Illus. by Marla Frazee. New York: Harcourt, 2000.

When a young girl has a series of mishaps at home one Saturday, her mother tries not to lose her temper—and does not quite succeed.

Inference: Harriet's mother is making a mighty effort not to yell. "Harriet, my *darling* child," she says instead, after she cleans up the spilled juice that dripped on the dog. Later, when too many incidents "happen just like that," mother's patience is sorely tried. "Harriet, sweetheart, what are we to do? Harriet Harris, I'm talking to *you*." One incident too many finally pushes mother over the edge, and "she yelled and yelled and yelled." Of course, she is later sorry. "But sometimes it happens, just like that." Mother can empathize with Harriet now. Soon they are remarking about the "big mess," the "very big mess" that has resulted when the pillow bursts and feathers fly all over. They "laughed and laughed and went on laughing as they picked up the feathers together." Things are ok again.

Other Devices: *Foreshadowing, Understatement*

Art Style: Pencil and transparent drawing ink cartoons wonderfully augment the spare text in this timeless story of childhood exuberance and parental restraint.

Curriculum Tie-in: Social Science (Family Relationships)

Garland, Michael. *Dinner at Magritte's.* New York: Dutton Children's Books (Penguin), 1995.

Young Pierre spends the day with surrealist artists René Magritte and Salvador Dali.

Inference: When he leaves to visit the Magrittes, Pierre's parents are sitting "as still as stone" in their cottage, reading the newspaper and knitting. A touch of gray stone color is creeping up their legs. When he returns, they are still sitting in their respective chairs, "as still as stone." These colorless people apparently have not moved since he left. In fact, their bodies have turned to stone while he was gone having an exciting day.

Other Devices: *Cliché, Foreshadowing*

Art Style: Normal routine is contrasted with surrealistic surprises as a young boy finds entertainment away from his boring family.

Curriculum Tie-in: Art (Biography)

Gibbons, Faye. *Mama and Me and the Model T.* Illus. by Ted Rand. New York: Morrow, 1999.

When Mr. Long says any man can drive a car, Mama gets behind the wheel to show women can drive, too.

Inference: Mr. Long knows something about what it takes to drive skillfully, not to mention safely. As his wife gets into the car for the first time, he shouts, "Get in the house, young'uns!" Clearly he fears they might be in danger from this unpredictable situation. When her wild drive is finally over, she tells the family that the motorcar has a mind of its own. Mr. Long replies, "It's not the only one," as he mops his face with a handkerchief. Come what may, he has learned that the car is not going to be the exclusive domain of the males in the family.

Other Devices: *Foreshadowing, Hyperbole, Imagery, Onomatopoeia, Parallelism, Stereotype, Understatement*

Art Style: Expressionistic watercolors exuberantly dramatize the mysterious intricacies of mastering the wondrous but tricky skills of automobile driving.

Curriculum Tie-in: Social Science (Family Relationships)

*Gralley, Jean. *Hogula, Dread Pig of Night.* New York: Henry Holt, 1999.

Although he lives high on the hog in his castle on Grimy Pork Chop Hill, Hogula is unhappy because he has no friends—until he meets Elvis Ann, Dread Queen of Kissyface.

Inference: When Elvis Ann follows Hogula home from the mall, the household believes she will become his next victim. "Excellent! Mahster's midnight snack has delivered itself to the door!" says the housekeeper, Igoretta. Even Hogula thinks so. He thanks her for returning his glove and says, "Won't you come in?" He smiles. "Never had he wanted to snort a tempting bit of mortal so badly." As he brings his twitching piggie snout to "that delicious spot on her neck," he notices "her lips were twitching, too!" She, it seems, has equally appalling designs on him!

Other Devices: *Alliteration, Allusion, Antihero, Aphorism, Cliché, Foreshadowing, Irony, Poetic Justice, Pun, Simile, Stereotype, Understatement*

Art Style: Appropriately repulsive expressionistic cartoons in gouache and ink on watercolor paper develop the characters of this humorously gentle Dracula-style relationship.

Curriculum Tie-in: Social Science (Friendship)

Greenfield, Karen. *Sister Yessa's Story.* Illus. by Claire Ewart. New York: Laura Geringer (HarperCollins), 1992.

Dark clouds gather as Yessa walks to her brother's place, telling a story as she goes about the early days of the earth, and the animals follow her, two by two, to listen.

Inference: "Storm clouds gathered as the animals followed along, listening to Yessa's story, on their way to Yessa's brother's place." When she arrives, "Brother Noah swung wide the doors to his ark. Yessa ushered in all the animals, two by two." This activity points to the famous biblical story about the Great Flood and its aftermath.

Other Devices: *Parallel Story*

Art Style: Gouache on watercolor paper in lush, expressionistic pictures majestically follow a myth of the beginning of animal life across the earth and the preservation of animal life later in earth's history.

Curriculum Tie-in: Literature (Legend)

Harris, Jim. *The Three Little Dinosaurs.* Gretna, LA: Pelican Publishing, 1999.

Three young dinosaurs set out on their own, only to be hassled by a Tyrannosaurus rex, who gets a big surprise in the end.

Inference: When the rex finally succeeds in demolishing the three dinosaurs' stone house, so many years have passed that they've grown up—and up. T-rex runs away to take up a "quiet, more peaceful life—fishing." But, as the reader turns the last page, the T-rex may not find the peace he desires. He is holding a puny fishing pole whose line is in the mouth of a very large and mad-looking sea monster, standing in the water directly in front of him.

Other Devices: *Antithesis, Foreshadowing, Parody, Poetic Justice, Tone*

Art Style: Lush, detailed acrylic expressionistic paintings provide satisfyingly humorous perspectives and points of view of aggressor and victim.

Hutchins, Hazel. *One Duck.* Illus. by Ruth Ohi. New York: Annick (Firefly Books), 1999.

A mother duck works to defend her nest of eggs from a marauding crow and a farmer's cultivator.

Inference: After a brief foray to a pond for food, a duck returns to her nest and eggs. She "settles down upon them knowing it is almost time and waits." She hears the approaching tractor in the field of stubble. She "stretches her long neck to see what can be seen, feels an uneasiness she cannot explain." When the farmer realizes the situation, he "reaches down with big hands careful not to touch the eggs . . . " and carries the nest "one row over, lays it down on land already turned . . . ." His intention is for the duck to find the eggs easily while getting them out of the way of his machinery. Later, success is proven when the reader sees "one duck waddling over the stubble field followed by twelve ducklings crossing the road sliding into the safety of the pond just doing what ducks do—one duck."

Other Devices: *Antithesis, Atmosphere, Imagery, Onomatopoeia, Parallelism, Tone*

Art Style: Expressionistic pen/ink watercolor drawings sensitively complement the lyrical text of this common farming drama.

Curriculum Tie-in: Science (Agriculture, Animal Behavior)

Johnson, Angela. *Down the Winding Road.* Illus. by Shane Evans. New York: DK Ink, 2000.

The annual summer visit to the country home of the Old Ones, the uncles and aunts who raised Daddy, brings joy and good times.

Inference: There is love and respect for each other—the city family arriving to visit and the Old Ones awaiting them. The Old Ones "are standing in line when we pull into the drive." They've clearly been waiting and looking forward to the arrival. There are hugs with creased faces "and warm hands to hold." The children splash in the lake as much for the amusement of the Old Ones as for themselves. They "chase each other in the water, then watch the trees and the Old Ones to know when it's time to go." When they walk back to the house along the winding road, they slow down a bit "for the Old Ones."

Other Devices: *Anachronism, Atmosphere, Irony*

Art Style: In expressionistic pen/ink and oil paintings, the gentle, loving life of a caring family is made believable.

Curriculum Tie-in: Social Science (Family Relationships)

Johnson, Paul Brett. *Old Dry Frye: A Deliciously Funny Tall Tale.* New York: Scholastic Press, 1999.

A humorous retelling of an Appalachian folktale about a preacher who chokes on a chicken bone.

Inference: While the area citizens are frantically trying to "get shed" of the preacher's body, he may not be as dead as they believe. When he is put on the back of a mean-spirited horse "that wasn't much 'count," the illustration shows that the horse bounces the chicken bone right out of Old Dry Frye's throat. Outside their kitchen windows, "On nights when the moon is full and there's a plate of chicken on the table, you can guess what folks are saying: 'Dad-fetch me! I believe that's Old Dry Frye.' "
Other Devices: *Black Humor, Cliché, Hyperbole, Poetic Justice, Serendipity, Tone, Understatement*
Art Style: Ebullient acrylic cartoons share the fortunes and misfortunes of the self-serving characters in this raucous Appalachian romp.
Curriculum Tie-in: Literature (Tall Tales), Social Science (Appalachian Culture)

Kajikawa, Kimiko. *Yoshi's Feast.* Illus. by Yumi Heo. New York: DK Ink, 2000.
When Yoshi's neighbor, Sabu, the eel broiler, attempts to charge him for the delicious-smelling aromas he has been enjoying, Yoshi hatches a plan to enrich them both.
Inference: Neighbor Sabu's business is not as robust as it could be because "his hibachi was difficult to find, for it was hidden away on a small street on the outskirts of the city." Sabu is angered because Yoshi refuses to pay for any of Sabu's delicious food and foolishly brags, "For me, smelling your expensive eels is as good as eating them. Because of your eels, I grow richer with every meal." Soon the good smell of eels broiling has been replaced with the evil smell of Samma, the "stinkiest fish in all of Japan."
Other Devices: *Antithesis, Aphorism, Foreshadowing, Onomatopoeia, Parallelism, Poetic Justice*
Art Style: Oil paint, pencil, and paper collage folk art come together in a satisfyingly expressionistic design to transmit the flavor of this ethnic quarrel.
Curriculum Tie-in: Literature (Folktales—Japan)

*Kaplan, Howard. *Waiting to Sing.* Illus. by Hervé Blondon. New York: DK Ink, 2000.
A family who loves music and spends many hours at the piano is devastated by the death of the mother, but those still living find consolation in the beautiful music that remains.
Inference: Months after the mother's death the boy plays in his first recital. "My sister came back from school for the recital and sat by my father in the first row, an empty seat between them." The spot would have belonged to the mother and wife. "I opened my music to my thousand birds." The boy, like his sister before him, will be playing the family favorite, Beethoven's *Für Elise*. As a little boy, he had tried counting all the notes

in this song. "The notes looked like a thousand birds had landed in front of us."

Other Devices: *Allusion, Antithesis, Aphorism, Atmosphere, Foreshadowing, Imagery, Metaphor, Parallelism, Simile, Symbol*

Art Style: Shadowy, full-page, sepia-tone pastel cartoon drawings expressionistically evoke a fragile emotional period in the life of a family coping with restructuring itself after the wrenching loss of one of its members.

Curriculum Tie-in: Music (Piano), Social Science (Death, Family Relationships, Feelings)

Kimmel, Eric A. *Grizz!* Illus. by Andrew Glass. New York: Holiday House, 2000. Cowboy Lucky Doolin makes a deal with the Devil, agreeing not to wash, shave, or change his clothes for seven years, thus earning a fortune and the hand of his true love.

> **Inference:** On the train to Denver, Lucky "fell in with a smooth-talking stranger. The stranger only had half his left foot. The part that remained looked a lot like a horse's hoof." Pictures show him with two distinctive bumps on his forehead. As time passes, Lucky grows rich. "That stranger with the bum foot sure kept his side of the bargain." Nothing is seen of this "stranger" until the end of the bargain draws near. Lucky rushes to a barbershop to get cleaned up. Oddly, "the barber walked with a limp. He only had half his foot." It seems the Devil has returned, and now he expects his due. When he is outwitted, he still finds a victim, the fellow who has been wooing Lucky's sweetheart. "As for Parmelee Jones, he was last seen talking to a stranger over by the railway station. The stranger was missing half his left foot."
>
> **Other Devices:** *Atmosphere, Hyperbole, Motif, Poetic Justice, Simile, Understatement*
>
> **Art Style:** Oil sticks and water color dust create exaggerated cartoons that complement this version of a soul-selling wager folktale.
>
> **Curriculum Tie-in:** Literature (Folktales—America)

Kirkpatrick, Katherine. *Redcoats and Petticoats.* Illus. by Ronald Himler. New York: Holiday House, 1999. Members of a family in the village of Setauket on Long Island are displaced by the Redcoats and serve as spies for the Revolutionary Army of George Washington.

> **Inference:** Mother begins to behave strangely with the laundry, sometimes hanging dry petticoats on the line. When her son helps her hang handkerchiefs, she says, "Only three handkerchiefs today." But when he asks her to tell him what's happening, she replies, "Sometimes it's not safe for me to tell you everything." She sends him on errands that seem pointless.

He is to watch for a whale boat. And he is not to ask questions. Clearly, more is going on than laundry and fishing.

Other Devices: *Foreshadowing*

Art Style: Impressionistic pen/ink watercolors illustrate the essence of the relationship between two political views. Bright red both ties together and contrasts the patriots and the loyalists.

Curriculum Tie-in: History (Revolutionary War)

Kitamura, Satoshi. *Me and My Cat?* New York: Farrar Straus Giroux, 2000.

A young boy spends an unusual day after awakening to find that he and his cat have switched bodies.

Inference: Late one night "an old lady in a pointed hat came in through my bedroom window. She brandished her broom at me and fired out some words." Whoever she may be, this visitor sets in motion the next day's events. Nicholas watches as his mother drags him away from his breakfast to catch the bus. He is gone; but he is still there. He thinks how strange this is as he "pulls his whiskers." What has happened to Nicholas? When the boy (cat) returns home from school, the cat (boy) notices Nicholas's behavior is quite catlike. "He didn't seem to like me at all." That's because the boy (cat) seems to the cat (Nicholas) to be a strange cat in his territory. That night the same pointed hat lady comes in through the window again. "Sorry, love. I got the wrong address," she says. There is more broom brandishing and more words are blurted out. The next morning Nicholas is Nicholas and the cat is the cat. But, strangely, at school that day, "Mr. McGough sat on the table. He scratched himself, licked his shirt, and fell asleep for the rest of the lesson."

Other Devices: *Antithesis, Irony, Parallelism, Point of View, Understatement*

Art Style: Busy, hilarious acrylic cartoons detail the daily life of a boy's thoughts in a cat's body as he watches a cat's activities in his boy's body.

Curriculum Tie-in: Social Science (Animal Companions, Values)

Lawson, Julie. *Emma and the Silk Train.* Illus. by Paul Mombourquette. Buffalo, NY: Kids Can Press, 1997.

After seeing the beautiful silk blouse her mother made, Emma dreams of having a piece of silk for herself, and when the opportunity arises, determinedly pursues it.

Inference: Emma has desired a silk garment so long that when her birthday comes, "she didn't need to make a wish. Her new silk dress rustled as she leaned forward to blow out the candles." Clearly, she already has her wish.

Other Devices: *Ambiguity, Foreshadowing, Imagery, Parallelism, Simile*

Art Style: Lush, impressionistic oil paintings capture the time and adventure of the silk train era.

Curriculum Tie-in: History (Railroads—Silk)

Littlesugar, Amy. *Tree of Hope.* Illus. by Floyd Cooper. New York: Philomel (Penguin Putnam), 1999.

> Florrie's daddy used to be a stage actor in Harlem before the Depression forced the Lafayette Theater to close, but he gets a chance to act again when Orson Welles reopens the theater to stage an all-black version of *Macbeth*.
>
>> **Inference:** When the story opens, Florrie's daddy is reminiscing about his stage acting days and how a pretty young woman came up to the stage after a performance to present him a red, red rose. "She was behind me being an actor in those days." But these days, Mama is irritated by such memories, calling them daydreams. Then fortunes change again when the old Lafayette reopens with a grand Shakespearean drama. Once again a woman brings an actor a red, red rose after the performance. Just as in the old days, Mama is in support of Daddy's career.
>>
>> **Other Devices:** *Cliché, Flashback, Foreshadowing, Paradox, Serendipity, Simile, Stereotype/Reverse Stereotype, Symbol*
>>
>> **Art Style:** Rich, oilwash impressionistic paintings suggest not only happier memories in more prosperous times, but also the temporary bleakness of the current Depression and the emerging hope for a better future.
>>
>> **Curriculum Tie-in:** History (Black Culture—Depression)

Lorbiecki, Marybeth. *Just One Flick of a Finger.* Illus. by David Diaz. New York: Dial (Penguin Putnam), 1996.

> A young boy takes a gun to school to scare off the bully who has been tormenting him, and the gun is accidentally fired during the scuffle.
>
>> **Inference:** The boy stole his dad's revolver "as he slept off his latest beer." The boy wonders briefly if his father would care "if something happened to me." This boy's minimal family support may be contributing to his poor choices. Later, when his best friend makes him realize what a mistake bringing a gun to school is, he closes his eyes in shame "and chucked at the nearest tree." His friend has walked away from him, disappointed in him, and he's overwhelmed with a sense of loss. Then, on top of his self-disgust, the bully makes an appearance. He tips the gun out of his pocket "so the bully could see it." Violence is in the making.
>>
>> **Other Devices:** *Antithesis, Foreshadowing, Internal Rhyme, Metaphor, Pun, Simile, Theme*
>>
>> **Art Style:** Acrylics, watercolor, and digitally manipulated photographic backgrounds blend to create powerful, stylized, expressionistic comic book images that evoke danger and tension.
>>
>> **Curriculum Tie-in:** Social Science (Bullies)

Lowell, Susan. *Little Red Cowboy Hat.* Illus. by Randy Cecil. New York: Henry Holt, 1997.

> Little Red rides her pony, Buck, to Grandma's ranch with a jar of cactus jelly in the saddlebag.

Inference: The wolf Little Red meets wears a black cowboy hat. Everyone knows the bad guys wear black hats. When he forces conversation with her, "she could count the teeth in his smile." There is danger in this stranger. While she speaks to the figure muffled up under the bedclothes, Little Red hears odd, thumping sounds outside. Grandma does her own wood chopping. She bursts through the door just in the nick of time. The wolf tries to escape, but Grandma's shotgun booms and pows, and soon there is a "splat!" "You'd look mighty good as a rug," Grandma says. The wolf is seen no more.

Other Devices: *Aphorism, Atmosphere, Caricature, Hyperbole, Onomatopoeia, Parody, Simile, Stereotype, Tone*

Art Style: Gouache cartoons in expressionistic naïve style humorously match this unique geographical version of a familiar fairy tale.

Lum, Kate. *What! Cried Granny: An Almost Bedtime Story.* Illus. by Adrian Johnson. New York: Dial (Penguin Putnam), 1998.

Granny can do whatever it takes to make Patrick's first sleepover a success.

Inference: As it begins to grow dark, it's "Patrick, dear boy" and "sail off to Dreamland" and "I'll kiss you good night." Later, and much later still, it's "turn out the light" and "GO TO SLEEP." Granny's patience, understandably, begins to wear a bit thin after several delaying tactics have successfully delayed Patrick's going to bed. He doesn't have a bed, a pillow, a blanket, or a teddy bear. Resourceful Granny makes everything that's missing. But this takes time, not to mention energy. There are trees to cut down, sheep to shear, chicken feathers to collect.

Other Devices: *Hyperbole*

Art Style: Bright acrylic expressionistic cartoons illustrate Granny's growingly jaundiced view of this child's stalling bedtime tactics.

Curriculum Tie-in: Social Science (Grandparents)

Lyon, George Ella. *One Lucky Girl.* Illus. by Irene Trivas. New York: DK Pub., 2000.

Even though their trailer is destroyed by a tornado, a young boy's family is grateful because they find his baby sister alive.

Inference: The baby's crib in sitting out in the middle of the racetrack greens. As the boy approaches cautiously, fearful of what he may discover, he hears squalling. "'Yahoo!' I yelled, and jumped for the sky." His dad calls him 'Hawkeye' because his famous eyesight has come through again. "There were tears on his face, too." Palpable relief is all around.

Other Devices: *Ambiguity, Antithesis, Foreshadowing, Imagery, Metaphor, Parallelism, Simile*

Art Style: Smudgy pastel illustrations impressionistically assist the story line through use of both dark and bright colors.

Curriculum Tie-in: Science (Tornadoes), Social Science (Family Relationships)

*Mamet, David. *Henrietta.* Illus. by Elizabeth Dahlie. Boston: Houghton Mifflin, 1999.

> Henrietta pig, rebuffed by the law school admissions office, like so many of her underprivileged kind before her, wanders aimlessly until a chance encounter with a vagabond philosopher enables her to pursue her dream of a scholarly future.
>
> > **Inference:** Because the president of the Great University (in disguise) grows to respect Henrietta's "well remembered and well read" knowledge, she ends up being admitted and distinguishing herself as a successful student. In her commencement address, she speaks of the need for simple justice. Then, through the artist's rendering of her sitting among nine black-robed, august-looking justices, the reader realizes "her work took her to that high place she enjoys today," a seat on the Supreme Court.
> >
> > **Other Devices:** *Irony, Personification, Pun, Satire, Serendipity, Tone*
> >
> > **Art Style:** Spare pastel crayon impressionistic cartoons highlight in subtle, playful satire the foibles of higher education's entrenched, short-sighted traditions.
> >
> > **Curriculum Tie-in:** Literature (Fable), Social Science (Diversity)

*Martin, Nora. *The Stone Dancers.* Illus. by Jill Kastner. New York: Atheneum Books for Young Readers (Simon & Schuster), 1995.

> A young girl uses an old legend about stone dancers to teach her mountain village a lesson in hospitality and sharing.
>
> > **Inference:** The village people have forgotten that when their ancestors arrived, they, too, were different and were not welcomed by the local communities. They at last found a safe haven, and a legend begins as they dance in celebration on their mountaintop to show others who need a refuge that they will be welcomed here. Now, many years later, when strangers do come seeking refuge, the villagers fear them because they are from a distant land. Anise reminds her family, "Perhaps they saw the stone dancers." Her papa and mama look at each other. "Without eating his supper, Papa puts on his black felt hat and leaves the house" to visit quietly with every neighbor. The unfriendly faces the strangers had met suddenly become much more welcoming.
> >
> > **Other Devices:** *Aphorism, Imagery, Irony, Metaphor, Parallel Story, Simile*
> >
> > **Art Style:** Impressionistic oil paintings show the interplay of light and shadow, melding the real with the enchanted in this nineteenth-century French peasant village.
> >
> > **Curriculum Tie-in:** History (Nineteenth-Century France), Literature (Legends), Social Science (Values)

*Meddaugh, Susan. *Hog-Eye.* New York: Walter Lorraine Books (Houghton Mifflin), 1995.

> A young pig uses her ability to read to outwit a wolf that intends to eat her.

Inference: A child doesn't like to ride the bus to school, because "the kids are terrible." She dawdles and misses her bus, and gets on one without any children. By the time she realizes her mistake and gets off, she is lost, explaining later that she had encountered a wolf who wanted to put her into a soup. The wolf pulls down a dusty book from the shelf to find the soup recipe his mother uses, and the pig "realized something very interesting." The wolf is holding a book titled *E-Z Car Care* upside down. Using this awareness to her advantage, she sends him on dangerous missions to secure ingredients. For one of them she even draws a picture of the "Green Threeleaf." He must bring back a lot of it. And he must crush the leaves and keep them warm by putting them inside his shirt next to his skin.

Other Devices: *Allusion, Antithesis, Flashback, Foreshadowing, Hyperbole, Irony, Understatement*

Art Style: Split-page watercolor cartoons tell the "true story" of a schoolchild who dislikes her daily bus ride.

Curriculum Tie-in: Literature (Tall Tale)

Meggs, Libby Phillips. *Go Home! The True Story of James the Cat.* Morton Grove, IL: Albert Whitman, 2000.

A homeless cat spends several seasons trying to survive the elements until at last a suburban family adopts him.

Inference: In earlier days he had been a strong and swift hunter. "These days, he looked for leftover food at the back doors of houses where other cats lived." He needs to be accepted and cared for. Will the family accept one more cat? "Before long, Charlotte and Emily came to see how friendly and good-natured the cat was."

Other Devices: *Ambiguity, Antithesis, Connotation, Metaphor, Point of View, Simile*

Art Style: Realistic pastel illustrations follow James' admittance into a family that provides what has been missing in his life for a long time.

Curriculum Tie-in: Social Science (Animal Companions)

Miller, William. *The Piano.* Illus. by Susan Keeter. New York: Lee & Low Books, 2000.

A young black girl's love of music leads her to a job in the house of an older white woman, who teaches her not only to play the piano, but also the reward of intergenerational friendship.

Inference: In this tale of mutual respect, Miss Hartwell tries to demonstrate piano playing to the eager Tia, but her hands are too arthritic to play. Tia immediately understands the pain the older woman is in, and although she would love to continue the lesson, quickly reacts, sparing the woman the embarrassment of acknowledging her frailty. "I better get back to work now." Later, when they're together at the piano again, Tia bathes Miss

Hartwell's hands in a warm solution of saltwater to ease her painful joints. Miss Hartwell returns the favor by bathing Tia's hands after Tia has done some unaccustomed chores. Miss Hartwell says, "A friend of mind taught me this trick."

Other Devices: *Theme*

Art Style: Oil paint in realistic expressionism captures mood and feelings between these two new friends as their love of music transcends their physical and cultural diversity.

Curriculum Tie-in: Social Science (Values)

Modarressi, Mitra. *Yard Sale.* New York: DK Pub., 2000.

When Mr. Flotsam has a yard sale in the quiet town of Spudville, his neighbors are first upset, then delighted by their purchases.

Inference: The first garage sale brought excitement and change. "As for Mr. Flotsam, the next time spring rolled around, he decided to hold another yard sale . . . ." One can only wonder what a new round of sale items will mean to the quiet lives of Spudville.

Other Devices: *Allusion, Antithesis, Connotation, Hyperbole, Paradox, Serendipity, Understatement*

Art Style: Lively, full-page, watercolor naïve art accompanies an understated text.

*Morrison, Toni, with Slade Morrison. *The Big Box,*. Illus. by Giselle Potter. New York: Hyperion, 1999.

To make three youngsters conform to their rules, grown-ups create a world inside a box, including treats and simulated nature, but all the kids really want is the freedom to be themselves.

Inference: Like pet animals caged in a pretend world, the children are living the adults' concept of a child's good life. Nevertheless, "The doors open only one way." And there are "three big locks." What terrible transgressions have made the grown-ups "nervous" about letting the children live naturally? Patty talked in the library and went to the toilet four times. Mickey hollered in the hall and played handball against the wall. Liza let the chickens keep their eggs and took the bit from the horse's mouth and fed honey to the bees. Say the adults, "We all agree, your parents and we," these kids can't handle their freedom. Parents visit, when it's convenient for them—right after their bingo game, and after their comedy show. And what is to be accomplished with this "cure" effected through life in a big box? It is so the "grown-up world can adore you . . . can abide you . . . to approve you."

Other Devices: *Antithesis, Internal Rhyme, Irony, Oxymoron, Satire, Theme*

Art Style: Naïve watercolors show the contrast between the real joy of simple outdoor amusements and the cloying dissatisfaction of adult-provided, commercial rubbish.

Curriculum Tie-in: Social Science (Values)

Nickle, John. *The Ant Bully.* New York: Scholastic Press, 1999.

Lucas learns a lesson about bullying by the ants he has been tormenting.

Inference: As a fellow colony worker, Lucas answers questions about his other life when he was a "giant." No, he was not the biggest giant. "Not compared with Sid the bully. He was always stealing my hat and spraying me with the hose." The ants reply, "Oh, like you did to us?" Then there is an awkward silence. Lucas experiences empathy for the ants.

Other Devices: *Antihero, Antithesis, Foreshadowing, Personification, Poetic Justice, Point of View*

Art Style: Expressionistic acrylic cartoons skillfully play with perspective as both the boy and the ants view the same environment.

Curriculum Tie-in: Social Science (Bullies, Values)

*Nolen, Jerdine. *Big Jabe.* Illus. by Kadir Nelson. New York: Lothrop, Lee & Shepard, 2000.

Momma Mary tells stories about a special young man who does wondrous things, especially for the slaves on the Plenty Plantation.

Inference: Addy eats a pear presented to her by a mysterious child called Jabe. It "must be the fruit of heaven," she enthuses. Seeds from the gift pear grow into a tree "full of luscious pears. And there, shining between them, the North Star sparkled overhead," the star that guides runaway slaves to freedom. The overseer is forbidden by the owner to interfere with Jabe's "calling," but "when he found Pot-Tim whistling as he worked in the stables, he whupped him good." The bully habitually takes out his frustration on someone accessible. Pot-Tim disappears. Only Addy deduces his a venue of escape. "Jabe took Pot-Tim to that pear tree," Addy whispers. "But no one heard." When other slaves disappear, Addy notes, "Jabe took them to that pear tree. This time people listened." They have begun to realize the tree's significance. Finally, it is Addy herself who faces the overseer's wrath. When the empty chains are all that are left of her presence, the people breathe the thought that no one would say aloud: "Jabe took Addy to that pear tree."

Other Devices: *Allusion, Anachronism, Antithesis, Flashback, Flash-forward, Foreshadowing, Hyperbole, Imagery, Parallelism, Simile, Symbol, Understatement*

Art Style: Strong, detailed pen/ink, watercolor, and gouache drawings provide wonderful expressionistic period ambience to this folktale.

Curriculum Tie-in: History (Slavery—America), Literature (Tall Tale)

O'Malley Kevin. *Bud.* New York: Walker & Company, 2000.

The orderly Sweet-Williams are dismayed at their son's fondness for the messy pastime of gardening.

Inference: His father "read to Bud from a variety of important books on a variety of subjects." His mother "showed him how to hold a paintbrush the right way and to keep the colors inside the lines." His parents are trying to guide Bud's development. But even with these diversionary tactics, Bud is showing signs of disorderly exuberance. His mother points out that sunflowers are yellow. Bud's are purple. And as he swings his paintbrush around, he joyfully proclaims "Paint Baby, Paint!" All the subterfuge to hide Bud's unconventional garden from Grandfather's view when he visits, proves to be unnecessary. When Bud explains about the many varieties of plants he is growing, and about his kitchen scrap compost piles, and how earthworms improve the soil, "Grandfather was impressed." Finally, Grandfather remarks, "Your grandmother used to grow roses just like this." It is clear that the messy garden is not going to upset Grandfather after all.

Other devices: *Antithesis, Aphorism, Foreshadowing, Irony, Pun, Theme, Understatement*

Art Style: Large, expressive gouache cartoons lovingly follow the development of tolerance, respect, and appreciation for a beloved child's unconventional approach to life.

Curriculum Tie-in: Science (Gardening), Social Science (Family Relationships, Values)

Osborne, Mary Pope. *Kate and the Beanstalk.* Illus. by Giselle Potter. New York: Atheneum Books for Young Readers (Simon & Schuster), 2000.

In this version of the classic tale, a girl climbs to the top of a giant beanstalk, where she uses her quick wit to outsmart a giant and make her and her mother's fortune.

Inference: When the girl reaches the top of the beanstalk, she encounters an old woman, who tells her the castle she sees used to belong to a noble knight and his fair wife and baby. A monstrous giant came to steal from them and killed the good man, taking over the castle. The wife and baby were visiting in the valley and feared to return home. "Alas, now they are very poor and close to starving." Kate is moved by the story and agrees to try to help "right the terrible wrongs that have occurred." Though she and her mother are starving, she does not make the connection, as the reader does, that the noble's wife and child are herself and her mother.

Other Devices: *Hyperbole, Motif, Poetic Justice, Simile, Stereotype/Reverse Stereotype*

Art Style: Naïve drawings in pencil, ink, gouache, and watercolor expressionistically tell the familiar tale of the thieving giant and the rescue of stolen treasure.

Curriculum Tie-in: Literature (Folktale), Social Science (Values)

Pawagi, Manijusha. *The Girl Who Hated Books.* Illus. by Leanne Franson. Hillsboro, OR: Beyond Words, 1998.

Although she lives in a house full of avid readers, Meena hates books—until she discovers the magic inside them.

Inference: A stack of fallen books opens and the characters inside fall out. Meena reads the stories to help the characters discover into which books they belong. By the time she finishes, she begins to feel lonely. "I'll never see those rabbits again!" she says. But, "then she noticed that the books were still there, lying around her. She started to smile." When her parents come home, "She was reading a book."

Other Devices: *Alliteration, Allusion, Antithesis, Foreshadowing, Hyperbole, Internal Rhyme, Pun, Tone*

Art Style: Pen/ink watercolor expressionistic cartoons emphasize emotion and background action.

Preston, Tim. *The Lonely Scarecrow.* Illus. by Maggie Kneen. New York: Dutton Children's Books (Penguin Books), 1999.

A lonely scarecrow with a scary face has trouble making friends with the animals who surround him, until a heavy snowfall transforms him into a jolly snowman.

Inference: The scarecrow, who has been surrounded by small creatures during heavy winter snows, worries that when the snow melts and reveals who he really is, his newfound friends will run away in fear. But "as the warmth of spring stirred the brown earth, the scarecrow felt a bird peck at his hat and a mouse nestle in the folds of his coat." He knows he'll never be lonely again. His outward appearance will not be an issue.

Other Devices: *Imagery, Metaphor, Paradox, Parallelism, Theme*

Art Style: Lavishly embossed, finely detailed, watercolor and acrylic cartoons fondly render scenes of seasonal changes.

Curriculum Tie-in: Science (Seasons), Social Science (Friendship)

Ruurs, Margriet. *Emma and the Coyote.* Illus. by Barbara Spurll. New York: Stoddart Kids, 1999.

Emma thinks chickens are smarter than coyotes, and she struts boldly where no chicken should go to prove it.

Inference: Emma tries to zigzag between trees in the orchard to elude the coyote and discovers there are no more trees behind which to hide. She knows she is in trouble. The farmer's children see her just before the coyote strikes. When they chide her about coyotes being smarter than chickens, "Emma had nothing to say—not even one tiny, little tok." She knows what a close call she had. But she continues to take unnecessary risks. The final time, she falls out of a tree right on the coyote, who leaps in surprise and accidentally jumps forward straight into a trap. "Emma fluffed herself up and looked down her beak at the coyote. Then, on legs that trembled just a little, she marched past . . . ." She might not be willing to admit to others the extent of her danger, but she can't hide reality from herself.

Other Devices: *Alliteration, Foreshadowing, Imagery, Irony, Motif, Parallelism, Serendipity, Simile*
Art Style: Bright primary color paintings expressionistically follow the fortunes of Emma and the barnyard animals.
Curriculum Tie-in: Social Science (Self-esteem)

*Say, Allen. *The Sign Painter.* Boston: Walter Lorraine Books (Houghton Mifflin), 2000.

An assignment to paint a large billboard in the desert changes the life of an aspiring artist.

Inference: The boy "hesitated, then straightened and tapped on the glass" of a sign shop. He seems needy but reluctant to stoop to the work of craftsman; he considers himself an artist. The man is pleased with the boy's work. "We'll make a good team. You won't go hungry." "The boy doesn't answer." His commitment to this kind of life is not forthcoming. The man later chastises him for wanting to add a few embellishments to the painting layout. "The boy looked away" when the man asks him if when he's paid to paint a woman, he will paint a landscape. The boy clearly would prefer individualizing his work. Then the two overhear a phone call that speaks to the reasons behind the amazing roller coaster they have found in the middle of the desert. "Imagine it, all lit up at night . . . . Had the name for years, before any of the building was done . . . the whole thing was riding on the highway coming through . . . who knows? But we'll advertise . . . billboards . . . we can only hope." "It was late when the boy said good-bye to the sign painter." The one-sided conversation convinces the boy to move on toward his own artistic goals and leave behind the financial security of being a sign painter.
Other Devices: *Ambiguity, Antithesis, Imagery, Point of View, Theme, Tone*
Art Style: Magnificent realistic acrylic paintings unfold the contrasts in this provocative story about personal choices between security and dreams.
Curriculum Tie-in: Philosophy (Quality of Life)

*Turner, Ann. *Red Flower Goes West.* Illus. by Dennis Nolan. New York: Hyperion Books for Children, 1999.

As they journey west, a family nurtures the red flower they have carried with them from their old home.

Inference: When Pa tells the family they are moving west to California, where there is gold and free land, he says, "A man can't let that go by." The children look at each other. They know what to expect. "Once Pa had an idea, no one could stop him." They have been through this before. As they begin their journey, Ma holds the red flower on her lap. "I wished I had something to hold on to, too," says the narrator. He would also like the comfort of holding on to a bit of home. When they finally arrive at their new homesite, the oxen "ran and bellowed just like Jenny and me." Clearly, everyone is relieved and joyful to have the journey end.

Other Devices: *Connotation, Metaphor, Parallelism, Simile, Symbol*

Art Style: Soft crayon and pastel realistic drawings, mostly in shades of gray, depict a stern pioneer experience accented by the bright red beacon of the family's talisman.

Curriculum Tie-in: History (Westward Expansion)

*Van Allsburg, Chris. *The Sweetest Fig.* Boston: Houghton Mifflin, 1993.

After being given two magical figs that make his dreams come true, Monsieur Bibot sees his plans for future wealth upset by his long-suffering dog.

Inference: The stiff, unrelenting Monsieur Bibot angrily dismisses two figs with which a poor patient pays her dental bill. By accident he discovers their true value. What he dreams at night comes true the following day after eating one of them. He had dreamed he stood in his underwear in front of a café. "The dentist looked up and saw the rest of his dream come true." "All the eyes of Paris were fixed on the Eiffel Tower, which slowly drooped over as if it were made of soft rubber." "He would not waste the second fig" as he thinks wealthy thoughts. But it is too late. He enters his kitchen just as his little dog finishes licking up the last of the second fig. Now the dog's dreams will come true.

Other Devices: *Irony, Poetic Justice*

Art Style: Pastel, sepia-tone realistic illustrations show the just deserts of a self-serving dentist and his patient dog.

White, Linda Arms. *Comes a Wind.* Illus. by Tom Curry. New York: DK Pub., 2000.

While visiting their mother's ranch, two brothers who constantly try to best each other swap tall tales about big winds, and are surprised by the fiercest wind they have ever seen.

Inference: Nothing till now has stopped the rivalry between the two brothers. But when Mama gets snagged up on the weather vane of the barn, they pull together for her sake. "Mama grinned ear to ear, watching her boys working." It's almost worth being snatched by the wind to see her sons lay aside their antagonism for one another. They find something they agree upon. "Now that—" said Clement. "—was a wind!" said Clyde.

Other Devices: *Atmosphere, Foreshadowing, Hyperbole, Parallelism, Simile*

Art Style: Painted acrylics in expressionistic naïve perspectives illustrate the peculiar and humorous effects of the forces of wind and imagination.

Curriculum Tie-in: Literature (Tall Tales)

*Wilkon, Piotr. *Rosie the Cool Cat.* Illus. by Jozef Wilkon. New York: Viking (Penguin Books), 1989.

Casper and Carolina are proud of their jet-black fur and despair trying to cope with their orange kitten, who likes to play with mice and sleep in the doghouse.

Inference: Having a kitten who will not conform, Rosie's father, Casper, gets gray hairs fretting over her behavior. Later, as an adult, Rosie becomes the star of a rock group. Her parents see her on TV. "I think I'm getting some more gray hairs," Casper moans. His difficult kitten is not following the family mold.

Other Devices: *Antithesis, Foreshadowing, Irony, Poetic Justice, Satire, Stereotype, Symbol*

Art Style: Pastel and colored pencil expressionistic cartoons capture the family pride in its uniqueness as well as its sense of puzzlement in the jolting difference of the odd one.

Curriculum Tie-in: Social Science (Family Relationships, Individuality, Values)

*Wisniewski, David. *Golem.* New York: Clarion Books (Houghton Mifflin), 1996. (Caldecott—1997)

A saintly rabbi miraculously brings to life a clay giant who helps him watch over the Jews of sixteenth-century Prague.

Inference: As the rabbi explains the conditions of his being alive, the Golem does not like what he hears. He will be allowed to live "until the Jews are no longer in danger," the rabbi tells him. "Then you will return to the earth from whence you came. Do you understand?" "Golem said nothing." He performs his duties well, in the process earning the Jews' respect. When he returns to clay, "Though Golem had not truly been a man, they recited Kaddish, the prayer for the dead."

Other Devices: *Analogy, Atmosphere, Foreshadowing, Imagery, Irony, Motif, Paradox, Simile*

Art Style: Paper cut in sophisticated expressionistic collage produces a powerful physical and emotional effect in this cautionary tale.

Curriculum Tie-in: Literature (Legend), Social Science (Values)

Zagwÿn, Deborah. *Apple Batter.* Berkeley, CA: Tricycle Press, 1999.

Because of their persistence, Delmore succeeds in learning to hit a baseball and his mother, Loretta, succeeds in growing apples.

Inference: Loretta's apple trees produce few apples; Delmore hits few fair balls. When one of Delmore's balls ricochets off the trunk of an apple tree and buries itself off to the side, his dog, who retrieves the balls, is confused. He looks all around and, finding no ball, mistakes the nearest round object he sees for the missing ball. "He stood on his hind paws and delicately nipped a low-hanging sphere off the tree." Loretta sighs, "If only dogs could see in color." Delmore notices that the single apple left on the tree is about the size of a baseball now. He swings and "sent his ball cleanly and swiftly in the direction of the last thing he'd looked at—Loretta's prized apple. He never expected them to meet." The "last apple said goodbye to its twig and went spinning over the garden gate."

Other Devices: *Alliteration, Analogy, Antithesis, Foreshadowing, Irony, Parallelism, Pun, Simile*

Art Style: Expressionistic watercolor cartoons compare the changing fortunes of mother and son as they struggle mutually toward their respective goals.

Curriculum Tie-in: Athletics (Baseball), Science (Apple Production)

INTERNAL RHYME

Two or more words rhyme within a line of text.

Example: "Once upon a midnight dreary, while I pondered, weak and
weary . . . ."

Edgar Allan Poe, *The Raven*

Bradbury, Ray. *Switch on the Night.* Illus. by Leo and Diane Dillon. New York: Alfred A. Knopf, 1983.

A lonely little boy, who is afraid of the dark, is introduced to a whole new world by his friend, a little girl.

Internal Rhyme: A stranger stood there in the middle of the "white lights, the bright lights, the hall lights, the small lights, the yellow lights, the mellow lights." The stranger told him that by turning out the lights, he could switch on the "light stars, the bright stars, the true stars, the blue stars!"

Other Devices: *Alliteration, Antithesis, Irony, Metaphor, Motif, Paradox, Simile, Symbol*

Art Style: Surrealistic pastel drawings match the rhythmical text of this slightly magical, slightly scientific, and quite ethereal night world.

Curriculum Tie-in: Science: (Astronomy), Social Science (Fears)

Dengler, Marianna. *Fiddlin' Sam.* Illus. by Sibyl Graber Gerig. Flagstaff, AZ: Rising Moon (Northland), 1999.

Wandering through the Ozarks and bringing joy to people with his music, Fiddlin' Sam seeks the right person to take up his fiddle and carry on the practice.

Internal Rhyme: "And folks all sat down at his *feet* as the single thread of the fiddle tune *reached* up and up . . . ." "Fiddlin' *Sam* was a happy *man* . . . ." "He fiddled high and *low*, fast and *slow*."

Other Devices: *Antithesis, Atmosphere, Foreshadow Inference, Parallelism, Serendipity*

Art Style: Exuberant realistic and expressionistic watercolors in shades of bright yellow, pink, and blue faithfully reveal the emotional and physical

details of this musician's life.
Curriculum Tie-in: Social Science (Missouri Ozarks)

Howe, James. *Horace and Morris but Mostly Dolores.* Illus. by Amy Walrod. New York: Atheneum Books for Young Readers (Simon & Schuster), 1999.
   Three mice friends learn that the best clubs include everyone.
   Internal Rhyme: Snappy signs that say "How to get a fella using mozzarella" or the "Frisky Whisker Club," and, of course, the characters' names: Chloris, Boris, Horace, Morris, and Dolores, add to a humorous story with an important cultural message.
   Other Devices: *Allusion, Parallelism, Pun, Stereotype, Theme*
   Art Style: Acrylics and collage cartoons illustrate a basic gender response to excitement and adventure by showing few physical or behavioral differences between the male and female mouse children.
   Curriculum Tie-in: Social Science (Gender Equality)

Johnston, Tony. *Alice Nizzy Nazzy, the Witch of Santa Fe.* Illus. by Tomie dePaola. New York: G.P. Putnam's Sons, 1995.
   When Manuela's sheep are stolen, she has to go to Alice Nizzy Nazzy's talking roadrunner-footed adobe house and try to get the witch to give the flock back.
   Internal Rhyme: Manuela shows the witch where the black cactus flower can be found. She points the way, up a canyon, *steep* and *deep*. Every one of the tea jars is stuffed with teas for *gashes*, for *rashes*, for *rickets*, for *crickets*.
   Other Devices: *Alliteration, Connotation, Foreshadowing, Hyperbole, Motif, Poetic Justice, Simile*
   Art Style: Bright pastel and acrylic folk cartoons illustrate the western lifestyle in this good vs. bad character tale.
   Curriculum Tie-in: Geography (New Mexico), Literature (Fairy Tales—America), Social Science (Values)

Lorbiecki, Marybeth. *Just One Flick of a Finger.* Illus. by David Diaz. New York: Dial (Penguin Putnam), 1996.
   A young boy takes a gun to school to scare off the bully who has been tormenting him, and the gun is accidentally fired during the scuffle.
   Internal Rhyme: The boy says, "The *rule* at my *school* is you're a *fool* if you can't get your hand on a gun." Then he says, "Reebo was in my face, calling me 'Fat *Jack*' and 'White *Rat*.'" He thinks about getting a gun. "I knew the *trick*—just one *flick* of his finger and Reebo would be off his case. He knew where his father kept the gun in a *box*, but he could trip the *lock*. His thoughts turn "to *steel* at the *feel* of the cold metal. His friend Sherms tells him about his brother "doing *time* without a *dime*." Eventually, he comes to understand the flimsy protection carrying a gun can be. "So the *cool* can *drool* for all I care."

Other Devices: *Antithesis, Foreshadowing, Inference, Metaphor, Pun, Simile, Theme*

Art Style: Acrylics, watercolors and digitally manipulated photographic backgrounds blend to create powerful stylized, expressionistic, comic book images that evoke danger and tension.

Curriculum Tie-in: Social Science (Bullies)

Lowell, Susan. *Cindy Ellen: A Wild Western Cinderella.* Illus. by Jane Manning. New York: Joanna Cotler Books (HarperCollins), 2000.

Cindy Ellen loses one of her diamond spurs at the square dance in the retelling of this classic fairytale.

Internal Rhyme: Cindy was a skilled cowgirl. She wrangled and *roped* and galloped and *loped* with the best buckaroos on the range. Her fairy godmother reminded her "there ain't no horse that can't be *rode*, and there ain't no man that can't be *throwed*. She danced at the square dance, *twirling, swirling,* and losing track of time.

Other Devices: *Alliteration, Aphorism, Foreshadowing, Parallelism, Parody, Simile, Tone*

Art Style: Action-packed, expressionistic acrylic cartoons hilariously support the story's western flavor.

Curriculum Tie-in: Social Science (Self-esteem)

Mahy, Margaret. *Simply Delicious.* Illus. by Jonathan Allen. New York: Orchard Books, 1999.

A resourceful father engages in all kinds of acrobatic moves to keep an assortment of jungle creatures from getting the double-dip, chocolate-chip-and-cherry ice cream cone he is taking home to his son.

Internal Rhyme: The special treat has rainbow *twinkles* and chopped-nut *sprinkles*. Before his son can have the ice cream, Mr. Minky must take a short cut down the *lumpy, bumpy*, jungle track to his back garden. He climbs on his bicycle and goes *lumping and bumping* along the trail.

Other Devices: *Alliteration, Foreshadowing, Hyperbole, Poetic Justice, Simile, Understatement*

Art Style: Lively line and gouache cartoons in lush jungle colors satisfyingly follow the father's adventures as he delivers his son an appreciated treat.

Curriculum Tie-in: Literature (Cumulative Tale)

***Morrison, Toni with Slade Morrison.** *The Big Box.* Illus. by Giselle Potter. New York: Hyperion, 1999.

To make three unique youngsters conform to their rules, grown-ups create a world inside a box, including treats and simulated nature, but all the kids really want is the freedom to be themselves.

Internal Rhyme: Parents come to visit after their comedy *show* with Blim*pies* and Frisbees and comic books and Matchbox cars that *go*. The children get "a butterfly under *glass* and an aquarium thing with plastic fish made so it would *last*." And Nikes and a Spice Girls *shirt*, and a jar of genuine *dirt*." "I eat my *beets* and on Saturday morning I change my *sheets*." Beavers chew trees when they *need 'em*, but those kids can't handle their *freedom*.

Other Devices: *Antithesis, Inference, Irony, Oxymoron, Satire, Theme*

Art Style: Naïve watercolors show the contrast between the real joy expressed by the children in their simple outdoor amusements and the cloying dissatisfaction with adult-provided commercial rubbish.

Curriculum Tie-in: Social Science (Values)

*Myers, Christopher. *Black Cat.* New York: Scholastic Press, 1999.

Black Cat ambles on an eye-opening journey, exploring feelings about identity, beauty, and home.

Internal Rhyme: Black Cat is "cousin to the *concrete* creeping down our city *streets;* where do you live, where will we *meet?*" Black Cat dances to the "banging *beats* of passing *jeeps*." Does he "nod hello to people he *meets* on the yellow subway *seats?*" We "want to *know*, where do you *go?*" He plays "*chain*-link *games*." He edges over rooftops ,seeking sun-soaked *spots*." "*Home* is anywhere I *roam*."

Other Devices: *Alliteration, Imagery, Metaphor, Simile*

Art Style: Bold combination of collage, ink, and gouache with striking perspectives lends an intensity to the peculiarities of metro life.

Curriculum Tie-in: Art (Medium and Technique)

Pawagi, Manjusha. *The Girl Who Hated Books.* Illus. by Leanne Franson. Hillsboro, OR: Beyond Words, 1998.

Although she lives in a house full of avid readers, Meena hates books—until she discovers the magic inside them.

Internal Rhyme: "There were books in dressers and drawers and *desks*, in closets and cupboards and *chests*." "There were books on the sofa and books on the *stairs*, books crammed in the fireplace and stacked on the *chairs*." When the creatures begin falling out of the toppled stack of books, "Humpty Dumpty went flying and then broke in *half*, behind Mother Goose and a purple *giraffe*." There are "elephants, emperors, emus and *elves* and an assortment of monkeys tangled up in them*selves*."

Other Devices: *Alliteration, Allusion, Antithesis, Foreshadowing, Hyperbole, Inference, Pun, Tone*

Art Style: Pen/ink watercolor expressionistic cartoons emphasize emotion and background action.

Steig, William. *Wizzil.* Illus. by Quentin Blake. New York: Farrar Straus Giroux, 2000.

A bored witch causes trouble when she decides to take revenge on an old man, but her mischief leads to a happy ending.

Internal Rhyme: The parrot, Beatrice, is pleased with the witch's plan to turn herself into a glove and take revenge on the Frimp family. "That's the way, *Wizzil*; make him *sizzle*." He has troubles when he begins wearing a glove he finds. When his daughter-in-law asks him if he's all right, he lies, "I'm *fine* as *wine*." Eventually, DeWitt "saw the *light*; Fred and Florence must be *right*" about the glove.

Other Devices: *Alliteration, Ambiguity, Connotation, Foreshadowing, Irony, Serendipity, Tone*

Art Style: Delightfully awful watercolor cartoons capture the personalities and behaviors of the rotten witch and the hillbilly family she pesters.

Curriculum Tie-in: Social Science (Love)

Strete, Craig Kee. *The Lost Boy and the Monster.* Illus. by Steve Johnson and Lou Fancher. New York: G.P. Putnam's Sons (Penguin Books for Young Readers), 1999.

With the help of a rattlesnake and a scorpion, a lost boy gains two names and defeats the horrible foot-eating monster.

Internal Rhyme: The rope that the monster uses to ensnare unsuspecting children is described as being *tangled* and *angled* and *coiled* and *oiled*, and *sticky-icky*. Eventually, the monster himself gets entrapped. That rope stuck to his *nose* and it stuck to his *toes*.

Other Devices: *Ambiguity, Connotation, Motif, Poetic Justice, Simile, Theme, Tone*

Art Style: Textured paste, oil paint, potato stamping, and scratching tools create expressionistic paintings in brown and yellow tones reminiscent of American Indian folk art.

Curriculum Tie-in: Art (American Indian), Literature (Folktales—American Indian)

Waite, Judy. *Mouse, Look Out!* Illus. by Norma Burgin. New York: Dutton Children's Books (Penguin Putnam), 1998.

Inside an old, abandoned house a mouse searches for a safe place to hide from a cat.

Internal Rhyme: Inside the *torn, worn* mattress, a little mouse is sleeping. Through the broken wood of the *ragged* and *jagged* door the mouse creeps.

Other Devices: *Alliteration, Atmosphere, Metaphor, Poetic Justice, Simile*

Art Style: Realistic acrylic paintings in detailed perspective are a perfect complement to the pleasingly ominous, gently scary text.

IRONY

The perception or awareness of a discrepancy or incongruity between words and their meaning, or between actions and their results, or between appearance and reality.

Example: And on the pedestal these words appear:
"My name is Ozymandias, king of kings:
Look on my works, ye Mighty, and despair!"
Nothing beside remains. Round the decay
Of that colossal wreck, boundless and bare
The lone and level sands stretch far away.

Percy Shelley, *Ozymandias*

Alexander, Lloyd. *The House Gobbaleen.* Illus. by Diane Goode. New York: Dutton Children's Books (Penguin Books), 1995.

Unhappy over what he considers his bad luck, Tooley ignores his cat's warnings and invites a greedy little man into his home in the mistaken hope of improving his fortunes.

Irony: When the little man tells Tooley that he never promised to bring him luck, Tooley finally realizes what a fool he'd been to invite the creature into his home. "What am I doing waiting on you hand and foot? And gobbled out of house and home! With never a decent night's sleep in my own bed! And no luck at the end of it!" Then he assesses his situation. "It's luck I wanted, and luck I got. All of it bad."

Other Devices: *Ambiguity, Foreshadowing, Hyperbole, Inference, Simile, Theme, Tone, Understatement*

Art Style: Humorous gouache and watercolor cartoons illustrate this modern folktale.

Curriculum Tie-in: Literature (Folktale), Social Science (Values)

*Armstrong, Jennifer. *Pierre's Dream.* Illus. by Susan Gaber. New York: Dial (Penguin Putnam), 1999.

Thinking he is dreaming, Pierre, a lazy, foolish, man, shows no fear as he performs many amazing and dangerous circus acts.

Irony: Because he thinks it's not real, Pierre finds himself capable of all kinds of marvelous things. The villager who is known and knows himself as an idler with no talent, stands out as the best circus performer among the troupe. They look up to him with respect; so does the audience. It takes waking from the dream that was not really a dream for Pierre to begin to respect himself and recognize his own potential.

Other Devices: *Antihero, Foreshadowing, Inference, Theme*

Art Style: Ethereal expressionistic acrylic paintings alternate between stunning perspectives and large close-ups.
Curriculum Tie-in: Social Science (Values)

Aylesworth, Jim. *The Full Belly Bowl.* Illus. by Wendy Anderson Halpern. New York: Atheneum Books for Young Readers (Simon & Schuster), 1999.
    In return for the kindness he showed a wee small man, a very old man is given a magical bowl that causes problems when it's not used properly.
    Irony: Before the full belly bowl enters his life, the old man is happy with his cat and his simple ways. Later, after discovering how anything in the bowl will multiply as it's taken out, he hopes to improve his lot by taking a carefully garnered bag of copper pennies to exchange for ten-dollar gold pieces. He forgets to put away the bowl properly. A mouse crawls inside and out again. It is followed by multiple mice. When the old man returns home and discovers his error, he hastily puts his cat into the bowl. Out she jumps. Out jump multiple cats, so many he can no longer tell his beloved Angelina from all the others. But the mice are gone now. Unfortunately, so is the full belly bowl. A cat has knocked it off the table, and it has broken. Still, despite the fact that he cannot tell which of the many cats is Angelina, he is not dissatisfied. He doesn't have the potential to be either rich or well-fed now, but it doesn't matter much. "The truth is, he loved them all. To him, they were just about the sweetest cats in the whole world." Contrary to expectations, he is not grief-stricken at his losses. He is sanguine. Life is still good.
    Other Devices: *Foreshadowing*
    Art Style: Pen/ink intricate, cartoon-style colored pencil drawings are delicate, beautifully whimsical and bordered in details that are perfect for this gentle cautionary folktale.
    Curriculum Tie-in: Social Science (Values)

*Baylor, Byrd. *The Table Where Rich People Sit.* Illus. by Peter Parnall. New York: Charles Scribner's Sons, 1994.
    A girl discovers that her impoverished family is rich in things that matter in life, especially being outdoors and experiencing nature.
    Irony: The girl questions her parents' lifestyle. "They don't mind planting fields of sweet corn or alfalfa. They like to pick chiles and squash and tomatoes. They'll put up strong fences or train wild young horses." Her father asks, "How many people are as lucky as we are?" She laments they won't take jobs in a building somewhere in town where they could make more money, because their number-one rule is that they "have to see the sky." And looking out a window is not adequate. These people aren't sensible, she complains. They traveled all over to find the "most beautiful mountain" just so her first sight at birth would be that mountainside at sunrise. Strangely, "the truth is, I still like sunrise quite a lot." And, her

little brother was born at the place where the "ocean meets the jungle under a certain kind of purple-blue night sky and the exact green waves they like." Now, he can't decide whether his favorite animal is a dolphin or a whale. As the family totals up the value of the natural world around them, the girl realizes she must include "wandering in open country, alone, free as a lizard, not following trails, not having a plan, just turning whatever way the wind turns me." She decides "the cash part doesn't seem to matter anymore." She thought she was disgruntled with their lack of material success; she comes to realize she really prizes the way of life her family leads.

Other Devices: *Antihero, Aphorism, Foreshadowing, Paradox*

Art Style: Sweeping pen/ink watercolors on white spaces flow majestically in expressionistic celebration of nature.

Curriculum Tie-in: Geography (American Southwest), Literature (Parable)

Bradbury, Ray. *Switch on the Night.* Illus. by Leo and Diane Dillon. New York: Alfred A. Knopf, 1983.

A lonely little boy, who is afraid of the dark, is introduced to a whole new world by his new friend, a little girl.

Irony: As an unfortunate by-product of fearing the dark, the boy is deprived of friendships and the joy of playing outside in the evening with the other children in his neighborhood. When he is at last introduced to the delights of the world of nighttime, he experiences not only new pleasure with the special offerings of the dark, but is also able, finally, to live a normal child's life as he runs and plays happily with other children.

Other Devices: *Alliteration, Antithesis, Internal Rhyme, Metaphor, Motif, Paradox, Simile, Symbol*

Art Style: Surrealistic pastel drawings match the rhythmical text of this slightly magical, slightly scientific, and quite ethereal night world.

Curriculum Tie-in: Science (Astronomy), Social Science (Fears)

Camp, Lindsay. *Why?* Illus. by Tony Ross. New York: G.P. Putnam's Sons (Penguin Putnam Books for Young Readers), 1998.

Lily's constant "why" questions drive her father crazy until one day he discovers that questioning the way things are, can be a very good thing.

Irony: When the frightening day at the park with the invading space aliens is over, at Lily's bedtime her father promises he won't ever get cranky with her again for asking endless "why" questions. He says, "I was very proud of you in the park today" for doing what usually annoys him. She had asked the Thargons why they wanted to destroy earth. This caused them to think about their reasons, and to decide it wasn't doing them any good.

Other Devices: *Inference, Paradox, Serendipity, Understatement*

Art Style: Colored pencil cartoons illustrate the repetitious, rapid-fire questions from Lily, and the answers she receives, that make up Lily's day and the day of those who suffer her presence.
Curriculum Tie-in: Social Science (Family Relationships)

Carrick, Carol. *Big Old Bones*. Illus. by Donald Carrick. New York: Clarion Books, 1989.

Professor Potts discovers some old bones and puts them together in various ways until he is satisfied he has discovered a dinosaur that once ruled the earth.
Irony: "The head is too big," he pronounces as he puts together what he first calls a Triceratops. So, he goes back to the pile of remaining bones and tries again. This time he shudders. "It gives me bad dreams. Besides, the front legs are too small." He calls this effort Tyrannosaurus rex. "Wrong again," thinks the professor as he looks at his third try. "An animal this size could never walk the earth." He has called it Brontosaurus. He can't show all these failures to the reporters and scientists. Perhaps one more try and some skin around the bones. He enlists his wife's help with the sewing. They are at last pleased with the outcome. They call their "giant lizard" Tribrontosaurus rex, a composite animal. In the end the professor has rejected what was closest to reality for a final effort that does not resemble the bones of any actual animal.
Other Devices: *Understatement*
Art Style: Pen line and watercolor cartoons fit the early efforts of a nineteenth-century scientist trying to make sense of extinct animal life.
Curriculum Tie-in: Science (Paleontology)

*Cole, Brock. *Buttons*. New York: Farrar Straus Giroux, 2000.

When their father eats so much that he pops the buttons off his britches, each of his three daughters tries a different plan to find replacements.
Irony: The oldest daughter intends to parade up and down the Palace Bridge in her finest clothes. Surely a rich man will fall in love with her and ask her to be his wife. She will consent if he gives her all his buttons. What really occurs is that she is set upon by a band of ruffians, who tear her gown and steal her purse and tip her over the balustrade so that she falls headfirst into the river below. A barge hauler pulls her from the water and falls in love with her despite the duckweed in her hair. She accepts his proposal, forgetting all about the buttons. The second daughter disguises herself and joins the army in order to secure a uniform with many buttons. Before she can carry out her plan, the soldiers come under siege. In the battle a handsome ensign falls senseless from his horse. She tends his wounds. In the process of tearing off his garments, "many buttons were lost and destroyed, but who could think of buttons at a time like this?" The third daughter runs around a meadow, holding out her apron to catch any buttons that might fall from the sky. A cowherd observes her pretty legs

and discovers what she is trying to accomplish. He tells her to hold her apron out under the thickest leaves of a tree, and when she does, "a set of used trouser buttons fell into her apron." The father now has a set of buttons for his britches but, strangely, a certain bridegroom must hold up his own pants with a "bit of string."

Other Devices: *Aphorism, Inference, Pun, Tone*

Art Style: Pen/ink and watercolor combine in humorous cartoons that complement this lighthearted spoof on courtship and family duty.

Curriculum Tie-in: Literature (Fairy Tale)

*Cronin, Doreen. *Click, Clack, Moo Cows That Type.* Illus. by Betsy Lewin. New York: Simon & Schuster, 2000.

Farmer Brown's cows find a typewriter in the barn and start making demands that result in their going on strike when he refuses to give them what they want.

Irony: Farmer Brown thinks he is finished with his animals' aberrant behavior when he concludes negotiations with a promise to give the cows the electric blankets they demand in exchange for the typewriter that started all his grief. Unfortunately, a Pandora's box of trouble is just beginning. Other farm animals—the ducks—have observed and learned how to get what they want, too. The typewriter is now in their possession. New demands are being sent to Farmer Brown.

Other Devices: *Inference, Symbol*

Art Style: Lampblack watercolor overlaid by watercolor washes creates simple cartoons with striking perspectives that illustrate the developing agreements.

Curriculum Tie-in: Economics (Unions)

*Deedy, Carmen Agra. *The Yellow Star: The Legend of King Christian X of Denmark.* Illus. by Henri Sorensen. Atlanta: Peachtree, 2000.

King Christian must abide by Nazi orders regarding the wearing of the identifying yellow star, but he must also protect all the Danes from harm.

Irony: It seems impossible to protect the Jews and also abide by Nazi discrimination until the king realizes the best way to hide a star-wearing Jew would be among all the citizenry. He first wears a yellow star as an example. Quickly all Danes grasp the message and also wear a yellow star. The symbol of division and shame backfires in Denmark. A hateful symbol of injustice is turned into a symbol of solidarity and, thus, an impotent weapon against Jewry.

Other Devices: *Antithesis, Aphorism, Atmosphere, Foreshadowing, Inference, Paradox, Parallelism, Pun, Simile, Symbol, Theme*

Art Style: Impressionistic oil paintings accompany the spare, terse text in this vignette showing the political reality of the Danes' circumstances during a very somber historical period.

> **Curriculum Tie-in**: History (World War II—Nazi Occupation—Denmark), Literature (Legend), Social Science (Values)

DePaola, Tomie. *The Art Lesson.* New York: G.P. Putnam's Sons, 1989.

Having learned to be creative in drawing pictures at home, young Tommy is dismayed when he goes to school and finds the art lesson there much more regimented.

> **Irony:** Tommy "couldn't wait to go to kindergarten." School means art lessons. Then he discovers the terrible truth. "Oh, you won't have your art lessons until next year." He is allowed to paint, but "it wasn't much fun." The paint quality is poor. The paper gets wrinkly. The paint cracks and flakes off. Tommy looks forward to next year. He has a new box of sixty-four crayons. He's ready for his art lessons. Then he finds out he can't use his wonderful colors. He has to use the school box of eight. And though he is to practice with them, he mustn't peel off the paper or wear down the points, because they are school property. Finally, he discovers he is to copy the art teacher's drawing. "Real artists don't copy." How sad! The thing that he looks forward to most about school becomes his greatest disappointment.
>
> **Other Devices:** *Atmosphere, Flash-forward, Inference, Parallelism, Serendipity, Theme*
>
> **Art Style:** Blocky pastel cartoons follow the fortunes and budding development of a young artist in a conformist world.
>
> **Curriculum Tie-in**: Social Science (Individuality)

Ernst, Lisa Campbell. *Goldilocks Returns.* New York: Simon & Schuster Books for Young Readers, 2000.

Fifty years after Goldilocks first met the three bears, she returns to fix up their cottage and soothe her guilty conscience.

> **Irony:** Though her intentions are honorable, the mature Goldi fails to right the wrongs of her past encounter with the bear family. Instead of making up for the messes she caused as a child, she succeeds only in making matters worse. She tosses out the food they like and replaces it with things they dislike. She tries to cobble up the chair she broke and messes with the others. She makes their beds uncomfortable, and she forces her décor on them. "A growl began to grow in Papa Bear's throat." Goldi doesn't notice. She hugs them and leaves, thinking she has at last wiped out her childhood debt. The bears are left traumatized—again.
>
> **Other Devices:** *Allusion, Antihero, Connotation, Flash-forward, Inference, Parallelism, Tone, Understatement*
>
> **Art Style:** Large bulky, cartoons reflect the story's original atmosphere intended for young listeners, while the language and picture complexity expand the interest level for more savvy audiences.

Fearnley, Jan. *Mr. Wolf's Pancakes.* Waukesha, WI: Little Tiger Press, 1999.
When Mr. Wolf seeks help from his neighbors about how to make pancakes, he is rudely rebuffed and must rely upon his own efforts.
> **Irony:** In this story it is the wolf who initially gets treated badly by the "good" characters. Mr. Wolf willingly offers to share with his neighbors if they will help him make his pancakes. But they rudely refuse, arriving only when they smell the delicious pancake aroma. They force their way inside to take what they want. What is a wolf to do? He shrugs, and follows them all into the kitchen. They could have shared companionship and a delicious meal with him; instead, they become part of his meal.
> **Other Devices:** *Allusion, Antihero, Black Humor, Poetic Justice, Stereotype*
> **Art Style:** Detailed cartoons in pen/ink and watercolor drawings delight the reader not only with only the story in progress but also with humorous nods to many Mother Goose rhymes and fairy-tale personalities.
> **Curriculum Tie-in:** Social Science (Conduct and Behavior)

Fitzpatrick, Marie-Louise. *Lizzy and Skunk.* New York: DK Ink, 2000.
When Lizzy's favorite puppet is lost, she overcomes her fears to find him.
> **Irony:** Skunk tells Lizzy that "Life is wonderful." Lizzy replies that it is scary, too. She uses her skunk puppet as a talisman the way Dumbo the big-eared baby circus elephant used a feather to enable him to fly. With Skunk on her hand, she is less fearful about the dark and spiders and making mistakes. But when Skunk becomes lost and then is found high in a tree, saving him becomes her first concern. Suddenly, she can climb a tree easily. Her newfound self-confidence is exhilarating. "Life is wonderful," she pronounces. "But scary, too," Skunk replies. Now it is the once-timid Izzy who tells Skunk not to worry. She can take care of him.
> **Other Devices:** *Parallelism, Personification*
> **Art Style:** Appealingly revealing watercolor cartoons support this tale of emerging self-esteem.
> **Curriculum Tie-in:** Social Science (Fears, Self-esteem)

*Gralley, Jean. *Hogula, Dread Pig of Night.* New York: Henry Holt, 1999.
Although he lives high on the hog in his castle on Grimy Pork Chop Hill, Hogula is unhappy because he has no friends—until he meets Elvis Ann, Dread Queen of Kissyface.
> **Irony:** When the "tempting bit of mortal" turns up on his doorstep, Hogula intends to snort her neck. Meanwhile Elvis Ann is thinking they will "make a perfect team." She intends to kissyface him. Each expects to use the other, and each finds that a sort of friendship is possible between them, as long as they swear off their obnoxious behavior toward each other.
> **Other Devices:** *Alliteration, Allusion, Antihero, Aphorism, Cliché, Foreshadowing, Inference, Poetic Justice, Pun, Simile, Stereotype, Understatement*
> **Art Style:** Appropriately repulsive expressionistic cartoons in gouache and ink on watercolor paper develop the characters of this humorously

gentle Dracula-style relationship.
Curriculum Tie-in: Social Science (Friendship)

Henkes, Kevin. *Wemberly Worried.* Greenwillow Books (HarperCollins), 2000.
A mouse named Wemberly, who worries about everything, finds that she has a whole list of things to worry about when she faces the first day of nursery school.
Irony: Wemberly and her new nursery school friend share things in common and have a very good time. Before she realizes it, the first day is over and the teacher is inviting the students to come back tomorrow. Wemberly says, "I will. Don't worry." Look who is telling someone else not to worry!
Other Devices: *Antithesis, Cliché, Parallelism, Pun*
Art Style: Watercolor and black pen cartoons with sidebar comments delightfully enhance the rhythmic text.
Curriculum Tie-in: Social Science (Fears)

Hoban, Russell. *Trouble on Thunder Mountain.* Illus. by Quentin Blake. New York: Orchard Books (Grolier), 2000.
When Megafright International flattens their beautiful mountain to put up a hi-tech plastic theme park, the O'Saurus family uses faith and lots of Monsta-Gloo to put things right.
Irony: A real mountain exists that would make a suitable tourist attraction. But the developer wants, instead, to take it down and erect a plastic imitation mountain in its place. When the fake mountain is finished, people say it looks like a plastic mountain. They prefer the restored dirt mountain. They don't mind the picnic ants or the creepy crawly things that the developer was trying to eliminate by erecting a clean, tidy, plastic mountain. Even the intended Tunnel of Terror is pronounced "boring." The developer has spent time and money creating something that was much better in its natural state.
Other Devices: *Aphorism, Connotation, Foreshadowing, Hyperbole, Poetic Justice, Satire, Understatement*
Art Style: Humorous pen/ink watercolor cartoons spiritedly produce a funny tribute to old-fashioned ingenuity and to nature.
Curriculum Tie-in: Science (Ecology)

Hopkinson, Deborah. *A Band of Angels: A Story Inspired by the Jubilee Singers.* Illus. by Raul Colón. New York: Atheneum Books for Young Readers (Simon & Schuster), 1999.
The daughter of a slave forms a gospel singing group and goes on tour to raise money to save Fisk University.
Irony: When the black singers try to sing "white" songs to a white audience, they have trouble filling theaters. In frustrated desperation they tentatively turn to their own freedom songs from the days of slavery. Surprisingly, "they could feel everyone in the hall leaning forward to listen." When they

finish, "the hall erupted with shouts and cheers and applause." From that moment on, "they were invited to sing for thousands of people all over the United States and Europe." Singing songs from their own culture brings white paying crowds to their concerts. These Fisk students raise money to renovate their school but are so busy they never return to finish their own education and graduate from the school they preserved.

Other Devices: *Antithesis, Foreshadowing, Simile*

Art Style: Watercolor/pencil expressionistic muted lines and shades of brown, yellow, and green with scratch lines illustrate the contrasts of loss and hope in this grand success story.

Curriculum Tie-in: History (Black Culture)

Johnson, Angela. *Down the Winding Road.* Illus. by Shane Evans. New York: DK Ink, 2000.

The annual summer visit to the country home of the Old Ones, the uncles and aunts who raised Daddy, brings joy and good times.

Irony: The Old Ones offer the same hospitality every visit: a family meal and a walk to the lake and the same old family stories. Yet, these city children can't wait to leave behind the highway and go down the winding road where there are no people except the Old Ones. For one afternoon every summer the city family steps back into the enfolding lives of these simple old folks who offer nothing but all their devotion. When they arrive, the Old Ones line up to welcome them. When they leave, the Old Ones line up to "wave us away to the city, and we are already missing them."

Other Devices: *Anachronism, Atmosphere, Inference*

Art Style: In expressionistic pen/ink and oil painting, the gentle loving life of a caring family is made enviously believable.

Curriculum Tie-in: Social Science (Family Relationships)

*Johnson, D.B. *Henry Hikes to Fitchburg.* Boston: Houghton Mifflin, 2000.

While his friend works hard to earn train fare to Fitchburg, young Henry Thoreau walks the thirty miles through woods and fields, enjoying nature.

Irony: Whose method will win the bet and bring arrival to Fitchburg first? While Henry enjoys a leisurely amble, complete with a swim and a taste of honey from a hive, his friend earns train fare by sweeping out the post office, painting the courthouse fence, filling a wood box, and even cleaning out Mrs. Thoreau's chicken house. Her own son is off amusing himself while the mother must pay an outsider to do her chores! Henry loses the bet by a few minutes, but he's had more fun arriving at Fitchburg than his friend, who spent his day unhappily engaged in drudgery to earn a few coins to ride on a crowded, uncomfortable train.

Other Devices: *Allusion, Paradox, Theme, Understatement*

Art Style: Colored pencil and acrylic paint in stylishly simple, expressionistic designs contrast interesting visual perspectives and provide period detail.
Curriculum Tie-in: Literature (Henry David Thoreau), Philosophy (Quality of Life)

Keller, Holly. *That's Mine, Horace.* New York: Greenwillow Books (HarperCollins), 2000.

Horace loves the little yellow truck that he finds in the school yard, but he has a problem when a classmate tries to claim it.

Irony: Horace discovers that the delight he takes in the special truck is ruined when he lies about owning it. He becomes ill thinking how disappointed those who love him will be when they discover the truth. Having the truck he desires has not made Horace happy.

Other Devices: *Parallelism, Serendipity*

Art Style: The simple, stylized watercolor and black pen cartoons focus on the important elements of this emotional situation as a child learns to value his character more than a toy.

Curriculum Tie-in: Social Science (Values)

Kitamura, Satoshi. *Me and My Cat?* New York: Farrar Straus Giroux, 2000.

A young boy spends an unusual day after awakening to find that he and his cat have switched bodies.

Irony: A witch comes into Nicholas's room, and the next morning life becomes peculiar. For the first time, Nicholas (in his cat's body) can observe the morning routine he and his mother go through to get him to school every day. After she drags him from bed, she hauls him to the bathroom and makes him wash and dress. "Downstairs she interrupted my breakfast. She was furious." Nicholas in the cat's body watches the cat in his body behave like the cat it really is. The boy-cat has opened a tin of cat food and is, of course, eating it out of the cat's dish, sticking his face directly into the bowl. Nicholas begins to develop a bit of empathy for his mother and for his pet cat. That evening the witch pays a second visit. It was all a mistake. Wrong house. At last, the spell is off, and things return to normal for Nicholas and for his cat, Leonardo. But at school that morning something peculiar, but familiar, happens. "Mr. McGough sat on the table. He scratched himself, licked his shirt, and fell asleep for the rest of the lesson."

Other Devices: *Antithesis, Inference, Parallelism, Point of View, Understatement*

Art Style: Busy, hilarious, acrylic cartoons detail the daily life of a boy's thoughts in a cat's body as he watches a cat's activities in his boy's body.

Curriculum Tie-in: Social Science (Animal Companions, Values)

Krensky, Stephen. *The Youngest Fairy Godmother Ever.* Illus. by Diana Cain Bluthenthal. New York: Simon & Schuster Books for Young Readers, 2000.

Mavis tries to pursue her goal of playing fairy godmother and granting wishes to those around her, but she finds the process trickier than she thought.

Irony: While Mavis is desperate to discover someone to whom she can grant a wish, her patient dog sets an assortment of toys before her and holds his walking leash in his mouth, hopeful for some attention. She is busy searching for a chance to grant a wish, and misses an obvious one. She pops up among piles of boxes in a store display, upsetting them and creating, not the answer to someone's wishes, but rather a nightmare to clean up. The same thing occurs in her classroom when she tries to turn the pet mouse into a coachman, like in the fairy tale. Another mess is all she accomplishes as Hector Mouse runs around the room. When her friend Cindy remarks that she needs a costume for Halloween, Mavis tries the magic wand first, but the results are not satisfactory. Next, she hunches over a sewing machine, finally granting her friend's wish the old-fashioned way, by hard labor.

Other Devices: *Allusion, Understatement*

Art Style: A mix of inks and paints produces lively cartoons that complement the wry humor in this funny tale of determination to succeed.

Curriculum Tie-in: Social Science (Values)

Lamstein, Sarah Marwil. *I Like Your Buttons!* Illus. by Nancy Cote. Morton Grove, IL: Albert Whitman & Co., 1999.

When a little girl compliments her teacher about the buttons on her outfit, it starts a chain reaction of goodwill, good deeds, and thoughtfulness throughout the day.

Irony: Cassandra's innocent, heartfelt compliment turns out not only to please a lot of others but to please her, too. By day's end, her father, one of the recipients of an act of goodwill, feels kindly about a stray kitten that hangs around the restaurant where he works. He decides to bring it home to his daughter. She is delighted with her gift and has no idea that, inadvertently, she set things in motion that resulted in her receiving it.

Other Devices: *Serendipity, Theme*

Art Style: Acrylic, gouache, and watercolor pencil cartoons emphasize happy faces that express the joy of having been recipients of simple compliments.

Curriculum Tie-in: Social Science (Values)

*Mamet, David. *Henrietta.* Illus. by Elizabeth Dahlie. Boston: Houghton Mifflin, 1999.

Henrietta Pig, rebuffed by the law school admissions office, like so many of her underprivileged kind before her, wanders aimlessly until a chance encounter with a vagabond philosopher enables her to pursue her dream of a scholarly future.

Irony: The school "could neither admit nor acknowledge her." She has no credentials. She has nothing but an "honest and inquiring mind." So the "school had no time for Henrietta." Even her efforts to attend classes without being on the class roll are "discovered one too many times." She is ejected and barred as a nuisance. But when she is finally legitimized by the institution's president as a bonafide student, and when she distinguishes herself in a brilliant career, "her accomplishments, of course, have been claimed by the School and the City."

Other Devices: *Inference, Personification, Pun, Satire, Serendipity, Tone*

Art Style: Spare pastel crayon impressionistic cartoons highlight the foibles of higher education's entrenched, shortsighted traditions through subtle, playful satire.

Curriculum Tie-in: Literature (Fable), Social Science (Diversity)

*Martin, Nora. *The Stone Dancers.* Illus. by Jill Kastner. New York: Atheneum Books for Young Readers (Simon & Schuster), 1995.

A young girl uses an old legend about stone dancers to teach her mountain village a lesson in hospitality and sharing.

Irony: Thanks to their ancestors the villagers have lived comfortably over the generations secure from persecutions. The old ones welcomed and accepted strangers. Now, it is the turn of their descendents to welcome oppressed peoples from a distant land. How will they react? They notice that the strangers do not look like them. They notice the strangers are dirty. They might be insane, since they are saying the mountain is calling out to them. "They could be dangerous." The villagers' forefathers knew rejection and offered refuge. But today's villagers have known only acceptance and offer rejection.

Other Devices: *Aphorism, Imagery, Inference, Metaphor, Parallel Story, Simile*

Art Style: Impressionistic oil paintings show the interplay of light and shadow, melding the real with the enchanted in this nineteenth-century French peasant village.

Curriculum Tie-in: History (Nineteenth-Century France), Social Science (Values)

*Meddaugh, Susan. *Hog-Eye.* New York: Walter Lorraine Books (Houghton Mifflin), 1995.

A young pig uses her ability to read to outwit a wolf that intends to eat her.

Irony: A young pig doesn't like her daily bus ride to school because the kids are so awful. Yet after her misadventure the day before, when she dawdled and missed her bus and then got lost after riding another bus, she is anxious to brag to everyone about her day. "Today I beat my brother to the corner."

Other Devices: *Allusion, Antithesis, Flashback, Foreshadowing, Hyperbole, Inference, Understatement*

Art Style: Split-page watercolor cartoons tell the "true story" of a schoolchild who dislikes her daily bus ride.

Curriculum Tie-in: Literature (Tall Tale)

Morimoto, Junko. *The Two Bullies.* Trans. by Isao Morimoto. New York: Crown (Random House), 1997.

Two bullies, one from China and one from Japan, inadvertently intimidate one another before meeting face to face, and never fight for supremacy as a result.

Irony: Ni-ou from Japan decides to challenge the other strong man, Dokkoi, from China. As Ni-ou waits for him to come home, he hears Dokkoi's earthquake-sounding footsteps "from miles away" and thinks he has "no chance of winning." He runs off and gets in his boat to paddle back to Japan. Upon arriving home, the Chinese strong man learns of Ni-ou's departure and rushes after the coward, flinging an anchor toward his boat. It catches the boat in the stern. He begins hauling it back to shore. But Ni-ou uses a file given to him by a priest and quickly saws through the anchor chain. He considers himself fortunate to have escaped the Chinese bully. Meanwhile, back in China, Dokkoi sighs with relief and assesses the situation differently. "How amazing to see him rip that chain apart—it's lucky I didn't fight him!" Both think the other too powerful to have been beaten.

Other Devices: *Serendipity*

Art Style: Gouache and pastel expressionistic cartoons humorously point out the pomposity of these two typical bullies.

Curriculum Tie-in: Literature (Folktales—Japan), Social Science (Bullies)

*Morrison, Toni with Slade Morrison. *The Big Box.* Illus. by Giselle Potter. New York: Hyperion, 1999.

To make three unique youngsters conform to their rules, grown-ups create a world inside a box, including treats and simulated nature, but all the kids really want is the freedom to be themselves.

Irony: The adults believe the children can't handle freedom because they don't follow adult-provided rules. While the adults are saying one thing, they are acting another. "You're a wonderful child and we really don't want to remove you." "You're an awfully nice kid with a wonderful future before you." "You're an awfully sweet girl with a lot of potential inside you." But "with a pat on the cheek," "a knowing smile," and "an understanding hug," into the box they all go. They are provided everything they need: a Princess phone and a jar of genuine dirt, an autographed basketball and a record that plays exactly the sound made by a living seagull. They have stuffed duck prepared by a restaurant cook and a film of a fresh running brook. The adults in their world are trying to correct problems the children do not have and are making problems that did not exist.

Other Devices: *Antithesis, Inference, Internal Rhyme, Oxymoron, Satire, Theme*

Art Style: Naïve watercolors show the contrast between the joy expressed naturally by the children in their simple outdoor amusements and the cloying dissatisfaction with adult-provided, commercial rubbish.

Curriculum Tie-in: Social Science (Values)

*Myers, Tim. *Basho and the Fox.* Illus. by Oki S. Han. New York: Marshall Cavendish, 2000.

A Japanese poet is challenged by a fox to create his best haiku.

Irony: Basho shares his best poems with the fox, and they are rejected. Even the fox kits can do better, he is told. "I had no idea foxes were such magnificent poets!" Finally, facing a deadline to produce, he dashes off a last-minute haiku. "It's not really a good one, he thought, but at least it's something." He is shocked when the fox is ecstatically pleased. What makes this one great? "This one has a fox in it!"—which is the only criterion of greatness that interests the foxes.

Other Devices: *Ambiguity, Antithesis, Aphorism, Imagery, Motif, Parallelism, Theme*

Art Style: Mischievous watercolor folk paintings convey the Eastern sensibility of feudal Japan.

Curriculum Tie-in: History (Japan), Social Science (Self-esteem)

O'Malley, Kevin. *Bud.* New York: Walker & Company, 2000.

The orderly Sweet-Williams are dismayed at their son's fondness for the messy pastime of gardening.

Irony: Bud's irrepressible gardening instincts are barely tolerated by his loving parents. His grandfather, they are certain, will never accept such messy activities. They do everything possible to shield Grandfather from sight of the yard when he visits. Then a storm intervenes. Grandfather sees the devastation that upsets Bud. He also notes the care with which Bud had created his garden. And he is especially touched when he discovers Bud is raising the same kind of roses his wife loved to grow. Instead of criticizing Bud's disorderly gardening passion, he joins Bud in the garden's restoration. Change, he proclaims, is inevitable!

Other Devices: *Antithesis, Aphorism, Foreshadowing, Inference, Pun, Theme, Understatement*

Art Style: Large, expressive gouache cartoons lovingly follow the development of tolerance, respect, and appreciation for a beloved child's unconventional approach to life.

Curriculum Tie-in: Science (Gardening), Social Science (Family Relationships, Values)

*Pacilio, V.J. *Ling Cho and His Three Friends.* Illus. by Scott Cook. New York: Farrar Straus Giroux, 2000.

> Through his plan to share the wealth of his wheat crop with three friends, a Chinese farmer teaches the importance of allowing other people to help in time of need.
>
> **Irony:** None of the three friends has any coins to share with Ling Cho after having taken to market the load of wheat each has been entrusted to sell for him. Two have clearly invented stories of woe to account for their failure to show up with payment. But, rather than accuse them of theft, Ling Cho plays along with their fabricated tales. He tells one he feels responsible for the ordeal he has undergone with the dragon that ate up the load of wheat. He assures the friend that such a thing will not happen next year at harvest time. "I shall not request your help. I'm too afraid that frightful beast might choose to reappear. I'll not be a party to your premature demise." And so the friend will have no chance to abscond with any more of Ling Cho's earnings. The second friend talks of a hole in the pocket that contained Ling Cho's share of the wheat sale profit. "If you had not sold my wheat at marketplace that day, no golden coins would you have had to lose along the way. And rest assured, you have my word, it won't occur again. That fate, once more, might be unkind is truly what I fear. Your friendship means much more to me than any coins of gold. I'll not chance that guilt and shame might turn that friendship cold." Ling Cho won't be asking this friend to sell wheat for him again. The third man kept the wheat for his starving family. Ling Cho pretends anger. "To justify what you have done with wheat you were to sell. To marketplace you were to go, but home you went instead." Therefore, this friend must work off his debt by helping Ling Cho plant, tend crops, and harvest. When all tasks are complete, "You shall receive, as just reward, two wagonloads of wheat." The first is for his consumption and the second is to sell at marketplace. The two friends he pretends to sympathize with receive no second chance. The one he appears to scold receives with his admonishment an opportunity to retain his pride and a better life for his family.
>
> **Other Devices:** *Alliteration, Aphorism, Paradox, Poetic Justice, Theme*
>
> **Art Style:** Impressionistic oil paintings in Chinese reds and golds suggest unstated meanings behind spoken words.
>
> **Curriculum Tie-in:** Social Science (Friendship, Values)

Ruurs, Margriet. *Emma and the Coyote.* Illus. by Barbara Spurll. New York: Stoddart Kids, 1999.

> Emma thinks chickens are smarter than coyotes, and she struts boldly where no chicken should go to prove it.
>
> **Irony:** Emma takes personal risks to draw the family's attention to the coyote. They respond by chasing it away, but warn her that a coyote is smarter than a chicken. She is flirting with danger. Emma doesn't get the

message. She foolishly continues to confront the enemy. Finally, after a particularly close call, even she realizes that only by the merest accident did she escape the jaws of the coyote. Though she will not admit an error of judgment, she is ready to retreat in dignity. Then she falls out of the magnolia tree and lands on the coyote. She pecks him hard on the backside, and, in surprise, he jumps forward into the trap he would never have walked into otherwise. The family is amazed. They think this was all Emma's planned strategy. "Well, what do you know, some chickens are smarter than coyotes!" they conclude.

Other Devices: *Alliteration, Foreshadowing, Imagery, Inference, Motif, Parallelism, Serendipity, Simile*

Art Style: Bright primary color paintings expressionistically follow the fortunes of Emma and the barnyard animals.

Curriculum Tie-in: Social Science (Self-esteem)

Sierra, Judy. *The Gift of the Crocodile: A Cinderella Story.* Illus. by Reynold Ruffins. New York: Simon and Schuster Books for Young Readers, 2000.

Damura of the Spice Islands escapes her cruel stepmother and stepsister, and marries a handsome prince, with the help of Grandmother Crocodile.

Irony: The stepsister wants a lovely sarong like the one Damura received as a gift from Grandmother Crocodile. But the river creature is not fooled by the greedy girl's tale of having lost her own sarong. "Give it to me!" she shouts. As she wraps it around her waist, "instantly it became a filthy rag swarming with leeches." And it sticks to her like glue. Later, the stepmother and daughter, in an effort to get the prince to marry the stepdaughter, devise a plan to try to get rid of Damura by taking her into the river and pushing her overboard. They come back saying, "A crocodile has swallowed her!" But, in the end, Damura is revived and invited to enjoy the river in safety. Grandmother Crocodile commands her relatives, "But if you see her stepmother or stepsister, you must eat them at once!" The two are forced to run into the "darkest part of the forest never to be seen again."

Other Devices: *Foreshadowing, Motif, Poetic Justice, Pun*

Art Style: Folk images painted in bright acrylics portray this Indonesian version of an international folktale.

Curriculum Tie-in: Literature (Folktale)

Steig, William. *Wizzil.* Illus. by Quentin Blake. New York: Farrar Straus Giroux, 2000.

A bored witch causes trouble when she decides to take revenge on an old man, but her mischief leads to a happy ending.

Irony: The witch, Wizzil, intends to "give him [De Witt] the works" for nearly "doing her in" when she had turned herself into a fly. She turns herself into a glove so that she can irritate him. But her plan goes awry. Wizzil and DeWitt end up falling in love. He flings the offending glove into a stream. Turned back into a witch, she "thrashed, gurgled, sputtered, and spat, and then she started to sink." DeWitt dives in and saves her life. She smiles her gratitude; he finds himself "hugging a surprisingly sweet old lady." They wind up "an old married couple who stayed on the farm."

Other Devices: *Alliteration, Ambiguity, Connotation, Foreshadowing, Internal Rhyme, Serendipity, Tone*

Art Style: Delightfully awful watercolor cartoons capture the personalities and behaviors of the rotten witch and the hillbilly family she pesters.

Curriculum Tie-in: Social Science (Love)

*Van Allsburg, Chris. *The Sweetest Fig.* Boston: Houghton Mifflin, 1993.

After being given two magical figs that make his dreams come true, Monsieur Bibot sees his plans for future wealth upset by his long-suffering dog.

Irony: Bibot discovers after eating one of the figs that it causes dreams to come true. Having wasted the first fig, he carefully prepares himself for the dreams he will have before he eats the remaining fig. It takes weeks to convince his psyche that he is rich so that his dreams will show him to be rich and then his dreams will come true. "Tomorrow he would wake up the richest man in the world. He looked down at Marcel and smiled. The little dog would not be coming along." A Great Dane would be more fitting. He is ready to eat the fig. But, when he turns his back to get some cheese, "he heard the crash of breaking china." He turns around in time to "see Marcel standing on a chair with his front paws on the table, chewing the last of the fig." Now it will be Marcel's dreams that come true.

Other Devices: *Inference, Poetic Justice*

Art Style: Pastel sepia-tone realistic illustrations show the just deserts of a self-serving dentist and his abused dog.

*Wilkon, Piotr. *Rosie the Cool Cat.* Illus. by Jozef Wilkon. New York: Viking (Penguin Books), 1989.

Casper and Carolina are proud of their jet-black fur and despair trying to cope with their orange kitten, who likes to play with mice and sleep in the doghouse.

Irony: Rosie has interests and behaviors that do not mesh with her family's values. Her parents despair. Then Rosie grows up and has kittens of her own. She is frustrated, because one of them "does everything differently from his sisters and brothers." Her father, meanwhile, has mellowed. "Now he only thinks about his grandchildren." They are perfect, of course.

Other Devices: *Antithesis, Foreshadowing, Inference, Poetic Justice, Satire, Stereotype, Symbol*

Art Style: Pastel and colored pencil expressionistic cartoons capture the family pride in its uniqueness as well as its sense of frustration in the jolting difference of the odd one.

Curriculum Tie-in: Social Science (Family Relationships, Individuality, Values)

*Wisniewski, David. *Golem.* New York: Clarion Books (Houghton Mifflin), 1996 (Caldecott—1997).

A saintly rabbi miraculously brings to life a clay giant who helps him watch over the Jews of sixteenth-century Prague.

Irony: The clay giant loves life but is returned to clay because he faithfully fulfilled his duty. " 'Please!' Golem cried. 'Please let me live! I did all that you asked of me! Life is so . . . precious . . . to me!' With that, he collapsed into clay." When the Jews are safe he no longer has a reason to exist. By doing well he has lost that which he cherishes most dearly.

Other Devices: *Analogy, Atmosphere, Foreshadowing, Imagery, Inference, Motif, Paradox, Simile*

Art Style: Paper cut in sophisticated, expressionistic collage produces a powerful physical and emotional effect for this cautionary tale.

Curriculum Tie-in: Literature (Legend), Social Science (Values)

*Yaccarino, Dan. *Deep in the Jungle.* New York: Anne Schwartz Book from Atheneum Books for Young Readers (Simon & Schuster), 2000.

After being tricked into joining the circus, an arrogant lion escapes and returns to the jungle, where he lives peacefully with the animals he used to terrorize.

Irony: Though used to commanding obedience from his fellow jungle animals, the lion willingly becomes submissive to the man when he thinks he shall become a famous circus star. He lowers his head for a leash. He walks into a cage and a gate slams shut on him. He performs tricks (though not the one he wanted to do), but the man gets all the applause. Disillusioned, he returns to the jungle in time to see more animals being loaded in circus wagons. While they hurl insults at him, for his prior behavior toward them, he swallows his pride and secures their freedom. Finally, with an appreciative audience at last, he performs for the animals the famous roar that he had hoped to be able to do in the circus and receives, at last, the accolade he desires.

Other Devices: *Anachronism, Antihero, Antithesis, Black Humor, Foreshadowing, Motif, Parallelism, Poetic Justice, Pun, Tone*

Art Style: Expressionistic gouache naïve cartoons against white backgrounds, reminiscent of the "Curious George" series, accent the droll language in this lesson in humility.

Curriculum Tie-in: Literature (Parable), Social Science (Values)

Zagwÿn, Deborah. *Apple Batter.* Berkeley, CA: Tricycle Press, 1999.

Because of their persistence, Delmore succeeds in learning to hit a baseball and his mother, Loretta, succeeds in growing apples.

Irony: Delmore can't hit a ball where he wants it to go, but it is getting faster and going forward now. Loretta can't get apples to grow on her trees, but there is one apple there. Delmore finally hits the ball toward the last thing he has focused his eyes on. He never thinks the ball would hit the apple. It does. Of all times to learn to focus and of all things to focus upon, the ball connects with the only apple Loretta had left on the tree. "What accuracy, Delmore," she says. "One apple for the future, and you hit it squarely and fairly off the tree!"

Other Devices: *Alliteration, Analogy, Antithesis, Foreshadowing, Inference, Parallelism, Pun, Simile*

Art Style: Expressionistic watercolor cartoons compare the changing fortunes of mother and son as they struggle toward their respective goals.

Curriculum Tie-in: Athletics (Baseball), Science (Apple Production)

METAPHOR

An implicit comparison between one thing as described in terms of another.

Example: Fog becomes a cat in the Carl Sandburg poem "Fog."
> The fog comes
> On little cat feet.
> It sits looking
> over harbor and city
> on silent haunches
> And then moves on.

Bradbury, Ray. *Switch on the Night.* Illus. by Leo and Diane Dillon. New York: Alfred A. Knopf, 1983.

A lonely little boy, who is afraid of the dark, is introduced to a whole new world by his new friend, a little girl.

Metaphor: The little girl told the boy, "Heaven is a house with porch lights . . . ." She said that switching on the dark allowed "Night to live in every room."

Other Devices: *Alliteration, Antithesis, Internal Rhyme, Irony, Motif, Paradox, Simile, Symbol*

Art Style: Surrealistic pastel drawings match the rhythmical text of this slightly magical, slightly scientific, and quite ethereal night world.

Curriculum Tie-in: Science (Astronomy), Social Science (Fears)

Carlstrom, Nancy. *Goodbye, Geese.* Illus. by Ed Young. New York: Philomel (Putnam Books), 1991.

A father describes the coming of winter to his little girl.

Metaphor: Winter is depicted as a person whose fingers touch every living thing with a frosty grip that "will tire the flowers" and put the garden to bed with a white blanket. Winter walks in through cracks rather than by turning a doorknob. Winter dances on top of the roof, stopping only to watch the stars and, with an icy stare, freezes rivers and ponds. Winter's body blocks out the sun and wraps us in swirling white. Winter listens to the beating wings and honking of geese flying south. When winter hears the geese leaving, winter comes.

Other Devices: *Simile*

Art Style: Glowing, misty chalk pastels in expressionistic, full-page illustrations suggest the effects of autumn changing into winter.

Curriculum Tie-in: Science (Seasons)

Givens, Terryl. *Dragon Scales and Willow Leaves.* Illus. by Andrew Portwood. New York: G.P. Putnam's Sons, 1997.

Although they are twins, Jonathan and Rachel neither look the same nor see things the same way—especially in the forest.

Metaphor: Jonathan slashes through the air with his sword, "striking and stabbing until the air was full of fluttering dragon scales." Rachel watches the leaves of a weeping willow softly float down, "making a colored carpet that shimmered and rustled in the breeze." When they reach the cornfield, they come upon "hundreds and thousands of tall figures with golden hair and suits of green." These Vikings are blocking their way through the cornfield.

Other Devices: *Alliteration, Antithesis, Imagery, Point of View, Simile*

Art Style: Impressionistic watercolor pictures expressionistically celebrate the varied ways we perceive our surroundings.

Curriculum Tie-in: Social Science (Individuality)

Hesse, Karen. *Come On, Rain!* Illus. by Jon J. Muth. New York: Scholastic Press, 1999.

A young girl eagerly awaits a coming rainstorm to bring relief from the oppressive summer heat.

Metaphor: When the girl sees rain clouds in the distance, "a creeper of hope circles 'round my bones." The smell of hot tar and garbage "bullies the air." The mother kneels over the "hot rump of a melon." Her friend Jackie-Joyce stands on her front steps with long legs that "sprout from her shorts." As the rain comes closer, the wind "grows bold and bolder." The first raindrops "plop down big, making dust dance all around us." Heavier rain "freckles our feet, glazes our toes." Soon everyone is laughing under "trinkets of silver rain."

Other Devices: *Alliteration, Foreshadowing, Hyperbole, Imagery, Paradox, Simile*

Art Style: Buoyant, ebullient expressionistic pen/ink watercolors lend emotional credibility to the nervous anxiety of relentless heat accompanied by worrisome drought, and the tremendous sense of relief that accompanies a thorough, nourishing rain.

Curriculum Tie-in: Science (Meteorology)

*Kaplan, Howard. *Waiting to Sing.* Illus. by Hervé Blondon. New York: DK Ink, 2000.

> A family who loves music and spends many hours at the piano is devastated by the death of the mother, but those still living find consolation in the beautiful music that remains.
>
> > **Metaphor:** The author describes the inside of the piano bench as "a hidden library that none of my friends knew about." The notes to the song he loves are "peeking over and below the margins." When he finally is able to turn back to piano playing after the death of his mother, he turns on the piano lamp, "and the light seemed to remember us. I felt as though we could quench our thirst on one bright drop."
> >
> > **Other Devices:** *Allusion, Antithesis, Aphorism, Atmosphere, Foreshadowing, Imagery, Inference, Parallelism, Simile, Symbol*
> >
> > **Art Style:** Shadowy, full-page sepia-tone pastel cartoons expressionistically evoke a fragile emotional period in the life of a family coping with restructuring itself after the wrenching loss of one of its members.
> >
> > **Curriculum Tie-in:** Music (Piano), Social Science (Death, Family Relationships, Feelings)

Kurtz, Jane. *Faraway Home.* Illus. by E.B. Lewis. New York: Gulliver Books (Harcourt), 2000.

> Desta's father, who needs to return briefly to his Ethiopian homeland, describes what it was like for him to grow up there.
>
> > **Metaphor:** In his youth, the father's family cooked over a fire "that lived in a scooped-out place in the middle of the floor." "Thousands of flamingos flap in a pink cloud over the Great Rift Valley lakes." His mother would show him that "sunsets were bright borders on the cloth of the evening sky. The moon and stars burned holes in the cloth to light the night." Desta can imagine the pink cloud of flamingos rippling up from a dark blue lake, "wrinkling the pale cloth of the evening sky."
> >
> > **Other Devices:** *Foreshadowing, Imagery, Simile*
> >
> > **Art Style:** Pen lines and watercolor expressionistic art capture the poignant reality immigrants face when they leave a beloved homeland for a new country.
> >
> > **Curriculum Tie-in:** Geography (Ethiopia), Social Science (Immigration—Ethiopia)

Kurtz, Jane. *River Friendly, River Wild.* Illus. by Neil Brennan. New York: Simon & Schuster Books for Young Readers, 2000.

> A family experiences a renewed appreciation for home and community after they are evacuated during a spring flood and then return to survey the damage.
>
> > **Metaphor:** The area before the flood is described as a "flat quilt" of the Red River Valley, "stitching North Dakota and Minnesota together." Spring "creeps into the city one toe at a time." The scene during the night

as refugees watch television, shows that "fire tongues lick the sky" during the burning of the downtown. When cleanup begins, "Every pile is someone's story." Inside the family's damaged home, they rummage among their belongings. "The paper dolls saw it all." Machinery comes to help pick up rubbish. "They call to each other in high yellow beeps." The family looks forward to getting their ruined things out of view. "I wish the machine with the mouth would get to our block and gobble all this garbage up."

Other Devices: *Antithesis, Aphorism, Atmosphere, Imagery, Onomatopoeia, Simile*

Art Style: Oil glaze of brown paint overlaid by thin layers of color in different areas and additional glazes for depth create fuzzy, impressionistic scenes that reflect the essence of this emotionally wrenching natural disaster.

Curriculum Tie-in: Geography (Flood—Grand Forks, North Dakota)

Lorbiecki, Marybeth. *Just One Flick of a Finger.* Illus. by David Diaz. New York: Dial (Penguin Putnam), 1996.

A young boy takes a gun to school to scare off the bully who has been tormenting him, and the gun is accidentally fired during the scuffle.

Metaphor: Sherms "has muscles where I have Twinkies." After the shooting accident the gun is referred to as a "killing machine." The prison where Sherms's brother is confined is "the old ice house" and "the pen."

Other Devices: *Antithesis, Foreshadowing, Inference, Internal Rhyme, Pun, Simile, Theme*

Art Style: Acrylics, watercolors, and digitally manipulated photographic backgrounds blend to create powerful, stylized expressionistic comic book images that evoke danger and tension.

Curriculum Tie-in: Social Science (Bullies)

Lyon, George Ella. *One Lucky Girl.* Illus. by Irene Trivas. New York: Dorling Kindersley, 2000.

Even though their trailer is destroyed by a tornado, a young boy's family is grateful because they find his baby sister alive.

Metaphor: The boy says of the impending tornado, "I could see a black finger of wind twisting toward us."

Other Devices: *Ambiguity, Antithesis, Foreshadowing, Imagery, Inference, Parallelism, Simile*

Art Style: Smudgy pastel illustrations impressionistically assist the story line through use of both dark and bright colors.

Curriculum Tie-in: Science (Tornadoes), Social Science (Family Relationships)

*Martin, Nora. *The Stone Dancers.* Illus. by Jill Kastner. New York: Atheneum Books for Young Readers (Simon & Schuster), 1995.

A young girl uses an old legend about stone dancers to teach her mountain village a lesson in hospitality and sharing.

>   **Metaphor:** "As moonlight shines between the clouds, she can see the stones unfurl long, heavy arms." These castle stones "rise on great stone legs and lift blank stone faces set on chiseled necks into the celestial light. Their boulder chests expand as they breathe in life. And after looking to one another as if in greeting, the huge bodies begin to dance." They "dance a caressing whisper dance, their long legs reaching in perfect honey slowness."
>
>   **Other Devices:** *Aphorism, Imagery, Inference, Irony, Parallel Story, Simile*
>
>   **Art Style:** Impressionistic oil paintings show the interplay of light and shadow, melding the real with the enchanted in this nineteenth-century French peasant village.
>
>   **Curriculum Tie-in:** History (Nineteenth-Century France), Literature (Legends), Social Science (Values)

Meggs, Libby Phillips. *Go Home! The True Story of James the Cat.* Morton Grove, IL: Albert Whitman, 2000.

A homeless cat spends several seasons trying to survive the elements until at last a suburban family adopts him.

>   **Metaphor:** One night a storm sent James running for cover under the people's shed. "Wind screamed, thunder shook the earth." At last, "the storm left, grumbling and snarling across the sky."
>
>   **Other Devices:** *Ambiguity, Antithesis, Connotation, Inference, Point of View, Simile*
>
>   **Art Style:** Realistic pastel illustrations follow James's admittance into a family that provides what has been missing in his life for a long time.
>
>   **Curriculum Tie-in:** Social Science (Animal Companions)

*Myers, Christopher. *Black Cat.* New York: Scholastic Press, 1999.

Black Cat ambles on an eye-opening journey of exploring feelings about identity, beauty, and home.

>   **Metaphor:** The city's "concrete creeps down our city streets." Black Cat listens to "brick music falling from project windows." Black Cat also hears the "quiet language of invisible trains." He lies on rooftop "hot tar beaches."
>
>   **Other Devices:** *Alliteration, Imagery, Internal Rhyme, Simile*
>
>   **Art Style:** Bold combination of collage, ink, and gouache with striking perspectives lends an intensity to the peculiarities of metro life.
>
>   **Curriculum Tie-in:** Art (Medium and Technique)

Preston, Tim. *The Lonely Scarecrow.* Illus. by Maggie Kneen. New York: Dutton Children's Books (Penguin Books), 1999.

A lonely scarecrow with a scary face has trouble making friends with the animals who surround him, until a heavy snowfall transforms him into a jolly snowman.

Metaphor: The "combine monster came to harvest the wheat. The animals hid from its churning jaws—and the ravaged acres of mud and stubble that it left behind." "From the north came a sly breeze that stole the leaves from the trees and the light from the days."
Other Devices: *Imagery, Inference, Paradox, Parallelism, Theme*
Art Style: Lavishly embossed, finely detailed watercolor and acrylic cartoons fondly render scenes of seasonal changes.
Curriculum Tie-in: Science (Seasons), Social Science (Friendship)

*Turner, Ann. *Red Flower Goes West*. Illus. by Dennis Nolan. New York: Hyperion Books for Children, 1999.
As they journey west, a family nurtures the red flower they have carried with them from their old home.
Metaphor: It is the narrator's sister who first personifies the flower as a beloved living being. "I bet this is the first red flower to cross this wide river. She's a traveler, like us." Though an Indian saves Pa's life in the river, "I know, too, that Red Flower helped somehow." Going down steep mountainsides requires careful control to avoid losing the wagon. After a particularly harrowing final slide down, the first thing the man asks his wife is, "How's your plant?" They all go to check on the plant's welfare. "Here she is!" they remark as they lift a pillow off it. Then they proceed, "patting that plant like it was an old dog."
Other Devices: *Connotation, Inference, Parallelism, Simile, Symbol*
Art Style: Soft crayon and pastel realistic drawings, mostly in shades of gray, depict a stern pioneer experience accented by the bright red beacon of the family's talisman.
Curriculum Tie-in: History (Westward Expansion)

Turner, Ann. *Secrets from the Dollhouse*. Illus. by Raúl Colón. New York: HarperCollins, 2000.
The life of a family of dolls and their servants living in a dollhouse in a young girl's room is told from the perspective of Emma, oldest of the doll children.
Metaphor: When the doll child finally has an adventure outside, "something fierce and cold blew my hair and clothes." "Tiny white handkerchiefs" fall from the sky. "When Girl talked, her words were clouds." She is left outside at night. Darkness is "floating down on the garden, catching on petals." Then "lights turned on in the sky and I saw they were pictures: someone dancing, a fish leaping, and a road."
Other Devices: *Foreshadowing, Imagery, Personification, Point of View, Simile*
Art Style: Stiff 1920s folk images in scratcher line pastels capture the whimsy of a toy world.

Waite, Judy. *Mouse, Look Out!* Illus. by Norma Burgin. New York: Dutton Children's Books (Penguin Putnam), 1998.

Inside an old, abandoned house a mouse searches for a safe place to hide from a cat.

Metaphor: The wind, like a menacing stranger, comes calling at the door, pounding, banging and bashing. It races through the drafty, derelict house. It wails through the kitchen, sweeping aside leaves and sticks. Then the wind climbs upstairs, "its soft breath" lingering in the room. Finally, the wind leaves the house.

Other Devices: *Alliteration, Atmosphere, Internal Rhyme, Poetic Justice, Simile*

Art Style: Realistic acrylic paintings in detailed perspective are a perfect complement to the pleasingly ominous, gently scary text.

MOTIF

A recurring theme, character, or verbal pattern.

Example: In folktales poor and meek characters have nothing but good-
ness and wit to prevail over the strong, rich, and evil characters.
"Little Pig, Little Pig, let me come in."
"Not by the hair of my chinny-chin-chin."

Alderson, Brian. *The Tale of the Turnip.* Illus. by Fritz Wegner. Cambridge, MA: Candlewick Press, 1999.

A humble farmer's garden produce pleases the king, who handsomely rewards his efforts, but an arrogant squire gets more than he bargained for when he attempts to claim a similar reward.

Motif: There is recurrence of the theme of rich but selfish contrasted to poor but generous in this story of just deserts. The poor man brings an offering of his biggest and best turnip to the wise king, who recognizes the spirit of the gift, if not its value. When the rich opportunist tries to curry favor with the king by bringing a gift that he expects will result in an even greater reward of gold, the king assesses the spirit in which it was given and provides a reward accordingly.

Other Devices: *Connotation, Hyperbole, Poetic Justice, Satire, Tone*

Art Style: Humorously detailed watercolor and ink cartoons delight the visual sense and the sense of justice.

Curriculum Tie-in: History (Nineteenth-Century England), Literature (Folktales—England)

Bradbury, Ray. *Switch on the Night.* Illus. by Leo and Diane Dillon. New York: Alfred A. Knopf, 1983.

A lonely little boy, who is afraid of the dark, is introduced to a whole new world by his new friend, a little girl.

Motif: A visitation by a stranger changes the boy's perception of nighttime. "All of a sudden he heard a rap at a window! Something dark was there. A knock at the screen door. Something dark was there! A tap at the back porch. Something dark was there!" The dark theme is continued with the stranger's appearance and even her name. "My name is Dark." She has "dark hair, dark eyes, and wore a dark dress and dark shoes." The "switching" concept is also used again and again in the text. The boy is taught that "It's not switching off the light. It's simply switching on the Night." The girl says that by doing this, "You switch on the crickets! You switch on the frogs! And, you switch on the stars!" She logically makes her case. "Who can hear the crickets with the lights on? Nobody. Who can hear the frogs with the lights on? Nobody. Who can see the stars with the lights on? Nobody. Who can see the moon with the lights on? Nobody."

Other Devices: *Alliteration, Antithesis, Internal Rhyme, Irony, Metaphor, Paradox, Simile, Symbol*

Art Style: Surrealistic pastel drawings match the rhythmical text of this slightly magical, slightly scientific, and quite ethereal night world.

Curriculum Tie-in: Science: (Astronomy), Social Science (Fears)

Glass, Andrew. *Bewildered for Three Days: As to Why Daniel Boone Never Wore His Coonskin Cap.* New York: Holiday House, 2000.

With the help of what he learned from a Delaware Indian boy and an accommodating mother raccoon, young Daniel Boone escapes danger when a bear steals his coonskin cap.

Motif: Boone begins by stating a personality trait: "I had the itching foot and was apt to wander off." His family restrains him enough to see to his chores, admonishing him to spend less time with the Indians. But "my foot itched." Fathers cannot always keep a watchful eye on their sons. Daniel and the Indian boy continue to play together. Daniel's family buys grazing land for some cows. Daniel is sent to search for strays. He promises to keep his wits and not to wander far. "But saying so set my foot itching, and I scratched it." This itchy foot penchant remains with him his whole life during his explorations.

Other Devices: *Atmosphere, Flashback, Foreshadowing, Point of View, Tone, Understatement*

Art Style: Impressionistic colored pencil and oil pastel humorously accompany this frontier yarn of a great adventurer told in a curious blend of humility and exaggeration.

Curriculum Tie-in: History (Biography—Daniel Boone), Literature (Tall Tale)

*Gregorowski, Christopher. *Fly, Eagle, Fly! An African Tale.* Illus. by Niki Daly. New York: Margaret K. McElderry books (Simon & Schuster), 2000.

A farmer finds an eagle and raises it to behave like a chicken, until a friend helps the eagle learn its rightful place in the sky.

Motif: The visitor speaks to the eagle, even though the farmer tells him it understands only chicken-talk. He tells the bird, "You belong not to the earth, but to the sky. Fly, Eagle, fly!" In the farmer's village, the eagle does not understand this. But once it is on a mountain ledge, the bird responds to its true nature.

Other Devices: *Analogy, Antithesis, Foreshadowing, Imagery, Parallelism*

Art Style: Expressionistic watercolor line washes in brown and blue tones satisfyingly re-create the ambience of an African village.

Curriculum Tie-in: Literature (Parable)

*****Hayes, Joe.** *A Spoon for Every Bite.* Illus. by Rebecca Lear. New York: Orchard Books, 1996.

A poor husband and wife ask their rich neighbor to be godfather to their child, and once they are compadres, prey upon his pride and extravagance to trick him out of his fortune.

Motif: The insensitive and foolish rich character is contrasted to the thoughtful and clever (opportunistic) poor characters in this story of arrogance gone amok. His pride will not allow the rich man to quit throwing away his spoons (and his wealth) until he is bankrupt in an attempt to show that he, too, can use a different spoon for every single bite he eats. All the poor couple must do to take advantage of his weakness is wait until the rich man has ruined himself, after which they can capitalize on his pride by gaining wealth through the sale of his discarded spoons.

Other Devices: *Ambiguity, Antihero, Antithesis, Foreshadowing, Hyperbole, Poetic Justice*

Art Style: Realistic pastel drawings contrast the striking differences in lifestyle between the compadres and their varied emotional responses to their circumstances.

Curriculum Tie-in: History (American Southwest), Literature (Folktales—Hispanic), Social Science (Values)

Johnston, Tony. *Alice Nizzy Nazzy, the Witch of Santa Fe.* Illus. by Tomie dePaola. New York: G.P. Putnam's Sons, 1995.

When Manuela's sheep are stolen, she has to go to Alice Nizzy Nazzy's talking roadrunner-footed adobe house and try to get the witch to give the flock back.

Motif: Whenever Manuela takes a bold, irreversible step or something frightening happens to her, the author punctuates her action with "Oh my!" As Manuela looks for her lost sheep, their tracks lead her straight to the witch woman's fence. She peers over it. "Oh, my!" When she walks through this fence that has opened up, "Oh, my!" And when she goes inside the witch's hut, "OH, MY!" Manuela gets popped into the cooking pot. "Oh, my!" When all weathers happen at once, "Oh, my!" Another phrase oft repeated is "Ay! Ay! Ay!" The horned lizard says it when he sees that the witch has crossed her fingers behind her back as she promises to give Manuela's sheep back to her. The lizard says it again in commiseration when Manuela is put in the stew pot, and again when a match is lit to begin the fire under the pot, and again as the water in the pot gets hot. Even the witch says it in frustration when she sees she is out of the magic black flower that brews into a youth-sustaining tea.

Other Devices: *Alliteration, Connotation, Foreshadowing, Hyperbole, Internal Rhyme, Poetic Justice, Simile*

Art Style: Bright pastel and acrylic folk cartoons illustrate the southwestern lifestyle in this good vs. bad character tale.

Curriculum Tie-in: Geography (New Mexico), Literature (Fairytales—America), Social Science (Values)

Kimmel, Eric A. *Grizz!* Illus. by Andrew Glass. New York: Holiday House, 2000. Cowboy Lucky Doolin makes a deal with the Devil, agreeing not to wash, shave, or change his clothes for seven years, thus earning a fortune and the hand of his true love.

> **Motif:** This typical comedy western has a poor but noble cowboy, a rich and disdainful ranch owner, a lovely, desirable ranch owner's daughter, a rich, opportunist lawyer who tries to buy the daughter's affections, and a slick stranger, who expects to take advantage of the gullible cowboy. To gain his heart's desire, the cowboy must forfeit wealth and present himself on the merits of his own character.
>
> **Other Devices:** *Atmosphere, Hyperbole, Inference, Poetic Justice, Simile, Understatement*
>
> **Art Style:** Oil sticks and watercolor dust create exaggerated cartoons that complement this version of a soul-selling wager folktale.
>
> **Curriculum Tie-in:** Literature (Folktales—America)

*Myers, Tim. *Basho and the Fox.* Illus. by Oki S. Han. New York: Marshall Cavendish, 2000. A Japanese poet is challenged by a fox to create his best haiku.

> **Motif:** This famous poet lives alone, interested only in living simply and creating his masterpiece poetry. On the island, when the cherries are in season, he "ate his food, slept his sleep, lived his life, and wrote his poems." He also does this in winter, when his mouth waters at the thought of late-summer cherries.
>
> **Other Devices:** *Ambiguity, Antithesis, Aphorism, Imagery, Irony, Parallelism, Theme*
>
> **Art Style:** Mischievous watercolor folk paintings convey the Eastern sensibility of feudal Japan.
>
> **Curriculum Tie-in:** History (Japan), Social Science (Self-esteem)

Osborne, Mary Pope. *Kate and the Beanstalk.* Illus. by Giselle Potter. New York: Atheneum Books for Young Readers (Simon & Schuster), 2000.

In this version of the classic tale, a girl climbs to the top of a giant beanstalk, where she uses her quick wit to outsmart a giant and make her and her mother's fortune.

Motif: Just as in the classic story of Jack's encounter with the giant, Kate comes from very poor circumstances. The family is down to its last possession of value. Kate trades the cow for beans. Mother is angry, and throws them out the window. A beanstalk grows overnight. Kate climbs it to the top. She sees a castle and learns of three treasures stolen from the castle's former owner. Clever Kate hides when the giant approaches. His chant is familiar. The last word of "Fee, Fi, Fo, Fum" is embellished to rhyme with "woman" (Fum'un). "I smell the blood of an Englishwoman./ Be she alive or be she dead,/ I'll grind her bones to make my bread." He falls asleep after his breakfast. Kate steals his stolen treasures: the hen that lays golden eggs, the bag of gold coins, and the magic harp. He chases Kate down the stalk. When she reaches the bottom, she yells for her mother to bring the axe. She chops down the stalk. The giant falls and breaks his neck. Kate and her mother assume their rightful places as restored owners of the castle.

Other Devices: *Hyperbole, Inference, Poetic Justice, Simile, Stereotype/Reverse Stereotype*

Art Style: Naïve drawings in pencil, ink, gouache, and watercolor expressionistically tell the familiar tale of the thieving giant and the rescue of stolen treasure.

Curriculum Tie-in: Literature (Folktale), Social Science (Values)

Ruurs, Margriet. *Emma and the Coyote.* Illus. by Barbara Spurll. New York: Stoddart Kids, 1999.

Emma thinks chickens are smarter than coyotes, and she struts boldly where no chicken should go to prove it.

Motif: The other chickens wisely run to the chicken coop at the first sign of the coyote. "But not Emma." She faces the enemy and puts her life at risk again and again. Each time she narrowly escapes disaster, the farm family tells her, "You watch out! Coyotes are smarter than chickens." Emma sniffs and walks off with her beak in the air until the time even she recognizes the truth of the saying.

Other Devices: *Alliteration, Foreshadowing, Imagery, Inference, Irony, Parallelism, Serendipity, Simile*

Art Style: Bright primary color paintings expressionistically follow the fortunes of Emma and the barnyard animals.

Curriculum Tie-in: Social Science (Self-esteem)

Sierra, Judy. *The Gift of the Crocodile: A Cinderella Story.* Illus. by Reynold Ruffins. New York: Simon and Schuster Books for Young Readers, 2000.

Damura of the Spice Islands escapes her cruel stepmother and stepsister, and marries a handsome prince with the help of Grandmother Crocodile.

Motif: Several elements of the classic Cinderella folktale appear in this island version. Damura becomes motherless until her father marries a woman with a child. She soon becomes the household drudge. The jungle animals like the little green parrot and the lorikeet befriend her as do the house mice in the English version. One creature serves as a magical benefactor like a fairy godmother. Grandmother Crocodile provides beautiful clothes to replace her rags. The stepmother and her daughter are jealous of these possessions, and take them from her before she can attend the palace ball, at which the prince will be selecting his bride. Grandmother Crocodile fixes her up with a sarong and blouse of pure gold with slippers to match. There is a shining carriage with a white horse to whisk her away. She is admonished to leave the palace before the first rooster crows, just as Cinderella must leave before the clock strikes twelve. Damura is the envy of all at the ball. The prince takes notice. In her haste to leave, she loses one gold slipper, just as Cinderella loses a glass slipper. A palace envoy goes with the slipper to all the village households. The stepmother and her daughter scoff at Damura trying on the slipper, but of course it fits. The mother and daughter must flee for their lives when their plot to eliminate Damura becomes known. Damura lives happily ever after with the prince and their children.

Other Devices: *Foreshadowing, Irony, Poetic Justice, Pun*

Art Style: Folk images painted in bright acrylics portray this Indonesian version of an international folktale.

Curriculum Tie-in: Literature (Folktale)

Souhami, Jessica. *No Dinner! The Story of the Old Woman and the Pumpkin.* New York: Marshall Cavendish, 1999.

A frail old woman sets out to visit her granddaughter on the other side of the forest and must outwit hungry animals that want to eat her.

Motif: An old woman faces strong, fierce adversaries all around. As each beast confronts her, it shouts, "Boo! Old Woman, I'm going to eat you up!" She tells them she's too skinny now. Later, when she comes back, she'll be nice and fat. Each beast says, "All right, but don't be long. I'm hungry!" On her way home, she tries to avoid the animals by hiding in a pumpkin and rolling along in it. The animals ask, "Pumpkin, have you seen a little old woman?" Each time the pumpkin replies, that it has not. The animals say, "Bother! No dinner!"

Other Devices: *Onomatopoeia*

Art Style: Watercolor, ink, and charcoal naïve Indian folk art illustrate the old woman's encounters in simple detail.

Curriculum Tie-in: Literature (Cumulative Tale, Folktales—India)

Strete, Craig Kee. *The Lost Boy and the Monster.* Illus. by Steve Johnson and Lou Fancher. New York: G.P. Putnam's Sons (Penguin Books for Young Readers), 1999.

With the help of a rattlesnake and a scorpion, a lost boy gains two names and defeats the horrible foot-eating monster.

Motif: The boy meets a snake first, and later a scorpion. Each creature asks him, "Aren't you going to hit me with a stick? Most people do, the minute they see me." The boy replies to each, "Why should I do that. Snakes (Scorpions) belong in this world just like me." Each creature thanks the boy for "letting me be me." Then each names the boy "Snake (Scorpion) Brother." This kindness on the part of the boy is later repaid by each grateful creature when the boy needs it most. Acting with good intent is always to one's advantage. Later, in a Tarbaby effect the child gets tangled in the sticky rope. "The more he struggled, the more tangled up he got." The monster accidentally steps on his own sticky rope. Then turn-about is fair play. He, too, gets stuck. But because he has not lived a life of kindness, there is no one to help him in his time of need. "To this day, they say he is stuck there still."

Other Devices: *Ambiguity, Connotation, Internal Rhyme, Poetic Justice, Simile, Theme, Tone*

Art Style: Textured paste, oil paint, potato stamping, and scratching tools create expressionistic paintings in brown and yellow tones reminiscent of American Indian folk art.

Curriculum Tie-in: Art (American Indian), Literature (Folktales—American Indian)

*Wisniewski, David. *Golem.* New York: Clarion Books (Houghton Mifflin), 1996 (Caldecott—1997).

A saintly rabbi miraculously brings to life a clay giant who helps him watch over the Jews of sixteenth-century Prague.

Motif: When an oppressed people have exhausted their own tactics and are in dire straits, a righteous member of the group has the right to invoke supernatural forces to save the good and punish the wicked.

Other Devices: *Analogy, Atmosphere, Foreshadowing, Imagery, Inference, Irony, Paradox, Simile*

Art Style: Paper cut in sophisticated expressionistic collage exerts a powerful physical and emotional effect on this cautionary tale.

Curriculum Tie-in: Literature (Legend), Social Science (Values)

*Yaccarino, Dan. *Deep in the Jungle.* New York: Anne Schwartz Book from Atheneum Books for Young Readers (Simon & Schuster), 2000.

After being tricked into joining the circus, an arrogant lion escapes and returns to the jungle where he lives peacefully with the animals he used to terrorize.

Motif: Using the matter-of-fact "I'm afraid I must . . ." phrase, the man is able to entice a lion into serving as a circus performer. "I'm afraid I must put this leash on you. It's the law, you know." "I'm afraid you must ride in the luggage car." "I'm afraid I must put you in here [cage]." "I'm afraid I must use this whip. Showbiz, you know." "I'm afraid you must always obey me. Showbiz, you know." The lion is finally free, and puts his own meaning to the phrase as he says it to the jungle animals: "I'm afraid I owe you an apology. Silly pride and all." Finally, the lion is invited to perform his famous roaring concert for them. He is only too happy to oblige. "Showbiz, you know."

Other Devices: *Anachronism, Antihero, Antithesis, Black Humor, Foreshadowing, Irony, Parallelism, Poetic Justice, Pun, Tone*

Art Style: Expressionistic gouache naïve cartoons against white backgrounds, reminiscent of the "Curious George" series, accent the droll language in this lesson in humility.

Curriculum Tie-in: Literature (Parable), Social Science (Values)

ONOMATOPOEIA

The use of words to represent or imitate natural sounds.

Example: The "crash" of symbols. The "ting" of a triangle. The "boom" of a bass drum. The "blare" of a horn. The "tootle" of a flute.

Gibbons, Faye. *Mama and Me and the Model T.* Illus. by Ted Rand. New York: Morrow, 1999.

When Mr. Long says any man can drive a car, Mama gets behind the wheel to show women can drive, too.

Onomatopoeia: They are sitting at the table for dinner when they first heard the distinctive "Put-put-pow! Rackety-put-pow." They dash to see a motorcar coming. It stops in the yard with a blow of its horn, "Urrh-ru-gah!" All over the farm these sounds indicate the car is still moving. "Clangabang-clangabang-pow" it goes over a woodpile. "Thumpety-thump" and "Bonkety-bonk" it runs all over the house yard, taking down bushes and saplings and fencing.

Other Devices: *Foreshadowing, Hyperbole, Imagery, Inference, Parallelism, Stereotype, Understatement*

Art Style: Expressionistic watercolors exuberantly dramatize the mysterious intricacies of mastering the wondrous but tricky skills of automobile driving.

Curriculum Tie-in: Social Science (Family Relationships)

Hutchins, Hazel. *One Duck.* Illus. by Ruth Ohi. New York: Annick (Firefly Books), 1999.

A mother duck works to defend her nest of eggs from a marauding crow and a farmer's cultivator.

Onomatopoeia: "Robbed! Robbed! Robbed!" cries the crow as the duck glides in low beneath him, just in time to defend her eggs.

Other Devices: *Antithesis, Atmosphere, Imagery, Inference, Parallelism, Tone*

Art Style: Expressionistic pen/ink watercolor drawings sensitively complement the lyrical text of this common farming drama.

Curriculum Tie-in: Science (Agriculture, Animal Behavior)

Kajikawa, Kimiko. *Yoshi's Feast.* Illus. by Yumi Heo. New York: DK Ink, 2000.

When Yoshi's neighbor, Sabu, the eel broiler, attempts to charge him for the delicious-smelling aromas he has been enjoying, Yoshi hatches a plan to enrich them both.

Onomatopoeia: Yoshi dances to lure customers and shakes his coin box like a tambourine: "chin chin jara jara."

Other Devices: *Antithesis, Aphorism, Foreshadowing, Inference, Parallelism, Poetic Justice*

Art Style: Oil paint, pencil, and paper collage folk art come together in a satisfyingly expressionistic design to transmit the flavor of this ethnic quarrel.

Curriculum Tie-in: Literature (Folktales—Japan)

Kurtz, Jane. *River Friendly, River Wild.* Illus. by Neil Brennan. New York: Simon & Schuster Books for Young Readers, 2000.

A family experiences a renewed appreciation for home and community after they are evacuated during a spring flood and then return to survey the damage.

Onomatopoeia: As the trucks rumble through town, delivering loads of sand, "scrape, scritch," sand is shoveled. "Swish, thump," sand is dropped in the bag. "Woooo wooo" sirens wake up families to flee. The Red Cross truck bringing food for lunch "beep beeps" to alert householders.

Other Devices: *Antithesis, Aphorism, Atmosphere, Imagery, Metaphor, Simile*

Art Style: Oil glaze of brown paint overlaid by thin layers of color in different areas and additional glazes for depth create fuzzy impressionistic scenes that suggest the essence of this emotionally wrenching natural disaster.

Curriculum Tie-in: Geography (Flood—Grand Forks, North Dakota)

Lowell, Susan. *Little Red Cowboy Hat.* Illus. by Randy Cecil. New York: Henry Holt, 1997.

Little Red rides her pony, Buck, to Grandma's ranch with a jar of cactus jelly in the saddlebag.

Onomatopoeia: Little Red takes her pony down the canyon. "Clink-clunk-crunch" go its feet, striking sparks from the rocks. At the ranch it is too quiet. The only sound is the windmill, going "skree, skree." Inside Grandma's bedroom the wolf and Little Red engage in the familiar conversation about big eyes, nose, and teeth; outside the ranch house are "Thump! Thump! Thump!" noises. Unknown to the two inside, grandma is chopping wood. Grandma grabs her shotgun to chase off the wolf. The chickens "tut-tut-tut!" The cattle "Nnoo! Nnnooo!" Her gun goes off. "Pow! Bam! Boom!" Then "Splat!" and there is no more mention of the wolf.

Other Devices: *Aphorism, Atmosphere, Caricature, Hyperbole, Inference, Parody, Simile, Stereotype, Tone*

Art Style: Gouache cartoons in expressionistic naïve style humorously match this unique geographical version of a familiar fairy tale.

Souhami, Jessica. *No Dinner! The Story of the Old Woman and the Pumpkin.* New York: Marshall Cavendish, 1999.

A frail old woman sets out to visit her granddaughter on the other side of the forest, and must outwit the hungry animals that want to eat her.

Onomatopoeia: In this rhythmic cumulative tale, the old woman walks along slowly, patting with her stick . . . "tagook . . . tagook . . . tagook." Later, when she hides inside a large pumpkin and it rolls her along, the pumpkin goes "galook . . . galook . . . galook."

Other Devices: *Motif*

Art Style: Watercolor, ink, and charcoal naïve Indian folk art illustrates with simple ethnic detail the trials the old woman encounters in her journey.

Curriculum Tie-in: (Folktales—India), Literature (Cumulative Tale)

OXYMORON

Two startling contradictory terms or ideas combined for special effect.

Example: "thunderous silence," "sweet sorrow," "bold conservatism," "conspicuous by his absence," "tough love," "no light, but rather darkness visible"

Morrison, Toni, with Slade Morrison. *The Big Box.* Illus. by Giselle Potter. New York: Hyperion, 1999.

To make three unique youngsters conform to their rules, grown-ups create a world inside a box, including treats and simulated nature, but all the kids really want is the freedom to be themselves.

Oxymoron: In the guise of helping them, the adults in these children's lives attempt to make them conform for their own good. So the teachers, the tenants, the neighbors "who loved" them try to cure them. They actually express neither love nor help. The scowls on their faces belie their words.

Other Devices: *Antithesis, Inference, Internal Rhyme, Irony, Satire, Theme*

Art Style: Naïve watercolors show the contrast between the real joy expressed naturally by the children in their simple outdoor amusements and the cloying dissatisfaction with adult-provided commercial rubbish.

Curriculum Tie-in: Social Science (Values)

PARADOX

A statement contrary to common belief that seems contradictory, unbelievable, or absurd but, upon closer inspection, may contain a truth reconciling the conflicting opposites.

Example: "Water, water everywhere, nor any drop to drink"
"I must be cruel only to be kind"

Ada, Alma Flor. *Friend Frog.* Illus. by Lori Lohstoeter. New York: Gulliver Books (Harcourt), 2000.

When he finds he cannot croak, jump, or swim like the frog he meets at a pond, Field Mouse wonders if, after all, they can be friends.

Paradox: Field Mouse sets out to find a friend and discovers Frog, with the beautiful big eyes and lovely voice. But what can a meadow animal and water animal have in common? Frog wants the active life. Field Mouse likes to sit and share secrets. It seems unlikely they will ever get together. Field Mouse, hidden in tall grass at the water's edge, watches and admires Frog in the water. Suddenly, "the ground around Field Mouse darkened" with a passing shadow. Field Mouse shouts a warning. Frog jumps just in time; she didn't know about Falcon. That evening Field Mouse and his new friend Frog sit together on a log, listening to old stories and secrets of the meadow and pond from Grandfather Mouse.

Art Style: Expressionistic, realistic acrylic paintings clearly detail the meadow world and water world inhabited by these two unlikely friends.

Curriculum Tie-in: Science (Animal Behavior)

*Baylor, Byrd. *The Table Where Rich People Sit.* Illus. by Peter Parnall. New York: Charles Scribner's Sons, 1994.

A girl discovers that her impoverished family is rich in things that matter in life, especially being outdoors and experiencing nature.

Paradox: The homemade table constructed from discarded wood serves a very rich family, though they have little money. They discover a monetary value can be placed on sunsets, telling the time of day by the changing colors of the mountains, seeing one-time-only color of a cactus in bloom, having both day and night birds around them, and the freedom to follow trails, hunt eagle nests, sleep under the stars, and smell rain coming. This family that can't count much in cash finds it's really worth about $4,060,000.
Other Devices: *Antihero, Aphorism, Foreshadowing, Irony*
Art Style: Sweeping pen/ink watercolors on white spaces flow majestically in expressionistic homage to nature.
Curriculum Tie-in: Geography (American Southwest), Literature (Parable)

Bradbury, Ray. *Switch on the Night.* Illus. by Leo and Diane Dillon. New York: Alfred A. Knopf, 1983.
A lonely little boy, who is afraid of the dark, is introduced to a whole new world by his new friend, a little girl.
Paradox: The stranger teaches the boy "It's not switching off the light. It's simply switching on the Night. You can turn the Night off and on, just like you can turn a light off and on." By switching on the Night, one switches on a new world populated by crickets, frogs, stars, and the moon. These nighttime elements depend on darkness to be noticed. The boy realizes what he has been missing by keeping his world light. By allowing darkness, he is introduced to the different delights associated with night. He is much happier. "Now he has a Night switch instead of a light switch!"
Other Devices: *Alliteration, Antithesis, Internal Rhyme, Irony, Metaphor, Motif, Simile, Symbol*
Art Style: Surrealistic pastel drawings match the rhythmical text of this slightly magical, slightly scientific, and quite ethereal night world.
Curriculum Tie-in: Science (Astronomy), Social Science (Fears)

Camp, Lindsay. *Why?* Illus. by Tony Ross. New York: G.P. Putnam's Sons (Penguin Putnam Books for Young Readers), 1998.
Lily's constant "why" questions drive her father crazy until one day he discovers that questioning the way things are, can be a very good thing.
Paradox: On the Friday the space invaders arrive at the park, Lily's "why?" questions suddenly are no longer irritating. In fact, her father displays remarkable appreciation for her habit. "I was proud of you in the park today," he tells her, and even promises never to get cranky with her again, "no matter how often she asks him why." Lily doesn't know why he values her behavior now when he didn't before, but the reader does.
Other Devices: *Inference, Irony, Serendipity, Understatement*
Art Style: Colored pencil cartoons illustrate the repetitious, rapid-fire questions from Lily and the answers she receives that make up Lily's day

and the day of those who suffer her presence.
Curriculum Tie-in: Social Science (Family Relationships)

Chorao, Kay. *Pig and Crow.* New York: Henry Holt, 2000.
Crow tricks Pig by trading him supposedly magic items for food, but in the process Pig discovers the value of hard work and patience, and an appreciation for beauty and joy.

> **Paradox:** Pig does a lot of baking to relieve his loneliness. When Crow comes with magic trades in mind, Pig remains hopeful even though the trades are not yielding him the friendship that Crow promises. Crow first trades Pig's chocolate swirl fudge cake for seeds. He works hard and receives pumpkins for his effort. Crow returns to trade a walnut pumpkin pie for a little worm. Pig follows directions and patiently waits for his loneliness to end. A beautiful butterfly is the reward for his dedicated patience. He is delighted, but it flies out the window and disappears. Crow returns one last time with an egg that he trades for apple-raisin bread pudding. The egg hatches into a baby Canada goose. Pig has learned hard work tending the seeds, patience tending the worm, and wisdom to appreciate the lovely butterfly. He now has all the skills he needs to care for the baby goose. It grows up, spreads its wings, and shows Pig (who rides along) the wide world. Pig realizes that "though Crow tried to fool me, his trades really were magic." Pig is never lonely again.

> **Art Style:** Gouache with ink cartoons lovingly celebrate the success of learning the skills for friendship.

> **Curriculum Tie-in:** Social Science (Friendship, Values)

*Deedy, Carmen Agra. *The Yellow Star: The Legend of King Christian X of Denmark.* Illus. by Henri Sorensen. Atlanta: Peachtree, 2000.
King Christian must abide by Nazi orders regarding the wearing of the identifying yellow star, but he must also protect all the Danes from harm.

> **Paradox:** Without the yellow star to identify them, the Jews look like any other Danes. With the Nazi yellow star, the Gentiles look like Jews. As the king gazes into the night sky, he thinks, "If you wished to hide a star, where would you place it?" Then the answer comes to him. "Of course! You would hide it among its sisters." Like the anonymity of stars in the heavens, the yellow stars that the Jews are required to wear would not single them out for harm if every Dane were to wear such a star. Safety in numbers becomes the method of successful defiance of the vicious Nazi edict.

> **Other Devices:** *Antithesis, Aphorism, Atmosphere, Foreshadowing, Inference, Irony, Parallelism, Pun, Simile, Symbol, Theme*

> **Art Style:** Impressionistic oil paintings accompany the spare terse text in this vignette showing the political reality of the Danes' circumstances during a very somber historical period.

Curriculum Tie-in: History (World War II—Nazi Occupation—Denmark), Literature (Legend), Social Science (Values)

Dórrie, Doris. *Lottie's Princess Dress.* Illus. by Julia Kaergel. New York: Dial (Penguin Putnam), 1998.

Lottie and mother disagree about suitable schoolday attire but resolve the matter agreeably, to the surprise of all.

Paradox: Lottie wakes up knowing this is going to be a very special day. And such a special day requires special clothing. A plain red sweater and blue skirt won't do. She must wear her princess dress and crown. Mother says it is too cold for that outfit. An argument ensues, the result of which is that both mother and daughter wear very special clothes on a very ordinary day. "It wasn't snowing anymore, and their glittery gold dresses kept them as warm as summer sunshine." Passers-by are happy for them. "Today must be a very special day!" they remark. The bus driver asks, "Where may I take your highnesses today?" People at work tell Lottie's mother how special she looks. At school Lottie and her best friend "made up a story about a king, a magic carpet, and a princess in a glittery gold dress." "Everyone agreed it was a perfectly special day."

Other Devices: *Antithesis, Theme, Understatement*

Art Style: Spare lines, bright colors through chalk pastels, and accent gold foil complement this expressionistic, naïve rendering of an emotional confrontation.

Curriculum Tie-in: Social Science (Conflict Resolution)

Hesse, Karen. *Come On, Rain!* Illus. by Jon J. Muth. New York: Scholastic Press, 1999.

A young girl eagerly awaits a coming rainstorm to bring relief from the oppressive summer heat.

Paradox: Following the refreshing shower, "the rain has made us new." Soothed spirits make everyone feel differently about life, enough to qualify as being "new."

Other Devices: *Alliteration, Foreshadowing, Hyperbole, Imagery, Metaphor, Simile*

Art Style: Buoyant, expressionistic pen/ink watercolors lend emotional credibility to the nervous anxiety of relentless heat accompanied by worrisome drought, and the tremendous sense of relief that accompanies a thorough, nourishing rain.

Curriculum Tie-in: Science (Meteorology)

*Johnson, D.B. *Henry Hikes to Fitchburg.* Boston: Houghton Mifflin, 2000.

While his friend works hard to earn train fare to Fitchburg, young Henry Thoreau walks the thirty miles through woods and fields, enjoying nature.

Paradox: Henry's friend arrives in Fitchburg by train an hour before Henry. But Henry's method of travel is more pleasant and seems less taxing. He has time to swim, press flowers in a book, carve a walking stick, paddle a raft, taste honey and blackberries, and even to nap. His friend has no time for pleasure as he spends most of the day filling a wood box, sweeping an office, painting a fence, and weeding a garden to earn the bit of money it takes for fare to ride a crowded, hot train. The goal was to go to Fitchburg to see the country. Henry experience the journey; his friend, who arrived first, did not.

Other Devices: *Allusion, Irony, Theme, Understatement*

Art Style: Colored pencil and acrylic paint in stylishly simple, expressionistic designs contrast interesting visual perspectives and provide period detail.

Curriculum Tie-in: Literature (Henry David Thoreau), Philosophy (Quality of Life)

Littlesugar, Amy. *Tree of Hope.* Illus. by Floyd Cooper. New York: Philomel (Penguin Putnam), 1999.

Florrie's daddy used to be a stage actor in Harlem before the Depression forced the Lafayette Theater to close, but he gets a chance to act again when Orson Welles reopens the theater to stage an all-black version of *Macbeth*.

Paradox: Some black residents of Harlem don't feel black people should be acting in *Macbeth*, because "Shakespeare's a white man. We oughta only be doin' plays written 'bout us. Them people at the Lafayette've come to Harlem just to laugh at us!" But Daddy says, "This is Harlem's 'Macbeth'—you'll see." Even he is surprised how true that turns out to be. This version of a greedy nobleman and his greedy wife who would stop at nothing to become king and queen, even murdering the good king in power, takes place on the island of Haiti, where the terrible King Christophe once ruled. Now it really is Harlem's own *Macbeth*.

Other Devices: *Cliché, Flashback, Foreshadowing, Inference, Serendipity, Simile, Stereotype/Reverse Stereotype, Symbol*

Art Style: Rich oilwash impressionistic paintings suggest not only happier memories of when times were more prosperous, but also the temporary bleakness of the current Depression and the emerging hope for a better future.

Curriculum Tie-in: History (Black Culture—Depression)

McKissack, Patricia. *The Honest to Goodness Truth.* Illus. by Giselle Potter. New York: Atheneum Books for Young Readers (Simon & Schuster), 2000.

After promising never to lie, Libby learns it's not always necessary to blurt out the whole truth.

Paradox: After she confesses the truth about not feeding the horse before she plans to go play with a friend, "Libby felt a lot better, even though Mama punished her double. For not tending to Ol' Boss, Libby couldn't go play with Ruthie Mae. And for lying, she had to stay on the porch the rest of the day." She is disappointed that she misses a chance to play with her friend, but she also feels relieved now that the lie had been cleared up and she has "spoken the truth and shamed the devil." In fact, the incident has made such a striking impression on her that she decides unilaterally, "From now on, only the truth." But her certainty about the truth always being right is shaken when her honesty makes the people around her angry. Finally, Mama helps her understand the difference between cold hard truth and honest-to-goodness truth. "Sometimes the truth is told at the wrong time or in the wrong way, or for the wrong reasons. And that can be hurtful. But the honest-to-*goodness* truth is never wrong." One can tell the truth, and be wrong to do so.

Other Devices: *Ambiguity, Antithesis, Aphorism, Foreshadowing, Simile, Understatement*

Art Style: Pencil, ink, gouache, and watercolor in a luxuriant, expressionistic naïve style illustrate this tale of honesty.

Curriculum Tie-in: Social Science (Values)

Modarressi, Mitra. *Yard Sale.* New York: DK Pub., 2000.

When Mr. Flotsam has a yard sale in the quiet town of Spudville, his neighbors are first upset, then delighted by their purchases.

Paradox: The purchases don't function correctly when the owners get them home. The Zings' living-room rug flies out the door with their son on it. Miss Milton's typewriter types its own pages. Mrs. Applebee's telephone brings calls from the deceased. The Frumkins' music box keeps folks dancing. Mr. Twitchett's garden seeds grow into a jungle of vegetables. Mr. Rotelli's pasta machine is never ending. The owners are not pleased until others point out fortuitous benefits and product potential they had not realized. Neighborhood kids take turns flying on the rug. A new spaghetti restaurant opens. Miss Milton becomes famous with the book her typewriter creates. Mrs. Applebee finds a new career as Madame Olga. And the quiet (dull) town of Spudville has weekly dancing parties.

Other Devices: *Allusion, Antithesis, Connotation, Hyperbole, Inference, Serendipity, Understatement*

Art Style: Lively full-page watercolors accompany an understated text.

*Pacilio, V.J. *Ling Cho and His Three Friends.* Illus. by Scott Cook. New York: Farrar Straus Giroux, 2000.

Through his plan to share the wealth of his wheat crop with three friends, a Chinese farmer teaches the importance of allowing other people to help in time of need.

Paradox: Ling Cho's friends will never accept outright charity. He must devise a means to enable them to receive his largess by earning it. He sends each of them to market with a load of wheat. When they return with coins from the sale, they are to split their profit with him. They fail his trust. One of them honestly explains why he kept the wheat for his starving family.

Still, Ling Cho scolds him. "Not once did you allow your friends to help in any way. You let your wife and children share the burden of your pride, rather than requesting help that I could well provide. You betrayed me by taking wheat I gladly would have given you." An honest admittance of need and allowing friends to help in time of need is more honorable than giving to one in need.

Other Devices: *Alliteration, Aphorism, Irony, Poetic Justice, Theme*
Art Style: Impressionistic folk oil paintings in Chinese reds and golds suggest unstated meanings behind spoken words.
Curriculum Tie-in: Social Science (Friendship, Values)

Preston, Tim. *The Lonely Scarecrow.* Illus. by Maggie Kneen. New York: Dutton Children's Books (Penguin Books), 1999.

A lonely scarecrow with a scary face has trouble making friends with the animals who surround him, until a heavy snowfall transforms him into a jolly snowman.

Paradox: A thick blanket of snow covers the frozen earth. "The scarecrow seemed to have vanished, too. In his place stood a jolly snowman!" He is happy when the animals scamper around him. As the snow melts, the animals look up in wonder. "Could the friendly snowman be the same scary creature they had feared for so long?" The relationship has changed. The "scarecrow knew that he would never be lonely again."

Other Devices: *Imagery, Inference, Metaphor, Parallelism, Theme*
Art Style: Lavishly embossed, finely detailed, watercolor and acrylic cartoons fondly render scenes of seasonal changes.
Curriculum Tie-in: Science (Seasons), Social Science (Friendship)

Scamell, Ragnhild. *Toby's Doll's House.* Illus. by Adrian Reynolds. London: Levinson Books, 1998.

Toby is clear about wanting a doll's house for his birthday, but the adults in his life reinterpret his wish to coincide with their own childhood preferences.

Paradox: Toby said he wants a doll's house for his birthday. "He doesn't mean a doll's house," his grandad, his aunt, and his father exclaim. They proceed to tell him what he really wants is a fort, a farmyard, and a multistory car-parking ramp. Since the adults give him the gifts they have decided he really means he wants, the reader might assume that Toby is disappointed in his gifts. But the resourceful child has found a way to get his heart's desire after all. "Everyone was happy." Grandad with his fort, Auntie with her farmyard, and Dad with his multistory car ramp. Most of all Toby. He collects the boxes the gifts have come in and the wrapping paper. By arranging the large box on the bottom, the two smaller ones on the top, the red paper for a roof, the green paper for grass, and the blue paper for carpeting, he has his doll's house.

Other Devices: *Serendipity, Stereotype/Reverse Stereotype*

Art Style: With colored pencil, crayon, pen/ink, and watercolor, the large, simple cartoon drawings show a loving family and a happy resolution to a touchy issue.
Curriculum Tie-in: Social Science (Families)

*Wisniewski, David. *Golem*. New York: Clarion Books (Houghton Mifflin), 1996. (Caldecott—1997).

A saintly rabbi miraculously brings to life a clay giant who helps him watch over the Jews of sixteenth-century Prague.

Paradox: The Golem appreciates small things in life, like sunrises. "The sky changes from black to blue. It is very beautiful." When attackers come to the ghetto gate, he "rakes great furrows in the crowd" with a battering ram he has snapped in two. When the mob flees in panic, he throws down the broken battering ram, lifts the shattered gates, and hangs them back on their ruined hinges. He possesses both awesome capacity for violence and delicate sensitivity for life.
Other Devices: *Analogy, Atmosphere, Foreshadowing, Imagery, Inference, Irony, Motif, Simile*
Art Style: Paper cut in sophisticated expressionistic collage art produces a powerful physical and emotional effect on this cautionary tale.
Curriculum Tie-in: Literature (Legend), Social Science (Values)

PARALLEL STORY

A narrative or picture story enclosed within another story upon which equal or primary interest is centered.

*Dengler, Marianna. *The Worry Stone*. Illus. by Sibyl Graber Gerig. Flagstaff, AZ: Rising Moon (Northland), 1996.

When a small, serious boy joins Amanda on the park bench, she remembers that once she was small and serious, too, but she had Grandfather—and his wonderful stories.

Parallel Story: Amanda recognizes in the boy something of her own youthful experiences. Her childhood memories become the story of the origin of the worry stone. Her grandfather said, "Long, long ago, before the white man came, there lived an Indian maiden of the peaceful Chumash tribe." At the conclusion of the legend, narration returns to Amanda's youth, and finally to Amanda as an old woman sitting on the bench as she befriends a lonely child, so like her former self.
Other Devices: *Antithesis, Flashback, Foreshadowing, Inference, Parallelism*
Art Style: Appealing, realistic watercolor paintings expressionistically maintain focus on the separate threads of this woman's past and present.

Curriculum Tie-in: History (Chumash Indians), Social Science (Grandparents, Intergenerational Relationships)

Greenfield, Karen. *Sister Yessa's Story.* Illus. by Claire Ewart. New York: Laura Geringer (HarperCollins), 1992.

Dark clouds gather as Yessa walks to her brother's place, telling a story as she goes about the early days of the earth. The animals follow her two by two to listen.

Parallel Story: Yessa calls as loudly as she can to the north, to the south, to the east, and to the west. Would anyone like to hear a story? Big gray clouds are gathering in the distance. Yessa "wanted to be at her brother's place before the rain." A story will make the journey easier, even though it is "going to be a long, long walk." First to arrive are two goldfinches flying overhead. They dip closer to hear the story. Other animals are collected as they walk. The story begins "Once upon a time when the world was very new, a Great Turtle walked the earth, carrying all the animals of the world on his back." As Yessa walks, the Great Turtle story progresses with animals dropping off the turtle's back at locations on earth where habitat suits them. By the time the story ends, the turtle has distributed all the animals across earth, and Yessa has arrived at her brother's ark with the animals that will go aboard during the duration of the earth's flood. This book mixes ancient creation myth with biblical lore.

Other Devices: *Inference*

Art Style: Gouache on watercolor paper in lush expressionistic pictures majestically follows both the beginnings of animal life across the earth and the preservation of animal life later in earth's history.

Curriculum Tie-in: Literature (Legends)

*Martin, Nora. *The Stone Dancers.* Illus. by Jill Kastner. New York: Atheneum Books for Young Readers (Simon & Schuster), 1995.

A young girl uses an old legend about stone dancers to teach her mountain village a lesson in hospitality and sharing.

Parallel Story: On the mountaintop are the ruins of an old castle. The villagers live at the base of a mountain, tending goats and planting fields. In winter, when chores are finished, there are stories in front of the fire. A favorite one is of their village long ago. This is a story of a king and his refugee subjects, who flee persecution to find a safe haven on a mountaintop. The triumphant people dance on their castle wall to celebrate. Over the years, a legend grows up around these forebears. Even now, it is possible to "see the stones on the ridge top come to life and take the form of the old king and his subjects" as they dance in joy. The villagers meet a refugee family from far away, seeking a safe place to live. The villagers must reconcile their natural fear of strangers with their open-minded heritage.

Other Devices: *Aphorism, Imagery, Inference, Irony, Metaphor, Simile*

Art Style: Impressionistic oil paintings show the interplay of light and shadow, melding the real with the enchanted in this nineteenth-century French peasant village.

Curriculum Tie-in: History (Nineteenth-Century France), Literature (Legends), Social Science (Values)

PARALLELISM

Arrangement of equally important ideas in similar grammatical constructions for emphasis.

> Example: The law of the Lord is perfect, it gives new strength.
> The commands of the Lord are trustworthy, giving wisdom
>   to those who lack it.
> The laws of the Lord are right, and those who obey them
>   are happy.
> The commands of the Lord are just and give understanding
>   to the mind.
>
> Psalms 19: 7–8

*Bunting, Eve. *The Memory String.* Illus. by Ted Rand. New York: Clarion Books (Houghton Mifflin), 2000.

While still grieving for her mother and unable to accept her stepmother, a girl clings to the memories represented by forty-three buttons on a string.

Parallelism: As they hunt in the lawn for the buttons that scattered when the cat broke the memory string, "Their knees were covered with dirt. Ants crawled over their hands and arms." In her bed that night, Laura lies, "listening to the crickets, listening to Whiskers purring beside her."

Other Devices: *Ambiguity, Antithesis, Aphorism, Foreshadowing, Imagery, Inference, Simile*

Art Style: Shadowy, impressionistic watercolor paintings detail the emotional changes the child experiences as she feels both separation and reconnection to her family.

Curriculum Tie-in: Social Science (Family Relationships, Grief)

*Burleigh, Robert. *Edna.* Illus. by Joanna Yardley. New York: Orchard Books, 2000.

Carefree meanderings during her time in New York City give Edna St. Vincent Millay grist for a famous poem she later pens.

Parallelism: "Oh, how I love this great big city! I love the crowds, I love the sounds, I love the lights at night!" These simple declarations set the tone for her rhapsody of city life. She later remembers a special night when she stayed up till dawn. "It all welled up—the sights, the sounds, the feelings."

Other Devices: *Atmosphere, Foreshadowing, Imagery, Simile*

Art Style: Expressionistic watercolors in vivid hues help re-create the marvelous feelings of expectation and freedom experienced by youthful artists in a city of promise that welcomes their enthusiasm.

Curriculum Tie-in: Literature (Biography—Poets)

**Deedy, Carmen Agra. *The Yellow Star: The Legend of King Christian X of Denmark*. Illus. by Henri Sorensen. Atlanta: Peachtree, 2000.*

King Christian must abide by Nazi orders regarding the wearing of the identifying yellow star, but he must also protect all the Danes from harm.

Parallelism: "If King Christian called on the tiny Danish army to fight, Danes would die. If he did nothing, Danes would die."

Other Devices: *Antithesis, Aphorism, Atmosphere, Foreshadowing, Inference, Irony, Paradox, Pun, Simile, Symbol, Theme*

Art Style: Impressionistic oil paintings accompany the spare terse text in this vignette showing the political reality of the Danes' circumstances during a very somber period of history.

Curriculum Tie-in: History (World War II—Nazi Occupation—Denmark), Literature (Legend), Social Science (Values)

Dengler, Marianna. *Fiddlin' Sam*. Illus. by Sibyl Graber Gerig. Flagstaff, AZ: Rising Moon (Northland), 1999.

Wandering through the Ozarks and bringing joy to people with his music, Fiddlin' Sam seeks the right person to take up his fiddle and carry on the practice.

Parallelism: Sam's gift brings pleasure to the folks he meets along the way. "He could fiddle away their cares. He could fiddle away the achin' in their bones." "Forgetting the boy, forgetting the snake, he fiddled on, long and sweet." "Some said it was Sam who brought the good fortune. Some said it was the fiddle. Some said it was the music." "More and more he was sleeping in the soft bed folks offered him. More and more he was remembering his pa's words."

Other Devices: *Antithesis, Atmosphere, Foreshadowing, Inference, Internal Rhyme, Serendipity*

Art Style: Exuberant, realistic, and expressionistic watercolors in shades of bright yellow, pink, and blue faithfully reveal the emotional and physical details of this musician's life.

Curriculum Tie-in: Social Science (Missouri Ozarks)

**Dengler, Marianna. *The Worry Stone*. Illus. by Sibyl Graber Gerig. Flagstaff, AZ: Rising Moon (Northland), 1996.*

When a small, serious boy joins Amanda on the park bench, she remembers that once she was small and serious too, but she had Grandfather—and his wonderful stories.

Parallelism: "When she counts the years, she knows she is old. When she looks around, she knows she is alone. So she doesn't count, and she doesn't look around." Concerning the boy, she notes, "Why doesn't he smile? Why doesn't he laugh? Why doesn't he play with the others?" Eventually, the boy speaks to her. She asks him why he comes to the park. "Mama says I have to. Mama says I need air." Amanda recalls her youth. "No one had much time for Amanda except Grandfather, and no one had much time for Grandfather except Amanda . . . ." "In the afternoons they played checkers. And in the evenings they told stories."

Other Devices: *Antithesis, Flashback, Foreshadowing, Inference, Parallel Story*

Art Style: Appealing, realistic watercolor paintings expressionistically maintain focus on the separate threads of this woman's past and present.

Curriculum Tie-in: History (Chumash Indians), Social Sciences (Grandparents, Intergenerational Relationships)

DePaola, Tomie. *The Art Lesson.* New York: G.P. Putnam's Sons, 1989.

Having learned to be creative in drawing pictures at home, young Tommy is dismayed when he goes to school and finds the art lesson there much more regimented.

Parallelism: When his art teacher comes up with a plan that promises not only to cover the school's objective but also to allow Tommy a chance to make art the way he wants to, Tommy agrees to give it a try. "And he did." He draws the teacher's assignment. "And he did." He draws his own choice. "And he still does." As an adult he practices his skills as an artist for his living.

Other Devices: *Atmosphere, Flash-forward, Inference, Irony, Serendipity, Theme*

Art Style: Blocky pastel cartoons follow the fortunes and budding development of a young artist in a conformist world.

Curriculum Tie-in: Social Science (Individuality)

Ernst, Lisa Campbell. *Goldilocks Returns.* New York: Simon & Schuster Books for Young Readers, 2000.

Fifty years after Goldilocks first met the three bears, she returns to fix up their cottage and soothe her guilty conscience.

Parallelism: Goldi is still interfering. "Someone has taken my porridge!" says Papa Bear. Mama repeats this observation. Baby Bear concludes the trio with "Someone has taken my porridge, and they've thrown it all away!" Then Papa Bear notices that, "Someone has been fooling with my chair!" Mama Bear echoes this. Baby Bear concludes, "Someone has been fooling with my chair, and they've put it back together!"

Other Devices: *Allusion, Antihero, Connotation, Flash-forward, Inference, Irony, Tone, Understatement*

Art Style: Large, bulky cartoons convey the story's original atmosphere, intended for young listeners, while the language and picture complexity expand the interest level for more savvy audiences.

Fitzpatrick, Marie-Louise. *Lizzy and Skunk.* New York: DK Ink, 2000.

When Lizzy's favorite puppet is lost, she overcomes her fears to find him.

Parallelism: "Lizzy was afraid of shadows in the dark . . . but Skunk wasn't. Izzy was afraid of falling down . . . but Skunk wasn't. Lizzy was afraid of spiders . . . but Skunk wasn't. Lizzy was afraid of making mistakes . . . but Skunk wasn't. Lizzy got stage fright at the school show . . . but Skunk didn't." "Lizzy climbed the tree. Everyone watched. She reached Skunk just as he started to fall. Everyone gasped. Lizzy caught Skunk. Everyone clapped."

Other Devices: *Irony, Personification*

Art Style: Appealingly revealing watercolor cartoons support this tale of emerging self-confidence.

Curriculum Tie-in: Social Science (Fears, Self-esteem)

Gibbons, Faye. *Mama and Me and the Model T.* Illus. by Ted Rand. New York: Morrow, 1999.

When Mr. Long says any man can drive a car, Mama gets behind the wheel to show women can drive, too.

Parallelism: Mr. Long makes the tactical mistake of assuming only the boys in the family need to know how to drive. He asks the girls to step back while he gives instruction to the boys about "what to push and what to pull and what to twist." Then he asks who remembers what he said. "I do," say all the boys together. "I do," say Mama and Kate Long and the narrator. Papa says to the boys, "Any man can drive." Mama adds, "Then so can any woman." " 'Yes,' said all us girls. 'No!' yelled the boys. 'Wait!' said Mr. Long." It was too late. Mama dodged around him and sprang into the motorcar.

Other Devices: *Foreshadowing, Hyperbole, Imagery, Inference, Onomatopoeia, Stereotype, Understatement*

Art Style: Expressionistic watercolors exuberantly dramatize the mysterious intricacies of mastering the wondrous but tricky skills of automobile driving.

Curriculum Tie-in: Social Science (Family Relationships)

*Gregorowski, Christopher. *Fly, Eagle, Fly! An African Tale.* Illus. by Niki Daly. New York: Margaret K. McElderry Books (Simon & Schuster), 2000.

A farmer finds an eagle and raises it to behave like a chicken, until a friend helps the eagle learn its rightful place in the sky.

Parallelism: "He searched by the riverbed. He searched among the reeds." "He searched in the long thatch grass, taller than his own head. He climbed the slopes of the high mountain with its rocky cliffs rising to the sky." "Of course it's a chicken, it walks like a chicken, it talks like a chicken, it eats like a chicken. Of course it's a chicken." "The eagle's head stretched up; its wings stretched outwards; its legs leaned forward."

Other Devices: *Analogy, Antithesis, Foreshadowing, Imagery, Motif*

Art Style: Expressionistic watercolor line washes in brown and blue tones satisfyingly recreate the ambience of an African village.

Curriculum Tie-in: Literature (Parable)

Henkes, Kevin. *Wemberly Worried.* New York: Greenwillow books (HarperCollins), 2000.

A mouse named Wemberly, who worries about everything, finds that she has a whole list of things to worry about when she faces the first day of nursery school.

Parallelism: "Wemberly worried in the morning. She worried at night. And she worried throughout the day." At the playground, she worries about "the chains on the swings, the bolts on the slide, and the bars on the jungle gym." "What if no one else has spots? What if no one else wears stripes? What if no one else brings a doll? What if the teacher is mean? What if the room smells bad? What if they make fun of my name? What if I can't find the bathroom? What if I hate the snack? What if I have to cry?" Wemberly meets someone at nursery school. "Her name was Jewel. She was standing by herself. She was wearing stripes. She was holding a doll." The two have things in common. They introduce their dolls. "This is Petal," says Wemberly. "This is Nibblet," says Jewel. "Petal waved. Nibblet waved back." "Hi," says Petal. "Hi," says Nibblet. "I rub her ears," says Wemberly. "I rub her nose," says Jewel.

Other Devices: *Antithesis, Cliché, Irony, Pun*

Art Style: Watercolor and black pen cartoons with sidebar comments delightfully enhance the rhythmic text.

Curriculum Tie-in: Social Science (Fears)

Hest, Amy. *Mabel Dancing.* Illus. by Christine Davenier. Cambridge, MA: Candlewick Press, 2000.

Mabel doesn't want to go to sleep while Mama and Papa are having a dance party downstairs.

Parallelism: Mabel has a way of "spinning past the guests," "floating through the rooms." On the night of the dancing party "Mama tucked her in" and "Papa closed the curtains." But soon dog and child go to the head of the steps to watch. "They sat down and lay down" on Mabel's yellow blanket. "Mama's gown swooshed and Papa's bow tie tickled" as they dance her back up the stairs to bed.

Other Devices: *Atmosphere, Foreshadowing, Imagery*

Art Style: Airy, expressionistic watercolor washes and ink line drawings capture the contrast of bright excitement and action downstairs with gloomy loneliness and boring isolation upstairs.

Curriculum Tie-in: Social Science (Values)

Howe, James. *Horace and Morris but Mostly Dolores.* Illus. by Amy Walrod. New York: Atheneum Books for Young Readers (Simon & Schuster), 1999.

Three mice friends learn that the best clubs include everyone.

Parallelism: The three friends never say "This is something we shouldn't do." Instead, they say, "This is something we've got to do!" And so "There was almost nothing they didn't do." They are "the greatest of friends, the truest of friends, the now-and-forever-I'm-yours sort of friends."

Other Devices: *Allusion, Internal Rhyme, Pun, Stereotype, Theme*

Art Style: Acrylics and collage cartoons illustrate similar basic gender responses to excitement and adventure by showing few physical or behavioral differences between the male and female mouse children.

Curriculum Tie-in: Social Science (Gender Equality)

Hutchins, Hazel. *One Duck.* Illus. by Ruth Ohi. New York: Annick (Firefly Books), 1999.

A mother duck works to defend her nest of eggs from a marauding crow and a farmer's cultivator.

Parallelism: "One duck at first light feeds on a prairie pond. Feeds only briefly." She returns to "Her nest. Her eggs." As she sees the approaching farm equipment, she "Watches. Waits." An annoying crow "alights before her, taunts and teases, scolds and flaps." The farmer "checks the tractor; checks the hitch; checks the sky." The duck still sits. "She sees, she hears, she feels" the machinery move closer. She "feels the pull of the eggs beneath her, feels the danger moving down upon her." The farmer "feels the earth cool on the backs of his hands, feels the warmth of life within his cupped palms." One duck and the ducklings are "crossing the road, sliding into the safety of the pond, just doing what ducks do."

Other Devices: *Antithesis, Atmosphere, Imagery, Inference, Onomatopoeia, Tone*

Art Style: Expressionistic pen/ink watercolor drawings sensitively complement the lyrical text of this common farming drama.

Curriculum Tie-in: Science (Agriculture, Animal Behavior)

Kajikawa, Kimiko. *Yoshi's Feast.* Illus. by Yumi Heo. New York: DK Ink, 2000.

When Yoshi's neighbor, Sabu, the eel broiler, attempts to charge him for the delicious-smelling aromas he has been enjoying, Yoshi hatches a plan to enrich them both.

Parallelism: "Every night Yoshi watches his neighbor, Sabu, go to catch eels. Every day Yoshi watches Sabu broil his eels and wait for customers. And every evening Yoshi watches a disappointed Sabu eat all the leftover eels." "Yoshi sniffed broiled eels for breakfast. He sniffed broiled eels for lunch. And he sniffed broiled eels for dinner." "You have charged me for the smell of your eels, and I have paid you with the sound of my money." "Yoshi sniffed stinky samma for breakfast. He sniffed stinky samma for lunch, And he sniffed stinky samma for dinner." "Every day after that,

Yoshi danced for happy crowds around Sabu's hibachi. And every evening
the two neighbors sat on Yoshi's proch—laughing and enjoying Sabu's
sizzling-hot eels."
Other Devices: *Antithesis, Aphorism, Foreshadowing, Inference,*
Onomatopoeia, Poetic Justice
Art Style: Oil paint, pencil, and paper collage come together in a satisfyingly
expressionistic design to transmit the flavor of this ethnic quarrel.
Curriculum Tie-in: Literature (Folktales—Japan)

*Kaplan, Howard. *Waiting to Sing.* Illus. by Hervé Blondon. New York: DK Ink,
2000.
A family who loves music and spends many hours at the piano is devastated
by the death of the mother, but those still living find consolation in the
beautiful music that remains.
Parallelism: After the mother's death, the boy tries to play the piano, but
it isn't the same. "I looked to the doorway where she once stood, but it was
empty. I looked behind me, but no one was there." "I missed my mother
tucking in my school shirts or trying to slick back my hair with a wet comb.
I missed the blue beach glass of her eyes."
Other Devices: *Allusion, Antithesis, Aphorism, Atmosphere, Foreshadowing,*
Imagery, Inference, Metaphor, Simile, Symbol
Art Style: Shadowy, full-page, sepia-tone pastel cartoon drawings
expressionistically evoke a fragile emotional period in the life of a family
coping with restructuring itself after the wrenching loss of one of its
members.
Curriculum Tie-in: Music (Piano), Social Science (Death, Family
Relationships, Feelings)

Keller, Holly. *That's Mine, Horace.* New York: Greenwillow Books (HarperCollins),
2000.
Horace loves the little yellow truck that he finds in the school yard, but he has
a problem when a classmate tries to claim it.
Parallelism: When Horace finds the toy, he looks around. "Nobody was
coming, and nobody was watching." The burden of his secret theft takes
its toll. "His head hurt, and he had a stomach ache." On the day he feels
better about going back to school, Horace allows himself to admire the
truck a last time. "He opened the doors and snapped them shut. He spun
the wheels. He put it in his pocket."
Other Devices: *Irony, Serendipity*
Art Style: The simple, stylized watercolor and black pen cartoons focus
on the important elements of this emotional situation as a child learns to
value his character more than a toy.
Curriculum Tie-in: Social Science (Values)

Kitamura, Satoshi. *Me and My Cat?* New York: Farrar Straus Giroux, 2000.
A young boy spends an unusual day after awakening to find that he and his cat have switched bodies.

> **Parallelism:** Nicholas isn't acting normal. And no wonder. He may look like a little boy, but he is really a cat. The body that looks like a cat is really harboring Nicholas. "I climbed on Leonardo-in-my-shape and stroked his cheek. He purred. Then Mom stroked me gently. I purred."
>
> **Other Devices:** *Antithesis, Inference, Irony, Point of View, Understatement*
>
> **Art Style:** Acrylic cartoons detail the daily life of a boy's thoughts in a cat's body as he watches a cat's activities in his boy's body.
>
> **Curriculum Tie-in:** Social Science (Animal Companions, Values)

Laden, Nina. *Roberto the Insect Architect.* San Francisco: Chronicle Books, 2000.
Roberto the architect, who also happens to be a termite, sets off to the city to find success.

> **Parallelism:** "He sketched houses and streets. He sketched stores and playgrounds." "Roberto hammered and nailed. He sawed and sanded. He worked day and night." All day long "bounty-hunting butterflies took wing. Paper wasps swarmed the streets. Bold weevils crawled out of the woodwork." Soon "architects offered him jobs. Book publishers wanted his story. Ladybugs sent him love letters."
>
> **Other Devices:** *Alliteration, Allusion, Antithesis, Cliché, Pun*
>
> **Art Style:** Astoundingly detailed mixed media collages of paper, wood, blueprints, and gouache paint creatively brings this carefully crafted witty text to life.
>
> **Curriculum Tie-in:** Social Science (Values)

Lawson, Julie. *Emma and the Silk Train.* Illus. by Paul Mombourquette. Buffalo, NY: Kids Can Press, 1997.
After seeing the beautiful silk blouse her mother made, Emma dreams of having a piece of silk for herself, and when the opportunity arises, determinedly pursues it.

> **Parallelism:** When the train derails, everyone begins the scramble to retrieve the silk rolls. "By the end of the day, everyone had caught something. A few people caught bales of raw silk. Charlie caught a salmon. Pa caught his fly-fishing hat. Mama caught a cold. And Emma caught silk-fishing fever." But long after everyone else stops searching, Emma keeps fishing. "Sometimes she fished from shore. Sometimes she fished from the wharf. Sometimes she fished from the rowboat." When she ends up beached on an island in the fast-flowing river, she remembers the trains never stop. "Not for regulars, not for royalty, not for her."
>
> **Other Devices:** *Ambiguity, Foreshadowing, Imagery, Inference, Simile*
>
> **Art Style:** Lush impressionistic oil painting capture the time and adventure of the silk train era.
>
> **Curriculum Tie-in:** History (Railroads—Silk)

Lowell, Susan. *Cindy Ellen: A Wild Western Cinderella.* Illus. by Jane Manning. New York: Joanna Cotler Books (HarperCollins), 2000.

Cindy Ellen loses one of her diamond spurs at the square dance in the retelling of this classic fairytale.

Parallelism: Cindy Ellen's stepmother loads her with work. "Mend those fences! Tend those cows! Shovel out the corral!" Her fairy godmother goes right to work preparing her for the square dance. "It looked like a cross between a comet and a dust storm. It sounded like silver bells mixed with dynamite." Glistening sparks of fairy dust are sprinkling down everywhere. "They turned Cindy's clothes from cotton to satin, and they put quite a twinkle in Joe's eye."

Other Devices: *Alliteration, Aphorism, Foreshadowing, Internal Rhyme, Parody, Simile, Tone*

Art Style: Action-packed, expressionistic acrylic cartoons hilariously support the story's western flavor.

Curriculum Tie-in: Social Science (Self-esteem)

Lyon, George Ella. *One Lucky Girl.* Illus. by Irene Trivas. New York: DK Pub., 2000.

Even though their trailer is destroyed by a tornado, a young boy's family is grateful because they find his baby sister alive.

Parallelism: "Dad was a jockey, Mom walked horses, and I played baseball." On the day of the tornado, the boy sets the scene. "Mom and Dad were sitting in the shade. I was oiling my glove. Becky was down for a nap."

Other Devices: *Ambiguity, Antithesis, Foreshadowing, Imagery, Inference, Metaphor, Simile*

Art Style: Smudgy pastel illustrations impressionistically assist the story line through use of both dark and bright colors.

Curriculum Tie-in: Science (Tornadoes), Social Science (Family Relationships)

Martin, Jacqueline Briggs. *Snowflake Bentley.* Illus. by Mary Azarian. Boston: Houghton Mifflin, 1998 (Caldecott—1999).

This is a biography of a self-taught scientist who photographed thousands of individual snowflakes in order to study their unique formations.

Parallelism: "He could net butterflies and show them to his older brother, Charlie. He could pick apple blossoms and take them to his mother." "If the shed were warm the snow would melt. If he breathed on the black tray the snow would melt. If he twitched a muscle as he held the snow crystal on the long wooden pick the snowflake would break."

Other Devices: *Antithesis, Imagery, Simile*

Art Style: Woodcuts, with hand-tinted watercolors, are presented in nineteenth-century folk art style.

Curriculum Tie-in: Science (Meteorology, Photography)

*Myers, Tim.** *Basho and the Fox.* Illus. by Oki S. Han. New York: Marshall Cavendish, 2000.

A Japanese poet is challenged by a fox to create his best haiku.

Parallelism: As a hermit Basho "ate his food, slept his sleep, lived his life, and wrote his poems." Basho works, "writing new poems, reading old ones, searching for a haiku so beautiful and powerful that the old fox would be amazed." He spends time "writing and re-writing, changing words and adding words and taking words away, reading and listening and considering." He works harder at his haiku, "letting poems flow into him and out of him, then polishing them till they seemed perfect."

Other Devices: *Ambiguity, Antithesis, Aphorism, Imagery, Irony, Motif, Theme*

Art Style: Mischievous watercolor folk paintings convey the Eastern sensibility of feudal Japan.

Curriculum Tie-in: History (Japan), Social Science (Self-esteem)

*Nolen, Jerdine.** *Big Jabe.* Illus. by Kadir Nelson. New York: Lothrop, Lee & Shepard, 2000.

Momma Mary tells stories about a special young man who does wondrous things, especially for the slaves on the Plenty Plantation.

Parallelism: The mysterious Jabe grew rapidly. "By May he'd left his boyhood behind and showed no signs of stopping. By June he was a full-grown man and had the strength of fifty." The pear tree Jabe had planted also grew swiftly. "One day it was a sprout, the next it was a sapling, the day after that it was a young tree full of pretty white blossoms." When Jabe picked the cotton crop, he worked so fast the sun couldn't shine through the flying cotton. "So the cock didn't crow. Not an animal in the barn stirred. And not a single person, in the Big House or the Quarters, knew that a new day had dawned." That summer Plenty Plantation lived up to its name. "The barn was bursting at its seams. Three more smokehouses had to be built to handle all the meat. The larder in the Big House was crammed full." Addy vanished from her chains, leaving Mr. Sorensen fit to be tied. "He searched the barn; he searched the Quarters; he searched the entire plantation."

Other Devices: *Allusion, Anachronism, Antithesis, Flashback, Flash-forward, Foreshadowing, Hyperbole, Imagery, Inference, Simile, Symbol, Understatement*

Art Style: Strong, detailed pen/ink, watercolor, and gouache drawings provide wonderful, expressionistic period ambience to this folktale.

Curriculum Tie-in: History (Slavery—America), Literature (Tall Tale)

Preston, Tim. *The Lonely Scarecrow.* Illus. by Maggie Kneen. New York: Dutton Children's Books (Penguin Books), 1999.

A lonely scarecrow with a scary face has trouble making friends with the animals who surround him, until a heavy snowfall transforms him into a jolly snowman.

Parallelism: As the combine harvests the field where the scarecrow was placed, "The animals hid from its churning jaws. They also hid from the scarecrow." As the creatures play around him, "the scarecrow was afraid of what would happen when he lost his snowy coat. He was afraid that the animals would shrink from his twisted shape. Most of all, he was afraid he would be alone again."

Other Devices: *Imagery, Inference, Metaphor, Paradox, Theme*

Art Style: Lavishly embossed, finely detailed, watercolor and acrylic cartoons are fondly rendered scenes of glorious seasonal changes.

Curriculum Tie-in: Science (Seasons), Social Science (Friendship)

Ruurs, Margriet. *Emma and the Coyote.* Illus. by Barbara Spurll. New York: Stoddart Kids, 1999.

Emma thinks chickens are smarter than coyotes, and she struts boldly where no chicken should go to prove it.

Parallelism: "The pigs snorted. The rooster crowed. The chickens clucked after him." Up in the magnolia tree, "She didn't notice the coyote creep into the yard. The coyote didn't see the giant magnolia either."

Other Devices: *Alliteration, Foreshadowing, Imagery, Inference, Irony, Motif, Serendipity, Simile*

Art Style: Bright primary color paintings expressionistically follow the fortunes of Emma and the barnyard animals.

Curriculum Tie-in: Social Science (Self-esteem)

*St. George, Judith. *So You Want to Be President?* Illus. by David Small. New York: Philomel (Penguin Putnam Books for Young Readers), 2000 (Caldecott—2000).

This is a lively assortment of facts about the qualifications and characteristics of U.S. Presidents from George Washington to Bill Clinton.

Parallelism: "The President has to be polite to everyone. The President can't go anywhere alone. The President has lots of homework. People get mad at the President." "Being President can be wanting to serve your country . . . . It can be looking toward the future . . . . It can be wanting to turn lives around . . . . It can be wanting to make the world a better place . . . ."

Other Devices: *Antithesis, Atmosphere, Caricature, Tone*

Art Style: In the cherished tradition of political commentary, foibles, quirks, and humanity are illustrated in hilarious cartoons.

Curriculum Tie-in: History (American Presidents)

*Turner, Ann. *Red Flower Goes West.* Illus. by Dennis Nolan. New York: Hyperion Books for Children, 1999.

As they journey west, a family nurtures the red flower they have carried with them from their old home.

Parallelism: As the boy begins his narration, he is ambivalent about the wisdom of leaving Missouri for California, and this shows up in his feelings about the father who instigates the journey. "He sold our farm, sold our horses, Nat and Pat, and got oxen." Along the way the family must cross rivers. "Water lapped the wagon bed, crept over my toes." When his father goes under the water, "I clutched Red Flower, told her to watch over Pa, then I saw an Indian dive in from the opposite bank." He reflects on the experience. "I know that Indian saved Pa's life, and I know, too, that Red Flower helped somehow." In the end, the plant survives. "Red flower will grow new leaves and buds. And so will we, so will we."

Other Devices: *Connotation, Inference, Metaphor, Simile, Symbol*

Art Style: Soft crayon and pastel realistic drawings, mostly in shades of gray, depict a stern pioneer experience accented by the bright red beacon of the family's talisman.

Curriculum Tie-in: History (Westward Expansion)

White, Linda Arms. *Comes a Wind.* Illus. by Tom Curry. New York: DK Pub., 2000.

While visiting their mother's ranch, two brothers who constantly try to best each other swap tall tales about big winds, and are surprised by the fiercest wind they have ever seen.

Parallelism: "When Clement learned to roast a hot dog nice and even over a campfire, Clyde served up a five-course meal complete with apple pie cooked on a stick." "When Clyde figured out how to rope a bucking bronco, Clement managed to ride one—bareback." "When Clement decided to raise the biggest pig at the county fair in order to win a blue ribbon, Clyde raised a bigger one and taught it to dance a jig and join in the 'E-I-E-I-O' as he sang Old Mac Donald Had a Farm." While they sit on the porch swapping tall tales, "the wind snatched Clyde's words out of his mouth." It "yanked the buttons from Clement's shirt." It "blew the leaves right off the trees." As the wind picks up, "their eyes grew bigger than hen eggs." Then, as the wind gets worse, "their eyes grew bigger than goose eggs." Finally, "their eyes grew bigger than ostrich eggs" when they have to cling fast to the porch rail like arrows on a weather vane. When their mother is caught on the roof, the boys rush to help. "Clement wrestled the ladder from the barn." "Clyde climbed to the top and boosted Clement to the roof."

Other Devices: *Atmosphere, Foreshadowing, Hyperbole, Inference, Simile*

Art Style: Painted acrylics in expressionistic naïve perspectives illustrate the peculiar and humorous effects of the forces of wind and imagination.

Curriculum Tie-in: Literature (Tall Tales)

*Yaccarino, Dan. *Deep in the Jungle.* New York: Anne Schwartz Book from Atheneum Books for Young Readers (Simon & Schuster), 2000.

After being tricked into joining the circus, an arrogant lion escapes and returns to the jungle where he lives peacefully with the animals he used to terrorize.

Parallelism: The lion finds circus procedures disagreeable. Says the man to him, "I'm afraid you must always obey me. Showbiz, you know." Says the lion to the man, "I'm afraid I must eat you up. Jungle law, you know."
Other Devices: *Anachronism, Antihero, Antithesis, Black Humor, Foreshadowing, Irony, Motif, Poetic Justice, Pun, Tone*
Art Style: Expressionistic gouache naïve cartoons against white backgrounds, reminiscent of the "Curious George" series, accent the droll language in this lesson in humility.
Curriculum Tie-in: Literature (Parable), Social Science (Values)

Zagwÿn, Deborah. *Apple Batter.* Berkeley, CA: Tricycle Press, 1999.
Because of their persistence, Delmore succeeds in learning to hit a baseball and his mother, Loretta, succeeds in growing apples.
Parallelism: One spring, Delmore "pulled his wrinkled ball shorts out of his drawer well ahead of baseball season." His mother, Loretta, "wheeled her barrow out from under the eaves long before growing season." Though he wished to very much, Delmore "couldn't whack the ball, hit a tater, smash the apple." But mother and son are dedicated in their efforts. A ball is balanced on an upright pole. "Delmore swung at his plumbing pipe and Loretta checked her trees for pests." Rain "knocked leaves off Loretta's fruit trees" and "filled up Delmore's plumbing pipe." "Every winter Loretta clipped them and every spring she mulched them." "She loved apple shapes. She loved apple colors. She loved how some apples were tarter and crunchier than others." "Loretta gently polished the last apple. Delmore polished his batting." At the final game of the season, "Delmore was quick in the field and Delmore showed fine form at the plate."
Other Devices: *Alliteration, Analogy, Antithesis, Foreshadowing, Inference, Irony, Pun, Simile*
Art Style: Expressionistic watercolor cartoons compare the changing fortunes of mother and son as they struggle toward their respective goals.
Curriculum Tie-in: Athletics (Baseball), Science (Apple Production)

PARODY

A humorous but recognizable imitation of another literary work to amuse or ridicule the other's style or subject matter.

Example: This humorous imitation of the plot in Edgar Allan Poe's gothic story "The Fall of the House of Usher" is a poem by Reed Wittenmore:
"It was a big boxy wreck of a house
Owned by a classmate of mine named Rod Usher,

Who lived in the thing with his twin sister.
He was a louse and she was a souse."

Harris, Jim. *The Three Little Dinosaurs.* Gretna, LA: Pelican Publishing, 1999.
Three young dinosaurs set out on their own, only to be hassled by a
Tyrannosaurus rex, who gets a big surprise in the end.

Parody: This story follows the plot and much of the same language as the
Three Little Pigs with a different cast of characters and a different setting.
The three dinosaurs also build themselves houses. The fierce enemy asks
each of them, "Little pig, little pig, let me come in." They reply, "Not by
the hair of my chinny chin, chin." Then they add, "Stop calling us pigs!"
Their enemy, a Tyrannosaurus rex, manages to destroy two of the three
homes, though the dinos escape with their lives. It takes Rex awhile, but
he gains access, at last, to the third, sturdier house. But by then, the little
dinosaurs have grown into huge creatures, frightening away the
Tyrannosaurus rex. "So the three brothers built new houses and lived
happily ever after. And they never saw hide nor hair of Rex again."
Other Devices: *Antithesis, Foreshadowing, Inference, Poetic Justice, Tone*
Art Style: Lush, detailed acrylic expressionistic paintings provide
satisfyingly humorous perspective and point of view between aggressor
and victim.

Lowell, Susan. *Cindy Ellen: A Wild Western Cinderella.* Illus. by Jane Manning.
New York: Joanna Cotler Books (HarperCollins), 2000.
Cindy Ellen loses one of her diamond spurs at the square dance in the retelling
of this classic fairytale.

Parody: A rancher takes a second wife with two daughters. The wife
makes Cindy Ellen do the dirty work. She mends fences, tends cows, and
shovels out the corral. A big cattle king invites his neighbors to a rodeo and
square dance. Cindy's fairy godmother shoots a golden pistol that spreads
glittery dust instead of waving a magic wand. She admonishes Cindy to get
gumption, stand up straight, and dust herself off. Dressed for the western
fandango, Cindy Ellen has a creamy white Stetson, golden buckskin chaps,
and new boots with diamond-studded spurs. Cindy's little gray horse
becomes a silver horse with a softly sparkling coat. The rancher's son, Joe
Prince, is impressed with Cindy's rodeo skills as she beats him and her
stepsisters. When it's time to go to the square dance, a squash becomes a
stagecoach, six cactus mice are turned into six dappled horses, a fat pack
rat becomes a stagecoach driver, and a horned toad rides shotgun beside
the driver. After dancing all the squares, Cindy rushes off before midnight
and leaves behind one of her diamond spurs. Joe goes around the following
day, trying to fit the spur to all the ladies' boots. All ends well when the
spur fits Cindy's boot and she produces its match. They live together
happily ever after at the ranch house full of love and rodeo trophies.
Cindy's stepsisters both marry city slickers.

Other Devices: *Alliteration, Aphorism, Foreshadowing, Internal Rhyme, Parallelism, Simile, Tone*
Art Style: Action-packed, expressionistic acrylic cartoons hilariously support the story's western flavor.
Curriculum Tie-in: Social Science (Self-esteem)

Lowell, Susan. *Little Red Cowboy Hat.* Illus. by Randy Cecil. New York: Henry Holt, 1997.
Little Red rides her pony, Buck, to Grandma's ranch with a jar of cactus jelly in the saddlebag.
Parody: Instead of wearing her new red hood, living in the woods, and walking down the path to grandma's house as she carries a basket of goodies, this Little Red wears a red cowboy hat, lives in the desert country, rides her pony down the canyon and across the mesa, and takes a jar of cactus jelly to grandma. Her persona is not that of a helpless victim. This modern wolf tries to come on to Little Red. She leaps on her horse and races off to Grandma's ranch. But the wolf must have found a shortcut. He's already there in bed, wearing the missing Grandma's clothes. Little Red finds herself a victim, but not for long. It is Grandma who wields the ax. Together the women get on their horses and chase off the wolf.
Other Devices: *Aphorism, Atmosphere, Caricature, Hyperbole, Inference, Onomatopoeia, Simile, Stereotype, Tone*
Art Style: Gouache cartoons in expressionistic, naïve style humorously match this unique geographical version of a familiar fairy tale.

*Wisniewski, David. *Tough Cookie.* New York: Lothrop, Lee & Shepard (William Morrow), 1999.
When his friend Chips is snatched and chewed, Tough Cookie sets out to stop Fingers.
Parody: Tough Cookie is a stereotypical Sergeant Joe Friday detective. He speaks in unemotional, terse statements, telling just the facts. When romance occurs, it's tinged with regret and loss. "I'm knocking back a cup of java when this classy blond rolls up. Store-bought. Easy on the eyes. We used to be an item. Didn't work. Still hurts." Tough Cookie spurns help when he must face a hard opponent. "This is between Fingers and me." He stands alone against the bad guy. His crime-fighting professional friend fails him. "The guy can't take the pressure. Starts to snap. That's when the trouble starts." It looks bad for Tough Cookie, crime fighter. "Darkness covers me like a damp sponge. Can't move. Can't breathe. It's the end . . . ." But help comes from an unexpected source. The neighborhood crumbs rally in the nick of time.
Other Devices: *Analogy, Pun, Satire, Simile, Stereotype, Theme*
Art Style: Complex cut-paper illustrations in an expressionistic collage work amazingly well to support this munchable mystery.
Curriculum Tie-in: Social Science (Friendship)

PERSONIFICATION

Inanimate objects, natural forces, or abstract ideas are endowed with human qualities, characteristics, personalities, or actions.

Example: "The wind whistled." "Bright April shakes out her rain-drenched hair."

Sara Teasdale

"Time, the subtle thief of youth . . ."

John Milton

Fitzpatrick, Marie-Louise. *Lizzy and Skunk.* New York: DK Ink, 2000.
When Lizzy's favorite puppet is lost, she overcomes her fears to find him.
Personification: Her hand puppet Skunk speaks to Lizzy. "Isn't life wonderful?" he enthuses. "But scary," Lizzy responds. Things go ok as long as Skunk lends support through Lizzy's fearful day. When he becomes lost, she must look for Skunk "all by herself." Courageously she climbs a tree to rescue him. The results of catching him in front of a gasping, clapping audience does wonders for Lizzy's self-esteem. Having conquered her fears, she now says to Skunk, "Life is wonderful." "But scary, too," Skunk replies. "I'll take care of you," she promises.
Other Devices: *Irony, Parallelism*
Art Style: Appealingly revealing watercolor cartoons support this tale of emerging self-confidence.
Curriculum Tie-in: Social Science (Fears, Self-esteem)

Jones, Joy. *Tambourine Moon.* Illus. by Terry Widener. New York: Simon & Schuster Books for Young readers, 1999.
Noni is afraid as she and her grandaddy walk home, until he tells her how he met her Grandma Ismay one dark night in Alabama, and how the big yellow moon came to light up the sky.
Personification: On dark nights the "houses all have mean expressions on their faces." It is said in Alabama that "the moon works the night shift so that the sun can get some rest." Soon Noni is able to look at the moon and "see a friendly face."
Other Devices: *Antithesis, Hyperbole, Imagery, Simile*
Art Style: Acrylic art in expressionistic, ethnic folk designs employ both sharp angles and puffy, rounded curves.
Curriculum Tie-in: Social Science (Ethnicity—African-American, Grandparents)

*Mamet, David. *Henrietta.* Illus. by Elizabeth Dahlie. Boston: Houghton Mifflin, 1999.

Henrietta Pig, rebuffed by the law school admissions office, like so many of her underprivileged kind before her, wanders aimlessly until a chance encounter with a vagabond philosopher enables her to pursue her dream of a scholarly future.

Personification: This pig functions in a world of humans with all the characteristics of humans. Yet she is aware of her "minority" status. "Having seen the barriers to the Professions crumble before, she presented herself at the institution of her choice." It could "neither admit nor acknowledge her." She ends up being barred as a nuisance as she tries to enter the learning environment informally. The one human who speaks on an equal level with her is temporarily blinded due to the loss of his glasses. Once he is fitted with his spare spectacles, "Henrietta waited for the effect her identity might have on him." He rises above the level of his kind and, nonchalantly, takes her for the individual she is. "You've been of service to me, miss. Now how may I reciprocate?" Eventually, she distinguishes herself among the human population and stands out as the unique porcine face in the photograph of the Supreme Court justices.

Other Devices: *Inference, Irony, Pun, Satire, Serendipity, Tone*

Art Style: Spare, pastel crayon impressionistic cartoons highlight in subtle, playful satire the foibles of higher education's entrenched, shortsighted traditions.

Curriculum Tie-in: Literature (Fable), Social Science (Diversity)

Nickle, John. *The Ant Bully.* New York: Scholastic Press, 1999.

Lucas learns a lesson about bullying from the ants he has been tormenting.

Personification: Lucas is stunned to find himself shrunk down to ant size inside an ant colony after spraying them with his squirt gun. The queen asks him, "Don't you realize how long and hard we work to build what you destroy in seconds?" His silence is taken as further insult, and he is sentenced to hard labor. As he works with the colony members to bring in food and defend against enemies, they ask him what it is like to be a giant and is he the biggest giant. Later, on a foray into his own house to bring candy back to the queen, Lucas displays bravery. He jumps at his father's face in order to stop him from swatting the ants, so they can escape. Their sense of fair play helps restore Lucas to his freedom.

Other Devices: *Antihero, Antithesis, Foreshadowing, Inference, Poetic Justice, Point of View*

Art Style: Expressionistic acrylic cartoons skillfully play with perspective as both the boy and the ants view the same environment.

Curriculum Tie-in: Social Science (Bullies, Values)

Turner, Ann. *Secrets from the Dollhouse.* Illus. by Raúl Colón. New York: HarperCollins, 2000.

The life of a family of dolls and their servants living in a dollhouse in a young girl's room is told from the perspective of Emma, oldest of the doll children.

Personification: These dolls abide by the "Laws of Wood" that say they must not move when either Girl or Boy is around. They have limited movement, though they can rock forward and fall on invading mice to frighten them. And they do exhibit human feelings. Emma describes Papa as serious. But once, "when Girl put Baby in his arms, I saw him smile and wink his eye." Emma would like to go outside "to the place where the tree grows" that she can see from girl's room window. Once Girl does take her outside. Emma is "so excited I squeaked, but She did not hear." Emma "was sad to go inside" again. They all plan strategy against the possible invasion of Cat. "Buster and Butler will guard the door, Cook has her spoon, and Papa knocked four splinters from the wall for spears." But Emma is afraid. How can they fight a cat with clawed feet? When Baby is stolen, Emma says, "I wish I could run like Girl and find my sister!" "Stiffly I jerked out the door, calling, 'Baby? Can you hear me?'" When Baby is found at last, "A happiness so fierce and deep made my stiff arms pick her up, where she settled and sniffed against my shoulder, and Papa and Mama cried tears of welcome."

Other Devices: *Foreshadowing, Imagery, Metaphor, Point of View, Simile*

Art Style: Stiff 1920s folk images in scratcher line pastels capture the whimsy of a toy world.

POETIC JUSTICE

An outcome in which vice is punished and virtue rewarded in a manner appropriate to the situation.

> Example: The wolf who would eat the three little pigs, himself falls victim to the cooking pot when he lands in boiling water while trying to crawl down the third little pig's chimney.

Alderson, Brian. *The Tale of the Turnip.* Illus. by Fritz Wegner. Cambridge, MA: Candlewick Press, 1999.

A humble farmer's garden produce pleases the king, who handsomely rewards his efforts, but an arrogant squire gets more than he bargained for when he attempts to claim a similar reward.

Poetic Justice: When the farmer discovers a huge turnip in his garden, he immediately thinks such a prize should go to the king. The king recognizes the farmer's generosity and bestows upon him a wagonload of gold. The sly, greedy squire denigrates such a lowly gift and imagines how much more gold he will be given if he presents the king with one of his many excellent horses. When he delivers the animal to the king, the king recognizes the level of generosity in this gift and offers a fitting reward to the giver—the champion turnip.

Other Devices: *Connotation, Hyperbole, Motif, Satire, Tone*
Art Style: Humorously detailed watercolor and ink cartoons delight the visual sense and the sense of justice.
Curriculum Tie-in: History (Nineteenth-Century England), Literature (Folktales—England)

Fearnley, Jan. *Mr. Wolf's Pancakes.* Waukesha, WI: Little Tiger Press, 1999.
When Mr. Wolf seeks help from his neighbors about how to make pancakes, he is rudely rebuffed and must rely upon his own efforts.
Poetic Justice: His neighbors won't help to make the pancakes, but later they want to eat them. So, for their cruel rejection during his time of need, they are eaten, instead.
Other Devices: *Allusion, Antihero, Black Humor, Irony, Stereotype*
Art Style: Detailed cartoons in pen/ink and watercolor drawings delight the reader not only with the story in progress but also with humorous nods to many Mother Goose rhymes and fairy-tale personalities.
Curriculum Tie-in: Social Science (Conduct and Behavior)

*Gralley, Jean. *Hogula, Dread Pig of Night.* New York: Henry Holt, 1999.
Although he lives high on the hog in his castle on Grimy Pork Chop Hill, Hogula is unhappy because he has no friends—until he meets Elvis Ann, Dread Queen of Kissyface.
Poetic Justice: Hogula gives no quarter. He finds his victims, brings his twitching piggie snout to their necks and snorts them into a deep snooze. But Elvis Ann is a match. She plants wet smooches on her victims. Before he can scream and jump out of the way—too late, Hogula realizes who she is. There's nothing to do but make a friendship pact. She won't smooch him; he won't snort her.
Other Devices: *Alliteration, Allusion, Antihero, Aphorism, Cliché, Foreshadowing, Inference, Irony, Pun, Simile, Stereotype, Understatement*
Art Style: Appropriately repulsive expressionistic cartoons in gouache and ink on watercolor paper develop the characters of this humorously gentle Dracula-style relationship.
Curriculum Tie-in: Social Science (Friendship)

Harris, Jim. *The Three Little Dinosaurs.* Gretna, LA: Pelican Publishing, 1999.
Three young dinosaurs set out on their own, only to be hassled by a Tyrannosaurus rex who gets a big surprise in the end.
Poetic Justice: The rex uses his superior strength and size to intimidate the little dinosaurs. But his small brain is his downfall. By the time he figures out how to gain access to the little dinosaurs in their house of stone, they have grown up and cannot be harmed by the comparatively small T-rex. Furthermore, when the rex runs away to live a quiet life of fishing, he casts his line and snags a very, very large sea serpent to whom he will have to answer.

Other Devices: *Antithesis, Foreshadowing, Inference, Parody, Tone*
Art Style: Lush, detailed acrylic expressionistic paintings provide satisfyingly humorous perspective and point of view of aggressor and victims.

*Hayes, Joe. *A Spoon for Every Bite.* Illus. by Rebecca Lear. New York: Orchard Books, 1996.

A poor husband and wife ask their rich neighbor to be godfather to their child, and once they are compadres, prey upon his pride and extravagance to trick him out of his fortune.

Poetic Justice: When the poor couple mentions that they only have two spoons and had to buy a third in order to invite the rich man to dinner, he responds with ridicule. He brags about his wealth, saying he could eat with a different spoon every day of the year. The insulted poor couple gets back at him by telling him they have a friend who can use a different spoon with every bite. The rich man sets out to prove he can do the same thing. The result is that he loses his wealth buying spoons, and the poor couple becomes wealthy selling his discarded spoons.

Other Devices: *Ambiguity, Antihero, Antithesis, Foreshadowing, Hyperbole, Motif*

Art Style: Realistic pastel drawings contrast the striking differences in lifestyles between the compadres, and their varied emotional responses to their circumstances.

Curriculum Tie-in: History (American Southwest), Literature (Folktales—Hispanic), Social Science (Values)

Hoban, Russell. *Trouble on Thunder Mountain.* Illus. by Quentin Blake. New York: Orchard Books (Grolier), 2000.

When Megafright International flattens their beautiful mountain to put up a hi-tech plastic theme park, the O'Saurus family uses faith and lots of Monsta-Gloo to put things right.

Poetic Justice: Mr. Flatbrain kicks the O'Saurus family off their beloved mountain home in order to tear it down. When his own plastic mountain project fails, he must face the wrath of the tourists, who find his Tunnel of Terror boring. Now he is a gardener who makes rock gardens in the shape of little mountains, through which he sometimes makes tunnels.

Other Devices: *Aphorism, Connotation, Foreshadowing, Hyperbole, Irony, Satire, Understatement*

Art Style: Humorous pen/ink watercolor cartoons spiritedly produce a funny tribute to old-fashioned ingenuity and to nature.

Curriculum Tie-in: Science (Ecology)

Johnson, Paul Brett. *Bearhide and Crow.* New York: Holiday House, 2000.

After Sam tricks Amos into swapping a prize-winning gourd for a smelly old bearhide, Amos decides to give Sam a taste of his own medicine by negotiating an even more worthless trade.

Poetic Justice: It starts when Amos's wife sends him to the garden to get a gourd from which to carve a new water dipper. Sam gets to him first and promptly trades for Amos's dipper gourd with a moth-eaten old bearhide that is supposed to be magical. Amos's wife isn't happy about the trade. Amos needs to unload that hide, and decides to work a trade to give it back to Sam. He overhears thieves say where they have hidden gold on Sam's property. When a crow lands on the hide, Amos knows what to do. He tells Sam the crow can tell him where gold on Sam's land or anyone's land is hidden. Then he proceeds to prove it by "talking" to the crow and going to the site where the gold is buried. Amos is willing to let his crow go for half the bag of gold that is found on the site. Since Sam expects to get much more gold using the crow, he eagerly agrees to the trade. Soon, however, he is back when the crow fails to tell him where more gold is buried. Amos says Sam just needs to learn crow talk. The way to do that is to cover up with "this magical bearhide." Sam is doubtful, but it *did* come from a Gypsy woman, "and gypsies were known to deal in spells and conjuring." Amos is willing to trade back the bearhide to him for the other half of the found bag of gold. And that's how Amos ends up with all the robbers' gold, while Sam gets back his worthless bearhide and a crow of no special use. Amos uses some of his gold to buy his wife a metal dipper.

Other Devices: *Atmosphere, Serendipity*

Art Style: Pencil sketches and acrylic painted cartoons humorously illustrate the changing fortunes and effects of greed upon these mountain swappers.

Johnson, Paul Brett. *Old Dry Frye: A Deliciously Funny Tall Tale.* New York: Scholastic Press, 1999.

A humorous retelling of an Appalachian folktale about a preacher who chokes on a chicken bone.

Poetic Justice: While the community members have been going to great lengths to avoid any personal responsibility for the death of Old Dry Frye, he has managed to rally from their ministrations and has survived their best efforts to "get shed of him." "On nights when the moon is full and there's a plate of chicken on the table, you can guess what folks are saying: 'Dad-fetch me! I believe that's Old Dry Frye.'" To their horror, he still turns up to help himself to his favorite food.

Other Devices: *Black Humor, Cliché, Hyperbole, Inference, Serendipity, Tone, Understatement*

Art Style: Ebullient acrylic cartoons share the fortunes and misfortunes of the self-serving characters in this raucous Appalachian romp.

Curriculum Tie-in: Literatuare (Tall Tales), Social Science (Appalachian Culture)

Johnston, Tony. *Alice Nizzy Nazzy, the Witch of Santa Fe.* Illus. by Tomie dePaola. New York: G.P. Putnam's Sons, 1995.

When Manuela's sheep are stolen, she has to go to Alice Nizzy Nazzy's talking roadrunner-footed adobe house and try to get the witch to give the flock back.

Poetic Justice: Not only does the witch intend to keep Manuela's sheep, she also intends to eat Manuela. "Naughty children are so tasty," she comments. But when she tastes the soup in which Manuela is standing, she puckers her face and spits it out in disgust. "You are a good child. Good children taste so sour!" Off she flies in her mortar to find a naughty child. Manuela hops out of the pot, and the witch's spell in broken. The dirty pillows lying about the hut become sheep again. Manuela happily takes them home.

Other Devices: *Alliteration, Connotation, Foreshadowing, Hyperbole, Internal Rhyme, Motif, Simile*

Art Style: Bright pastel and acrylic folk cartoons illustrate the southwestern lifestyle in this good vs. bad character tale.

Curriculum Tie-in: Geography (New Mexico), Literature (Fairytales— America), Social Science (Values)

Kajikawa, Kimiko. *Yoshi's Feast.* Illus. by Yumi Heo. New York: DK Ink, 2000.

When Yoshi's neighbor, Sabu, the eel broiler, attempts to charge him for the delicious-smelling aromas he has been enjoying, Yoshi hatches a plan to enrich them both.

Poetic Justice: When Yoshi, who enjoys the aromas of his neighbor's eel broiling, refuses to pay for this pleasure, Sabu pays him back by cooking stinky fish that Yoshi must now smell. Yoshi comes up with a plan to settle their differences. "All day long, hungry people gathered to watch Yoshi's fiery dances and to buy Sabu's sizzling eels." And in the evening "the two neighbors sat on Yoshi's porch—laughing and enjoying Sabu's sizzling-hot eels."

Other Devices: *Antithesis, Aphorism, Foreshadowing, Inference, Onomatopoeia, Parallelism*

Art Style: Oil paint, pencil, and paper collage folk art come together in a satisfyingly expressionistic design to transmit the flavor of this ethnic quarrel.

Curriculum Tie-in: Literature (Folktales—Japan)

Kimmel, Eric A. *Grizz!* Illus. by Andrew Glass. New York: Holiday House, 2000.

Cowboy Lucky Doolin makes a deal with the Devil, agreeing not to wash, shave, or change his clothes for seven years, thus earning a fortune and the hand of his true love.

Poetic Justice: While the lawyer Parmelee Jones plots to marry the ranch owner's daughter, Lucky is trying to save her. He thinks he is slightly short of the seven years necessary to bring a fortune into the marriage, but he must act to prevent Jones from getting her. So he forfeits the fortune and promises that after he puts the ring on her finger, the Devil can do with him what he likes. Lawyer Jones tries to interfere by telling them at the last minute that he has just reread the will. The girl won't inherit Aunt Agatha's money if she marries a cowboy. Jones doesn't know Lucky is rich enough through his own labors not to need Aunt Agatha's fortune so he fails to stop the impending wedding. "As for Parmelee Jones, he was last seen talking to a stranger over by the railway station. The stranger was missing half his left foot. That was seven years ago. Nobody's heard from him since." He was apparently offered a deal he couldn't refuse by the same stranger who had hoped to win the soul of Lucky Doolin. For his greed, Jones has received his just reward.

Other Devices: *Atmosphere, Hyperbole, Inference, Motif, Simile, Understatement*

Art Style: Oil sticks and watercolor dust create exaggerated cartoons that complement this folktale version of a soul-selling wager.

Curriculum Tie-in: Literature (Folktales—America)

Krudop, Walter Lyon. *The Man Who Caught Fish.* New York: Farrar Straus Giroux, 2000.

A stranger with a pole magically catches fish and hands them out to villagers one at a time, but the king will not be content until he receives a whole basket of fish.

Poetic Justice: The stranger is scrupulous about "one person, one fish." His mission seems to be to dip his pole in water and to hand out fish to people he meets. He draws the attention of the king, who also becomes a recipient of the stranger's gift. Because of his arrogance, the king feels he should have more than one fish, and commands the stranger to catch him a basketful. The stranger ignores the command. This impudence infuriates the king, who tries various means to get a full basket of fish from the stranger. He orders his strongmen to take away the stranger's fishing pole. They cannot get it away from the stranger's hand. Eventually, the stranger is imprisoned for his disobedience. Still he does not comply. Finally, the king resorts to trickery. He disguises himself in rags and thinks to present himself to the stranger for another fish, returning again and again dressed as beggars. But the stranger does an odd thing. Instead of pulling out a fish, he hands the king the pole. A spell has been broken. Now it is the king who must do the fishing for "one person, one fish." He cannot drop the pole. His arrogance condemns him to take over the stranger's curse.

Other Devices: *Foreshadowing, Theme*

Art Style: Exquisite impressionistic folk paintings bring to life a culture of long ago.
Curriculum Tie-in: History (Thailand), Literature (Folktales—Thailand)

Mahy, Margaret. *Simply Delicious.* Illus. by Jonathan Allen. New York: Orchard Books, 1999.

A resourceful father engages in all kinds of acrobatic moves to keep an assortment of jungle creatures from getting the double-dip, chocolate-chip-and-cherry ice cream cone he is taking home to his son.

Poetic Justice: Each creature, from the butterflies to crocodile, is ready to flutter, dive, swoop, spring, and lunge for the ice cream cone. Only the deft action of Mr. Minky protects the ice cream from these marauders. In the end, he safely delivers the treat. For his efforts he goes in to his dinner—spicy pie and scrumptious pudding. The would-be thieves get nothing, though they look with intent upon each other and "began chasing one another back through the jungle."

Other Devices: *Alliteration, Foreshadowing, Hyperbole, Internal Rhyme, Simile, Understatement*

Art Style: Lively line and gouache cartoons in lush jungle colors satisfyingly follow the father's adventures as he delivers his son an appreciated treat.

Curriculum Tie-in: Literature (Cumulative Tale)

Mitchell, Adrian. *Nobody Rides the Unicorn.* Illus. by Stephen Lambert. New York: Arthur A. Levine Books (Scholastic), 1999.

Having been used by the king to trick a unicorn into imprisonment, Zoe decides to set him free again.

Poetic Justice: The cunning Doctor Slythe advises the king that to avoid being poisoned, he must drink and eat his meals from a unicorn's horn. The way to trap one is through a "quiet young girl with a gentle voice." The girl they choose lives alone and is nobody's child. She is not told the true reason she is being asked to sing sweetly and softly, so that "perhaps, a unicorn will appear and come lay his head in your lap." When the king's men use her efforts to capture the unicorn, she is angered. Since she feels responsible, she awaits evening and frees him before he comes to harm. Banished by the king, she is welcomed among the unicorns. The unicorn she saved asks her who she is. She says, "I'm nobody." It promptly invites her to climb up on its back, for "Nobody rides the unicorn."

Other Devices: *Pun, Simile*

Art Style: Naïve pastels in hazy earth tones contrast, in light and shadow, innocent childhood bravery with lurking, self-centered, devious authority figures.

Curriculum Tie-in: Social Science (Values)

Nickle, John. *The Ant Bully.* New York: Scholastic Press, 1999.

Lucas learns a lesson about bullying by the ants he has been tormenting.

Poetic Justice: Lucas must be made to realize the harm he causes when he floods the ant colony with his squirt gun, so they shrink him to their size and sentence him to hard labor. Soon he is bringing in food and defending the colony against enemies, as well as tending the queen. As a reward for his work and bravery, they restore him to his original size and give him his freedom . . . just in time to face his own bully, Sid. But the ants have also seen Sid. They reduce Sid to ant size. Now Lucas can teach a lesson to Sid.

Other Devices: *Antihero, Antithesis, Foreshadowing, Inference, Personification, Point of View*

Art Style: Expressionistic acrylic cartoons skillfully play with perspective as both the boy and the ants view the same environment.

Curriculum Tie-in: Social Science (Bullies, Values)

Osborne, Mary Pope. *Kate and the Beanstalk.* Illus. by Giselle Potter. New York: Atheneum Books for Young Readers (Simon & Schuster), 2000.

In this version of the classic tale, a girl climbs to the top of a giant beanstalk, where she uses her quick wit to outsmart a giant and make her and her mother's fortune.

Poetic Justice: The giant stole the noble knight's castle and treasures, and killed him. It is fair that the noble's daughter should one day return to the castle and steal back the treasures that belonged to her family and, in the process, cause the death of the wicked giant by cutting down the beanstalk.

Other Devices: *Hyperbole, Inference, Motif, Simile, Stereotype/Reverse Stereotype*

Art Style: Naïve drawings in pencil, ink, gouache, and watercolor expressionistically tell the familiar tale of the thieving giant and the rescue of stolen treasure.

Curriculum Tie-in: Literature (Folktale), Social Science (Values)

*Pacilio, V.J. *Ling Cho and His Three Friends.* Illus. by Scott Cook. New York: Farrar Straus Giroux, 2000.

Through his plan to share the wealth of his wheat crop with three friends, a Chinese farmer teaches the importance of allowing other people to help in time of need.

Poetic Justice: The two friends who make up tales about why they were unable to share coins with Ling Cho from the sale of wheat entrusted to them are told their services next year at harvest time will not be needed. He knows they have stolen from him. The friend who admits he needed the wheat for his family will be tied closely to Ling Cho during the coming year's planting and harvesting, and will earn his share in the marketing of the grain. Ling Cho will be able to help him without making it charity.

Other Devices: *Alliteration, Aphorism, Irony, Paradox, Theme*

Art Style: Impressionistic folk oil paintings in Chinese reds and golds suggest unstated meanings behind spoken words.

Curriculum Tie-in: Social Science (Friendship, Values)

Sierra, Judy. *The Gift of the Crocodile: A Cinderella Story.* Illus. by Reynold Ruffins. New York: Simon and Schuster Books for Young Readers, 2000.

Damura of the Spice Islands escapes her cruel stepmother and stepsister, and marries a handsome prince with the help of Grandmother Crocodile.

Poetic Justice: Damura receives a beautiful silver cloth sarong from Grandmother Crocodile when she lost her own rag while washing clothes at the river. Her greedy stepsister tries to fake losing her own sarong so that she, too, can have such a lovely gift. But for her, the sarong becomes a filthy rag swarming with leeches when she puts it on. The jealous mother and daughter try to feed Damura to the river crocodiles so that the prince will forget her and marry the stepdaughter. Grandmother Crocodile steps in to save Damura and to chase off the stepmother and her daughter. Damura wins the Prince and lives happily ever after. The wicked stepmother and her daughter go into the deep woods, "never to be seen again."

Other Devices: *Foreshadowing, Irony, Motif, Pun*

Art Style: Folk images painted in bright acrylics portray this Indonesian version of an international folktale.

Curriculum Tie-in: Literature (Folktale)

Strete, Craig Kee. *The Lost Boy and the Monster.* Illus. by Steve Johnson and Lou Fancher. New York: G.P. Putnam's Sons (Penguin Books for Young Readers), 1999.

With the help of a rattlesnake and a scorpion, a lost boy gains two names and defeats the horrible foot-eating monster.

Poetic Justice: The monster loves to eat little children's feet. The lost boy uses "the medicine bag with the sting in it," as the scorpion has instructed him. Where the sting hits the ground, "it turned into a desert of thick spiny cactus." The monster runs right into it. He howls with pain and cannot continue to chase the boy due to all the stickers in his feet. Furthermore, he is so distracted by his pain that he forgets about the sticky rope trap he has devised and steps on it. The same device he uses on his victims has caught him, and the cactus stickers are appropriately punishing a foot-eating monster.

Other Devices: *Ambiguity, Connotation, Internal Rhyme, Motif, Simile, Theme, Tone*

Art Style: Textured paste, oil paint, potato stamping, and scratching tools create expressionistic paintings in brown and yellow tones reminiscent of American Indian folk art.

Curriculum Tie-in: Art (American Indian), Literature (Folktales— American Indian)

*Van Allsburg, Chris. *The Sweetest Fig.* Boston: Houghton Mifflin, 1993.
>   After being given two magical figs that make his dreams come true, Monsieur
>   Bibot sees his plans for future wealth upset by his long-suffering dog.
>   **Poetic Justice:** Bibot is always teaching his dog "a lesson he will never
>   forget." He drags Marcel down the stairs for his morning walk. "The steep
>   steps were hard for the short-legged dog, but Bilbot wouldn't think of
>   carrying his pet. He hated to get Marcel's white hairs on his beautiful blue
>   suit." Bibot considers how it will be when he is rich. "The little dog would
>   not be coming along. In his dreams Bibot had Great Danes." Marcel gobbles
>   the last fig while Bibot's back is turned. The next morning, Bibot finds
>   himself under the bed in his dog's body. He looks out at Marcel, who is in
>   his body and demanding to go on their morning walk together.
>   **Other Devices:** *Inference, Irony*
>   **Art Style:** Pastel sepia-tone realistic illustrations show the just deserts of
>   a self-serving dentist and his patient dog.

Waite, Judy. *Mouse, Look Out!* Illus. by Norma Burgin. New York: Dutton Children's
Books (Penguin Putnam), 1998.
>   Inside an old, abandoned house a mouse searches for a safe place to hide from
>   a cat.
>   **Poetic Justice:** While the unsuspecting mouse goes about searching for
>   something to eat and a warm place to sleep, a cat is only a few steps, leaps,
>   and lunges behind. At last the mouse is ensconced in a bit of torn mattress,
>   sleeping and apparently not alert to the cat, who is finally about to pounce.
>   Just as the mouse is most at danger, a dog erupts from his place of rest in
>   the same room. Suddenly it is the cat who must look out as the dog chases
>   it out of the house.
>   **Other Devices:** *Alliteration, Atmosphere, Internal Rhyme, Metaphor, Simile*
>   **Art Style:** Realistic acrylic paintings in detailed perspective are a perfect
>   complement to the pleasingly ominous, gently scary text.

*Wilkon, Piotr. *Rosie the Cool Cat.* Illus. by Jozef Wilkon. New York: Viking (Penguin Books), 1989.
>   Casper and Carolina are proud of their jet-black fur and despair trying to cope
>   with their orange kitten, who likes to play with mice and sleep in the doghouse.
>   **Poetic Justice:** Rosie does not realize, until she has kittens, how hard it
>   is living with one who behaves differently. She has one black kitten among
>   the orange ones. And, he seems to be just as much a trial for her as she was
>   for her parents. "I don't know what's to become of him. Little Caz does
>   everything differently from his sisters and brothers."
>   **Other Devices:** *Antithesis, Foreshadowing, Inference, Irony, Satire, Stereotype/*
>   *Reverse Stereotype, Symbol*
>   **Art Style:** Pastel and colored pencil expressionistic cartoons capture the
>   family pride in its uniqueness as well as its sense of frustration in the jolting
>   difference of the odd one.

Curriculum Tie-in: Social Science (Family Relationships, Individuality, Values)

*****Yaccarino, Dan.** *Deep in the Jungle.* New York: Anne Schwartz Book from Atheneum Books for Young Readers (Simon & Schuster), 2000.

After being tricked into joining the circus, an arrogant lion escapes and returns to the jungle, where he lives peacefully with the animals he used to terrorize.

Poetic Justice: The lion discovers he has made an error in judgment when he goes with the circus man. He endures humiliation and abuse. Finally, when the man tells him he must always obey him because "that's showbiz, you know," the lion promptly eats him up, because "that's jungle law, you know." And when the lion discovers that his fellow jungle creatures are about to be herded into the same life he has escaped from, he lures their captor into participating in his famous "man's-head-in-the-lion's-mouth" trick. So the man did, and "you can figure out the rest." While he was denied his chance at stardom in the circus, the lion eventually is able to perform his favorite trick. An appreciative jungle animal audience cheers and throws roses and demands encores when he does his famous roar.

Other Devices: *Anachronism, Antihero, Antithesis, Black Humor, Foreshadowing, Irony, Motif, Parallelism, Pun, Tone*

Art Style: Expressionistic gouache naïve cartoons against white backgrounds, reminiscent of the "Curious George" series, accent the droll language in this lesson in humility.

Curriculum Tie-in: Literature (Parable), Social Science (Values)

POINT OF VIEW

Perspective from which the story is seen and told.

Example: I sniffed the strange object. The message it gave me was one of danger. I did not touch it. I gave her a warning look. Together, we left it alone and traveled on. (first person)

The wolf sniffed the trap, hackles raised, and turned to give his mate a warning look. Together they ignored the dangerous object and traveled on. (limited third person)

The male wolf sniffed the trap, hackles raised, and turned to give a warning look to his mate. She understood that the strange object meant danger. Together they traveled on. (omniscient)

*****Browne, Anthony.** *Voices in the Park.* New York: DK Pub., 1998.

Lives briefly intertwine when two youngsters meet in the park.

Point of View: The perspectives of four individuals vary greatly regarding their time at the park. The mother considers the venture a duty among many obligations to perform, and of equal benefit to her dog and her son. She finds the man and girl unsuitable, and their dog, a nuisance. The boy is subdued but tentatively pleased when he meets another child to play with. The other child is glad her dad's mind is off his joblessness for a little while, and she finds the boy okay but the mother a twit. The man is glad his daughter has a good time and wishes he were as carefree as the romping dogs.

Other Devices: *Connotation, Foreshadowing, Inference*

Art Style: The story moves from one voice to another. Each character's perspective is reflected in the shifting landscape and seasons with bright acrylic surrealistic paintings that match the bossy woman, the sad man, the lonely boy, and the cheerful girl.

Curriculum Tie-in: Social Science (Feelings)

Givens, Terryl. *Dragon Scales and Willow Leaves.* Illus. by Andrew Portwood. New York: G.P. Putnam's Sons, 1997.

Although they are twins, Jonathan and Rachel neither look the same, nor do they see things the same way—especially in the forest.

Point of View: There is a "flicker of red and a stirring, rustling." Rachel sees leaves of a weeping willow float softly down in a shimmery carpet. Jonathan sees a dragon to be subdued with slashes of his sword. There are "shrieks and howls from treetops high above." Jonathan sees an ambush by forest trolls. They throw down rocks. Rachel sees quarreling blue jays and frisky squirrels that shake loose some pine needles and an occasional acorn. The "hundreds and thousands of tall figures with golden hair and suits of green" that block their way are Viking warriors to Jonathan and rows of corn to Rachel. And when they return after their walk, Jonathan "ran to meet three knights, who bowed and ushered him into the presence of the queen." Rachel ran past the cornstalks and her father on the tractor to her mother waiting at the door with supper.

Other Devices: *Alliteration, Antithesis, Imagery, Metaphor, Simile*

Art Style: Impressionistic watercolor pictures expressionistically celebrate the different ways we perceive our surroundings.

Curriculum Tie-in: Social Science (Individuality)

Glass, Andrew. *Bewildered for Three Days: As to Why Daniel Boone Never Wore His Coonskin Cap.* New York: Holiday House, 2000.

With the help of what he learned from a Delaware Indian boy and an accommodating mother raccoon, young Daniel Boone escapes danger when a bear steals his coonskin cap.

Point of View: Before Daniel can bolt out the door to play, his papa grabs him by the belt. "See to thy chores and spend less time among Indians." His playmate finds him pounding corn into meal, and helps him tote water from a distant spring and collect wood chips for kindling. The Indian boy's father is not pleased. "It's time Little Beaver proved himself in the company of young Delaware braves." Their paths separate as Little Beaver takes his place as a Delaware brave and Daniel learns the homesteader's tasks. His father tells him, "The Delaware live in the forest and love the savage wilderness as their mother. When we ask them to honor our fences, it is an unreasonable thing we ask. I fear there is no way to share a land so differently understood."

Other Devices: *Atmosphere, Flashback, Foreshadowing, Motif, Tone, Understatement*

Art Style: Impressionistic colored pencil and oil pastel humorously accompany this frontier yarn of a great adventurer told in a curious blend of humility and exaggeration.

Curriculum Tie-in: History (Biography—Daniel Boone), Literature (Tall Tale)

Kitamura, Satoshi. *Me and My Cat?* New York: Farrar Straus Giroux, 2000.

A young boy spends an unusual day after awakening to find that he and his cat have switched bodies.

Point of View: Nicholas in his cat's (Leonardo's) body discovers that for animals, "Life was as tough and complicated as it was for humans." He gets thrown out of the house when he leaps from one cupboard to another on the other side of the room, and knocks it over. "Mom threw me out of the house" and, of course, does not recognize him. He learns the neighbor's friendly dog is not at all friendly to him in his cat body. "Of course! He couldn't recognize me." He tries to walk along a wall and is told by other cats it's their wall. Before he can explain the wall belongs to everyone, they are "all over me." He recalls that Leonardo was Heloise's kitten, but when he calls a tentative greeting, she ignores him completely. Later, when his cat, in the body of Nicholas, returns home from school, he notices how strangely, like a cat, the "boy" acts. The boy-cat goes through the cat flap, licks his sweater clean, sharpens his nails on the woodwork, and scratches himself earnestly. He feels sorry for his mother, who is trying to cope with her strange-acting "son." "She became so worried that she called the doctor and asked him to come at once." He is thankful to awaken in his own body the next morning.

Other Devices: *Antithesis, Inference, Irony, Parallelism, Understatement*

Art Style: Busy, hilarious acrylic cartoons detail the daily life of a boy's thoughts in a cat's body as he watches a cat's activities in his boy's body.

Curriculum Tie-in: Social Science (Animal Companions, Values)

Meggs, Libby Phillips. *Go Home! The True Story of James the Cat.* Morton Grove, IL: Albert Whitman, 2000.

A homeless cat spends several seasons trying to survive the elements until at last a suburban family adopts him.

Point of View: "The black cat could not remember who had put the collar around his neck, or when." He likes the way this family talks to their cats when they are upset. "He listened to the kindness in their voices." It has been "so long since anyone had petted him!" The family "didn't know how tight the collar was, how hungry he felt, or how their friendly words and kind hands made him wish he were their cat." He makes overtures to them, and gets squirted with a hose and told to go home. He "stumbled back to the woods, confused. He did not know where 'Home' was." Later, the family does take him to a veterinarian's office, where he hears that he "should become a House Cat." The black cat "wondered what a House Cat was." The family brings him inside their house. "The children put a cozy blanket in the sun for the black cat. He had not felt anything so warm and soft since he was a kitten snuggled close to his mother. He loved his toys, too. Being a House Cat was not bad!" Later, when the people discover his name, he comes to the woman "purring grandly, as if to say, 'Yes. I am James, Your Cat from now on.' "

Other Devices: *Ambiguity, Antithesis, Connotation, Inference, Metaphor, Simile*

Art Style: Realistic pastel illustrations follow James's admittance into a family that provides what has been missing in his life for a long time.

Curriculum Tie-in: Social Science (Animal Companions)

Mochizuki, Ken. *Passage to Freedom: The Sugihara Story.* Illus. by Dom Lee. Afterword by Hiroki Sugihara. New York: Lee & Low, 1997.

Following refusal by the Japanese government to issue visas to Jewish refugees from Poland, Consul Sugihara and his family make a crucial decision that saves thousands of lives.

Point of View: Narration through Consul Sugihara's small son shows how the presence of refugees creates disorder and disruption in his family life. "I grew tired of staying indoors. I asked my father constantly, 'Why are these people here? What do they want? Why do they have to be here? Who are they?'" Once he understands the situation, the solution seems, in his child's perspective, to be simple. "If we don't help them, won't they die?" The narrator admits that at the time he "did not fully understand what the three of them had done, or why it was so important. I do now."

Other Devices: *Antithesis, Aphorism, Foreshadowing, Theme*

Art Style: The stark fear of survival is shown in realistic, photograph-like, sepia-tone oil paint and pencil over scratched beeswax paper. Emotionally charged, unrelenting shades of brown shadowing focus on the grim refugee predicament—their barely contained explosive violence, and the terrible decision facing the diplomat.

Curriculum Tie-in: History (World War II)

Nickle, John. *The Ant Bully.* New York: Scholastic Press, 1999.

Lucas learns a lesson about bullying from the ants he has been tormenting.

Point of View: Because the big neighbor kid Sid is mean to him, smaller Lucas takes out his frustration on still smaller ants by spraying them with his squirt gun. But when he is shrunk to their tiny size and becomes part of their colony, he quickly learns to see things from the ants' perspective. They work hard to bring in food, defend themselves from wasps and spiders, and tend the queen. He even feels loyalty for them. Back at his own home, he diverts his father's attention away from swatting the ants so they can escape. He is rewarded with his freedom just in time to face Sid. The ants, however, know how to repay courage and loyalty. Sid's power has been greatly "reduced."

Other Devices: *Antihero, Antithesis, Foreshadowing, Inference, Personification, Poetic Justice*

Art Style: Expressionistic acrylic cartoons skillfully play with perspective as both the boy and the ants view the same environment.

Curriculum Tie-in: Social Science (Bullies, Values)

*Say, Allen. *The Sign Painter.* Boston: Walter Lorraine Books (Houghton Mifflin), 2000.

An assignment to paint a large billboard in the desert changes the life of an aspiring artist.

Point of View: The man has settled for pragmatic reality; the boy still dreams of a career as an artist. "Now, there's a canvas for you," the man says to the boy when they arrive at their first blank billboard. The boy tries to put an artistic slant to it. "It'll be like painting a mural," he rationalizes. "But who's going to see it way out here?" The man is unconcerned. "That's not our problem." Later, the man asks him, "How does it feel to be a wage earner?" The boy does not think in economic terms. "I am a painter," he replies. The man remembers how it was. "We all have dreams. What made you want to paint?" The boy replies, "It's what I love." The man quickly dismisses that attitude. "But you found out you had to make a living." The boy's terse "Yes" in no way acknowledges a readiness to relinquish his pursuit of pure art. One works to live; the other lives to work.

Other Devices: *Ambiguity, Antithesis, Imagery, Inference, Theme, Tone*

Art Style: Magnificent realistic acrylic paintings unfold the contrasts in this provocative story about personal choices between issues of security versus dreams.

Curriculum Tie-in: Philosophy (Quality of Life)

Turner, Ann. *Drummer Boy: Marching to the Civil War.* Illus. by Mark Hess. New York: HarperCollins, 1998.

A thirteen-year-old soldier, coming of age during the American Civil War, beats his drum to raise tunes and spirits, and muffle the sounds of the dying.

Point of View: Who would ever have thought it would be the "crow boy," the one who threw rocks at birds in the corn, who would go to war? The young narrator reacts to ugly newspaper pictures making fun of President Lincoln. He "had to go to war somehow." He observes that "our horses live better" than do slaves. At training camp he learns to rap out bright, marching tunes "to put the spirit into our boys." His drum "makes them brave" and "covers the first sounds of battle. So I guess I am some use after all." He learns to "march out with the drum bouncing, rattling my sticks on the hide so hard the sound flies up into the sky." "If I kept beating my drum I couldn't always hear the men crying out or the horses dying, 'cept the ground shook when they fell." Months later he decides that when the war is over, "I'll stop to talk to Mr. Lincoln and tell him how it's his fault, how his great, sad eyes made me go and see things no boy should ever see."
Other Devices: *Atmosphere, Imagery, Simile*
Art Style: Stunningly realistic paintings bring to life what it must have been like to be a very young boy in an uncommon situation.
Curriculum Tie-in: History (Civil War)

Turner, Ann. *Secrets from the Dollhouse.* Illus. by Raúl Colón. New York: HarperCollins, 2000.

The life of a family of dolls and their servants living in a dollhouse in a young girl's room is told from the perspective of Emma, oldest of the doll children.

Point of View: Emma is excited to go outside for an adventure and is delighted with snow, which seems to her like tiny white handkerchiefs falling from the sky. Boy takes the dolls outside to play war. They wonder what this is. "He put us in the tall grass where thunder boomed, something roared, and Boy crashed Mama and Papa together." Emma says she now knows what War is: "The hats hide your eyes, it is noisy, and you fall down too much." When Baby goes missing, Emma thinks "Cat took her and will chew her for breakfast." When the family is together again, they are happy, "all bunched up on two beds under one spread."
Other Devices: *Foreshadowing, Imagery, Metaphor, Personification, Simile*
Art Style: Stiff 1920s folk images in scratcher line pastels capture the whimsy of a toy world.

PUN

Word play when two meanings appear in one word, or in two words of identical sound but different spelling, or in words of similar sound but different meaning.

Example: 1. Words spelled or pronounced the same but with different meanings.

Example: "Now we must all 'hang' together or we will surely 'hang'
separately." (Ben Franklin),
(If the revolutionaries did not remain united, their
individual lives would be in danger.)
2. Words that are homonyms.
Example: lone/loan
3. Words that have close similarities in sound or meaning.
Example: First line of song: "O, say, can you see . . . ."
Hosea: "Yes, I see fine . . . ."

*Cole, Brock. *Buttons*. New York: Farrar Straus Giroux, 2000.
When their father eats so much that he pops the buttons off his britches, each
of his three daughters tries a different plan to find replacements.
Pun: His buttons pop off and fly into the stove. "We are *undone!*" he
laments. The pants fall down, and the man cannot earn a living.
Other Devices: *Aphorism, Inference, Irony, Tone*
Art Style: Pen/ink and watercolor combine in humorous cartoons that
complement this lighthearted spoof on courtship and family duty.
Curriculum Tie-in: Literature (Fairy Tale)

*Deedy, Carmen Agra. *The Yellow Star: The Legend of King Christian X of Den-
mark*. Illus. by Henri Sorensen. Atlanta: Peachtree, 2000.
King Christian must abide by the Nazi orders regarding the wearing of the
identifying yellow star, but he must also protect all the Danes from harm.
Pun: As the story opens, there is a description of all the Danes. Tall Danes,
stout Danes, old Danes, silly Danes, cranky Danes, and "even some Great
Danes." A photo of a large dog appears among the Danish dignitaries.
Other Devices: *Antithesis, Aphorism, Atmosphere, Foreshadowing, Inference,
Irony, Paradox, Parallelism, Simile, Symbol, Theme*
Art Style: Impressionistic oil paintings accompany the spare, terse text in
this vignette showing the political reality of the Danes' circumstances
during a very somber historical period.
Curriculum Tie-in: History (World War II—Nazi Occupation—
Denmark), Literature (Legend), Social Science (Values)

*Gralley, Jean. *Hogula, Dread Pig of Night*. New York: Henry Holt, 1999.
Although he lives high on the hog in his castle on Grimy Pork Chop Hill,
Hogula is unhappy because he has no friends—until he meets Elvis Ann,
Dread Queen of Kissyface.
Pun: When Hogula finishes with a victim, he says, "Heh-Heh, *fang* you
very much!" He has no friends except several thousand bats to *"hang* with"
upside down, as bats do. Together Hogula (snort snort!) and Elvis Ann
(kissy slurp!) say "Good *Bite!*" to each other.

Other Devices: *Alliteration, Allusion, Antihero, Aphorism, Cliché, Foreshadowing, Inference, Irony, Poetic Justice, Simile, Stereotype, Understatement*
Art Style: Appropriately repulsive expressionistic cartoons in gouache and ink on watercolor paper develop the characters of this humorously gentle Dracula-style relationship.
Curriculum Tie-in: Social Science (Friendship)

*Hamanaka, Sheila. *Peace Crane.* New York: Morrow Junior Books, 1995.
    After learning about the Peace Crane created by Sadako, a survivor of the bombing of Hiroshima, a young African-American girl wishes it would carry her away from the violence of her own world.
    Pun: The girl describes the bomb's effect as "when the *sun* fell on Hiroshima." Similarly, in her own country the terror that comes during nighttime violence occurs "when the *sun* falls in the city."
    Other Devices: *Allusion, Antithesis, Flash-forward, Imagery, Simile, Symbol*
    Art Style: Luminous, expressionistic oil paintings on canvas celebrate the spirit of the Peace Crane's hope for a troubled world.
    Curriculum Tie-in: History (War and Peace—Japan and America)

Howe, James. *Horace and Morris but Mostly Dolores.* Illus. by Amy Walrod. New York: Atheneum Books for Young Readers (Simon & Schuster), 1999.
    Three mice friends learn that the best clubs include everyone.
    Pun: Dolores joins an all-girls' club and discovers them engaged in discovering the many uses of cheese. They call themselves "Cheese Puffs," a name denoting a feminine stereotype of delicate and rather minimal worth. Dolores is not that kind of girl. Maybe the girls can be persuaded to do something really fun. She asks her fellow members, "Anybody here want to build a fort? How about a *Roque-Fort?*"
    Other Devices: *Allusion, Internal Rhyme, Parallelism, Stereotype, Theme*
    Art Style: Acrylics and collage cartoons illustrate a basic gender response to excitement and adventure by showing few physical or behavioral differences between the male and female mouse children.
    Curriculum Tie-in: Social Science (Gender Equality)

Laden, Nina. *Roberto the Insect Architect.* San Francisco: Chronicle Books, 2000.
    Roberto the architect, who also happens to be a termite, sets off to the city to find success.
    Pun: Even when he is little, Roberto "went against the grain" of termite behavior. He "played" with his food, stacking it instead of eating it. He "pined for pine" and "melted over maple." Since his family does not understand his attitude toward wood, he was "hungry to start a new life." He wants to "build" his dreams in a place where other termites won't "bug" him. Without money, he has to rent a room in a "flea-bag" hotel run by

a "nervous tick." Soon he is feeling like a "pest." He is nearly "nailed" by a carpenter ant. He helps a homeless fly become a "house fly" again. Headlines in the Insect Inquirer read "Termite Chips New Homes Out of Old Blocks!"
Other Devices: *Alliteration, Allusion, Antithesis, Cliché, Parallelism*
Art Style: Astoundingly detailed mixed-media collage of paper, wood, blueprints, and gouache paint creatively bring this carefully crafted, witty text to life.
Curriculum Tie-in: Social Science (Values)

Lorbiecki, Marybeth. *Just One Flick of a Finger.* Illus. by David Diaz. New York: Dial (Penguin Putnam), 1996.
A young boy takes a gun to school to scare off the bully who has been tormenting him, and the gun is accidentally fired during the scuffle.
Pun: When two friends realize a bully is not going to back off, they "made a blood brothers' pact to stick together." Later, after the boy's friend is shot, they become actual blood brothers, "cause I begged to share, and they let me give him the blood I could spare."
Other Devices: *Antithesis, Foreshadowing, Inference, Internal Rhyme, Metaphor, Simile, Theme*
Art Style: Acrylics, watercolors, and digitally manipulated photographic backgrounds blend to create powerful, stylized expressionistic images that evoke danger and tension.
Curriculum Tie-in: Social Science (Bullies)

McNaughton, Colin. *Yum!* New York; Harcourt Brace, 1998.
Preston Pig suggests that Mr. Wolf get a job so he can buy what he wants to eat, but as he considers different lines of work, Mr. Wolf has a one-track mind.
Pun: Preston Pig asks Mr. Wolf what he would like to be. Mr. Wolf responds, "*Full.*" Preston Pig suggests Mr. Wolf could become a soccer player. Mr. Wolf declares he wouldn't mind "a *shot* at that" as he imagines kicking a fat, round pig to "*soften him up.*" Mr. Wolf imagines what it might be like to teach school with a room full of little pigs that are so *sweet.* As a pilot, Mr. Wolf can picture himself having "an in-flight snack" as he contemplates *pie in the sky.* All these career suggestions are "food for thought."
Other Devices: *Allusion, Ambiguity, Satire, Tone, Understatement*
Art Style: Detailed cartoons and humorous asides add to the impish joy of this wolf and pig encounter.
Curriculum Tie-in: Social Science (Values)

*Mamet, David. *Henrietta.* Illus. by Elizabeth Dahlie. Boston: Houghton Mifflin, 1999.

Henrietta Pig, rebuffed by the law school admissions office, like so many of her underprivileged kind before her, wanders aimlessly until a chance encounter with a vagabond philosopher enables her to pursue her dream of a scholarly future.

Pun: There is a play on the many meanings of the word "justice" in this fable. Remembering her earlier experiences of trying to gain access to the university, during her commencement address Henrietta places the emphasis less on her accomplishments as one from a disadvantaged group and more on a call for society to "work for social justice" in admissions policies and in life's opportunities. Ultimately, she does indeed place "social justice" as a high priority in her own life's work. She becomes a "justice" on the United States Supreme Court, where her job is literally to dispense justice for the sake of all.

Other Devices: *Inference, Irony, Personification, Satire, Serendipity, Tone*

Art Style: Spare pastel crayon impressionistic cartoons highlight in subtle, playful satire the foibles of higher education's entrenched, shortsighted traditions.

Curriculum Tie-in: Literature (Fable), Social Science (Diversity)

Mitchell, Adrian. *Nobody Rides the Unicorn.* Illus. by Stephen Lambert. New York: Arthur A. Levine Books (Scholastic), 1999.

Having been used by the king to trick a unicorn into imprisonment, Zoe decides to set him free again.

Pun: In her kingdom, Zoe is acknowledged to be "nobody." She has no parents, is unimportant, and is considered useful to the king only because she has been identified as having the necessary qualities to attract the unicorn. When she discovers she has been tricked into luring it into capture, she frees the animal. In gratitude, it asks her name. She says, "I'm nobody." It replies, "Climb on my back, kind Nobody, for nobody rides the unicorn."

Other Devices: *Poetic Justice, Simile*

Art Style: Naïve pastels in hazy earth tones contrast, in light and shadow, innocent childhood bravery with lurking, self-centered, devious authority figures.

Curriculum Tie-in: Social Science (Values)

O'Malley, Kevin. *Bud.* New York: Walker & Company, 2000.

The orderly Sweet-Williams are dismayed at their son's fondness for the messy pastime of gardening.

Pun: The staid, very proper Grandfather has suddenly been transformed into a head-to-toe dirty gardener, having a wonderful time rebuilding what a storm has messed up. His son, Bud's father, is puzzled. "Change is inevitable, Son," laughs Grandfather, "except from a vending machine."

Other Devices: *Antithesis, Aphorism, Foreshadowing, Inference, Irony, Theme, Understatement*

Art Style: Large expressive gouache cartoons lovingly follow the development of tolerance, respect, and appreciation for a beloved child's unconventional approach to life.

Curriculum Tie-in: Science (Gardening), Social Science (Family Relationships, Values)

Pawagi, Manjusha. *The Girl Who Hated Books.* Illus. by Leanne Franson. Hillsboro, OR: Beyond Words, 1998.

Although she lives in a house full of avid readers, Meena hates books—until she discovers the magic inside them.

Pun: Meena's cat Max does not like books either. When he was a kitten, an atlas fell on his tail, bending the tip like a pipe cleaner. "Ever since, he's tried to *stay on top of the books* rather than below them." He literally crawls on top of book piles.

Other Devices: *Alliteration, Allusion, Antithesis, Foreshadowing, Hyperbole, Inference, Internal Rhyme, Tone*

Art Style: Pen/ink watercolor expressionistic cartoons emphasize emotion and background action.

Sierra, Judy. *The Gift of the Crocodile: A Cinderella Story.* Illus. by Reynold Ruffins. New York: Simon and Schuster Books for Young Readers, 2000.

Damura of the Spice Islands escapes her cruel stepmother and stepsister, and marries a handsome prince with the help of Grandmother Crocodile.

Pun: Damura's stepmother and stepsister were "eaten up" with jealousy and devise a plan to throw her out of the boat to the crocodiles. But it is the stepmother and stepsister who find themselves in danger. If they ever show up at the river, "Eat them at once!" says Grandmother Crocodile.

Other Devices: *Foreshadowing, Irony, Motif, Poetic Justice*

Art Style: Folk images painted in bright acrylics portray this Indonesian version of an international folktale.

Curriculum Tie-in: Literature (Folktale)

Wallace, Karen. *Scarlette Beane.* Illus. by Jon Berkeley. New York: Dial Books for Young Readers (Penguin Putnam), 2000.

When family members give five-year-old Scarlette a garden, she succeeds in growing gigantic vegetables and creating something wonderful.

Pun: This family is totally devoted to the gardening life. Their house looks like a garden shed. They give their daughter, aged five, a garden of her own. Naturally, what surname could be better for such aficionados than "Beane"?

Other Devices: *Foreshadowing, Hyperbole, Simile*

Art Style: Bright primary colors and muted shadowy hues combine in expressionistic acrylic paintings on textured paper to illustrate a fantastic world of prodigious vegetable growth.

Curriculum Tie-in: Literature (Tall Tales)

*Wisniewski, David. *Tough Cookie.* New York: Lothrop, Lee and Shepard (William Morrow), 1999.

When his friend Chips is snatched and chewed, Tough Cookie sets out to stop Fingers.

Pun: "Tough Cookie" has been in the jar a long time. He may no longer be fresh, but he describes himself as having come from a "regular batch" with "lots of dough." He lives a rough life, but it's "still sweet," just a "little stale." The bottom of the jar is loaded with nice folks, sometimes called "crumbs." His girl friend, "Pecan Sandy" is one "cookie that doesn't crumble." His friend "Chips" gets "chewed up" pretty bad when "Fingers" attacks him. The other cops talk big, but "inside, they're marshmallows." Tough Cookie goes after the dreaded Fingers, then wonders if he's a "nutbar" to do this alone. Fingers gives the crumbs "the brush-off." After her timely assistance, Tough Cookie pays his girlfriend, Pecan Sandy, the compliment of calling her a "smart cookie."

Other Devices: *Analogy, Parody, Satire, Simile, Stereotype, Theme*

Art Style: Complex cut-paper illustrations in expressionistic collage work amazingly well to support this munchable mystery.

Curriculum Tie-in: Social Science (Friendship)

*Yaccarino, Dan. *Deep in the Jungle.* New York: Anne Schwartz Book from Atheneum books for Young Readers (Simon & Schuster), 2000.

After being tricked into joining the circus, an arrogant lion escapes and returns to the jungle, where he lives peacefully with the animals he used to terrorize.

Pun: The lion learns that he is not going to be allowed to perform his act solo, so he decides to end the arrangement. The man tells him he will always have to obey him, and he cracks the whip for good measure. The lion thinks a moment, and replies that he will then have to eat him up. "He swallowed the man, one gulp, right down." He's had a *bellyful* of show business.

Other Devices: *Anachronism, Antihero, Antithesis, Black Humor, Foreshadowing, Irony, Motif, Parallelism, Poetic Justice, Tone*

Art Style: Expressionistic gouache naïve cartoons against white backgrounds, reminiscent of the "Curious George" series, accent the droll language in this lesson in humility.

Curriculum Tie-in: Literature (Parable), Social Science (Values)

Zagwÿn, Deborah. *Apple Batter.* Berkeley, CA: Tricycle Press, 1999.

Because of their persistence, Delmore succeeds in learning to hit a baseball and his mother, Loretta succeeds in growing apples.

Pun: Delmore has put into the ground a plumbing pipe from which he practices hitting a baseball that he places on top of the pipe. As he begins to get control of his aim, "a good swing was no longer a *pipe* dream for him." Batting has been his stumbling block. "Batting drove him *batty*."

Other Devices: *Alliteration, Analogy, Antithesis, Foreshadowing, Inference, Irony, Parallelism, Simile*
Art Style: Expressionistic watercolor cartoons compare the changing fortunes of mother and son as they struggle toward their respective goals.
Curriculum Tie-in: Athletics (Baseball), Science (Apple Production)

SATIRE

Criticizing humanity or institutions with sarcasm, wit, and humor for the purpose of showing their absurdity and need of improvement.

Alderson, Brian. *The Tale of the Turnip.* Illus. by Fritz Wegner. Cambridge, MA: Candlewick Press, 1999.

A humble farmer's garden produce pleases the king, who handsomely rewards his efforts, but an arrogant squire gets more than he bargained for when he attempts to claim a similar reward.

Satire: The humble farmer, unused to expecting much from life, is happily surprised by a magnificent reward for his simple, generous nature. The rich and calculating squire is never satisfied with all that he has. His manipulating greed results in unhappy surprise and disappointment.

Other Devices: *Connotation, Hyperbole, Motif, Poetic Justice, Tone*
Art Style: Humorously detailed watercolor and ink cartoons delight the visual sense and the sense of justice.
Curriculum Tie-in: History (Nineteenth-Century England), Literature (Folktales—England)

Cowley, Joy. *The Video Shop Sparrow.* Illus. by Gavin Bishop. Honesdale, PA: Boyds Mills Press, 1999.

When George and Harry try to return a video, they find the shop closed. Trapped inside is a sparrow, which they try to rescue.

Satire: The boys turn to the adults in their town for help in opening the video shop and releasing a trapped bird. Their parents, the waitress, and the police are dismissive. One less sparrow is not worth fussing about in the grand scheme of life. So the boys, who know only that help is needed, go to "the top." The mayor is having a press conference. When she hears the boys' problem, "she smiled a big warm smile." This matter can be turned to her advantage. Forget the problems with the road taxes and sewer system. She has a self-serving story for the press. Using her influence, she soon gains access to the locked video store. The boys rush in to gather up the distressed sparrow "while the cameras went flash, flash, flash," and the mayor tells the newspaper people "that no job was too small for a caring mayor." George says, "She's a very nice lady." His father wryly notes, "And very smart." Above the newspaper photo are the words, "The Champion of Sparrows and Children."

Other Devices: *Inference, Theme, Tone*

Art Style: Pen/ink line watercolor style cartoons show the innocent intentions of the children in contrast to the distinctly disinterested attitude of the adults except where personal advantage may be gained.

Curriculum Tie-in: Social Science (Values)

Hoban, Russell. *Trouble on Thunder Mountain.* Illus. by Quentin Blake. New York: Ordhard Books (Grolier), 2000.

When Megafright International flattens their beautiful mountain to put up a hi-tech plastic theme park, the O'Saurus family uses faith and lots of Monsta-Gloo to put things right.

Satire: President J.M. Flatbrain is "delighted to tell you" that Thunder Mountain will be torn down. "Thunder Mountain is just a lot of dirt and rocks, with creepy-crawlies under the rocks and animals running around loose all over the place. Megafright Mountain will be clean and tidy, with entertainment for the whole family and no ants when they picnic." The O'Saurus family will be resettled at a "garbage dump reserved for you." The Flatbrain organization concludes its announcement letter with "We hope you will be pleased with this improvement . . . . Betterly yours, A. Worser." The dirt mountain is blasted apart. The pieces are taken to a beautiful valley. "Dump everything here, and we will fill in this valley and make it flat," says the project president. But the finished fake mountain disappoints tourists, who prefer to explore the real thing. Even the Tunnel of Terror is boring. Meanwhile, after carefully restoring it, the O'Saurus family is able to sell tourists packed picnic lunches and the pleasure of "interactive ants" for picnickers who want to explore a real dirt mountain.

Other Devices: *Aphorism, Connotation, Foreshadowing, Hyperbole, Irony, Poetic Justice, Understatement*

Art Style: Humorous pen/ink watercolor cartoons spiritedly produce a funny tribute to old-fashioned ingenuity and to nature.

Curriculum Tie-in: Science (Ecology)

Krudop, Walter Lyon. *Something Is Growing.* New York: Atheneum Books for Young Readers (Simon & Schuster), 1995.

When Peter plants a seed near a city street, things quickly change.

Satire: This city of the future is suspicious of and quite unfamiliar with anything "growing." When a neighborhood snoop notices the plant Peter has cultivated, she calls upon a professor to evaluate the situation. The "Gigantus floriticus" admittedly has unusual growing habits. It sends out spores that create other plant species. Now there are grass, vines, hedges. Can it be stopped? They will study the matter to "get to the bottom of this." The plant "is an eyesore." "We can't have trees hold up traffic." Though they admit, "the water looks cleaner." And people to seem to like the change. They gather to cheer Peter's efforts. They photograph him proudly to record the unusual event. They put the picture on a museum wall "for the world to see."

Other Devices: *Foreshadowing*

Art Style: Impressionistic acrylic paintings soften the shocking effects of plant life gone lushly abundant.

Curriculum Tie-in: Science (Ecology)

McNaughton, Colin. *Yum!* New York: Harcourt Brace, 1998.

Preston Pig suggests that Mr. Wolf get a job so he can buy what he wants to eat, but as he considers different lines of work, Mr. Wolf has a one-track mind.

Satire: The wolf knows what he wants, but takes no practical action to achieve it. "People don't realize what hard work it is catching pigs! All that scheming and creeping around . . . ." The wolf is lounging beneath a window carelessly left open by a foolish little pig. But the inattentive wolf is so busy feeling sorry for himself he fails to take advantage. Meanwhile, from inside the house, clearly audible through the open window: "Preston! Have you left that window open?" Still no practical action from Mr. Wolf, who fails to see his opportunity. "A wolf could starve! It's not fair—he's inside stuffing his snout while I'm out here with a rumbling tummy. When do I ever get to win?"

Other Devices: *Allusion, Ambiguity, Pun, Tone, Understatement*

Art Style: Detailed cartoons and humorous asides add to the impish joy of this wolf-and-pig encounter.

Curriculum Tie-in: Social Science (Values)

*Mamet, David. *Henrietta.* Illus. by Elizabeth Dahlie. Boston: Houghton Mifflin, 1999.

Henrietta Pig, rebuffed by the law school admissions office, like so many of her underprivileged kind before her, wanders aimlessly until a chance encounter with a vagabond philosopher enables her to pursue her dream of a scholarly future.

Satire: She has "no credentials save an honest and inquiring mind," so "the school had no time for Henrietta." She is in despair, having come to the "Athens of the North" precisely because "Boston sets itself up as our Seat of Learning, and have not the Luminaries in all the fields issued from there these last three hundred years?" The "Old Man," with whom she has her chance encounter, is impressed by her literary knowledge as they amuse each other exchanging quotes in their conversation. He asks her where she received her education. She replies by quoting the author Henry Fielding, "Education is most often useless, save in those cases it is near superfluous."

Other Devices: *Inference, Irony, Personification, Pun, Serendipity, Tone*

Art Style: Spare pastel crayon impressionistic cartoons highlight in subtle, playful satire the foibles of higher education's entrenched, shortsighted traditions.

Curriculum Tie-in: Social Science (Diversity), Literature (Fable)

Martin, Bill. *Chicken Chuck.* Illus. by Steven Salerno. New York: Winslow Press, 2000.

Chicken Chuck the rooster, who has set himself up as boss of the barnyard by virtue of the special blue feather in the middle of his forehead, finds his authority undermined by a circus horse with two blue feathers.

Satire: A thing is special only because it is rare. Once it becomes common, its desirability diminishes. "I'm the boss of the barnyard, for only *I* have a bright blue feather." And Chicken Chuck becomes very bossy indeed. Naturally, everyone else wants what has made him unique. They copy him by tying on blue feathers. How will Chicken Chuck remain special now? He must wear two blue feathers! Still, it doesn't seem quite as satisfying as was his original legitimate blue feather.

Other Devices: *Symbol*

Art Style: Energetic mixed media collages playfully illustrate the foolish pursuit of material possessions in the absence of values.

Curriculum Tie-in: Social Science (Values)

*Morrison, Toni, with Slade Morrison. *The Big Box.* Illus. by Giselle Potter. New York: Hyperion, 1999.

To make three unique youngsters conform to their rules, grown-ups create a world inside a box, including treats and simulated nature, but all the kids really want is the freedom to be themselves.

Satire: This is a scathing indictment of self-centered adults who haven't a clue how to react to children behaving normally. The children must be cured of having too much fun. One girl sang in class and wouldn't play with dolls and spoiled the pledge to the flag. A boy wrote his name on the apartment mailbox lid and sat on the apartment super's Honda and hollered in the hall. A third child upset the rural way of life by letting squirrels into the fruit trees, taking a bit from the horse's mouth, and feeding honey to bees. For such obvious transgressions, adults feel compelled to throttle their uniqueness before they are ruined. The children try to make their case by saying, "If freedom is handled just your way then it's not my freedom or free." Typically, the adults disregard each child's well-spoken argument. One child receives an "understanding hug"; another, a "knowing smile"; and the third, a "pat on the cheek" as they are put in "a big brown box." To keep them quiet, they are plied with treats considered by adults to please all children—store-bought cake, a four-color TV set, Bubble Yum, dolls with names, commercial endorsement items, popcorn, and Chee-tos. And, finally, as a sop to their childhood, their parents generously come to visit them on Wednesday nights, after the parents' favorite activities are finished.

Other Devices: *Antithesis, Inference, Internal Rhyme, Irony, Oxymoron, Theme*

Art Style: Naïve watercolors show the contrast between the real joy expressed naturally by the children in their simple outdoor amusements, and the cloying dissatisfaction with adult-provided commercial rubbish.

Curriculum Tie-in: Social Science (Values)

***Wilkon, Piotr.** *Rosie the Cool Cat.* Illus. by Jozef Wilkon. New York: Viking (Penguin Books), 1989.

Casper and Carolina are proud of their jet-black fur and despair trying to cope with their orange kitten, who likes to play with mice and sleep in the doghouse.

Satire: "This is terrible!" father Casper laments about his daughter's fur color. But crying and sobbing do not help. Rosie refuses to behave like a proper cat. Her parents' disapproval drives her away. She hangs out with red and even piebald cats. Her parents blame the dog for being a bad influence. Then they see her on television as the star of a rock group. "She's famous!" Neighbors are impressed. Rosie returns home. Casper is delighted. All his old objections to Rosie's behavior become insignificant in light of his beautiful grandkittens. One of them is even black, "the spitting image of me," Casper observes. And, wouldn't you know! He's the one who "does everything differently from his sisters and brothers."

Other Devices: *Antithesis, Foreshadowing, Inference, Irony, Poetic Justice, Stereotype/Reverse Stereotype, Symbol*

Art Style: Pastel and colored pencil expressionistic cartoons capture the family pride in its conformity as well as its frustration in the jolting difference of the odd one.

Curriculum Tie-in: Social Science (Family Relationships, Individuality, Values)

***Wisniewski, David.** *Tough Cookie.* New York: Lothrop, Lee & Shepard (William Morrow), 1999.

When his friend Chips is snatched and chewed, Tough Cookie sets out to stop Fingers.

Satire: Crime fighting, the law of the land, and social status get a bit of humorous ridicule. "You have to carry your ID card and sell-by date with you at all times. Freshness determines your level within the Jar. It's the law." Tough Cookie is on the force to help those with no power. The world calls them crumbs; he calls them friends. Once you're at the bottom of the jar, you never leave. Then his partner (they worked together on the Pfefferneusse case) gets chewed. At the police station they serve "lousy coffee and bad advice." Fellow officers tell him, "Nobody stops Fingers." Tough Cookie sets out alone to fight crime. He rejects neighborhood offers of help, but he learns that it takes community support to deter crime.

Other Devices: *Analogy, Parody, Pun, Simile, Stereotype, Theme*
Art Style: Complex cut-paper illustrations in an expressionistic collage work amazingly well to support this munchable mystery.
Curriculum Tie-in: Social Science (Friendship)

SERENDIPITY

Accidental good fortune that occurs just when it's needed.

Example: The fall roars from cloud
                Down the canyon wall . . . then ends
                In a maze of rainbows.
                                                                    Anon.

Altman, Linda Jacobs. *Amelia's Road.* Illus. by Enrique O. Sanchez. New York: Lee & Low, 1993.
　　Tired of moving around so much, Amelia, the daughter of migrant farmworkers, dreams of a stable home.
　　　Serendipity: After a wonderful first day of school, Amelia can't wait to tell her mother about it. She looks for a shortcut home and finds the "accidental road." It ends in a most wondrous tree, the sturdiest, most permanent thing Amelia has ever seen. She wants "to belong to this place and know that it belongs to her." What will happen when her family moves on? Amelia finds an old metal box, "the answer to her problem." She fills it with "Amelia-things" like a hair ribbon, her school name tag, the picture she'd drawn in class of her dearest wishes, and a photograph of her family. She buries the box under the tree at "a place where she could come back to."
　　　Other Devices: *Alliteration, Antithesis, Connotation, Simile, Symbol*
　　　Art Style: Acrylics on canvas in blocky folk style depict the farm laborers' nomadic life.
　　　Curriculum Tie-in: Social Science (Migrant Workers)

Camp, Lindsay. *Why?* Illus. by Tony Ross. New York: G.P. Putnam's Sons (Penguin Putnam Books for Young Readers), 1998.
　　Lily's constant "why" questions drive her father crazy until one day he discovers that questioning the way things are can be a very good thing.
　　　Serendipity: How fortunate it is that when the invading space aliens land at the park, it is Lily they speak to. They frighten everyone else when they emerge from their ship saying, "Tremble, earthlings! We have come to destroy your planet!" The unflappable Lily simply does what she always does. She asks, "Why?" This begins a dialogue that makes the Thargons

reflect upon their mission. Her persistence results in their decision to abandon their original intention and to return home. Earth is saved.

Other Devices: *Inference, Irony, Paradox, Understatement*

Art Style: Colored pencil cartoons illustrate the repetitious, rapid-fire questions from Lily and the answers she receives, that make up Lily's day and the day of those who suffer her presence.

Curriculum Tie-in: Social Science (Family Relationships)

Dengler, Marianna. *Fiddlin' Sam.* Illus. by Sibyl Graber Gerig. Flagstaff, AZ: Rising Moon (Northland), 1999.

Wandering through the Ozarks and bringing joy to people with his music, Fiddlin' Sam seeks the right person to take up his fiddle and carry on the practice.

Serendipity: Sam has spent his life sharing his fiddle music throughout the mountains. But now, in his old age, he still has one responsibility left. He must find someone to pass it on to. He is becoming anxious because he has found no one, and his time is growing short. Then he sees a boy trudging along the road. This boy seems vaguely familiar. When he learns where the lad is going, "things commenced to come together." "This boy sitting here next to him was a ringer for that other boy." And he, like Sam, is a restless wanderer. Even better, "the boy's fingers were moving. His hands itched to try the fiddle." Sam has at last stumbled upon the one to whom he can pass it on, the son of that first boy.

Other Devices: *Antithesis, Atmosphere, Foreshadowing, Inference, Internal Rhyme, Parallelism*

Art Style: Exuberant realistic and expressionistic watercolors in shades of bright yellow, pink, and blue faithfully reveal the emotional and physical details of this musician's life.

Curriculum Tie-in: Social Science (Missouri Ozarks)

DePaola, Tomie. *The Art Lesson.* New York: G.P. Putnam's Sons, 1989.

Having learned to be creative in drawing pictures at home, young Tommy is dismayed when he goes to school and finds the art lesson there much more regimented.

Serendipity: Tommy's love for art might have been stifled forever if the school's rigid rules had not been compromised by a sensitive art teacher. She tells him, "It wouldn't be fair to let you do something different from the rest of the class." But, to acknowledge his individuality, she adds, "If you draw the Pilgrim man and woman and the turkey, and if there's any time left, I'll give you another piece of paper and you can do your own picture with your own crayons." This is a plan Tommy can live with.

Other Devices: *Atmosphere, Flash-forward, Inference, Irony, Parallelism, Theme*

Art Style: Blocky pastel cartoons follow the fortunes and budding development of a young artist in a conformist world.
Curriculum Tie-in: Social Science (Individuality)

Johnson, Paul Brett. *Bearhide and Crow.* New York: Holiday House, 2000.
After Sam tricks Amos into swapping a prize-winning gourd for a smelly old bearhide, Amos decides to give Sam a taste of his own medicine by negotiating an even more worthless trade.
Serendipity: Amos brings home the bearhide, draping it over his shoulders. His angry wife chases him off for frightening her and for swapping the good water dipper gourd for the worthless hide. Amos holes up inside a culvert, and overhears two thieves discussing where they have hidden a bag of gold. He later uses this bit of fortuitous information to work some clever trades with Sam, who ends up with the bearhide again while Amos gets the gold.
Other Devices: *Atmosphere, Poetic Justice*
Art Style: Pencil sketches and acrylic painted cartoons humorously illustrate the changing fortunes and effects of greed upon these mountain swappers.

Johnson, Paul Brett. *Old Dry Frye: A Deliciously Funny Tall Tale.* New York: Scholastic Press, 1999.
A humorous retelling of an Appalachian folktale about a preacher who chokes on a chicken bone.
Serendipity: Determined to avoid blame for killing the preacher, one couple hoists Old Dry Frye on top of a mean-spirited horse "that wasn't much 'count." They then take a broom and slap the horse on the rear end. It takes off bouncing and bucking from side to side. Old Dry Frye's chin was "a-bobbin' and his elbows a-flappin'." This vigorous shaking process dislodges the chicken bone, and it flies out of Old Dry Frye's mouth. He's back among the living again, and the community is none the wiser. Now he is free to make mysterious mealtime visitations whenever he chooses, especially when fried chicken is on the menu.
Other Devices: *Black Humor, Cliché, Hyperbole, Inference, Poetic Justice, Tone, Understatement*
Art Style: Ebullient acrylic cartoons share the fortunes and misfortunes of the self-serving characters in this raucous Appalachian romp.
Curriculum Tie-in: Literature (Tall Tales), Social Science (Appalachian Culture)

Keller, Holly. *That's Mine, Horace.* New York: Greenwillow Books (HarperCollins), 2000.
Horace loves the little yellow truck that he finds in the school yard, but he has a problem when a classmate tries to claim it.

Serendipity: Once he says the truck is his, Horace is stuck with his lie and feels miserable about it. Unaware of the reason, everyone is kind to him when he makes himself sick with shame over his deed. Then, suddenly something happens that offers him a graceful way out. The real owner of the toy writes him a get-well note that tells him, "It's ok for you to keep the truck until you're all better. Then you have to give it back." Horace feels much better. At school recess the next day, Horace takes out the toy truck and lets it roll all the way down the slide to the truck's owner at the bottom. They play together with it in the sandbox, making roads and tunnels. When the bell rings, the friend takes the truck and they run back to class.

Other Devices: *Irony, Parallelism*

Art Style: The simple, stylized watercolor and black pen cartoons focus on the important elements of this emotionally charged situation as a child learns to value his character more than a toy.

Curriculum Tie-in: Social Science (Values)

Lamstein, Sarah Marwil. *I Like Your Buttons!* Illus. by Nancy Cote. Morton Grove, IL: Albert Whitman & Co., 1999.

When a little girl compliments her teacher about the buttons on her outfit, it starts a chain reaction of goodwill, good deeds, and thoughtfulness throughout the day.

Serendipity: As the day begins, Cassandra admires her teacher's buttons. When the day ends, Cassandra is delighted to curl up in bed with a brand-new kitten. "His eyes are so big and bright," she says, "I think I'll call him Buttons." In between, and unknown to Cassandra, many good feelings were spun off from her original compliment. The last person affected by someone's thoughtfulness was her father, who was moved to bring home the stray kitten as a gift to her.

Other Devices: *Irony, Theme*

Art Style: Acrylics, gouache, and watercolor pencil cartoons emphasize happy faces and bright eyes that express the joy of having been recipients of kind words.

Curriculum Tie-in: Social Science (Values)

Littlesugar, Amy. *Tree of Hope.* Illus. by Floyd Cooper. New York: Philomel (Penguin Putnam), 1999.

Florrie's daddy used to be a stage actor in Harlem before the Depression forced the Lafayette Theater to close, but he gets a chance to act again when Orson Welles reopens the theater to stage an all-black version of *Macbeth.*

Serendipity: Florrie knows how much acting means to her father, who is reduced these days to working in the Allnight Bakery. She wishes on the theater's old Tree of Hope, "Please, let my daddy be an actor again!" And the very next day it happens. "By order of President Roosevelt himself.

The old Lafayette Theatre was opening its doors once more." It seems Florrie's wish has come true.

Other Devices: *Cliché, Flashback, Foreshadowing, Inference, Paradox, Simile, Stereotype/Reverse Stereotype, Symbol*

Art Style: Rich oilwash impressionistic paintings suggest not only happier memories of when times were more prosperous, but also the temporary bleakness of the current Depression and the emerging hope for a better future.

Curriculum Tie-in: History (Black Culture—Depression)

*Mamet, David. *Henrietta.* Illus. by Elizabeth Dahlie. Boston: Houghton Mifflin, 1999.

Henrietta Pig, rebuffed by the law school admissions office, like so many of her underprivileged kind before her, wanders aimlessly until a chance encounter with a vagabond philosopher enables her to pursue her dream of a scholarly future.

Serendipity: What might have happened to Henrietta, were it not for the Old Vagabond, can only be speculated. However, with her "resources diminished," she is reduced to sleeping underneath bridges at night. Her kind nature comes to the fore as she observes an old man on a park bench, searching for his glasses. "The day was drawing in and it was cold, and she saw the Old Man was anxious." So she joins in the search. When it "proved bootless," she asks if she may see him home. The rest is history. He is impressed by her "well remembered and well read" knowledge, and reveals himself to be the president of the Great University. Because she has been of service to him, he asks her, "How may I reciprocate?" She is admitted as a student, and soon distinguishes herself in a brilliant career.

Other Devices: *Inference, Irony, Personification, Pun, Satire, Tone*

Art Style: Spare pastel crayon impressionistic cartoons highlight in subtle, playful satire the foibles of higher education's entrenched, shortsighted traditions.

Curriculum Tie-in: Literature (Fable), Social Science (Diversity)

Modarressi, Mitra. *Yard Sale.* New York: DK Pub., 2000.

When Mr. Flotsam has a yard sale in the quiet town of Spudville, his neighbors are first upset, then delighted by their purchases.

Serendipity: The Zings' rug becomes a magic carpet for neighborhood kids. The typewriter that zips off page after page of its own writing makes a best-seller for the owner. The telephone that rings up with messages from long-dead people enables its owner to begin a new career as a medium, Madame Olga. Mr. Rotelli opens a restaurant with his never-ending pasta maker. Mr. Twitchett supplies mountains of vegetables for the restaurant from his garden jungle. Everyone unexpectedly benefits from the amazing purchases they take from the yard sale.

Other Devices: *Allusion, Antithesis, Connotation, Hyperbole, Inference, Paradox, Understatement*

Art Style: Lively full-page watercolor naïve art accompanies an understated text.

Morimoto, Junko. *The Two Bullies.* Trans. by Isao Morimoto. New York: Crown (Random House), 1997.

Two bullies, one from China and one from Japan, inadvertently intimidate one another before meeting face to face, and never fight for supremacy as a result.

Serendipity: The Japanese strong man Ni-ou hears the footsteps of the approaching Chinese strong man, Dokkoi, and is frightened. He wants only to return home to Japan. But the Chinese bully flings an anchor into his boat and begins pulling him back to shore. Ni-ou paddles as hard as he can, but he gets nowhere as Dokkoi slowly reels him back. Ni-ou uses a rasp to saw through one of the anchor chain links. When it breaks, the pressure release makes Dokkoi lose his balance and fall into the water. "The earth shook and shook and created an enormous tidal wave that carried Ni-ou all the way to Japan."

Other Devices: *Irony*

Art Style: Gouache and pastel expressionistic cartoons humorously point out the pomposity of these two typical bullies.

Curriculum Tie-in: Literature (Folktales—Japan), Social Science (Bullies)

Ruurs, Margriet. *Emma and the Coyote.* Illus. by Barbara Spurll. New York: Stoddart Kids, 1999.

Emma thinks chickens are smarter than coyotes, and she struts boldly where no chicken should go to prove it.

Serendipity: Emma is able to use a fortuitous circumstance not only to frighten off the enemy but also to impress the farm family with her "intelligence." She climbs into a magnolia tree, under which the coyote trap had been placed. But the branch sways under her weight in the wind, and she falls out of the tree just as the coyote underneath is inspecting the trap. She lands on him and pecks his backside. The "coyote yelped and jumped forward—straight into the trap." Thanks to her fall, the enemy, who is too smart to walk into the trap, is propelled into it by a fortunate accident.

Other Devices: *Alliteration, Foreshadowing, Imagery, Inference, Irony, Motif, Parallelism, Simile*

Art Style: Bright primary color paintings expressionistically follow the fortunes of Emma and the barnyard animals.

Curriculum Tie-in: Social Science (Self-esteem)

Scamell, Ragnhild. *Toby's Doll's House.* Illus. by Adrian Reynolds. London: Levinson Books, 1998.

Toby is clear about wanting a doll's house for his birthday, but the adults in his life reinterpret his wish to coincide with their own childhood preferences.

Serendipity: Toby thanks his family members with hugs when he opens their gifts of a fort, a farmyard, and a car-parking ramp. But when he blows out the candles on his birthday cake, he wishes he had a doll's house. "And when he opened his eyes again, he could hardly believe what he saw. There it was, a beautiful doll's house, with an upstairs, and a downstairs, and a front that opened up." Toby has seen potential in the boxes that his other gifts came wrapped in. He can arrange them to become the doll's house he really wanted.

Other Devices: *Paradox, Stereotype/Reverse Stereotype*

Art Style: In colored pencil, crayon, pen/ink, and watercolor, the large, simple, cartoon drawings show a loving family and a happy resolution to a touchy issue.

Curriculum Tie-in: Social Science (Families)

Steig, William. *Wizzil.* Illus. by Quentin Blake. New York: Farrar Straus Giroux, 2000.

A bored witch causes trouble when she decides to take revenge on an old man, but her mischief leads to a happy ending.

Serendipity: DeWitt takes off the bad-luck glove and throws it into the stream under the bridge. He watches it turn into a repulsive witch, who is unable to swim. But she is also a fellow creature in need of help. He discovers something amazing as he dives in to rescue her. "Wizzil had been so thoroughly cleansed by the crystal-clear water that all her vicious nastiness was whirled away downstream."

Other Devices: *Alliteration, Ambiguity, Connotation, Foreshadowing, Internal Rhyme, Irony, Tone*

Art Style: Delightfully awful watercolor cartoons capture the personalities and behaviors of the rotten witch and the hillbilly family she pesters.

Curriculum Tie-in: Social Science (Love)

SIMILE

Comparison between two unlike things for purposes of pointing out an attribute found in them both. This comparison is signaled by the terms "like" or "as" or "than."

Example: Laughed like a hyena; mad as a hornet; lower than a snake's belly in a wagon rut.

Alexander, Lloyd. *The House Gobbaleen.* Illus. by Diane Goode. New York: Dutton Children's Books (Penguin Books), 1995.

Unhappy over what he considers his bad luck, Tooley ignores his cat's warnings and invites a greedy little man into his home in the mistaken hope of improving his fortunes.

Simile: The more the little man partakes of Tooley's hospitality, the fatter he becomes, until he is round "as a pumpkin." The cat frightens the little man with tales of the Gobbaleen, who has eyes "big as saucers" and teeth "sharp as pitchforks." When the cat feigns fear of the "monster" Gobbaleen, his tail is "like a bottlebrush." Soon the idea of a Gobbaleen is stuck in the little man's head "like a burr." Nervous and susceptible, he is terrified when the cat bursts out of the food pot "like a jack-in-the-box." This is too much for the fat man. He rolls out the front door "like a cannonball."

Other Devices: *Ambiguity, Foreshadowing, Hyperbole, Inference, Irony, Theme, Tone, Understatement*

Art Style: Humorous gouache and watercolor cartoons illustrate this modern folktale.

Curriculum Tie-in: Literature (Folktale), Social Science (Values)

Altman, Linda Jacobs. *Amelia's Road.* Illus. by Enrique O. Sanchez. New York: Lee & Low, 1993.

Tired of moving around so much, Amelia, the daughter of migrant farmworkers, dreams of a stable home.

Simile: After a wonderful first day of school, Amelia is feeling "as bright as the sky."

Other Devices: *Alliteration, Antithesis, Connotation, Serendipity, Symbol*

Curriculum Tie-in: Social Science (Migrant Workers)

Baker, Jeannie. *The Hidden Forest.* New York: Greenwillow Books (Harper Collins), 2000.

When a friend helps him retrieve the fish trap he lost while trying to fish off the coast of eastern Tasmania, Ben comes to see the giant kelp forest he had feared in a new light.

Simile: The surface of the water is "like a mirror." The kelp is "like velvet" swirling against his skin.

Other Devices: *Connotation, Imagery, Inference*

Art Style: Photographed collages are multidimensional constructions of natural materials, such as pressed seaweeds, sponges, and sand, that create the enchanting world of ocean life.

Curriculum Tie-in: Science (Ocean Ecology)

Battle-Lavert, Gwendolyn. *The Music in Derrick's Heart.* Illus. by Colin Bootman. New York: Holiday House, 2000.

Uncle Booker T., who makes magic by playing his harmonica music from his heart, spends the summer teaching Derrick how to play.

Simile: The summer heat lay on Derrick's front porch "like a wool coat." Uncle Booker T.'s eyes flashed "as dark as his patent-leather shoes." At the neighborhood park, Derrick imagines running up and down the slide "like moving his fingers across the harmonica."
Other Devices: *Aphorism, Atmosphere, Inference, Tone*
Art Style: Expressionistic oil paintings show an appreciation of small-town African-American music played from the heart.
Curriculum Tie-in: Social Science (Ethnicity—African-American)

Bradbury, Ray. *Switch on the Night.* Illus. by Leo and Diane Dillon. New York: Alfred A. Knopf, 1983.
A lonely little boy, who is afraid of the dark, is introduced to a whole new world by his new friend, a little girl.
Simile: The lonely boy spent his evenings switching on all kinds of house lights. The house looked "like it was on fire!" Then he had a visitor. The girl's face was "as white as the moon." The light in her eyes shone "like white stars."
Other Devices: *Alliteration, Antithesis, Internal Rhyme, Irony, Metaphor, Motif, Paradox, Symbol*
Art Style: Surrealistic pastel drawings match the rhythmical text of this slightly magical, slightly scientific, and quite ethereal night world.
Curriculum Tie-in: Science: (Astronomy), Social Science (Fears)

*Bunting, Eve. *The Memory String.* Illus. by Ted Rand. New York: Clarion Books (Houghton Mifflin), 2000.
While still grieving for her mother and unable to accept her stepmother, a girl clings to the memories represented by forty-three buttons on a string.
Simile: Laura's cat breaks the memory string. Whisker's claws catch on the string, scattering buttons "like sunflower seeds." When the last button is at last found, it is Laura's stepmother, Jane, who discovers it. Jane knows Laura is uncomfortable with her presence in the household. She suggests to Laura's father, "Let's just leave it on the porch. Like a gift from a good fairy."
Other Devices: *Ambiguity, Antithesis, Aphorism, Foreshadowing, Imagery, Inference, Parallelism*
Art Style: Shadowy, impressionistic watercolor paintings detail the emotional changes the child experiences as she feels both separation and reconnection to her family.
Curriculum Tie-in: Social Science (Family Relationships, Grief)

*Bunting, Eve. *Swan in Love.* Illus. by Jo Ellen McAllister Stammen. New York: Atheneum Books for Young Readers (Simon & Schuster), 2000.
Despite ridicule of the other animals, Swan persists in his adoration for a swan-shaped boat named Dora.

Simile: Once a hand, "soft as neck down," reached out to stroke his feathers. Over the years, the boat deveops cracks, "thin as spiders' webs." The boat owner is "as fat as a bear in his bundle of a coat." Swan's life on earth ends. He drifts through waves of time, "his body light as mist."
Other Devices: *Antithesis, Aphorism, Foreshadowing, Imagery, Inference, Theme*
Art Style: Resplendent pastel expressionistic illustrations shimmer with grace as they illuminate the story of transforming love.
Curriculum Tie-in: Social Science (Love)

*Burleigh, Robert. *Edna.* Illus. by Joanna Yardley. New York: Orchard Books, 2000.
Carefree meanderings during her time in New York City give Edna St. Vincent Millay grist for a famous poem she later pens.
Simile: On the ferry were "rough old wooden seats that looked like church pews." The night out till dawn "stayed for a long time inside me, like a seed," until it welled up in sights, sounds and feelings in her writings.
Other Devices: *Atmosphere, Foreshadowing, Imagery, Parallelism*
Art Style: Expressionistic watercolors in vivid hues help re-create the marvelous feelings of expectation and freedom experienced by youthful artists in a city of promise that welcomes their enthusiasm.
Curriculum Tie-in: Literature (Biography—Poets)

Carlstrom, Nancy. *Goodbye, Geese.* Illus. by Ed Young. New York: Philomel (Putnam Books), 1991.
A father describes the coming of winter to his little girl.
Simile: The song of winter is "as clean as new snow." Winter wraps us in white "like the fields and the forest." Winter's arms are "as strong as the wind's spirit" but "as quiet as the moon holding its breath."
Other Devices: *Metaphor*
Curriculum Tie-in: Science (Seasons)

*Deedy, Carmen Agra. *The Yellow Star: The Legend of King Christian X of Denmark.* Illus. by Henri Sorensen. Atlanta: Peachtree, 2000.
King Christian must abide by Nazi orders regarding the wearing of the identifying yellow star, but he must also protect all the Danes from harm.
Simile: "Like a fierce storm," war was spreading across Europe. Soon Nazi soldiers gathered "like dark clouds" at the Danish border.
Other Devices: *Antithesis, Aphorism, Atmosphere, Foreshadowing, Inference, Irony, Paradox, Parallelism, Pun, Symbol, Theme*
Art Style: Impressionistic oil paintings accompany the spare, terse text in this vignette showing the political reality of the Danes' circumstances during a very somber period of history.
Curriculum Tie-in: History (World War II—Nazi Occupation—Denmark), Literature (Legend), Social Science (Values)

Givens, Terryl. *Dragon Scales and Willow Leaves.* Illus. by Andrew Portwood. New York: G.P. Putnam's Sons, 1997.

Although they are twins, Jonathan and Rachel neither look the same nor see things the same way—especially in the forest.

Simile: Jonathan's shield is "like a wall," and his sword "like an angry bee," as he defends his sister from the forest trolls, the dragon, the pirates, and the Vikings while out on their walk.

Other Devices: *Alliteration, Antithesis, Imagery, Metaphor, Point of View*

Art Style: Impressionistic watercolor pictures expressionistically celebrate the different ways we perceive our surroundings.

Curriculum Tie-in: Social Science (Individuality)

*Gralley, Jean. *Hogula, Dread Pig of Night.* New York: Henry Holt, 1999.

Although he lives high on the hog in his castle on Grimy Pork Chop Hill, Hogula is unhappy because he has no friends—until he meets Elvis Ann, Dread Queen of Kissyface.

Simile: When Elvis Ann smooches, her lips leave her face "like a water balloon shot from a bazooka."

Other Devices: *Alliteration, Allusion, Antihero, Aphorism, Cliché, Foreshadowing, Inference, Irony, Poetic Justice, Pun, Stereotype/Reverse Stereotype, Understatement*

Art Style: Appropriately repulsive expressionistic cartoons in gouache and ink on watercolor paper develop the characters of this humorously gentle Dracula-style relationship.

Curriculum Tie-in: Social Science (Friendship)

*Hamanaka, Sheila. *Peace Crane.* New York: Morrow Junior Books, 1995.

After learning about the Peace Crane created by Sadako, a survivor of the bombing of Hiroshima, a young African-American girl wishes it would carry her away from the violence of her own world.

Simile: The Peace Crane is described as rising "like a phoenix" from the fire of the atomic destruction. And the quarter-million souls killed in the bombing went soaring up "like a cloud."

Other Devices: *Allusion, Antithesis, Flash-forward, Imagery, Pun, Symbol*

Art Style: Luminous expressionistic oil paintings on canvas celebrate the spirit of the Peace Crane's hope for a troubled world.

Curriculum Tie-in: History (War and Peace—Japan and America)

Hesse, Karen. *Come On, Rain!* Illus. by Jon J. Muth. New York: Scholastic Press, 1999.

A young girl eagerly awaits a coming rainstorm to bring relief from the oppressive summer heat.

Simile: The heat makes the girl feel she's sizzling "like a hot potato." Her friend's long legs look "like two brown string beans." The phonograph music shimmies and sparkles and streaks "like night lightning." After the rain everyone feels "fresh as dew."

Other Devices: *Alliteration, Foreshadowing, Hyperbole, Imagery, Metaphor, Paradox*

Art Style: Buoyant, ebullient expressionistic pen/ink watercolors lend emotional credibility to the nervous anxiety of relentless heat accompanied by worrisome drought, and the tremendous sense of relief that accompanies a thorough, nourishing rain.

Curriculum Tie-in: Science (Meteorology)

Hopkinson, Deborah. *A Band of Angels: A Story Inspired by the Jubilee Singers.* Illus. by Raúl Colón. New York: Atheneum Books for Young Readers (Simon & Schuster), 1999.

The daughter of a slave forms a gospel singing group and goes on tour to raise money to save Fisk University.

Simile: It was said of Grandma Ella that "singing was part of that child the way swallows are part of the sky." She had a love of learning inside her that glowed "like a warm, bright flame." Her leadership enabled other students to begin to sing the old slave songs, too. Their voices joined hers, "like streams flowing into a deep river."

Other Devices: *Antithesis, Foreshadowing, Irony*

Art Style: Watercolor/pencil expressionistic muted lines and shades of brown, yellow, and green with scratch lines illustrate the contrasts of loss and hope in this grand success story.

Curriculum Tie-in: History (Black Culture)

Johnston, Tony. *Alice Nizzy Nazzy, the Witch of Santa Fe.* Illus. by Tomie dePaola. New York: G.P. Putnam's Sons, 1995.

When Manuela's sheep are stolen, she has to go to Alice Nizzy Nazzy's talking roadrunner-footed adobe house and try to get the witch to give the flock back.

Simile: The witch is "as old as rivers," "as old as hills, "as old as sandstone cliffs." Her voice scrapes "like gritty sand." Her face is "withered as a walnut," and her skin is "yellow as squash." Her teeth are "black as night." Her belt is conchos, "shiny as moons." And her velvet skirt "swishes like water" when she moves. Her brow grows "dark as a thunderhead." Her eyes get "big as sopaipillas." She crawls into her mortar, swirling off "like a storm."

Other Devices: *Alliteration, Connotation, Foreshadowing, Hyperbole, Internal Rhyme, Motif, Poetic Justice*

Art Style: Bright pastel and acrylic folk cartoons illustrate the southwestern lifestyle in this good vs. bad character tale.

Curriculum Tie-in: Geography (New Mexico), Literature (Fairy Tales— America), Social Science (Values)

Jones, Joy. *Tambourine Moon.* Illus. by Terry Widener. New York: Simon & Schuster
Books for Young Readers, 1999.

Noni is afraid as she and her granddaddy walk home, until he tells her how he
met her Grandma Ismay one dark night in Alabama, and how the big yellow
moon came to light up the sky.

Simile: The shadows of parked cars are "as huge as giants, as gray as rats
and twice as creepy." Car headlights look "like two miniature moons
riding on the front of the car." The choir members sing off-key, "like rocks
hitting a rusty can." Ismay, however, sings "like a brook in the Alabama
woods." Her voice is "low as twilight, light as a halo." In the scary woods,
every twig sounds "like a firecracker going off and every screech owl's hoot
sounded like a call to the haints." The night is lonelier "than a grave
without a tombstone." The tambourine moon hangs there, "like butter
running down the sides of a hot biscuit."

Other Devices: *Antithesis, Hyperbole, Imagery, Personification*

Art Style: Acrylic art in expressionistic, ethnic folk designs employs both
sharp angles and puffy, rounded curves.

Curriculum Tie-in: Social Science (Ethnicity—African-American,
Grandparents)

*****Kaplan, Howard.** *Waiting to Sing.* Illus. by Hervé Blondon. New York: DK Ink,
2000.

A family who loves music and spends many hours at the piano is devastated
by the death of the mother, but those still living find consolation in the
beautiful music that remains.

Simile: The windows of the boy's apartment are "flung wide open like the
little squares on my third best friend's advent calendar." His mother in her
flowery dress "looked like summer." Even in bed the boy thinks his family's
piano playing covered him gently, "like the whisper of an August blanket."
His and his father's hands on the keyboard together are "like skimming
stones, smoothing over the foamy white keys, navigating the black ones
as if they were rocks." When his father opens a sheet of music, the notes
look "like a thousand birds had landed in front of us." The cool, gray sky
"looked the way I felt inside." Before stepping up to play his solo, he runs
his fingers through his hair, "like a comb."

Other Devices: *Allusion, Antithesis, Aphorism, Atmosphere, Foreshadowing,
Imagery, Inference, Metaphor, Parallelism, Symbol*

Art Style: Shadowy, full-page sepia-tone pastel drawings expressionistically
evoke a fragile emotional period in the life of a family coping with
restructuring itself after the wrenching loss of one of its members.

Curriculum Tie-in: Music (Piano), Social Science (Death, Family
Relationships, Grief)

Kimmel, Eric A. *Grizz!* Illus. by Andrew Glass. New York: Holiday House, 2000.
Cowboy Lucky Doolin makes a deal with the Devil, agreeing not to wash,
shave, or change his clothes for seven years, thus earning a fortune and the
hand of his true love.

> **Simile:** The lovely Shelby is "sweet as huckleberry pie." During his exile,
> Lucky has hair that "looked like a buzzard's nest." He looks "like a grizzly
> bear. He smelled like one." He has a "beard like a mountain man." Shelby
> and her father are "as broke as a busted-down wagon" when the ranch
> comes upon hard times. The ranch owner accuses his lawyer of being
> "lower than a rattlesnake's belt buckle."
> **Other Devices:** *Atmosphere, Hyperbole, Inference, Motif, Poetic Justice,
> Understatement*
> **Art Style:** Oil sticks and watercolor dust create exaggerated cartoons that
> complement this version of a soul-selling wager folktale.
> **Curriculum Tie-in:** Literature (Folktales—America)

Kurtz, Jane. *Faraway Home.* Illus. by E.B. Lewis. New York: Gulliver Books,
(Harcourt), 2000.
Desta's father, who needs to return briefly to his Ethiopian homeland, describes
what it was like for him to grow up there.

> **Simile:** Evening comes "soft as a curtain closing." Her father tells her
> sometimes at night the "wind whooshed cold as old bones" through the
> trees outside his home. In this country there are white blossoms on her
> bedroom windowsill, "blossoms that look like snow."
> **Other Devices:** *Foreshadowing, Imagery, Metaphor*
> **Art Style:** Pen lines and watercolor expressionistic art capture the poignant
> reality immigrants face when they leave a beloved homeland for a new
> country.
> **Curriculum Tie-in:** Geography (Ethiopia), Social Science (Immigration—
> Ethiopia)

Kurtz, Jane. *River Friendly, River Wild.* Illus. by Neil Brennan. New York: Simon &
Schuster Books for Young Readers, 2000.
A family experiences a renewed appreciation for home and community after
they are evacuated during a spring flood and then return to survey the damage.

> **Simile:** The river wiggles "like a fat brown thread" along the flat quilt of
> the Red River Valley. Spring brings days warm "as the boots that snuggled
> my feet all winter." Melting water soon comes from the south "like a
> pickup truck in overdrive." When danger threatens, everyone is "as quiet
> as unturned pages in a book." The narrator lies in bed while her heart
> "pumps like a rowing machine." Her parents wander around helplessly
> "like balls of string, winding and unwinding." Later, when they return to
> inspect the damage, they stumble around "like a car that's lost its steering."

Soggy carpet "feels like an elephant" as they work to drag it out. The school windows look back "like empty eyes." Workers are "as dirty as smudge pots."

Other Devices: *Antithesis, Aphorism, Atmosphere, Imagery, Metaphor, Onomatopoeia*

Art Style: Oil glaze of brown paint overlaid by thin layers of color in different areas and additional glazes for depth create fuzzy, impressionistic scenes that suggest the essence of this emotionally wrenching natural disaster.

Curriculum Tie-in: Geography (Flood—Grand Forks, North Dakota)

Lawson, Julie. *Emma and the Silk Train.* Illus. by Paul Mombourquette. Buffalo, NY: Kids Can Press, 1997.

After seeing the beautiful silk blouse her mother made, Emma dreams of having a piece of silk for herself, and when the opportunity arises, determinedly pursues it.

Simile: Long shadows play tricks, making bushes and branches look "like people waving from shore and walking along the tracks." Emma ties her silk so it flows "like a banner between two trees" in an attempt to signal a passing train.

Other Devices: *Ambiguity, Foreshadowing, Imagery, Inference, Parallelism*

Art Style: Lush, impressionistic oil paintings capture the time and adventure of the silk train era.

Curriculum Tie-in: History (Railroads—Silk)

Littlesugar, Amy. *Tree of Hope.* Illus. by Floyd Cooper. New York: Philomel (Penguin Putnam), 1999.

Florrie's daddy used to be a stage actor in Harlem before the Depression forced the Lafayette Theater to close, but he gets a chance to act again when Orson Welles reopens the theater to stage an all-black version of *Macbeth.*

Simile: Florrie's daddy reaches out his hand to the wishing tree "like it was an old friend." Florrie imagines her wish "like a leaf, twirling and fluttering past those peddlers' wagons and empty buildings all the way up Seventh Avenue—to the Tree of Hope."

Other Devices: *Cliché, Flashback, Foreshadowing, Inference, Paradox, Serendipity, Stereotype/Reserve Stereotype, Symbol*

Art Style: Rich oilwash impressionistic paintings suggest not only happier memories of the past, when times were more prosperous, but also the temporary bleakness of the current Depression and the emerging hope for a better future.

Curriculum Tie-in: History (Black Culture—Depression)

Lorbiecki, Marybeth. *Just One Flick of a Finger.* Illus. by David Diaz. New York: Dial (Penguin Putnam), 1996.

A young boy takes a gun to school to scare off the bully who has been tormenting him, and the gun is accidentally fired during the scuffle.

Simile: The boy and his friend stick together "like a pair of Reeboks." The bully is "mean as a needle and thin as a weenie." When Reebo, the bully, smiles, it's "like ice sliced thin." The boy thinks that having a gun will make him "swift as lightning and hot as a racing engine." When he carries the gun, it hits him in the ribs "like a big heartbeat." He practices drawing it in front of the bathroom mirror "like a cowboy or a TV cop." After the gun goes off, his head feels "heavy as a bowling ball." His friend's older brother knows the score and is going to keep the boys "straight as a church steeple and proud as a Masai."

Other Devices: *Antithesis, Foreshadowing, Inference, Internal Rhyme, Metaphor, Pun, Theme*

Art Style: Acrylics, watercolors and digitally manipulated photographic backgrounds blend to create powerful, stylized expressionistic comic book images that evoke danger and tension.

Curriculum Tie-in: Social Science (Bullies)

Lowell, Susan. *Cindy Ellen: A Wild Western Cinderella.* Illus. by Jane Manning. New York: Joanna Cotler Books (HarperCollins), 2000.

Cindy Ellen loses one of her diamond spurs at the square dance in the retelling of this classic fairy tale.

Simile: Underneath her dirty old clothes, Cindy Ellen is "as pretty as a peach," while her stepsisters are puffed up "like two turkey gobblers" and dressed up "like a sore thumb." Cindy's fairy godmother chastises her for being "down and dirty as a flop-eared hound dog." Cindy's spurs are set with diamonds "as big as sugar lumps." She is a good bronc rider and stays stuck to the saddle "like a postage stamp." Fairy dust creates a dress that shines "like the sun, the moon, and all the stars together." Her skirt floats over petticoats "as soft and puffy as summer clouds." When the stepsisters try to make the spur fit their boots, the boots split open, and toes pop out "like puppies from a basket."

Other Devices: *Alliteration, Aphorism, Foreshadowing, Internal Rhyme, Parallelism, Parody, Tone*

Art Style: Action-packed, expressionistic acrylic cartoons hilariously support the story's western flavor.

Curriculum Tie-in: Social Science (Self-esteem)

Lowell, Susan. *Little Red Cowboy Hat.* Illus. by Randy Cecil. New York: Henry Holt, 1997.

Little Red rides her pony, Buck, to Grandma's ranch with a jar of cactus jelly in the saddlebag.

Simile: The wolf wears a cowboy hat "three shades blacker than a locomotive." It is too quiet at the ranch when Little Red arrives. It is "quiet

as a tree full of owls." When confronted by Grandma, the wolf drops Little
Red "like a hot potato."
Other Devices: *Aphorism, Atmosphere, Caricature, Hyperbole, Inference,*
Onomatopoeia, Parody, Stereotype/Reverse Stereotype, Tone
Art Style: Gouache cartoons in expressionistic naïve style humorously
match this unique geographical version of a familiar fairy tale.

Lyon, George Ella. *One Lucky Girl.* Illus. by Irene Trivas. New York: DK Pub.,
2000.
Even though their trailer is destroyed by a tornado, a young boy's family is
grateful because they find his baby sister alive.
Simile: The boy lives at a racetrack and describes the coming of the
tornado. The world goes dark, and it sounds "like we were under a stampede
of horses." In the aftermath, they find parts of their trailer strung along the
ground "like a road of crumpled tinfoil." Eventually the boy finds his
sister's crib on the racing greens, "right there in the green grass, plain as
cake on a plate."
Other Devices: *Ambiguity, Antithesis, Foreshadowing, Imagery, Inference,*
Metaphor, Parallelism
Art Style: Smudgy pastel illustrations impressionistically assist the story
line through use of both dark and bright colors.
Curriculum Tie-in: Science (Tornadoes), Social Science (Family
Relationships)

McKissack, Patricia. *The Honest to Goodness Truth.* Illus. by Giselle Potter. New
York: Atheneum Books for Young Readers (Simon & Schuster), 2000.
After promising never to lie, Libby learns it's not always necessary to blurt out
the whole truth.
Simile: The lie "slid out of her mouth, like it was greased with warm
butter." Mama's persistent questions make her feel "like she'd swallowed
a handful of chicken feathers." She gets into trouble when she pronounces
Miss Tusselbury's garden looks "like a jungle." Libby's horse is "older than
black pepper."
Other Devices: *Ambiguity, Antithesis, Aphorism, Foreshadowing, Paradox,*
Understatement
Art Style: A mix of pencil, ink, gouache, and watercolor gives a luxuriant,
expressionistic, naïve style to this tale of honesty.
Curriculum Tie-in: Social Science (Values)

Mahy, Margaret. *Simply Delicious.* Illus. by Jonathan Allen. New York: Orchard
Books, 1999.
A resourceful father engages in all kinds of acrobatic moves to keep an
assortment of jungle creatures from getting the double-dip, chocolate-chip-
and-cherry ice cream cone he is taking home to his son.

Simile: On the jungle path giant bamboos arch over his head with leaves "as large as dinner plates."

Other Devices: *Alliteration, Foreshadowing, Hyperbole, Internal Rhyme, Poetic Justice, Understatement*

Art Style: Lively line and gouache cartoons in lush jungle colors satisfyingly follow the father's adventures as he delivers his son an appreciated treat.

Curriculum Tie-in: Literature (Cumulative Tale)

Martin, Jacqueline Briggs. *Snowflake Bentley.* Illus. by Mary Azarian. Boston: Houghton Mifflin, 1998 (Caldecott—1999).

This is a biography of a self-taught scientist who photographed thousands of individual snowflakes in order to study their unique formations.

Simile: Bentley thinks snow is "as beautiful as butterflies or apple blossoms." His first camera is "taller than a newborn calf," and costs "as much as his father's herd of ten cows." Snow in Vermont is "as common as dirt."

Other Devices: *Antithesis, Imagery, Parallelism*

Art Style: Woodcuts with hand-tinted watercolors serve this nineteenth-century folk art well.

Curriculum Tie-in: Science (Meteorology, Photography)

*Martin, Nora. *The Stone Dancers.* Illus. by Jill Kastner. New York: Atheneum Books for Young Readers (Simon & Schuster), 1995.

A young girl uses an old legend about stone dancers to teach her mountain village a lesson in hospitality and sharing.

Simile: The ancients live until the armies of other kings come "like a great river" to attack them. It seems to the child Anise that the great castle stones unfurl long, heavy arms "as softly as a deep sigh." Their great weight "crashes like thunder."

Other Devices: *Aphorism, Imagery, Inference, Irony, Metaphor, Parallel Story*

Art Style: Impressionistic oil paintings show the interplay of light and shadow, melding the real with the enchanted in this Nineteenth-century French peasant village.

Curriculum Tie-in: History (Nineteenth-Century France), Literature (Legends), Social Science (Values)

Meggs, Libby Phillips. *Go Home! The True Story of James the Cat.* Morton Grove, IL: Albert Whitman, 2000.

A homeless cat spends several seasons trying to survive the elements until at last a suburban family adopts him.

Simile: On the night of the terrible storm, the lightning "crackles like white fire."

Other Devices: *Ambiguity, Antithesis, Connotation, Inference, Metaphor, Point of View*
Art Style: Realistic pastel illustrations follow James's admittance into a family that provides what has been missing in his life for a long time.
Curriculum Tie-in: Social Science (Animal Companions)

Mitchell, Adrian. *Nobody Rides the Unicorn.* Illus. by Stephen Lambert. New York: Arthur A. Levine Books (Scholastic), 1999.
Having been used by the king to trick a unicorn into imprisonment, Zoe decides to set him free again.
Simile: In a dream, Zoe learns a song about the unicorn that states he "flows like milk." His mind is "peaceful as the grass."
Other Devices: *Poetic Justice, Pun*
Art Style: Naïve pastels in hazy earth tones contrast, in light and shadow, innocent childhood bravery with lurking, self-centered, devious authority figures.
Curriculum Tie-in: Social Science (Values)

*Myers, Christopher. *Black Cat.* New York: Scholastic Press, 1999.
Black Cat ambles on an eye-opening journey of exploring feelings about identity, beauty, and home.
Simile: Black Cat saunters "like rainwater down storm drains." He balances "like bottles somebody left on a wall." His eyes are "like the green of empty glass bottles."
Other Devices: *Alliteration, Imagery, Internal Rhyme, Metaphor*
Art Style: Bold combination of collage, ink, and gouache with striking perspectives lends an intensity to the peculiarities of metro life.
Curriculum Tie-in: Art (Medium and Technique)

*Nolen, Jerdine. *Big Jabe.* Illus. by Kadir Nelson. New York: Lothrop, Lee & Shepard, 2000.
Momma Mary tells stories about a special young man who does wondrous things, especially for the slaves on the Plenty Plantation.
Simile: Addie finds a boy child in a basket in the stream and scoops him up, discovering that where he's been sitting is a plump round pear, "as golden as the noonday sun." Jabe moves so fast picking cotton that the field looks "like a snowstorm in the dead of winter!" During a twister, full-grown trees are lifted out of the ground and tossed around "like they were no more than dry leaves." The story of a missing horse spreads through the Quarters "like fire set to dry kindling."
Other Devices: *Allusion, Anachronism, Antithesis, Flashback, Flash-forward, Foreshadowing, Hyperbole, Imagery, Inference, Parallelism, Symbol, Understatement*

Art Style: Strong, detailed pen/ink, watercolor, and gouache drawings wonderful expressionistic ambience to this folktale.

Curriculum Tie-in: History (Slavery—America), Literature (Tall Tale)

Osborne, Mary Pope. *Kate and the Beanstalk*. Illus. by Giselle Potter. New York: Atheneum Books for Young Readers (Simon & Schuster), 2000.

In this version of the classic tale, a girl climbs to the top of a giant beanstalk, where she uses her quick wit to outsmart a giant and make her and her mother's fortune.

Simile: The giant's footsteps sound "like the booms of a cannon." His snoring is "as loud as thunder." When he falls from the beanstalk, the ground shakes "like an earthquake." One biscuit is "as big as a cow."

Other Devices: *Hyperbole, Inference, Motif, Poetic Justice, Stereotype/Reverse Stereotype*

Art Style: Naïve drawings in pencil, ink, gouache, and watercolor expressionistically tell the familiar tale of the thieving giant and the rescue of stolen treasure.

Curriculum Tie-in: Literature (Folktale), Social Science (Values)

Ruurs, Margriet. *Emma and the Coyote*. Illus. by Barbara Spurll. New York: Stoddart Kids, 1999.

Emma thinks chickens are smarter than coyotes, and she struts boldly where no chicken should go to prove it.

Simile: Emma fits on her nest "like the lid on a cookie jar." She warns the farm family about the encroaching coyote by hopping up and down on an apple crate under the kitchen window, "bouncing like a ball!"

Other Devices: *Alliteration, Foreshadowing, Imagery, Inference, Irony, Motif, Parallelism, Serendipity*

Art Style: Bright primary color paintings expressionistically follow the fortunes of Emma and the barnyard animals.

Curriculum Tie-in: Social Science (Self-esteem)

Strete, Craig Kee. *The Lost Boy and the Monster*. Illus. by Steve Johnson and Lou Fancher. New York: G.P. Putnam's Sons (Penguin Books for Young Readers), 1999.

With the help of a rattlesnake and a scorpion, a lost boy gains two names and defeats the horrible foot-eating monster.

Simile: The monster's teeth are "hard as stone"; his eyes are "as big and bulgy as old tires."

Other Devices: *Ambiguity, Connotation, Internal Rhyme, Motif, Poetic Justice, Theme, Tone*

Art Style: Textured paste, oil paint, potato stamping, and scratching tools create expressionistic paintings in brown and yellow tones reminiscent of American Indian folk art.

Curriculum Tie-in: Art (American Indian), Literature (Folktales—American Indian)

Turner, Ann. *Drummer Boy*, Marching to the Civil War. Illus. by Mark Hess. New York: HarperCollins, 1998.

A thirteen-year-old soldier, coming of age during the American Civil War, beats his drum to raise tunes and spirits, and muffle the sounds of the dying.

Simile: The young boy is impressed by the appearance of President Lincoln, who towers up into the sky "like a black tree." The boy watches the enemy move "like a herd of beasts, with the dust smoking up." He sees men fall "like grain cut down." Soon the battles run together in his mind "like a story too long for telling."

Other Devices: *Atmosphere, Imagery, Point of View*

Art Style: Stunningly realistic paintings bring to life what it must have been like to be a very young boy in an uncommon situation.

Curriculum Tie-in: History (Civil War)

*Turner, Ann. *Red Flower Goes West*. Illus. by Dennis Nolan. New York: Hyperion Books for Children, 1999.

As they journey west, a family nurtures the red flower they have carried with them from their old home.

Simile: The narrator describes the red flower as glowing warm and bright, "like a lantern to show us the way." The family is so tied to the welfare of the plant that when they arrive at their destination, they immediately search through their wagon for it, and when they find it unharmed, begin patting it "like it was an old dog." The land they choose for their new home is a green meadow stretched out "like Ma's flowered calico."

Other Devices: *Connotation, Inference, Metaphor, Parallelism, Symbol*

Art Style: Soft crayon and pastel realistic drawings, mostly in shades of gray, depict a stern pioneer experience accented by the bright red beacon of the family's talisman.

Curriculum Tie-in: History (Westward Expansion)

Turner, Ann. *Secrets from the Dollhouse*. Illus. by Raúl Colón. New York: HarperCollins, 2000.

The life of a family of dolls and their servants living in a dollhouse in a young girl's room is told from the perspective of Emma, oldest of the doll children.

Simile: Emma says she and her mother lean together whispering secrets "like two trees in the yard." Serious Papa is described as wearing his face "like a stiff hat." When Cook is in an uproar, all the flounces on her dress stick out "like angry tongues." When cat breathes, "it felt like fire on my hand." His eyes shine "like green lamps." Outside in the darkness, the night chill covers her face "like a cold blanket." The stars turn on in the sky "like lamps in a faraway ceiling." Some of them seem to be a road "like white dust shining." The doll household fears the cat with "teeth like knives." At Christmas wreaths hang on the door "like hard green candies."

Other Devices: *Foreshadowing, Imagery, Metaphor, Personification, Point of View*

Art Style: Stiff 1920s folk images in scratcher line pastels capture the whimsy of a toy world.

Waite, Judy. *Mouse, Look Out!* Illus. by Norma Burgin. New York: Dutton Children's Books (Penguin Putnam), 1998.

Inside an old abandoned house a mouse searches for a safe place to hide from a cat.

Simile: While a mouse tries to seek shelter and food a shadow comes creeping, "silent as the sunset."

Other Devices: *Alliteration, Atmosphere, Internal Rhyme, Metaphor, Poetic Justice*

Art Style: Realistic acrylic paintings in detailed perspective are a perfect complement to the pleasingly ominous, gently scary text.

Wallace, Karen. *Scarlette Beane.* Illus. by Jon Berkeley. New York: Dial Books for Young Readers (Penguin Putnam), 2000.

When family members give five-year-old Scarlette a garden, she succeeds in growing gigantic vegetables and creating something wonderful.

Simile: Most babies at birth are red-faced. Scarlette's face is described, by this gardening family, as "red as a beet." The house the family lives in looks "like a garden shed." When she receives her own garden, Scarlette digs in the soil until it is "crumbly as chocolate cake." Soon her special abilities produce carrots "as huge as tree trunks," onions "as big as hot-air balloons," and parsley "as thick as a jungle." The moon hangs "like a pearl in the sky." Scarlette's fingers flash "like green stars." The sun rises "like a huge golden coin."

Other Devices: *Foreshadowing, Hyperbole, Pun*

Art Style: Bright primary colors and muted, shadowy hues combine in expressionistic acrylic paintings on textured paper to illustrate a fantastic world of prodigious vegetable growth.

Curriculum Tie-in: Literature (Tall Tales)

White, Linda Arms. *Comes a Wind.* Illus. by Tom Curry. New York: DK Pub., 2000.

While visiting their mother's ranch, two brothers, who constantly try to best each other, swap tall tales about big winds and are surprised by the fiercest wind they have ever seen.

Simile: Clement shambles toward the house "like a hound dog on its way to a flea dip." Clyde shuffles toward the house "like a calf on the end of a branding rope." Clyde tries to keep still, but words shoot out of him "like

a cork out of sody water." Having her boys get along makes Mama "happy as an armadillo with an anthill all her own." When the big wind comes, their eyes grow "bigger than hen's eggs." When a herd of longhorns fly by, their eyes grow "bigger than goose eggs." And, their eyes grow "bigger than ostrich eggs" when they see Clement's red barn whip past. The wind brings a two-hole outhouse, doors flapping "like the wings of a dizzy duck." The boys cling fast to the porch rail, stretched head-to-toe "like arrows on a weather vane." The wind catches Mama's skirt, and it billows out "like a ship's sail at full mast." Flapping "like a broody hen," she calls for help to get down off the barn weather vane. Finally, in order to rescue her, her boys work "like two mules hitched to the same load."
Other Devices: *Atmosphere, Foreshadowing, Hyperbole, Inference, Parallelism*
Art Style: Painted acrylics in expressionistic naïve perspectives illustrate the peculiar and humorous effects of the forces of wind and imagination.
Curriculum Tie-in: Literature (Tall Tales)

*Wisniewski, David. *Golem.* New York: Clarion Books (Houghton Mifflin), 1996 (Caldecott—1997)
A saintly rabbi miraculously brings to life a clay giant who helps him watch over the Jews of sixteenth-century Prague.
Simile: The giant's chest expanded "like bellows." Shouted curses and drunken threats hurtled over the ghetto wall "like stones."
Other Devices: *Analogy, Atmosphere, Foreshadowing, Imagery, Inference, Irony, Motif, Paradox*
Art Style: Paper cut in sophisticated, expressionistic collage produces a powerful physical and emotional effect on this cautionary tale.
Curriculum Tie-in: Literature (Legend), Social Science (Values)

*Wisniewski, David. *Tough Cookie.* New York: Lothrop, Lee and Shepard (William Morrow), 1999.
When his friend Chips is snatched and chewed, Tough Cookie sets out to stop Fingers.
Simile: A slap stings his cheek "like a velvet bee." Darkness covers him "like a damp sponge."
Other Devices: *Analogy, Parody, Pun, Satire, Stereotype/Reverse Stereotype, Theme*
Art Style: Complex cut-paper illustrations in an expressionistic collage work amazingly well to support this munchable mystery.
Curriculum Tie-in: Social Science (Friendship)

Zagwÿn, Deborah. *Apple Batter.* Berkeley, CA: Tricycle Press, 1999.
Because of their persistence, Delmore succeeds in learning to hit a baseball and his mother, Loretta, succeeds in growing apples.

Simile: As the baseball season advances, Delmore becomes more anxious to improve his batting. The weather grows "dark as Delmore's mood." The one remaining apple on Loretta's tree is "round as a smile on the tree."
Other Devices: *Alliteration, Analogy, Antithesis, Foreshadowing, Inference, Irony, Parallelism, Pun*
Art Style: Expressionistic watercolor cartoons compare the changing fortunes of mother and son as they struggle toward their respective goals.
Curriculum Tie-in: Athletics (Baseball), Science (Apple Production)

STEREOTYPE/REVERSE STEREOTYPE

Predictable, oversimplified patterns of thinking or reacting. Reverse stereotype is the opposite of the expected.

Example: A stereotypical response to danger in an action adventure plot would be intervention by a strong male protagonist to save the life of a helpless female character. In reverse stereotype a female character would use her wit and intellect to get herself out of a dangerous situation, saving the male character as well.

Fearnley, Jan. *Mr. Wolf's Pancakes.* Waukesha, WI: Little Tiger Press, 1999.
When Mr. Wolf seeks help from his neighbors about how to make pancakes, he is rudely rebuffed and must rely upon his own efforts.
Stereotype: In a reversal of the usual plot, the polite and generous wolf in this story is the victim of his rude neighbors. Chicken Little slams the door in Mr. Wolf's face. So does Wee Willy Winkie. The Gingerbread Man shouts that he is too busy to bother with Mr. Wolf. Little Red Riding Hood tells him to "Get out of here! I'm not lending my basket to you!" The Three Little Pigs say, "Forget about it!" when he asks for assistance cooking his pancakes. To their regret, they won't accept the kinder, gentler wolf. They push him to the edge by shoving their way into his kitchen to help themselves to his pancakes. So be it. In a flash he eats them up.
Other Devices: *Allusion, Antihero, Black Humor, Irony, Poetic Justice*
Art Style: Detailed cartoons in pen/ink and watercolor drawings delight the reader not only with the story in progress but also with humorous nods to many Mother Goose rhymes and fairy-tale personalities.
Curriculum Tie-in: Social Science (Conduct and Behavior)

Gibbons, Faye. *Mama and Me and the Model T.* Illus. by Ted Rand. New York: Morrow, 1999.
When Mr. Long says any man can drive a car, Mama gets behind the wheel to show women can drive, too.

Stereotype: Mr. Long addresses himself to the boys. "Now gather round, boys. You'll be driving this motorcar someday. You girls step back." The boys agree. "Cars are for boys," one of them says. The males fail to see the frown of denial on Mama's face and the dissatisfaction among the females. After his driving instructions, Mr. Long asks who remembers what he said. The boys say they do. Mama says she does. "Mr. Long edged us girls aside. 'Pay attention, boys, while I show you again. Men need to learn to drive.' " One of the boys remarks, "And girls don't. Girls just ride." That is all it takes for Mama to take over. Everyone learns from this lesson, especially Mr. Long. After Mama's wild drive, he says, "I guess this Model T belongs to all of us."

Other Devices: *Foreshadowing, Hyperbole, Imagery, Inference, Onomatopoeia, Parallelism, Understatement*

Art Style: Expressionistic watercolors exuberantly dramatize the mysterious intricacies of mastering the wondrous but tricky skills of automobile driving.

Curriculum Tie-in: Social Science (Family Relationships)

*Gralley, Jean. *Hogula, Dread Pig of Night.* New York: Henry Holt, 1999.

Although he lives high on the hog in his castle on Grimy Pork Chop Hill, Hogula is unhappy because he has no friends—until he meets Elvis Ann, Dread Queen of Kissyface.

Stereotype: Hogula's home is, of course, on *Grimy* Pork Chop Hill. And he packs his castle with *mud and swill and old garbagey things* a pig is expected to like.

Other Devices: *Alliteration, Allusion, Antihero, Aphorism, Cliché, Foreshadowing, Inference, Irony, Poetic Justice, Pun, Simile, Understatement*

Art Style: Appropriately repulsive expressionistic cartoons in gouache and ink on watercolor paper develop the characters of this humorously gentle Dracula-style relationship.

Curriculum Tie-in: Social Science (Friendship)

Howe, James. *Horace and Morris but Mostly Dolores.* Illus. by Amy Walrod. New York: Atheneum Books for Young Readers (Simon & Schuster), 1999.

Three mice friends learn that the best clubs include everyone.

Stereotype: The three have a lot in common and enjoy each other's company, but "a boy mouse must do what a boy mouse must do." So Horace and Morris make a decision to leave Dolores and join the "Mega-Mice" boys' club, where they play combat games and sports. No girls are allowed. Soon Dolores also finds a club, the "Cheese Puffs" girls' club, no boys allowed. She figures "a girl mouse must do what a girl mouse must do." She finds herself making gifts for mother from Muenster and learning how to get a fella with Mozzarella. She is bored. She asks if anyone would like to build a fort. Her club members gasp in shock. So Dolores quits. She is joined by another girl mouse, Chloris, also tired of doing "girl" stuff. They go to the boys' club and ask the members, "Who wants to go exploring?" Most of the boys say, "yuck!!" and "with girls?" and "no way!" But Horace and Morris and another boy named Boris say, "I do." So the five friends go off to have fun. The next day they build a clubhouse of their own and allow everyone to join.

Other Devices: *Allusion, Internal Rhyme, Parallelism, Pun, Theme*

Art Style: Acrylics and collage cartoons illustrate a basic gender response to excitement and adventure by showing few physical or behavioral differences between the male and female mouse children.

Curriculum Tie-in: Social Science (Gender Equality)

Littlesugar, Amy. *Tree of Hope.* Illus. by Floyd Cooper. New York: Philomel (Penguin Putnam), 1999.

Florrie's daddy used to be a stage actor in Harlem before the Depression forced the Lafayette Theater to close, but he gets a chance to act again when Orson Welles reopens the theater to stage an all-black version of *Macbeth*.

Stereotype/Reverse Stereotype: Some folks in Harlem are angry that black actors are willing to work in a white man's play. "We oughta only be doin' plays written 'bout us. Them people at the Lafayette've come to Harlem just to laugh at us!" But Orson Welles's *Macbeth* is about black people's experience. He sets the play not on the Scottish heath but on the island of Haiti, where King Christophe once ruled. The monstrous castle is surrounded by a dark green jungle. The "conjure men" come from western Africa and use drums made from goat skins to tell Macbeth's terrible fortune. The play's timeless theme of greed overcomes ethnic differences.

Other Devices: *Cliché, Flashback, Foreshadowing, Inference, Paradox, Serendipity, Simile, Symbol*

Art Style: Rich oilwash impressionistic paintings suggest not only happier memories of the past, when times were more prosperous, but also the temporary bleakness of the current Depression and the emerging hope for a better future.

Curriculum Tie-in: History (Black Culture—Depression)

Lowell, Susan. *Little Red Cowboy Hat.* Illus. by Randy Cecil. New York: Henry Holt, 1997.

Little Red rides her pony, Buck, to Grandma's ranch with a jar of cactus jelly in the saddlebag.

Stereotype/Reverse Stereotype: Grandma is not a helpless victim in this version of the Little Red story. She, not a rescuing man, is the ax-wielding defender of the child. And together girl and woman chase off the wolf, who behaves very much like the predator he is.

Other Devices: *Aphorism, Atmosphere, Caricature, Hyperbole, Inference, Onomatopoeia, Parody, Simile, Tone*

Art Style: Gouache cartoons in expressionistic naïve style humorously match this unique geographical version of a familiar fairy tale.

Osborne, Mary Pope. *Kate and the Beanstalk.* Illus. by Giselle Potter. New York: Atheneum Books for Young Readers (Simon & Schuster), 2000.

In this version of the classic tale, a girl climbs to the top of a giant beanstalk, where she uses her quick wit to outsmart a giant and make her and her mother's fortune.

Stereotype/Reverse Stereotype: In the familiar rendition of the beanstalk story, Jack is somewhat thickheaded and foolishly loses the family's last hope against starvation when he trades possessions for beans. Kate is described as "plucky" and loving to help out. When her mother sends her out to sell the family cow, she says, "Don't worry, I'll take care of everything." For all her fine intentions, she, too, trades the last possession for the enticing beans. Her mother is as upset as Jack's mother was, and predicts, "Now we will surely starve!" When her help is requested, Kate bravely steals back from the giant the valuable items he had taken from the owner of the castle at the top of the beanstalk. Like the boy Jack, she saves the day by chopping down the beanstalk, causing the giant to fall to his death and thereby ridding the valley of an evil presence. She proves able to use her wits as well as a boy.

Other Devices: *Hyperbole, Inference, Motif, Poetic Justice, Simile*

Art Style: Naïve drawings in pencil, ink, gouache, and watercolor expressionistically tell the familiar tale of the thieving giant and the rescue of stolen treasure.

Curriculum Tie-in: Literature (Folktale), Social Science (Values)

Scamell, Ragnhild. *Toby's Doll's House.* Illus. by Adrian Reynolds. London: Levinson Books, 1998.

Toby is clear about wanting a doll's house for his birthday, but the adults in his life reinterpret his wish to coincide with their own childhood preferences.

Stereotype: Toby has drawn a house plan. He wants his doll's house to have an upstairs and a downstairs and a front that opens up. He has even made furniture from empty matchboxes and bits of cardboard and plastic. He has made people cut out from a magazine. It is all ready to move into a doll's house when he gets one for this birthday. But nobody hears Toby when he tells them, "All I want is a doll's house." Grandad says, "He means a fort. I always wanted a fort when I was a boy." Auntie says, "He means a farmyard, with horses and cows, and pigs and sheep." Dad says, "What Toby wants is a multistory car-park full of toy cars." This family is trying to reinvent Toby. No boy would really want a doll's house. But Toby does, and he's a boy. And, as any typical boy might do under similar circumstances, he finally makes one from the gift boxes and wrapping paper that the fort, the farmyard, and the parking garage were packed in.

Other Devices: *Paradox, Serendipity*
Art Style: With colored pencil, crayon, pen/ink, and watercolor, the large, simple cartoon drawings show a loving family and a happy resolution to a touchy issue.
Curriculum Tie-in: Social Science (Family Relationships)

*Wilkon, Piotr. *Rosie the Cool Cat.* Illus. by Jozef Wilkon. New York: Viking (Penguin Books), 1989.

Casper and Carolina are proud of their jet-black fur and despair trying to cope with their orange kitten, who likes to play with mice and sleep in the doghouse.
Stereotype: Her parents want Rosie to learn to "behave like a proper cat." Cats are supposed to catch mice, not play with them. But the final straw is her relationship with the dog. "A friendship between a dog and a cat was not allowed."
Other Devices: *Antithesis, Foreshadowing, Inference, Irony, Poetic Justice, Satire, Symbol*
Art Style: Pastel and colored pencil expressionistic cartoons capture the family pride in its conformity as well as its sense of frustration at the jolting difference of the odd one.
Curriculum Tie-in: Social Science (Family Relationships, Individuality, Values)

*Wisniewski, David. *Tough Cookie.* New York: Lothrop, Lee and Shepard (William Morrow), 1999.

When his friend Chips is snatched and chewed, Tough Cookie sets out to stop Fingers.
Stereotype: This story has the classic hard-boiled detective; the classy, beautiful, but smart blond; loyal common folk; and inept police. It's up to the detective to stand alone against the bad guy, whom everyone else fears to face. The tough detective has a soft spot for the underdog and puts his life on the line. But in the end, he admits he needs the help of loyal friends to help save the situation.
Other Devices: *Analogy, Parody, Pun, Satire, Simile, Theme*
Art Style: Complex cut-paper illustrations in an expressionistic collage work amazingly well to support this munchable mystery.
Curriculum Tie-in: Social Science (Friendship)

SYMBOL

Any person, object, or action that has additional meaning beyond itself to represent or stand for a more abstract emotion or idea.

Example: Great Conestogas, white against the sky:
          Listen to the rumble as the East goes by.
                              Jessamyn West, "Conestoga Wagons"

Altman, Linda Jacobs. *Amelia's Road.* Illus. by Enrique O. Sanchez. New York: Lee & Low, 1993.
> Tired of moving around so much, Amelia, the daughter of migrant farmworkers, dreams of a stable home.
>> **Symbol:** Amelia hates roads so much, that she cries every time her father takes out the map. Roads are long and cheerless, and lead to labor camps instead of a permanent home. Then she finds a different kind of road, an "accidental road," which is more a rocky footpath. It ends at a most wondrous tree, "quite the sturdiest, most permanent thing Amelia had ever seen." She closes her eyes and pictures it in front of a tidy, white dream house. So determined to come back to this special spot again, she doesn't even mind when it's time to move on. She has found a homesite.
>> **Other Devices:** *Alliteration, Antithesis, Connotation, Serendipity, Simile*
>> **Art Style:** Acrylics on canvas in blocky, ethnic folk style depict the familiar farm labor nomadic life.
>> **Curriculum Tie-in:** Social Science (Migrant Workers)

*Berkeley, Laura. *The Spirit of the Maasai Man.* New York: Barefoot Books, 2000.
> Locked inside their cages, the zoo animals have given up hope until the spirit of the Maasai Man hums his haunting songs of their homeland.
>> **Symbol:** The spirit of the Maasai Man is the best spirit that lives in all of us and communicates the need of the animal world to be free to follow their natural earth-songs. Like the animals in their zoo cages, our spirits, too, can be transported in our minds beyond the walls of our present life to an understanding of the needs of other beings.
>> **Other Devices:** *Imagery, Theme, Tone*
>> **Art Style:** Realistic acrylic and crayon drawings touchingly illuminate the plight of captive wild animals in expressionistic settings.
>> **Curriculum Tie-in:** Geography (Animal Habitats), Science (Zoos)

Bradbury, Ray. *Switch on the Night.* Illus. by Leo and Diane Dillon. New York: Alfred A. Knopf, 1983.
> A lonely little boy, who is afraid of the dark, is introduced to a whole new world by his new friend, a little girl.
>> **Symbol:** When the story opens, the boy doesn't like light switches. They turn off light, and he fears the dark. "He wouldn't touch a light switch." After the stranger's visit, he is able to perceive light switches as not shutting out light, but rather as turning on the night. His fear of the dark has been turned into love of nighttime offerings.

Other Devices: *Alliteration, Antithesis, Internal Rhyme, Irony, Metaphor, Motif, Paradox, Simile*
Art Style: Surrealistic pastel drawings match the rhythmical text of this slightly magical, slightly scientific, and quite ethereal night world.
Curriculum Tie-in: Science (Astronomy), Social Science (Fears)

*Cronin, Doreen. *Click, Clack, Moo Cows That Type.* Illus. by Betsy Lewin. New York: Simon & Schuster, 2000.
Farmer Brown's cows find a typewriter in the barn and start making demands that result in their going on strike when he refuses to give them what they want.
Symbol: This classic tale of union operation has both employees and a company boss. The cows and chickens work for Farmer Brown. They want their conditions improved. They are cold and ask for electric blankets. Farmer Brown considers them impudent to make such a request. He refuses to give them what they want. They go on strike, refusing to give him milk and eggs. Negotiation begins. They compromise. The typewriter will be returned if Farmer Brown provides electric blankets. The matter is on its way to being resolved. Other employees learn about the power of forming a union. Soon they, too, are making their own demands for improvements.
Other Devices: *Inference, Irony*
Art Style: Lampblack watercolor overlaid by watercolor washes creates simple cartoons with striking perspectives that illustrate the developing agreements finally reached.
Curriculum Tie-in: Economics (Unions)

*Deedy, Carmen Agra. *The Yellow Star: The Legend of King Christian X of Denmark.* Illus. by Henri Sorensen. Atlanta: Peachtree, 2000.
King Christian must abide by Nazi orders regarding the wearing of the identifying yellow star, but he must also protect all the Danes from harm.
Symbol: The Nazi flag flying over the Danes' palace is a hated symbol of fear and abuse. When they win the small victory of its removal, the Danes look upon the place where it used to fly as a powerful symbol of resistance. The yellow stars that Jews are forced to wear are embraced by every Dane, thereby becoming a symbol of unity and hope against violations of human rights.
Other Devices: *Antithesis, Aphorism, Atmosphere, Foreshadowing, Inference, Irony, Paradox, Parallelism, Pun, Simile, Theme*
Art Style: Impressionistic oil paintings accompany the spare, terse text in this vignette showing the political reality of the Danes' circumstances during a very somber period of history.
Curriculum Tie-in: History (World War II—Nazi Occupation—Denmark), Literature (Legend), Social Science (Values)

*Hamanaka, Sheila. *Peace Crane.* New York: Morrow Junior Books, 1995.

After learning about the Peace Crane created by Sadako, a survivor of the bombing of Hiroshima, a young African-American girl wishes it would carry her away from the violence of her own world.

Symbol: The crane, a Japanese symbol of long life, is borrowed by the American child. She wonders, "Are you flying still?" If a thousand paper cranes represented wishes for life and for peace, could she, too, fold her "dreams inside the wings of a crisp white paper crane?" She asks whether the souls that fall to violence in the city have flown up to heaven. She sees the crane as the embodiment of hope and peace for all times, its home "in my heart" and "with the homeless."

Other Devices: *Allusion, Antithesis, Flash-forward, Imagery, Pun, Simile*

Art Style: Luminous, expressionistic oil paintings on canvas celebrate the spirit of the Peace Crane's hope for a troubled world.

Curriculum Tie-in: History (War and Peace—Japan and America)

*Kaplan, Howard. *Waiting to Sing.* Illus. by Hervé Blondon. New York: DK Ink, 2000.

A family who loves music and spends many hours at the piano is devastated by the death of the mother, but those still living find consolation in the beautiful music that remains.

Symbol: As the family flounders to find itself again, there is the ever-present piano. "I walked from my bedroom to the piano bench, as if holding on to the music for balance, and sat by my father's side. We let the piano speak for us. It was our way of crying, the way it had once been our way of laughing." Beethoven's *Für Elise* is the special piece of music that connects the family's past and present. The boy's older sister learned to play it by heart for her first recital. The boy recalls that the notes first looked to him like a thousand birds. His father patiently placed his hands over the boy's as he learned to play the piece. Later, after the mother's death and when they are ready to begin living again, the father tentatively turns to this familiar piece and plays the first two notes of *Für Elise.* The boy is drawn to the sounds, and the family's healing begins. He starts to practice for his own first recital. And the reader knows that he will be playing the family's special song. When he opens his sheet music, ready to perform at the recital, "my thousand birds were waiting to sing." Both the piano and the Beethoven music represent the delights that life offers even after joy in living has nearly been extinguished.

Other Devices: *Allusion, Antithesis, Aphorism, Atmosphere, Foreshadowing, Imagery, Inference, Metaphor, Parallelism, Simile*

Art Style: Shadowy, full-page sepia-tone pastel drawings expressionistically evoke a fragile emotional period in the life of a family coping with restructuring itself after the wrenching loss of one of its members.

Curriculum Tie-in: Music (Piano), Social Science (Death, Family Relationships, Feelings)

Littlesugar, Amy. *Tree of Hope.* Illus. by Floyd Cooper. New York; Philomel (Penguin Putnam), 1999.

Florrie's daddy used to be a stage actor in Harlem before the Depression forced the Lafayette Theater to close, but he gets a chance to act again when Orson Welles reopens the theater to stage an all-black version of *Macbeth*.

Symbol: Only one thing remains of those old, golden theater days. "One twisted and crooked thing. It was a tree." When almost everything in Harlem seems to have died, theater people give it a special name, Tree of Hope. One wish on it will bring good luck, even in hard times. Florrie wishes hard that her daddy can become an actor again. The government reopens the theater to give work to dancers, singers, stage hands, and actors. The Tree of Hope becomes a symbol of their second chance. As does the one long-stemmed red rose that Florrie's mother presents to her daddy on opening night, just as she did when the two first met.

Other Devices: *Cliché, Flashback, Foreshadowing, Inference, Paradox, Serendipity, Simile, Stereotype/Reverse Stereotype*

Art Style: Rich oilwash impressionistic paintings suggest not only happier memories of the past, when times were more prosperous, but also the temporary bleakness of the current Depression and the emerging hope for a better future.

Curriculum Tie-in: History (Black Culture—Depression)

Martin, Bill. *Chicken Chuck.* Illus. by Steven Salerno. New York: Winslow Press, 2000.

Chicken Chuck the rooster, who has set himself up as boss of the barnyard by virtue of the special blue feather in the middle of his forehead, finds his authority undermined by a circus horse with two blue feathers.

Symbol: The blue feather that unexpectedly grows out of Chicken Chuck's forehead accords him special status. He becomes bossy, and the other barnyard animals become envious. When they report that a circus horse has two such feathers, Chicken Chuck is threatened. An investigation reveals the feathers are merely tied on. He finds a source for many blue feathers even as his own is accidentally lost. But no number of blue feathers restores the feeling of power he used to feel. True authority does not rest in outward pomp and appearance.

Other Devices: *Satire*

Art Style: Energetic mixed media collages playfully illustrate the foolish pursuit of status in the absence of values.

Curriculum Tie-in: Social Science (Values)

*Nolen, Jerdine. *Big Jabe*. Illus. by Kadir Nelson. New York: Lothrop, Lee & Shepard, 2000.

Momma Mary tells stories about a special young man who does wondrous things, especially for the slaves on the Plenty Plantation.

Symbol: Addy rescues the mystery boy from the basket in the stream, and a pear appears where he had been. She bites into it and pronounces it "must be the fruit of heaven." The boy plants the pear seeds, saying, "They want to grow." The tree that sprouts grows quickly, until it looks as if "it had been rooted there forever." Shining between its branches, "the North Star sparkled overhead." Thereafter, whenever a slave is mistreated, Jabe, the boy from the basket, brings the person to the pear tree. That slave disappears to freedom, leaving no trace to follow. Slowly, Addy begins to associate the pear tree with the disappearance of slaves. She mentions this to her fellow slaves, who at first don't listen. Finally, when Addy herself disappears, they think what none among them will say aloud: "Jabe took Addy to that pear tree."

Other Devices: *Allusion, Anachronism, Antithesis, Flashback, Flash-forward, Foreshadowing, Hyperbole, Imagery, Inference, Parallelism, Simile, Understatement*

Art Style: Strong, detailed pen/ink, watercolor, and gouache drawings provide expressionistic period ambience to this folktale.

Curriculum Tie-in: History (Slavery—America), Literature (Tall Tale)

*Turner, Ann. *Red Flower Goes West*. Illus. by Dennis Nolan. New York: Hyperion Books for Children, 1999.

As they journey west, a family nurtures the red flower they have carried with them from their old home.

Symbol: Packed to bursting though the wagon is, Ma is adamant that "Where I go, this flower goes too." From that moment on, it represents their hope for survival. "If that flower dies, we'll never get to California," the boy narrator believes. It wilts, as they do, during the endless miles over desert and mountains. But as spirits droop, "I saw a small new leaf," the boy notes, which prompts his sister to predict their good fortune. "We're going to make it!" she shouts. Even Pa recognizes the geranium's significance to their success. During a harrowing slide down a mountain, during which his own life is at peril, he asks at the bottom, "How's your plant?" The narrator observes, "We were like that red flower; dug up from our home soil, ferried over rivers, jolted over plains, drylands, and killer mountains." Ma pronounces the family will thrive. "Red flower will grow new leaves and buds. And so will we, so will we."

Other Devices: *Connotation, Inference, Metaphor, Parallelism, Simile*

Art Style: Soft crayon and pastel realistic drawings, mostly in shades of gray, depict a stern pioneer experience accented by the bright red beacon of the family's talisman.

Curriculum Tie-in: History (Westward Expansion)

*Wilkon, Piotr. *Rosie the Cool Cat*. Illus. by Jozef Wilkon. New York: Viking (Penguin Books), 1989.

> Casper and Carolina are proud of their jet-black fur and despair trying to cope with their orange kitten, who likes to play with mice and sleep in the doghouse.
>
> > **Symbol:** The orange kitten represents individuality that needs to be nurtured, not repressed. When she cannot conform to family standards, she leaves in frustration and discovers talents she can contribute to society. She exhibits not only admirable musical skills, but also tolerance, a positive value that her culture is lacking.
> >
> > **Other Devices:** *Antithesis, Foreshadowing, Inference, Irony, Poetic Justice, Satire, Stereotype/Reverse Stereotype*
> >
> > **Art Style:** Pastel and colored pencil expressionistic cartoons capture the family pride in its conformity as well as its sense of frustration in the jolting difference of the odd one.
> >
> > **Curriculum Tie-in:** Social Science (Family Relationships, Individuality, Values)

THEME

The underlying meaning or truth about life or humanity as revealed in a literary work's plot and characterization.

> Example: Refusing to accept commonly held tenets about race relations and choosing, instead, to make judgments based upon character values becomes the theme in Mark Twain's *Huckleberry Finn*.

Alexander, Lloyd. *The House Gobbaleen*. Illus. by Diane Goode. New York: Dutton Children's Books (Penguin Books), 1995.

> Unhappy over what he considers his bad luck, Tooley ignores his cat's warnings and invites a greedy little man into his home in the mistaken hope of improving his fortunes.
>
> > **Theme:** "If cats trusted to luck," said Gladsake, "we'd still be sitting begging on doorsteps. Stop blubbering, Tooley, and make your own luck for a change. Your luck's no better nor worse than anyone else's." And that is what Tooley comes to understand. "Nothing went better or worse than it had before," but "Tooley never again complained of his luck." His experience trying to get the fat little man out of his house helps him see the error in his attitude.
> >
> > **Other Devices:** *Ambiguity, Foreshadowing, Hyperbole, Inference, Irony, Simile, Tone, Understatement*
> >
> > **Art Style:** Humorous gouache and watercolor cartoons illustrate this modern tale.
> >
> > **Curriculum Tie-in:** Literature (Folktale), Social Science (Values)

*Armstrong, Jennifer. *Pierre's Dream.* Illus. by Susan Gaber. New York: Dial (Penguin Putnam), 1999.

Thinking he is dreaming, Pierre, a lazy, foolish man, shows no fear as he performs many amazing and dangerous circus acts.

Theme: Nothing is expected of the town's idler. And he expects nothing of himself, for he is jobless, has no interests, no hobbies, and thinks of nothing much except his next meal. How could such a one become a star circus performer? Pierre does believe anything is possible, in a dream. Since this is a dream, he will show his town they are wrong about him. A bit of confidence can do wonders for one's self-esteem.

Other Devices: *Antihero, Foreshadowing, Inference, Irony*

Art Style: Ethereal, expressionistic acrylic paintings alternate between stunning perspectives and large close-ups.

Curriculum Tie-in: Social Science (Values)

*Berkeley, Laura. *The Spirit of the Maasai Man.* New York: Barefoot Books, 2000.

Locked inside their cages, the zoo animals have given up hope until the spirit of the Maasai Man hums his haunting songs of their homeland.

Theme: Captive animals cry for their freedom. Those provided a sense of their natural environment sing for having felt this vital freedom. The Maasai Man "sang his songs and the imprisoned beasts felt the freedom of the wild." The Maasai Man in all of us understands the need for each creature to live naturally.

Other Devices: *Imagery, Symbol, Tone*

Art Style: Realistic acrylic and crayon drawings touchingly illuminate the plight of captive wild animals in expressionistic settings.

Curriculum Tie-in: Geography (Animal Habitats), Science (Zoos)

Bunting, Eve. *Can You Do This, Old Badger?* Illus. by Le Uyen Pham. New York: Harcourt, 1999.

Although Old Badger cannot do some things as easily as he used to, he can still teach Little Badger the many things he knows about finding good things to eat and staying safe and happy.

Theme: Little Badger is amazed. "How do you know so much?" Old Badger tells him, "Because I have been around for a long time. And because, many years ago, an old badger taught me. Someday you will be an old badger and you will teach a little badger what you know." This is the Creator's Plan, with badgers and with children, too. It is the responsibility of adults of all species to pass on to youth the knowledge they need to know to survive and prosper.

Other Devices: *Ambiguity, Foreshadowing*

Art Style: Detailed, expressionistic gouache on watercolor paper lovingly shows this special age/youth relationship.

Curriculum Tie-in: Social Science (Intergenerational Relationships)

*Bunting, Eve. *Swan in Love.* Illus. by Jo Ellen McAllister Stammen. New York: Atheneum Books for Young Readers (Simon & Schuster), 2000.

Despite ridicule of the other animals, Swan persists in his adoration for a swan-shaped boat named Dora.

Theme: With no logic on his side and no hope of affection's return, Swan remains faithful to his love. He asks for nothing. He is reminded by the animals that the object of his love is different, that this kind of love is wrong, that it would be wiser to give his love to a swan, that he will be alone. Swan is undeterred. All that matters is his love for Dora. The creator approves of his simple faithfulness and provides the means, in another dimension, for the happy fulfillment that was denied to Swan during his life. Love makes all things possible.

Other Devices: *Antithesis, Aphorism, Foreshadowing, Imagery, Inference, Simile*

Art Style: Resplendent pastel expressionistic illustrations shimmer with grace as they illuminate the story of transforming love.

Curriculum Tie-in: Social Science (Love)

Cowley, Joy. *The Video Shop Sparrow.* Illus. by Gavin Bishop. Honesdale, PA: Boyds Mills Press, 1999.

When George and Harry try to return a video, they find the shop closed. Trapped inside is a sparrow, which they try to rescue.

Theme: The boys think they see a "special trusting look" in the eye of the trapped sparrow. That "look" may be the workings of their own conscience, calling for action in behalf of a helpless creature. Doing good for the sake of goodness is their simple motivation. The same cannot be said about the adults in this matter.

Other Devices: *Inference, Satire, Tone*

Art Style: Pen/ink line watercolor cartoons show the innocent intentions of the children in contrast to the distinctly uninterested attitude of the adults except where personal advantage may be gained.

Curriculum Tie-in: Social Science (Values)

*Deedy, Carmen Agra. *The Yellow Star: The Legend of King Christian X of Denmark.* Illus. by Henri Sorensen. Atlanta: Peachtree, 2000.

King Christian must abide by Nazi orders regarding the wearing of the identifying yellow star, but he must also protect all the Danes from harm.

Theme: The story begins with the statement that "in the country of Denmark, there were only Danes." Everyone, regardless of religion, is the beloved King Christian's loyal subject. Though the Nazis try to divide the Danes, in the end they find the means to defy injustice against some of their citizenry. The story ends, "And, once again, in the country of Denmark, there were only Danes." The people of one nation refused to allow Nazi poison to separate them.

Other Devices: *Antithesis, Aphorism, Atmosphere, Foreshadowing, Inference, Irony, Paradox, Parallelism, Pun, Simile, Symbol*
Art Style: Impressionistic oil paintings accompany the spare, terse text in this vignette showing the political reality of the Danes' circumstances during a very somber historical period.
Curriculum Tie-in: History (World War II—Nazi Occupation—Denmark), Literature (Legend), Social Science (Values)

DePaola, Tomie. *The Art Lesson.* New York: G.P. Putnam's Sons, 1989.
Having learned to be creative in drawing pictures at home, young Tommy is dismayed when he goes to school and finds the art lesson there much more regimented.
Theme: In their effort to provide consistent education, schools are not especially good at providing individualized education. A perceptive art teacher realizes Tommy's level of ability is beyond the structured school art lesson. Compromise between the classroom teacher, the art teacher, and Tommy enables each to accomplish his/her respective goal. Tommy learns that "it wouldn't be fair to let you do something different from the rest of the class." The school system realizes a limit of one sheet of paper is too restrictive for this child. Permitting him to use his expanded box of crayons would be good for his creativity. Schools exercise wisdom in accommodating potential.
Other Devices: *Atmosphere, Flash-forward, Inference, Irony, Parallelism, Serendipity*
Art Style: Blocky pastel cartoons follow the fortunes and budding development of a young artist in a conformist world.
Curriculum Tie-in: Social Science (Individuality)

Dórrie, Doris. *Lottie's Princess Dress.* Illus. by Julia Kaergel. New York: Dial (Penguin Putnam), 1998.
Lottie and Mother disagree about suitable schoolday attire but resolve the matter agreeably, to the surprise of all.
Theme: The routines of life must sometimes give way momentarily to more important goals. For a "special" day, change is necessary. A daughter's happiness outweighs any disadvantage of coping with party clothes in a nonparty setting.
Other Devices: *Antithesis, Paradox, Understatement*
Art Style: Spare lines and bright colors through chalk pastels and accent gold foil complement this expressionistic, naïve rendering of an emotional confrontation.
Curriculum Tie-in: Social Science (Conflict Resolution)

Howe, James. *Horace and Morris but Mostly Dolores.* Illus. by Amy Walrod. New York: Atheneum Books for Young Readers (Simon & Schuster), 1999.
Three mice friends learn that the best clubs include everyone.

Theme: When three good friends think they must follow established expectations for their respective genders, they discover that they are not as happy as when they did things together that they liked doing. They discover that basing friendship upon mutual interests is more important to a satisfying life than adhering to social stereotypes.

Other Devices: *Allusion, Internal Rhyme, Parallelism, Pun, Stereotype*

Art Style: Acrylics and collage cartoons illustrate a basic gender response to excitement and adventure by showing few physical or behavioral differences between the male and female mouse children.

Curriculum Tie-in: Social Science (Gender Equality)

*Johnson, D.B. *Henry Hikes to Fitchburg*. Boston: Houghton Mifflin, 2000.
While his friend works hard to earn train fare to Fitchburg, young Henry Thoreau walks the thirty miles through woods and fields, enjoying nature.

Theme: Life is meant to be enjoyed while it's being lived, each moment of the day. Henry's journey to Fitchburg is as pleasurable as his being there. His friend exhausts himself working to earn train fare for the dubious pleasure of riding in a crowded coach and arriving first at the destination. He does not enjoy his day of work nor his ride to Fitchburg. He does not meet the goal of "going to Fitchburg to see the country."

Other Devices: *Allusion, Irony, Paradox, Understatement*

Art Style: Colored pencil and acrylic paint in stylishly simple, expressionistic designs contrast interesting visual perspectives and provide period detail.

Curriculum Tie-in: Literature (Henry David Thoreau), Philosophy (Quality of Life)

Krudop, Walter Lyon. *The Man Who Caught Fish*. New York: Farrar Straus Giroux, 2000.
A stranger with a pole magically catches fish and hands them out to villagers one at a time, but the king will not be content until he receives a whole basket of fish.

Theme: Be content with a fair share of earth's riches and avoid expending energy to garner more than is one's due. The stranger explains how he came to carry the pole. "Like you, I was not content with just one fish. My arrogance condemned me to take over the stranger's curse until I found another person as proud as I once was." Now, the king is that person, and he must fish for those he meets.

Other Devices: *Foreshadowing, Poetic Justice*

Art Style: Exquisite impressionistic folk paintings bring to life a culture of long ago.

Curriculum Tie-in: History (Thailand), Literature (Folktales—Thailand)

Lamstein, Sarah Marwil. *I Like Your Buttons!* Illus. by Nancy Cote. Morton Grove, IL: Albert Whitman & Co., 1999.

When a little girl compliments her teacher about the buttons on her outfit, it starts a chain reaction of goodwill, good deeds, and thoughtfulness throughout the day.

Theme: Passing on kindness received can have a far-reaching positive effect, as is shown by all the different people who experience pleasure because someone started it with a thoughtful remark.

Other Devices: *Irony, Serendipity*

Art Style: Acrylics, gouache, and watercolor pencil cartoons emphasize happy faces and bright eyes that express the joy of having been recipients of kind words.

Curriculum Tie-in: Social Science (Values)

Lorbiecki, Marybeth. *Just One Flick of a Finger.* Illus. by David Diaz. New York: Dial (Penguin Putnam), 1996.

A young boy takes a gun to school to scare off the bully who has been tormenting him, and the gun is accidentally fired during the scuffle.

Theme: The boy thinks, "You're a fool if you can't get your hand on a gun." He also believes that with a gun, he would be "so bad no one would mess with me." He loses the respect of his best friend, who calls him a coward and walks away from him. Then an accidental shooting nearly takes the life of his friend. He becomes strong enough to shun the "cool who can drool for all I care." Carrying a gun is not what makes him "swift as lightning." He comes to understand the "lightning" is in his mind, now that he has his life straight.

Other Devices: *Antithesis, Foreshadowing, Inference, Internal Rhyme, Metaphor, Pun, Simile*

Art Style: Acrylics, watercolors, and digitally manipulated photographic backgrounds blend to create powerful, stylized, expressionistic images that evoke danger and tension.

Curriculum Tie-in: Social Science (Bullies)

Miller, William. *The Piano.* Illus. by Susan Keeter. New York: Lee & Low Books, 2000.

A young black girl's love of music leads her to a job in the house of an older white woman, who teaches her not only to play the piano but also the rewards of intergenerational friendship.

Theme: Relations between the races are based on economics. Working for one white person is the same as for another, the only difference being better pay at one place over the other. For Tia and Miss Hartwell two other elements enter the equation. They care about each other's welfare because they share a love of music. Miss Hartwell can share her knowledge with Tia; Tia can be an appreciative pupil who brings freshness to the musical setting. A mutual interest and sensitive respect can transcend traditional boundaries of age, race, and economic status.

Other Devices: *Inference*
Art Style: Oil paintings in realistic expressionism capture mood and feelings between these two new friends.
Curriculum Tie-in: Social Science (Values)

Mochizuki, Ken. *Passage to Freedom: The Sugihara Story*. Illus. by Dom Lee. Afterward by Hiroki Sugihara. New York: Lee & Low, 1997.

Following refusal by the Japanese government to issue visas to Jewish refugees from Poland, Consul Sugihara and his family make a crucial decision that saved thousands of lives.

Theme: Responding to human need transcends political boundaries and sometimes even personal welfare. The Jews want a chance to escape their terrible plight. The Japanese consul has a family to consider. While children enjoy innocent moments of play, adults are not afforded such casual luxury. And so, in the end, adults have only one choice, to act with determined compassion, regardless of personal consequences.

Other Devices: *Antithesis, Aphorism, Foreshadowing, Point of View*

Art Style: The stark fear of survival is shown in realistic, photograph-like oil paint and pencil over scratched beeswax paper. Emotionally charged, unrelenting shades of brown shadowing focus on the grim refugee predicament—their barely contained explosive violence, and the terrible decision facing the diplomat.

Curriculum Tie-in: History (World War II)

*Morrison, Toni, with Slade Morrison. *The Big Box*. Illus. by Giselle Potter. New York: Hyperion, 1999.

To make three unique youngsters conform to their rules, grown-ups create a world inside a box, including treats and simulated nature, but all the kids really want is the freedom to be themselves.

Theme: Adults learn that while they are trying to teach children how to "handle" their freedom, they are in need of some lessons in developing mutual respect. Take a clue from the animal world. Rabbits hop; beavers chew trees. It's what they do. Creatures, including children, ought to be permitted to behave naturally, without penalty.

Other Devices: *Antithesis, Inference, Internal Rhyme, Irony, Oxymoron, Satire*

Art Style: Naïve watercolors show the contrast between the real joy expressed naturally by the children in their simple outdoor amusements, and the cloying dissatisfaction with adult-provided commercial rubbish.

Curriculum Tie-in: Social Science (Values)

*Myers, Tim. *Basho and the Fox*. Illus. by Oki S. Han. New York: Marshall Cavendish, 2000.

A Japanese poet is challenged by a fox to create his best haiku.

Theme: Basho questions his skills when a fox brags that foxes are far better poets than are humans. Then he learns that what constitutes excellence in a fox's opinion is nothing more than a poem that has a fox in it. Basho realizes one must not bow to a critic's view of what is good and what is not. Art must be created for its own sake, not to seek acclaim.

Other Devices: *Ambiguity, Antithesis, Aphorism, Imagery, Irony, Motif, Parallelism*

Art Style: Mischievous watercolor folk paintings convey the Eastern sensibility of feudal Japan.

Curriculum Tie-in: History (Japan), Social Science (Self-esteem)

O'Malley, Kevin. *Bud.* New York; Walker & Company, 2000.

The orderly Sweet-Williams are dismayed at their son's fondness for the messy pastime of gardening.

> **Theme:** The adults learn that long-established views can succumb to love and an open mind. Bud teaches his family that there is joy and value in less structured approaches to life.
>
> **Other Devices:** *Antithesis, Aphorism, Foreshadowing, Inference, Irony, Pun, Understatement*
>
> **Art Style:** Large expressive gouache cartoons lovingly follow the development of tolerance, respect, and appreciation for a beloved child's unconventional approach to life.
>
> **Curriculum Tie-in:** Science (Gardening), Social Science (Family Relationships, Values)

*Pacilio, V.J. *Ling Cho and His Three Friends.* Illus. by Scott Cook. New York: Farrar Straus Giroux, 2000.

Through his plan to share the wealth of his wheat crop with three friends, a Chinese farmer teaches the importance of allowing other people to help in time of need.

> **Theme:** Ling Cho's three friends are not as wealthy as he is. He tries to find a means of helping them without letting them believe it is charity. He allows them to keep half the proceeds from the sale of a load of wheat. Two of the friends keep all the profits and make up a story about why there are no coins to share. One tells him frankly that he has kept the load of wheat for his family. Ling Cho scolds this friend for the sin of pride in not admitting how desperately needy he is. Knowing when to accept help is as important as giving help. And a friend who is able to admit his need is a valued friend.
>
> **Other Devices:** *Alliteration, Aphorism, Irony, Paradox, Poetic Justice*
>
> **Art Style:** Impressionistic folk oil paintings in Chinese reds and golds suggest unstated meanings behind spoken words.
>
> **Curriculum Tie-in:** Social Science (Friendship, Values)

Preston, Tim. *The Lonely Scarecrow.* Illus. by Maggie Kneen. New York: Dutton
Children's Books (Penguin Books), 1999.

A lonely scarecrow with a scary face has trouble making friends with the
animals who surround him, until a heavy snowfall transforms him into a jolly
snowman.

> **Theme:** When the animals become familiar with the scarecrow as a
> snowman, they enjoy his presence. As the snow melts off, revealing the
> scarecrow they used to fear, they realize the friendly snowman and the
> scary-looking scarecrow are one and the same. How could they ever have
> feared him? Relationships ought not to be based on outward appearances.
> **Other Devices:** *Imagery, Inference, Metaphor, Paradox, Parallelism*
> **Art Style:** Lavishly embossed, finely detailed, watercolor and acrylic
> cartoons fondly render scenes of seasonal changes.
> **Curriculum Tie-in:** Science (Seasons), Social Science (Friendship)

*Say, Allen. *The Sign Painter.* Boston: Walter Lorraine Books (Houghton Mifflin),
2000.

An assignment to paint a large billboard in the desert changes the life of an
aspiring artist.

> **Theme:** A boy arrives in a town needing a job. He reluctantly agrees to
> assist a sign painter. The boy has skills and is conscientious. The man
> pronounces them a good team, but, the boy visualizes himself as a painter.
> Out in the desert they accidentally witness the beginnings of someone's
> grand dream. The man is amused; the boy is energized. Someone else has
> demonstrated courage in the pursuit of an impractical goal; the boy no
> longer has any regrets leaving behind the temptation of a safe choice for
> the uncertainties of following a personal dream.
> **Other Devices:** *Ambiguity, Antithesis, Imagery, Inference, Point of View,
> Tone*
> **Art Style:** Magnificent realistic acrylic paintings unfold the contrasts in
> this provocative story about personal choices between issues of security
> versus dreams.
> **Curriculum Tie-in:** Philosophy (Quality of Life)

Strete, Craig Kee. *The Lost Boy and the Monster.* Illus. by Steve Johnson and Lou
Fancher. New York: G.P. Putnam's Sons (Penguin Books for Young Readers),
1999.

With the help of a rattlesnake and a scorpion, a lost boy gains two names and
defeats the horrible foot-eating monster.

> **Theme:** Kindness to others, without thought of reward, will be its own
> reward. Cruelty will also, in the end, receive its just deserts. The monster,
> who traps children with a sticky rope so he can eat their feet, is himself
> caught in the rope after injuring his feet running through cactus stickers.

Other Devices: *Ambiguity, Connotation, Internal Rhyme, Motif, Poetic Justice, Simile, Tone*
Art Style: Textured paste, oil paint, potato stamping, and scratching tools create expressionistic paintings in brown and yellow tones reminiscent of American Indian folk art.
Curriculum Tie-in: Art (American Indian), Literature (Folktales— American Indian)

*Wisniewski, David. *Tough Cookie.* New York: Lothrop, Lee and Shepard (William Morrow), 1999.

When his friend Chips is snatched and chewed, Tough Cookie sets out to stop Fingers.
Theme: Best results happen through cooperation and trust. Tough Cookie thinks only he can save the Jar residents from the dreaded Fingers. When he learns his partner has been attacked, his "raisins turn to ice." It's time to put Fingers away for keeps. But he figures he must do it alone. Soon he is in deep trouble. Darkness covers him. He can't move, can't breathe. It's the end. Just in time help arrives. Thousands of his friends, the crumbs, send Fingers away, proving that his girlfriend is right. "You're a smart cookie," he tells her. "Maybe being a tough cookie isn't enough." She replies, "You don't learn quick, but you learn."
Other Devices: *Analogy, Parody, Pun, Satire, Simile, Stereotype/Reverse Stereotype*
Art Style: Complex cut-paper illustrations in an expressionistic collage work amazingly well to support this munchable mystery.
Curriculum Tie-in: Social Science (Friendship)

TONE

The attitude of a writer toward a literary work's subject and its audience as revealed by choice of words and details.

Example: "Afoot and light-hearted I take to the open road, healthy, free,
the world before me."

Walt Whitman, *Song of the Open Road*

Alderson, Brian. *The Tale of the Turnip.* Illus. by Fritz Wegner. Cambridge, MA: Candlewick Press, 1999.

A humble farmer's garden produce pleases the king, who handsomely rewards his efforts, but an arrogant squire gets more than he bargained for when he attempts to claim a similar reward.

Tone: Whimsical, folksy humor is the hallmark of this tale of contrasts. The farmer "lived in a ramshackle cottage, with a few chickens and suchlike." The squire has a big house, stables, gardens, fields, meadows, chickens, pigs, cows, horses, "and who knows what else." When the farmer discovers his huge turnip, he announces "to his missus": "Hen's teeth! This is a right champion turnip." When the king sees it, he agrees "Stone the crows! That's the most champion turnip I ever did see." The king is also properly impressed with the squire's fine horse. "By gum! That's the most gussied-up horse I ever did see."

Other Devices: *Connotation, Hyperbole, Motif, Poetic Justice, Satire*

Art Style: Humorously detailed watercolor and ink cartoons delight the visual sense and the sense of justice.

Curriculum Tie-in: History (Nineteenth-Century England), Literature (Folktales—England)

Alexander, Lloyd. *The House Gobbaleen.* Illus. by Diane Goode. New York: Dutton Children's Books (Penguin Books), 1995.

Unhappy over what he considers his bad luck, Tooley ignores his cat's warnings and invites a greedy little man into his home in the mistaken hope of improving his fortunes.

Tone: The cat offers his hilarious, no-nonsense view of the stranger. "He's got a lopsided, squinny-eyed look to him I don't care for at all." The fellow had been found on the doorstep, "tucking into the kipper and washing it down with the cider as fast as he could swallow." He uses tobacco liberally, "puffing away and making a dreadful stink." Tooley waits on the scamp in hopes of receiving the gift of good luck. "I know your honor has something big in store for me. You needn't tell anything ahead of time. Only just give a little bit of a nod if I'm on to it. The biggest of all, isn't it? The pot of gold!" After indulging himself with Tooley's hospitality, the fat creature has the audacity to take his bed. "Without so much as a good night, he waddled into Tooley's bed chamber, climbed into Tooley's bed, pulled Tooley's quilt over his head, and fell sound asleep that instant, snoring loud enough to shake the roof. Tooley spent a restless night on some straw on the floor." Each day the obnoxious little man plants himself in Tooley's chair, "bawling for bacon, kippers, more jugs of cider; scooping fistfuls of tobacco from the jar; and puffing such clouds of smoke that the cat could hardly stop coughing and sneezing."

Other Devices: *Ambiguity, Foreshadowing, Hyperbole, Inference, Irony, Simile, Theme, Understatement*

Art Style: Humorous gouache and watercolor cartoons illustrate this modern folktale.

Curriculum Tie-in: Literature (Folktale), Social Science (Values)

Battle-Lavert, Gwendolyn. *The Music in Derrick's Heart.* Illus. by Colin Bootman. New York: Holiday House, 2000.

> Uncle Booker T., who makes magic by playing his harmonica music from his heart, spends the summer teaching Derrick how to play.
>
> **Tone:** These ethnic characters are energetic in their dedication to finding spirit in their music. "The music got in their hands and feet." Big Mama asks Booker T. to "play my favorite hymn, I need a song to lift my spirits." When Uncle Booker T. plays, he concentrates "so hard it hurt to watch him. Soft and slow. Slow and soft." Big Mama tells Derrick, as she "moaned in time with the beat," that his "songs just set my soul on fire. I'm thinking of all our kinfolk who have gone on to glory." Aunt Agnes needs to hear jazz, "colorful notes that Uncle Booker T. dragged up and down the yard. Smooth and swinging. Short and choppy." She tells them, "I've danced to Duke Ellington from can't-see at night to can-see in the morning."
>
> **Other Devices:** *Aphorism, Atmosphere, Inference, Simile*
>
> **Art Style:** Expressionistic oil paintings show an appreciation of small-town African-American music played from the heart.
>
> **Curriculum Tie-in:** Social Science (Ethnicity—African-American)

*Berkeley, Laura. *The Spirit of the Maasai Man.* New York: Barefoot Books, 2000.

> Locked inside their cages, the zoo animals have given up hope until the spirit of the Maasai Man hums his haunting songs of their homeland.
>
> **Tone:** The author's deep respect for the trapped animals is expressed in the actions of the Maasai Man. He says the zoo beasts cry "because they cannot hear the songs of the wild." He stands at the zoo's entrance and "hummed his haunting earth-songs and the voices of the trapped souls sang out in harmony." Why do the beasts sing? "Because they are free." The songs have enabled the imprisoned beasts to feel the freedom of the wild.
>
> **Other Devices:** *Imagery, Symbol, Theme*
>
> **Art Style:** Realistic acrylic and crayon drawings touchingly illuminate the plight of captive wild animals in expressionistic settings.
>
> **Curriculum Tie-in:** Geography: (Animal Habitats), Science (Zoos)

*Cole, Brock. *Buttons.* New York: Farrar Straus Giroux, 2000.

> When their father eats so much that he pops the buttons off his britches, each of his three daughters tries a different plan to find replacements.
>
> **Tone:** The author playfully comments directly to the reader in frolicsome asides about this family of noodleheads. Regarding the youngest daughter, he remarks, "She was young and rabbity and still picked her nose when she thought no one was looking." When she reveals her plan to replace her father's trouser buttons, "Privately the old woman had her doubts, but since the older girls had such marvelous ideas, it hardly seemed to matter what the youngest did." As they each set out to try their plan, the author

says, "And now we shall hear what happened to them all." The eldest daughter's plan goes awry, but her beauty catches the attention of a barge hauler, who saves her life. When he asks to marry her, she agrees. "It seemed only decent under the circumstances." The girl forgets to ask her savior for buttons. So does the second daughter, who saves the life of a handsome soldier. "They talked of many silly things: babies and cottages and birds and nests, but not once did anyone mention buttons." The third daughter is having no luck in her attempts to catch buttons falling from the sky in her apron. "It was enough to discourage a saint, but still she got up every morning and did her best." A young cowherd steps in to assist. "So the next morning she did as he had told her and ran round and round under the old oak. And what do you think?" She is successful, even though the cowherd goes to his wedding with a bit of string tying up his trousers. "Here is a picture of their wedding party. There is the bride's father and mother. Doesn't he look proud with all his buttons done up?" As for the cowherd and the youngest daughter, "He doesn't seem to have enough buttons, but she doesn't care. It's a small fault and seems to run in the family."

Other Devices: *Aphorism, Inference, Irony, Pun*

Art Style: Pen/ink and watercolor combine in humorous cartoons that complement this lighthearted spoof on courtship and family duty.

Curriculum Tie-in: Literature (Fairy Tale)

Cowley, Joy. *The Video Shop Sparrow.* Illus. by Gavin Bishop. Honesdale, PA: Boyds Mills Press, 1999.

When George and Harry try to return a video, they find the shop closed. Trapped inside is a sparrow, which they try to rescue.

Tone: The adults do not attach the same amount of significance to the problem of the trapped bird as do the boys. When they ask a waitress where the video man lives, she says, "He's gone on vacation. But don't worry, kids. It's only a sparrow. Plenty more where that came from." Their father tries to call the store man and gets no answer. "He's gone all right. Forget it. Sparrows aren't exactly an endangered species." The police are annoyed to be bothered by such a trivial problem. "On New Year's Eve I don't get much sleep. Now buzz off, both of you, before you find out what I can be like when I'm tired." As far as the officer is concerned, the bird "can tweet in bird heaven." Their mother tries to distract the boys with meaningless platitudes about life and death. "Everybody dies. That's life. Great-grandpa died. The cat died. Don't worry about it. There are millions of sparrows in the world." Their father suggests they divert their minds by feeding the sparrows in the garden. "It will make you realize that sparrows are like ants. One more or less doesn't matter all that much."

Other Devices: *Inference, Satire, Theme*

Art Style: Pen/ink line watercolor style cartoons show the innocent intentions of the children in contrast to the distinctly uninterested attitude of the adults, except where personal advantage may be gained.
Curriculum Tie-in: Social Science (Values)

Ernst, Lisa Campbell. *Goldilocks Returns.* New York: Simon & Schuster Books for Young Readers, 2000.
  Fifty years after Goldilocks first met the three bears, she returns to fix up their cottage and soothe her guilty conscience.
  Tone: "Her favorite hobby was snooping in houses where no one was at home—until, of course, all that dreadful trouble with the bears." As she grew up, "no matter how she tried to leave her life of crime behind, it haunted her day and night." Meanwhile, nothing much has changed in the lives of the bears. "Their breakfast as usual was porridge, and as it had been every day since any of them could remember, it was much too hot to eat." The scene is set for the return of Goldi to make amends for her childhood destruction. She, unfortunately, hasn't changed much either. She sweeps away their cereal. "They won't have to eat this nasty tasting stuff anymore." Plowing forward, she "hung hoity-toity drapes, scattered pillows, and covered all the furniture with shiny plastic covers." Then she pronounces it all "perfect at last." But for the long-suffering bears, there is a hint that life as they prefer it could be restored. They see a "mischievous looking little girl, skipping along the path that led straight to their cottage. She could eat their food, mess up their fancy things, and break the repaired chair. Yes!" This irreverent sequel to the Three Bears is no sentimental journey of remembrance.
  Other Devices: *Allusion, Antihero, Connotation, Flash-forward, Inference, Irony, Parallelism, Understatement*
  Art Style: Large, bulky cartoons depict the story's original atmosphere, intended for young listeners, while the language and picture complexity expand the interest level for more savvy audiences.

Glass, Andrew. *Bewildered for Three Days: As to Why Daniel Boone Never Wore His Coonskin Cap.* New York: Holiday House, 2000.
  With the help of what he learned from a Delaware Indian boy and an accommodating mother raccoon, young Daniel Boone escapes danger when a bear steals his coonskin cap.
  Tone: The author eloquently respects the differences between the white and Indian cultures. Daniel's father and mother tell him it will soon be time for "thee and Little Beaver to part ways." Then his father explains, "The Delaware are our betters in the ways of the wilderness. None can teach thee woodcraft as they can, but we measure off fields for farming and build fences. When we ask them to honor our fences, it is an unreasonable thing we ask. I fear there is no way to share a land so differently understood."

The author also enjoys the trappings of the tall tale style of storytelling. A bear snatches off Daniel's coonskin cap. "Now you'd likely think that I'd just have let that big old bear have the raggedy cap and count myself lucky that my head wasn't still in it." Indian braves come upon him. "Arrows whizzed by. When the braves got to throwing distance, a hatchet toppled past, end over end. What was I to do?" He chooses to hide in a hollow log. "I had no hankering to drop in unexpected on a mama raccoon. She can be a scrappy critter if her little 'uns are in danger. But there I was and there was no telling how long I'd be staying."

Other Devices: *Atmosphere, Flashback, Foreshadowing, Motif, Point of View, Understatement*

Art Style: Impressionistic colored pencil and oil pastel humorously accompany this frontier yarn of a great adventurer told in a curious blend of humility and exaggeration.

Curriculum Tie-in: History (Biography—Daniel Boone), Literature (Tall Tale)

Harris, Jim. *The Three Little Dinosaurs.* Gretna, LA: Pelican Publishing, 1999.

Three young dinosaurs set out on their own, only to be hassled by a Tyrannosaurus rex who gets a big surprise in the end.

Tone: This version of an old favorite opens with mother saying, "It's time you went out into the world and make it on your own. But, be careful of the big bad Tyrannosaurus rex, or he will make dino-burgers out of you." The first young dinosaur "grabbed some snacks, plugged in his favorite video game, and plopped down in his comfy chair." When the thumping sound he hears is not the pizza deliveryman, the little dinosaur refuses to open the door. He shouts, "No way, Jose." Fortunately, as with previous versions, the little dino in this story escapes when his home is demolished. He "snuck out" and runs off to find his brothers. So goes this updated classic, which adds, for old time's sake, much of the familiar language used in the Three Little Pigs story—"Little pig, little pig, let me come in!" and "I'll huff, and I'll puff, and I'll blow your house in."

Other Devices: *Antithesis, Foreshadowing, Parody, Poetic Justice*

Art Style: Lush detailed acrylic expressionistic paintings provide satisfyingly humorous perspective and point of view between aggressor and victim.

Hutchins, Hazel. *One Duck.* Illus. by Ruth Ohi. New York: Annick (Firefly Books), 1999.

A mother duck works to defend her nest of eggs from a marauding crow and a farmer's cultivator.

Tone: The author's rhythmic, choppy style perfectly juxtaposes the duck's situation with the farmer's. A duck is "hidden perfectly in a hollow of ground down-lined, down-covered, still warm one nest with twelve olive eggs." She "settles down upon them knowing it is almost time and waits."

Meanwhile, a farmer thinks about his day. "Cultivator to hook up and pull onto the stubble field to till the soil for the wheat he'll plant and tend and sell to feed and clothe his family." His work involves orderly progress. "Slowly, steadily, the cultivator cuts and lifts and turns the soil the first row of a pattern." The farmer recognizes the duck's priority over the ground. He makes concessions for her. He carries the nest one row over and "lays it down on land already turned." He proceeds with his work, she with hers. In the grand scheme of life there is room for both the duck's business and the farmer's business.

Other Devices: *Antithesis, Atmosphere, Imagery, Inference, Onomatopoeia, Parallelism*

Art Style: Expressionistic pen/ink watercolor drawings sensitively complement the lyrical text of this common farming drama.

Curriculum Tie-in: Science (Agriculture, Animal Behavior)

Johnson, Paul Brett. *Old Dry Frye: A Deliciously Funny Tall Tale.* New York: Scholastic Press, 1999.

A humorous retelling of an Appalachian folktale about a preacher who chokes on a chicken bone.

Tone: The author's yarn-telling Appalachian twang begins this amazing account of accident and cover-up. "A while back there was this preacher man who was plumb crazy about fried chicken. Now, all preachers like chicken, but Old Dry Frye was the chicken-eatingest sermonizer that ever laid fire to a pulpit." Wherever fried chicken is being served, "Old Dry Frye with his nose a-twitchin' and his false teeth a-snappin'" would be sure to show up. "You could just count on it." After a series of incidents that ends without resolution to the problem of how to get rid of the body of Old Dry Frye, the author sums up with "They say Old Dry Frye is still tearing around the countryside. On nights when the moon is full and there's a plate of chicken on the table, you can guess what folks are saying—'Dad-fetch me! I believe that's Old Dry Frye.'"

Other Devices: *Black Humor, Cliché, Hyperbole, Inference, Poetic Justice, Serendipity, Understatement*

Art Style: Ebullient acrylic cartoons share the fortunes and misfortunes of the self-serving characters in this raucous Appalachian romp.

Curriculum Tie-in: Literature (Tall Tales), Social Science (Appalachian Culture)

Lowell, Susan. *Cindy Ellen: A Wild Western Cinderella.* Illus. by Jane Manning. New York: Joanna Cotler Books (HarperCollins), 2000.

Cindy Ellen loses one of her diamond spurs at the square dance in the retelling of this classic fairytale.

Tone: This rough, straight-talking western version shows a beaten down Cindy Ellen nicknamed Cinderbottom and Sanderella by her sneering stepsisters. Cindy gets dirty doing all the dirty jobs on the ranch, and her self-esteem is low. Fortunately, her fairy godmother assesses the situation correctly and appeals to her strengths. "Say hello to your fairy godmother, sugarfoot," she begins. She admonishes Cindy to stand up straight and dust herself off. "Magic is plumb worthless without gumption." The girl needs "some gravel in your gizzard. Grit! Guts! Stop that tomfool blubbering, and let's get busy. Time's a-wastin'." Cindy is sent off to the rodeo to show her mettle. Her godmother's gift of gumption helps her star at bronc riding and provides her a new "daredevil grin." This Cinderella stands up for herself and wins not only the cowboy, but something much more important, her self-respect.

Other Devices: *Alliteration, Aphorism, Foreshadowing, Internal Rhyme, Parallelism, Parody, Simile*

Art Style: Action-packed expressionistic acrylic cartoons hilariously support the story's western flavor.

Curriculum Tie-in: Social Science (Self-esteem)

Lowell, Susan. *Little Red Cowboy Hat.* Illus. by Randy Cecil. New York: Henry Holt, 1997.

Little Red rides her pony, Buck, to Grandma's ranch with a jar of cactus jelly in the saddlebag.

Tone: This is self-sufficient western country. Folks are savvy and resourceful. "Now Little Red Cowboy Hat knew perfectly well that this was not her grandmother. But where was Grandma? She decided to string the wolf along until she found out." Together, the women successfully defend themselves from this predator, and "they never had any wolf trouble around her ranch again."

Other Devices: *Aphorism, Atmosphere, Caricature, Hyperbole, Inference, Onomatopoeia, Parody, Simile, Stereotype/Reverse Stereotype*

Art Style: Gouache cartoons in expressionistic naïve style humorously match this unique geographical version of a familiar fairy tale.

McNaughton, Colin. *Yum!* New York: Harcourt Brace, 1998.

Preston Pig suggests that Mr. Wolf get a job so he can buy what he wants to eat, but as he considers different lines of work, Mr. Wolf has a one-track mind.

Tone: The author begins with this sidebar. "No animals were hurt in the making of this book. Oh, except Mr. Wolf, of course." Then, when the story begins with "One fine day . . . " a little pig asks the wolf what he's doing napping on the ground under the window. The reply is "If you must know, nosy pig, I'm waiting for you to come out so I can gobble you up!" The exchange continues with the pig asking why he wants to do that, and the wolf responding, "Because I'm hungry, stupid!" Dialogue is quite irreverent and funny. The author is having lots of fun spoofing a naïve pig and a less than clever wolf.

Other Devices: *Allusion, Ambiguity, Pun, Satire, Understatement*
Art Style: Detailed cartoons and humorous asides add to the impish joy of this wolf-and-pig encounter.
Curriculum Tie-in: Social Science (Values)

*Mamet, David. Henrietta. Illus. by Elizabeth Dahlie. Boston: Houghton Mifflin, 1999.

Henrietta, rebuffed by the law school admissions office, like so many of her underprivileged kind before her, wanders aimlessly until a chance encounter with a vagabond philosopher enables her to pursue her dream of a scholarly future.

Tone: The author speaks as though the reader is an insider to his exposure of education's missteps. When Henrietta is officially "ejected and barred as a nuisance" from the libraries and backs of lecture halls, she despairs "until that day the absence of which would deservedly decrease your admiration of this book," she encounters the Old Vagabond. Upon graduation, "it will not surprise you," she stands on the dais to give the commencement address. And "her accomplishments, of course, have been claimed by the School and the City."

Other Devices: *Inference, Irony, Personification, Pun, Satire, Serendipity*
Art Style: Spare pastel crayon impressionistic cartoons highlight in subtle, playful satire the foibles of higher education's entrenched shortsighted traditions.
Curriculum Tie-in: Literature (Fable), Social Science (Diversity)

Pawagi, Manjusha. *The Girl Who Hated Books.* Illus. by Leanne Franson. Hillsboro, OR: Beyond Words, 1998.

Although she lives in a house full of avid readers, Meena hates books—until she discovers the magic inside them.

Tone: Her name is Meena. The author says, "If you looked up her name in a book, you would find that it means 'fish' in ancient Sanskrit. But Meena didn't know that because she never looked up anything anywhere. She hated to read, and she hated books." The author admits that Meena has a point when she complains, "They're always in the way." In her house books are everywhere. Illustrations show them on lamp shades, in the bird cage, and sitting on the toilet as well as on all the chairs. This is a rollicking tale of conversion from nonreader to book lover. When a particularly tall stack of books topples over, the book characters spill out. There is a sobbing wolf who can't remember if he's from Little Red Riding Hood or The Three Little Pigs. Then he "blew his nose on the table cloth." When her parents return, they can't believe their eyes. "Not because the curtains were gone and the dishes were broken and the table legs were chewed up" (due to all the book animals running at large). They are amazed because Meena is reading a book.

Other Devices: *Alliteration, Allusion, Antithesis, Foreshadowing, Hyperbole, Inference, Internal Rhyme, Pun*
Art Style: Pen/ink watercolor expressionistic cartoons emphasize emotion and background action.

*Say, Allen. *The Sign Painter*. Boston: Walter Lorraine Books (Houghton Mifflin), 2000.

An assignment to paint a large billboard in the desert changes the life of an aspiring artist.

Tone: In this emotionally subdued tale of two workers on assignment, there is not much talk. The awe-inspiring desert landscape enfolds them. "As time went on, they spoke less, as if their voices would disturb the silence around them." But there is a moment of gentle levity between them. In the beginning, the 12 billboards seem a monotonous task to the boy, who prefers expressing individuality in his painting instead of following a strict, never-changing layout. But after the man chastises him for wishing to add embellishments to the design, he settles into the routine. One morning the man announces, "One more to go." The boy replies, "One more what?" The man laughs. He acknowledges the boy's joke.
Other Devices: *Ambiguity, Antithesis, Imagery, Inference, Point of View, Theme*
Art Style: Magnificent realistic acrylic paintings unfold the contrasts in this provocative story about personal choices between issues of security versus dreams.
Curriculum Tie-in: Philosophy (Quality of Life)

Steig, William. *Wizzil*. Illus. by Quentin Blake. New York: Farrar Straus Giroux, 2000.

A bored witch causes trouble when she decides to take revenge on an old man, but her mischief leads to a happy ending.

Tone: Irreverent fun sparkles through the text and illustrations. A witch receives advice from her parrot. "You've been perched on your behind for so long you're stinking the place up. Now, go make somebody suffer!" Wizzil is resolved on revenge. "That bald-headed fuddy-dud with his crazy swatter darn near did me in!" She turns herself into a glove. DeWitt "took to wearing his new glove all the time, except when he washed or shaved or had to wind his watch or pick his nose." DeWitt can't hit the flies when he wears his new glove. It made him "dippy sometimes—he'd let out a war cry and chase the little devils all over the house." His family wants him to remove the glove, because weird things have been happening since he put it on. His son says, "You've been acting nutty ever since you found that glove." DeWitt retaliates, "Nutty? If anyone around here's nutty, it's you." Eventually, all turns out well. Wizzil's parrot resigns herself to living with "humdrum humans." She figures "It'll be a whole new hayride."

Other Devices: *Alliteration, Ambiguity, Connotation, Foreshadowing, Internal Rhyme, Irony, Serendipity*
Art Style: Delightfully awful watercolor cartoons capture the personalities and behaviors of the rotten witch and the hillbilly family she pesters.
Curriculum Tie-in: Social Science (Love)

*St. George, Judith. *So You Want to Be President?* Illus. by David Small. New York: Philomel (Penguin Putnam Books for Young Readers), 2000 (Caldecott—2000).
This is a lively assortment of facts about the qualifications and characteristics of U.S. Presidents from George Washington to Bill Clinton.
Tone: A personal conversational approach defines this textual style. "You probably weren't born in a log cabin. That's too bad. People are crazy about log-cabin Presidents." "If you want to be President, your size doesn't matter." "Don't worry about your looks." "Do you have pesky brothers and sisters? Every one of our Presidents did. Benjamin Harrison takes the prize—he had eleven!" "Do you have a pet? All kinds of pets have lived in the White House, mostly dogs." "If you want to be President, you might consider joining the army . . . . If you can't be a general, be a hero like Theodore Roosevelt or John Kennedy . . . . Don't be a Franklin Pierce." "One thing is certain, if you want to be President—and stay President— be honest."
Other Devices: *Antithesis, Atmosphere, Caricature, Parallelism*
Art Style: In the cherished tradition of political commentary, foibles, quirks, and humanity are illustrated in these hilarious cartoons.
Curriculum Tie-in: History (American Presidents)

Strete, Craig Kee. *The Lost Boy and the Monster.* Illus. by Steve Johnson and Lou Fancher. New York: G.P. Putnam's Sons (Penguin Books for Young Readers), 1999.
With the help of a rattlesnake and a scorpion, a lost boy gains two names and defeats the horrible foot-eating monster.
Tone: In a personal storytelling speaking voice, the author tells the reader, " . . . and what did he like to eat? Well, my goodness, he liked to eat little children's feet!" But, as in all fairy tales, the monster is punished, and with his own sticky rope, too. "And to this day, they say he is stuck there still."
Other Devices: *Ambiguity, Connotation, Internal Rhyme, Motif, Poetic Justice, Simile, Theme*
Art Style: Textured paste, oil paint, potato stamping, and scratching tools create expressionistic paintings in brown and yellow tones reminiscent of American Indian folk art.
Curriculum Tie-in: Art (American Indian), Literature (Folktales— American Indian)

*Yaccarino, Dan.** *Deep in the Jungle.* New York: Anne Schwartz Book from Atheneum Books for Young Readers (Simon & Schuster), 2000.

> After being tricked into joining the circus, an arrogant lion escapes and returns to the jungle, where he lives peacefully with the animals he used to terrorize.
>
> **Tone:** Dry humor marks this author's style. "Deep in the jungle, the mighty lion roared for the monkeys to fan him faster. 'I'm afraid I must eat you,' he explained, 'if you don't obey me.' The monkeys fanned faster." He is offered a chance to become a famous movie star. "The lion, who never thought he was much appreciated anyway, agreed." The man puts him into a cage. "It'll be a good career move for you. Trust me." Later, the "man stuck his head right in the lion's mouth, and, well, you can figure out the rest." The lion apologizes to the jungle animals. "I'm afraid I owe you an apology," he says to every one of them. "Silly pride and all."
>
> **Other Devices:** *Anachronism, Antihero, Antithesis, Black Humor, Foreshadowing, Irony, Motif, Parallelism, Poetic Justice, Pun*
>
> **Art Style:** Expressionistic gouache naïve cartoons against white backgrounds, reminiscent of the "Curious George" series, accent the droll language in this lesson in humility.
>
> **Curriculum Tie-in:** Literature (Parable), Social Science (Values)

UNDERSTATEMENT

Intentionally representing something as less than in fact it is.

Example: *Hamlet* is a play "of some interest."

Alexander, Lloyd. *The House Gobbaleen.* Illus. by Diane Goode. New York: Dutton Children's Books (Penguin Books), 1995.

> Unhappy over what he considers his bad luck, Tooley ignores his cat's warnings and invites a greedy little man into his home in the mistaken hope of improving his fortunes.
>
> **Understatement:** "Now, Tooley was by no means the quickest-witted fellow in the world. But seeing his larder grow barer by the hours, and himself turned out of his own chair and chamber, he began thinking how his luck was a little slow in coming."
>
> **Other Devices:** *Ambiguity, Foreshadowing, Hyperbole, Inference, Irony, Simile, Theme, Tone*
>
> **Art Style:** Humorous gouache and watercolor cartoons illustrate this modern folktale.
>
> **Curriculum Tie-in:** Literature (Folktale), Social Science (Values)

Camp, Lindsay. *Why?* Illus. by Tony Ross. New York: G.P. Putnam's Sons (Penguin Putnam Books for Young Readers), 1998.

Lily's constant "why" questions drive her father crazy until one day he discovers that questioning the way things are can be a very good thing.

Understatement: Lily asks "why," and her father tries not to get cranky answering her. That is pretty much how every day goes. "Then, one Friday, something rather unusual happened." Earth is nearly destroyed by alien invaders. While families innocently enjoy a day at the park, the Thargons land and announce their mission. After they have a talk with Lily, they change their minds and go home. Lily is just being Lily, and that is a very good thing for earthlings.

Other Devices: *Inference, Irony, Paradox, Serendipity*

Art Style: Colored pencil cartoons illustrate the repetitious, rapid-fire questions from Lily, and the answers she receives, that make up Lily's day and the day of those who suffer her presence.

Curriculum Tie-in: Social Science (Family Relationships)

Carrick, Carol. *Big Old Bones.* Illus. by Donald Carrick. New York: Clarion Books, 1989.

Professor Potts discovers some old bones and puts them together in various ways until he is satisfied he has discovered a dinosaur that once ruled the earth.

Understatement: While the professor and his family were on an outing across country "when the Old West was new," the train stopped for water. His little dog "found a bone." It was very old and very big. "He decided to stay a few days and explore." The result was a pile of bones so huge it filled the train on the way back to the laboratory, and required an extension on the building where he pieced them back together to resemble what some "giant lizards" might have looked like.

Other Devices: *Irony*

Art Style: Pen line and watercolor cartoons fit the early efforts of nineteenth-century scientists trying to make sense of extinct animal life.

Curriculum Tie-in: Science (Paleontology)

Dahan, André. *Squiggle's Tale.* San Francisco: Chronicle, 2000.

Squiggle sends a letter assuring his parents that he is being good while visiting his cousins in Paris, but the pictures tell another story.

Understatement: At the park Squiggle and her pig friends find a huge fountain and "dipped our toes in just a tiny bit." Actually, they play in the fountain. Afterward, they "sit on the grass while our toes dried." They really roll down the grassy banks. They noticed a statue and "stood on our tippy toes to get a better look." They really climb the statue, and come down only when a policeman blows a whistle at them. They find ponies to ride. But they don't pay for their amusement. "That man with the cap raced all the way around with us, and he wasn't even on a horse!" They "got a little bit of cotton candy—but not too much." The illustration shows them wallowing in the stuff. They "took a nice, quiet stroll through the park until it was closing time!" The art shows them racing along on a skateboard.

Other Devices: *Ambiguity*

Art Style: Impressionistic pastels and pencil serve nicely to gloss over the truth of Squiggle's Parisian adventures.

Dórrie, Doris. *Lottie's Princess Dress.* Illus. by Julia Kaergel. New York: Dial (Penguin Putnam), 1998.

Lottie and Mother disagree about suitable schoolday attire but resolve the matter agreeably, to the surprise of all.

Understatement: Lottie is slow to get up. She has just had a nice dream. When she crawls out of bed at last, Mother says, "I see you got the getting-up part right. Did you forget the getting-dressed part?" Lottie's unreasonable determination to wear a princess dress to kindergarten on a cold day frustrates Mother. She yells angrily. Lottie replies, "You are too big for tantrums." But "to Lottie's surprise, she wasn't." At work, dressed in party finery, Mother's colleagues tell her how special she looks. Mother happily replies, "You should see my daughter."

Other Devices: *Antithesis, Paradox, Theme*

Art Style: Spare lines and bright colors through chalk pastels and accent gold foil complement this expressionistic naïve rendering of an emotional confrontation.

Curriculum Tie-in: Social Science (Conflict Resolution)

Ernst, Lisa Campbell. *Goldilocks Returns.* New York: Simon & Schuster Books for Young Readers, 2000.

Fifty years after Goldilocks first met the three bears, she returns to fix up their cottage and soothe her guilty conscience.

Understatement: Goldi uses her dubious talents to spruce up what she considers the pokey old bear cottage. She pulls out "three bolts of pom-pom fringe and her staple gun. The results were stunning." When the bears return from their walk, they see Goldi's truck parked out front. "They hadn't had much luck with visitors in the past."

Other Devices: *Allusion, Antihero, Connotation, Flash-forward, Inference, Irony, Parallelism, Tone*

Art Style: Large, bulky cartoons emulate the story's original atmosphere, intended to amuse young listeners, while the language and art detail expand the interest level for more savvy audiences.

Fox, Mem. *Harriet, You'll Drive Me Wild.* Illus. by Marla Frazee. New York: Harcourt, 2000.

When a young girl has a series of mishaps at home one Saturday, her mother tries not to lose her temper—and does not quite succeed.

Understatement: "One morning at breakfast, she knocked over a glass of juice, just like that." The illustration shows the purple liquid flowing off the table onto the back of the family dog, who then, of course, shakes himself, spreading the sticky mess farther afield. "At snack time, she dribbled jam all over her jeans, just like that." The illustration shows a cupboard door open with cookies from the tin spread out on the floor, an open box of graham crackers, a spilled box of cereal, and the dog licking jam from a spoon Harriet is holding for him. "Before lunch, when Harriet was painting a picture, she dripped paint onto the carpet, just like that." The illustration shows paint running off the bottom of a drenched piece of paper. The dog is tracking through it, out the front door and down the steps. "At lunch, Harriet slid off her chair and the tablecloth came with her, just like that." Again, plates break, food falls, and a vase of flowers crashes. When she is meant to be napping, "she ripped open a pillow, just like that." She and the dog are tugging together on it.

Other Devices: *Foreshadowing, Inference*

Art Style: Pencil and transparent drawing ink cartoons wonderfully augment the spare text in this timeless story of childhood exuberance and parental restraint.

Curriculum Tie-in: Social Science (Family Relationships)

Gibbons, Faye. *Mama and Me and the Model T.* Illus. by Ted Rand. New York: Morrow, 1999.

When Mr. Long says any man can drive a car, Mama gets behind the wheel to show women can drive, too.

Understatement: Mama defiantly springs into the car and tears around the farm, smashing into and over things. When she can turn the steering wheel and the car swings into a wide half-circle, she is convinced she has finally mastered the machine. "I'm learning!" she yells as she leaves a trail of destruction in her wake. Her daughter agrees, but points to the road "over there." When they finally bring the car to a stop in the front yard, Mama comments innocently, "This motorcar has a mind of its own." Her relieved husband is glad the car is intact and no one was hurt. "It's not the only one," he mutters.

Other Devices: *Foreshadowing, Hyperbole, Imagery, Inference, Onomatopoeia, Parallelism, Stereotype/Reverse Stereotype*

Art Style: Expressionistic watercolors exuberantly dramatize the mysterious intricacies of mastering the wondrous but tricky skills of automobile driving.

Curriculum Tie-in: Social Science (Family Relationships)

Glass, Andrew. *Bewildered for Three Days: As to Why Daniel Boone Never Wore His Coonskin Cap.* New York: Holiday House, 2000.

With the help of what he learned from a Delaware Indian boy and an accommodating mother raccoon, young Daniel Boone escapes danger when a bear steals his coonskin cap.

Understatement: In typical tall tale form, less is said than is warranted by circumstances. Daniel Boone has his heart set upon becoming a guide into the nation's wilderness. But in the telling of this, he has a healthy respect for his youthful foolishness. His Indian companion teaches him to track and listen to animals. "Is this how I will find the heart of a brave?" he asks. "No, it is the way to catch a squirrel," his friend responds. One day as he awakens from a nap in a mossy glade, he finds a bear looming over him. The creature "opened his hairy jaws wide and showed me his long teeth." As he flees from enemy warriors, "the band of young braves was in good spirits, laughing heedlessly and hollering. A hiding place seemed the best course of action." Reflecting upon this incident many years later, Daniel Boone admitted he lost his bearings "and bedded down two more nights in the forest before finding my way home to Mama." An astonished portrait painter asks him if the "great Daniel Boone was lost in the woods." Boone is quick to respond, "I can't say that I was ever truly lost, only that I was bewildered for three days."

Other Devices: *Atmosphere, Flashback, Foreshadowing, Motif, Point of View, Tone*

Art Style: Impressionistic colored pencil and oil pastel humorously accompany this frontier yarn of a great adventurer told in a curious blend of humility and exaggeration.

Curriculum Tie-in: History (Biography—Daniel Boone), Literature (Tall Tale)

**Gralley, Jean. *Hogula, Dread Pig of Night.* New York: Henry Holt, 1999.*
Although he lives high on the hog in his castle on Grimy Pork Chop Hill, Hogula is unhappy because he has no friends—until he meets Elvis Ann, Dread Queen of Kissyface.

Understatement: Hogula happens to choose the evening of October 31 to go to the mall to seek a friend. "He liked it right away." Folks are dressed in weird costumes to which the awful Hogula finds he can relate quite satisfactorily. Elvis Ann knows the two are made for each other. "She wasn't sure about these other two," Hogula's companions, who resemble creatures from a Frankenstein movie. They welcome her by measuring her neck, presumably for the nefarious purposes of their master, Hogula.

Other Devices: *Alliteration, Allusion, Antihero, Aphorism, Cliché, Foreshadowing, Inference, Irony, Poetic Justice, Pun, Simile, Stereotype/Reverse Stereotype*

Art Style: Appropriately repulsive expressionistic cartoons in gouache and ink on watercolor paper develop the characters of this humorously gentle Dracula-style relationship.

Curriculum Tie-in: Social Science (Friendship)

Hoban, Russell. *Trouble on Thunder Mountain.* Illus. by Quentin Blake. New York: Orchard Books (Grolier), 2000.

> When Megafright International flattens their beautiful mountain to put up a hi-tech plastic theme park, the O'Saurus family uses faith and lots of Monsta-Gloo to put things right.

> > **Understatement:** When the O'Sauruses learn their mountain home is to be torn down so a plastic mountain can be put in its place, son Jim pronounces, "It takes a man named Flatbrain to think of something like that." Dad says he will think of something to avoid this disaster, but the bulldozers have arrived and are running over the garden. Mom says, "Better do it soon, there go the parsnips." Then the family looks at the paper that describes their new residence. It turns out to be a garbage dump. "We hope you will be pleased with this impravement." It is signed A. Worser. Son Jim observes, "Worser could do better with his spelling." Flatbrain sends his robot-monster foreman to see what is behind the curtain the O'Sauruses have erected to hide their restoration of the dirt mountain. The robot says he has no software to lift the curtain. "Mr. Flatbrain kicked the robot-monster foreman. 'Try,' he said."

> > **Other Devices:** *Aphorism, Connotation, Foreshadowing, Hyperbole, Irony, Poetic Justice, Satire*

> > **Art Style:** Humorous pen/ink watercolor cartoons spiritedly produce a funny tribute to old-fashioned ingenuity and to nature.

> > **Curriculum Tie-in:** Science (Ecology)

*Johnson, D.B. *Henry Hikes to Fitchburg.* Boston: Houghton Mifflin, 2000.

> While his friend works hard to earn train fare to Fitchburg, young Henry Thoreau walks the thirty miles through woods and fields, enjoying nature.

> > **Understatement:** Who wins the bet? The two friends decide one morning to "go to Fitchburg to see the country." Henry thinks walking is the fastest way to travel. His friend will work and buy a ticket to ride the train. When Henry arrives in the evening, he finds his friend waiting for him in the moonlight. His friend announces that the train was faster. "I know," Henry says. Then he takes a small pail from his pack. "I stopped for blackberries." That doesn't begin to describe his enjoyable experiences on the way to Fitchburg.

> > **Other Devices:** *Allusion, Irony, Paradox, Theme*

> > **Art Style:** Colored pencil and acrylic paint in stylishly simple, expressionistic designs contrast interesting visual perspectives and provide period detail.

> > **Curriculum Tie-in:** Literature (Henry David Thoreau), Philosophy (Quality of Life)

Johnson, Paul Brett. *Old Dry Frye: A Deliciously Funny Tall Tale.* New York: Scholastic Press, 1999.

A humorous retelling of an Appalachian folktale about a preacher who chokes on a chicken bone.

Understatement: When a man carrying a sack of hog meat home, pauses to take a swim in a creek, he retrieves his sack afterward. "It seemed a bit heavier than it used to." That's because he picks up the sack that has Old Dry Frye inside. When two brothers notice what they believe are the eyes of a possum up in a tree, they think it would be good to have possum stew for supper. They chuck a rock at it, and down it falls. "Mighty big possum," one of them remarks. That's because the "possum" is really Old Dry Frye, who had been flung into the tree when a wheel barrow carrying him stubbed up against a rock in the road.

Other Devices: *Black Humor, Cliché, Hyperbole, Inference, Poetic Justice, Serendipity, Tone*

Art Style: Ebullient acrylic cartoons share the fortunes and misfortunes of the self-serving characters in this raucous Appalachian romp.

Curriculum Tie-in: Literature (Tall Tales), Social Science (Appalachian Culture)

Kimmel, Eric A. *Grizz!* Illus. by Andrew Glass. New York: Holiday House, 2000. Cowboy Lucky Doolin makes a deal with the Devil, agreeing not to wash, shave, or change his clothes for seven years, thus earning a fortune and the hand of his true love.

Understatement: For a while Lucky's lack of hygiene isn't noticed. "But by the time the fifth year rolled around, he had become distinctly unpleasant." Enough to send dogs howling and buzzards weeping. When he decides to end the wager because of his sweetheart's dilemma holding on to the mortgaged ranch, he tells the barber to "draw me a bath, hot as you can make it. I need to soak for a spell."

Other Devices: *Atmosphere, Hyperbole, Inference, Motif, Poetic Justice, Simile*

Art Style: Oil sticks and watercolor dust create exaggerated cartoons that complement this version of a soul-selling wager folktale.

Curriculum Tie-in: Literature (Folktales—America)

Kitamura, Satoshi. *Me and My Cat?* New York: Farrar Straus Giroux, 2000. A young boy spends an unusual day after awakening to find that he and his cat have switched bodies.

Understatement: When Nicholas finds himself in the body of his cat, he realizes he can jump to the top of shelves. He chooses to try for a cupboard on the other side of the room. But, he lands poorly and it falls over. "Mom threw me out of the house." Nicholas observes his boy's body behaving like a cat. "He found the radiator and the litter box irresistible." "He found the goldfish particularly fascinating." Finally, when the witch's spell is broken, the next morning Nicholas's mother shouts at him to wake up or he'll be late for school. "Everything was back to normal."

Other Devices: *Antithesis, Inference, Irony, Parallelism, Point of View*
Art Style: Busy, hilarious acrylic cartoons detail the daily life of a boy's thoughts in a cat's body as he watches a cat's activities in his boy's body.
Curriculum Tie-in: Social Science (Animal Companions, Values)

Krensky, Stephen. *The Youngest Fairy Godmother Ever.* Illus. by Diana Cain Bluthenthal. New York: Simon & Schuster Books for Young Readers, 2000.
   Mavis tries to pursue her goal of playing fairy godmother and granting wishes to those around her, but she finds the process trickier than she thought.
      Understatement: Mavis's parents like the idea of her granting wishes. They begin by wishing she would empty the trash and clean up her room. Mavis is sure these wishes don't count. Her friend Laura warns her she may have to work day and night to perfect her trade. As Laura lugs a huge bag of trash to the curb, she remarks, "It'll be worth it." Laura would like to be a circus star doing a high wire act. Mavis puts up the clothes line for her and waves the wand. Kids go "Oooh" when Laura steps out on the line. They go "Aaah" when the parasol breaks her fall. Mavis "could see Laura was not pleased" with the results of her wish. When she closes her eyes to wave her wand over Hector, the class pet mouse, the class doesn't see Hector. "She didn't see Hector, either." Hector is loose in the room. Eventually, Mavis is well on her way to granting wishes. It seems sewing the costume for a classmate is more dependable than waving the wand to grant wishes.
      Other Devices: *Allusion, Irony*
      Art Style: A mix of inks and paints produces lively cartoons that complement the wry humor in this funny tale of determination to succeed.
      Curriculum Tie-in: Social Science (Values)

McKissack, Patricia. *The Honest to Goodness Truth.* Illus. by Giselle Potter. Atheneum Books for Young Readers (Simon & Schuster), 2000.
   After promising never to lie, Libby learns it's not always necessary to blurt out the whole truth.
      Understatement: "Before lunchtime, Libby had told a lot of truths." She managed to upset most of her friends, telling how Daisy had forgotten her Christmas speech and cried in front of all the parents, and how Charlesetta had gotten a spanking for stealing peaches, and how Thomas didn't have lunch money and had to borrow from his teacher. "By the time school was out, hardly anyone would talk to her."
      Other Devices: *Ambiguity, Antithesis, Aphorism, Foreshadowing, Paradox, Simile*
      Art Style: Pencil, ink, gouache, and watercolor render a luxuriant, expressionistic naïve style to this tale of honesty.
      Curriculum Tie-in: Social Science (Values)

McNaughton, Colin. *Yum!* New York: Harcourt Brace, 1998.

    Preston Pig suggests that Mr. Wolf get a job so he can buy what he wants to eat, but as he considers different lines of work, Mr. Wolf has a one-track mind.

        Understatement: In the final cartoon frame father pig has overheard Mr. Wolf ask, "When do I ever get to win?" He replies, "Not in this book, buddy!" Then he drops a large pot (labeled "solid iron"). The wolf notes, "I could be wrong, but this looks like The End."

        Other Devices: *Allusion, Ambiguity, Pun, Satire, Tone*

        Art Style: Detailed cartoons and humorous asides add to the impish joy of this wolf and pig encounter.

        Curriculum Tie-in: Social Science (Values)

Mahy, Margaret. *Simply Delicious.* Illus. by Jonathan Allen. New York: Orchard Books, 1999.

    A resourceful father engages in all kinds of acrobatic moves to keep an assortment of jungle creatures from getting the double-dip, chocolate-chip-and-cherry ice cream cone he is taking home to his son.

        Understatement: Mr. Minky is harassed all the way home on his bicycle. He swings the cone to baffle butterflies. He holds the cone at knee level and waves it in circles to taunt the toucan. He holds it straight out in front of him and waves it up and down to muddle the monkey. He tosses it from his left hand to his right, holding it at arms' length to trick the tiger. He balances the cone on his toe and on his elbow and on his nose to keep it away from a lunging crocodile. In sight of his backyard he shoots up his homemade ramp and flies through the air across the back fence to glide down gracefully with the ice cream for his son. The boy sweeps his tongue across it in grand style and pronounces it "Simply delicious!" Then Mr. Minky, smiling at his son's joy, and having endured quite a workout, says simply, "I feel quite hungry myself." Off he goes to his supper.

        Other Devices: *Alliteration, Foreshadowing, Hyperbole, Internal Rhyme, Poetic Justice, Simile*

        Art Style: Lively line and gouache cartoons in lush jungle colors satisfyingly follow the father's adventures as he delivers his son an appreciated treat.

        Curriculum Tie-in: Literature (Cumulative Tale)

*Meddaugh, Susan. *Hog-Eye.* New York: Walter Lorraine Books (Houghton Mifflin), 1995.

    A young pig uses her ability to read to outwit a wolf that intends to eat her.

        Understatement: When a young pig realizes she has gotten onto a school bus that goes far past her school, she panics and yells for the driver to "Stop! Stop the bus!" When she tells this part of the story to her parents, she relates, "I went to the bus driver and calmly told him that I wanted to get off." When she is grabbed by a wolf and thrown into a sack, she hollers, "Help, Mommie!" But in the narration she reports, "I was scared but cool."

Other Devices: *Allusion, Antithesis, Flashback, Foreshadowing, Hyperbole, Inference, Irony*
Art Style: Split page watercolor cartoons tell the "true story" of a schoolchild who dislikes her daily bus ride.
Curriculum Tie-in: Literature (Tall Tale)

Modarressi, Mitra. *Yard Sale.* New York: DK Pub., 2000.
When Mr. Flotsam has a yard sale in the quiet town of Spudville, his neighbors are first upset, then delighted by their purchases.
> **Understatement:** Mr. Rotelli tries out his pasta maker, but "it seemed to be missing its OFF button." When Mrs. Applebee discovers the potential for a telephone that enables one to talk with dead people, she "was beginning to grow more fond" of her purchase. The townspeople agree the pages being turned out by the typewriter indicate it "had real talent." The Zings' "rug was always in great demand" because it takes the neighborhood kids on a magic carpet ride over their village. And as for the man who started all this, Mr. Flotsam, "the next time spring rolled around, he decided to hold another yard sale . . . ."
> **Other Devices:** *Allusion, Antithesis, Connotation, Hyperbole, Inference, Paradox, Serendipity*
> **Art Style:** Lively full-page watercolor naïve art accompanies an understated text.

*Nolen, Jerdine. *Big Jabe.* Illus. by Kadir Nelson. New York: Lothrop, Lee & Shepard, 2000.
Momma Mary tells stories about a special young man who does wondrous things, especially for the slaves on the Plenty Plantation.
> **Understatement:** The overseer becomes enraged when Jabe can weed a whole field of soybeans before sunup, hoe the back forty by midday, and mend ten miles of fence by sunset. "Life in the Quarters just didn't feel so burdensome with Jabe around."
> **Other Devices:** *Allusion, Anachronism, Antithesis, Flashback, Flash-forward, Foreshadowing, Hyperbole, Imagery, Inference, Parallelism, Simile, Symbol*
> **Art Style:** Strong, detailed pen/ink, watercolor, and gouache drawings provide wonderful expressionistic period ambience to this folk tale.
> **Curriculum Tie-in:** History (Slavery—America), Literature (Tall Tale)

O'Malley, Kevin. *Bud.* New York: Walker & Company, 2000.
The orderly Sweet-Williams are dismayed at their son's fondness for the messy pastime of gardening.
> **Understatement:** As the parents try to tame their son's gardening exuberance by clipping, spraying, and mowing in perfectly straight lines, Bud is planting flowers on dinner plates and in hats. "Was it supposed to rain today?" asks his father as Bud carelessly swings around a garden hose.

All this emphasis upon order comes straight from Grandfather Sweet-William. Each time he visits, he brings his usual presents: a classroom organizer for Bud and a bowl of silk flowers for his mother. Grandfather notes that silk flowers never drop their leaves. With a forced smile, Mrs. Sweet-Williams responds, "They are a wonder." While at their house, Grandfather insists upon doing the housework, commenting, "I have a special gift for finding dirt."

Other Devices: *Antithesis, Aphorism, Foreshadowing, Inference, Irony, Pun, Theme*

Art Style: Large, expressive gouache cartoons lovingly follow the development of tolerance, respect, and appreciation for a beloved child's unconventional approach to life.

Curriculum Tie-in: Science (Gardening), Social Science (Family Relationships, Values)

APPENDIX 1:
RESOURCES LISTED
BY AUTHOR

❖❖❖❖❖❖❖❖❖❖❖

Ada, Alma Flor. *Friend Frog*. Illus. by Lori Lohstoeter. New York: Gulliver Books (Harcourt), 2000.
Paradox

Alderson, Brian. *The Tale of the Turnip*. Illus. by Fritz Wegner. Cambridge, MA: Candlewick Press, 1999.
Connotation, Hyperbole, Motif, Poetic Justice, Satire, Tone

Alexander, Lloyd. *The House Gobbaleen*. Illus. by Diane Goode. New York: Dutton Children's Books (Penguin Books), 1995.
Ambiguity, Foreshadowing, Hyperbole, Inference, Irony, Simile, Theme, Tone, Understatement

Altman, Linda Jacobs. *Amelia's Road*. Illus. by Enrique O. Sanchez. New York: Lee & Low, 1993.
Alliteration, Antithesis, Connotation, Serendipity, Simile, Symbol

*Armstrong, Jennifer. *Pierre's Dream*. Illus. by Susan Gaber. New York: Dial (Penguin Putnam), 1999.
Antihero, Foreshadowing, Inference, Irony, Theme

Aylesworth, Jim. *The Full Belly Bowl*. Illus. by Wendy Anderson Halpern. New York: Atheneum Books for Young Readers (Simon & Schuster), 1999.
Foreshadowing, Irony

Baker, Jeannie. *The Hidden Forest*. New York: Greenwillow Books (HarperCollins), 2000.
Connotation, Imagery, Inference, Simile

Battle-Lavert, Gwendolyn. *The Music in Derrick's Heart*. Illus. by Colin Bootman. New York: Holiday House, 2000.
Aphorism, Atmosphere, Inference, Simile, Tone

*Baylor, Byrd. *The Table Where Rich People Sit*. Illus. by Peter Parnall. New York: Charles Scribner's Sons, 1994.
Antihero, Aphorism, Foreshadowing, Irony, Paradox

*Berkeley, Laura. *The Spirit of the Maasai Man*. New York: Barefoot Books, 2000.
Imagery, Symbol, Theme, Tone

Bradbury, Ray. *Switch on the Night*. Illus. by Leo and Diane Dillon. New York: Alfred A. Knopf, 1983.
Alliteration, Antithesis, Internal Rhyme, Irony, Metaphor, Motif, Paradox, Simile, Symbol

*Browne, Anthony. *Voices in the Park*. New York: DK Pub., 1998.
Connotation, Foreshadowing, Inference, Point of View

Bunting, Eve. *Can You Do This, Old Badger?* Illus. by Le Uyen Pham. New York: Harcourt, 1999.
Ambiguity, Foreshadowing, Theme

*Bunting, Eve. *The Memory String*. Illus. by Ted Rand. New York: Clarion Books (Houghton Mifflin), 2000.
Ambiguity, Antithesis, Aphorism, Foreshadowing, Imagery, Inference, Parallelism, Simile

*Bunting, Eve. *Swan in Love*. Illus. by Jo Ellen McAllister Stammen. New York: Atheneum Books for Young Readers (Simon & Schuster), 2000.
Antithesis, Aphorism, Foreshadowing, Imagery, Inference, Simile, Theme

*Burleigh, Robert. *Edna*. Illus. by Joanna Yardley. New York: Orchard Books, 2000.
Atmosphere, Foreshadowing, Imagery, Parallelism, Simile

Camp, Lindsay. *Why?* Illus. by Tony Ross. New York: G.P. Putnam's Sons (Penguin Putnam Books for Young Readers), 1998.
Inference, Irony, Paradox, Serendipity, Understatement

Carlstrom, Nancy. *Goodbye, Geese*. Illus. by Ed Young. New York: Philomel (Putnam Books), 1991.
Metaphor, Simile

Carrick, Carol. *Big Old Bones*. Illus. by Donald Carrick. New York: Clarion Books, 1989.
Irony, Understatement

Chorao, Kay. *Pig and Crow*. New York: Henry Holt, 2000.
Paradox

*Cole, Brock. *Buttons*. New York: Farrar Straus Giroux, 2000.
Aphorism, Inference, Irony, Pun, Tone

Cowley, Joy. *The Video Shop Sparrow*. Illus. by Gavin Bishop. Honesdale, PA: Boyds Mills Press, 1999.
Inference, Satire, Theme, Tone

*Cronin, Doreen. *Click, Clack Moo, Cows That Type*. Illus. by Betsy Lewin, New York: Simon & Schuster, 2000.
Inference, Irony, Symbol

Dahan, André. *Squiggle's Tale*. San Francisco: Chronicle, 2000.
Ambiguity, Understatement

*Deedy, Carmen Agra. *The Yellow Star: The Legend of King Christian X of Denmark*. Illus. by Henri Sorensen. Atlanta: Peachtree, 2000.
Antithesis, Aphorism, Atmosphere, Foreshadowing, Inference, Irony, Paradox, Parallelism, Pun, Simile, Symbol, Theme

Dengler, Marianna. *Fiddlin' Sam*. Illus. by Sibyl Graber Gerig. Flagstaff, AZ: Rising Moon (Northland), 1999.
Antithesis, Atmosphere, Foreshadowing, Inference, Internal Rhyme, Parallelism, Serendipity

*Dengler, Marianna. *The Worry Stone*. Illus. by Sibyl Graber Gerig. Flagstaff, AZ: Rising Moon (Northland), 1996.
Antithesis, Flashback, Foreshadowing, Inference, Parallel Story, Parallelism

DePaola, Tomie. *The Art Lesson*. New York: G.P. Putnam's Sons, 1989.
Atmosphere, Flash-Forward, Inference, Irony, Parallelism, Serendipity, Theme

Dórrie, Doris. *Lottie's Princess Dress*. Illus. by Julia Kaergel. New York: Dial (Penguin Putnam), 1998.
Antithesis, Paradox, Theme, Understatement

Ernst, Lisa Campbell. *Goldilocks Returns*. New York: Simon & Schuster Books for Young Readers, 2000.
Allusion, Antihero, Connotation, Flash-forward, Inference, Irony, Parallelism, Tone, Understatement

Fearnley, Jan. *Mr. Wolf's Pancakes*. Waukesha, WI: Little Tiger Press, 1999.
Allusion, Antihero, Black Humor, Irony, Poetic Justice, Stereotype/ Reverse Stereotype

Fitzpatrick, Marie-Louise. *Lizzy and Skunk*. New York: DK Ink, 2000.
Irony, Parallelism, Personification

Fox, Mem. *Harriet, You'll Drive Me Wild*. Illus. by Marla Frazee. New York: Harcourt, 2000.
Foreshadowing, Inference, Understatement

Garland, Michael. *Dinner at Magritte's*. New York: Dutton Children's Books (Penguin), 1995.
Cliché, Foreshadowing, Inference

Gibbons, Faye. *Mama and Me and the Model T*. Illus. by Ted Rand. New York: Morrow, 1999.
Foreshadowing, Hyperbole, Imagery, Inference, Onomatopoeia, Parallelism, Stereotype/Reverse Stereotype, Understatement

Givens, Terryl. *Dragon Scales and Willow Leaves*. Illus. by Andrew Portwood. New York: G.P. Putnam's Sons, 1997.
Alliteration, Antithesis, Imagery, Metaphor, Point of View, Simile

Glass, Andrew. *Bewildered for Three Days: As to Why Daniel Boone Never Wore His Coonskin Cap*. New York: Holiday House, 2000.
Atmosphere, Flashback, Foreshadowing, Motif, Point of View, Tone, Understatement

*Gralley, Jean. *Hogula, Dread Pig of Night*. New York: Henry Holt, 1999.
Alliteration, Allusion Antihero, Aphorism, Cliché, Foreshadowing, Inference, Irony, Poetic Justice, Pun, Simile, Stereotype/Reverse Stereotype, Understatement

Greenfield, Karen. *Sister Yessa's Story*. Illus. by Claire Ewart. New York: Laura Geringer (HarperCollins), 1992.
Inference, Parallel Story

*Gregorowski, Christopher. *Fly, Eagle, Fly! An African Tale*. Illus. by Niki Daly. New York: Margaret K. McElderry Books (Simon & Schuster), 2000.
Analogy, Antithesis, Foreshadowing, Imagery, Motif, Parallelism

*Hamanaka, Sheila. *Peace Crane*. New York: Morrow Junior Books, 1995.
Allusion, Antithesis, Flash-Forward, Imagery, Simile, Symbol

Harris, Jim. *The Three Little Dinosaurs*. Gretna, LA: Pelican Publishing, 1999.
Antithesis, Foreshadowing, Inference, Parody, Poetic Justice, Tone

*Hayes, Joe. *A Spoon for Every Bite*. Illus. by Rebecca Lear. New York: Orchard Books, 1996.
Ambiguity, Antihero, Antithesis, Foreshadowing, Hyperbole, Motif, Poetic Justice

Henkes, Kevin. *Wemberly Worried.* New York: Greenwillow Books (HarperCollins), 2000.
Antithesis, Cliché, Irony, Parallelism

Hesse, Karen. *Come On, Rain!* Illus. by Jon J. Muth. New York: Scholastic Press, 1999.
Alliteration, Foreshadowing, Hyperbole, Imagery, Metaphor, Paradox, Simile

Hest, Amy. *Mabel Dancing.* Illus. by Christine Davenier. Cambridge, MA: Candlewick Press, 2000.
Atmosphere, Foreshadowing, Imagery, Parallelism

Hoban, Russell. *Trouble on Thunder Mountain.* Illus. by Quentin Blake. New York: Orchard Books (Grolier), 2000.
Aphorism, Connotation, Foreshadowing, Hyperbole, Irony, Poetic Justice, Satire, Understatement

Hopkinson, Deborah. *A Band of Angels: A Story Inspired by the Jubilee Singers.* Illus. by Paul Colón. New York: Atheneum Books for Young Readers (Simon & Schuster), 1999.
Antithesis, Foreshadowing, Irony, Simile

Howe, James. *Horace and Morris but Mostly Dolores.* Illus. by Amy Walrod. New York: Atheneum Books for Young Readers (Simon & Schuster), 1999.
Allusion, Internal Rhyme, Parallelism, Pun, Stereotype/ Reverse Stereotype, Theme

Hutchins, Hazel. *One Duck.* Illus. by Ruth Ohi. New York: Annick (Firefly Books), 1999.
Antithesis, Atmosphere, Imagery, Inference, Onomatopoeia, Parallelism, Tone

Johnson, Angela. *Down the Winding Road.* Illus. by Shane Evans. New York: DK Ink, 2000.
Anachronism, Atmosphere, Inference, Irony

*Johnson, D.B. *Henry Hikes to Fitchburg.* Boston: Houghton Mifflin, 2000.
Allusion, Irony, Paradox, Theme, Understatement

Johnson, Paul Brett. *Bearhide and Crow.* New York: Holiday House, 2000.
Atmosphere, Poetic Justice, Serendipity

Johnson, Paul Brett. *Old Dry Frye: A Deliciously Funny Tall Tale.* New York: Scholastic Press, 1999.
Black Humor, Cliché, Hyperbole, Inference, Poetic Justice, Serendipity, Tone, Understatement

Johnston, Tony. *Alice Nizzy Nazzy, the Witch of Santa Fe.* Illus. by Tomie de Paola. New York: G.P. Putnam's Sons, 1995.
Alliteration, Connotation, Foreshadowing, Hyperbole, Internal Rhyme, Motif, Poetic Justice, Simile

Jones, Joy. *Tambourine Moon.* Illus. by Terry Widener. New York: Simon & Schuster Books for Young Readers, 1999.
Antithesis, Hyperbole, Imagery, Personification, Simile

Kajikawa, Kimiko. *Yoshi's Feast.* Illus. by Yumi Heo. New York: DK Ink, 2000.
Antithesis, Aphorism, Foreshadowing, Inference, Onomatopoeia, Parallelism, Poetic Justice

*Kaplan, Howard. *Waiting to Sing.* Illus. by Hervé Blondon. New York: DK Ink, 2000.
Allusion, Antithesis, Aphorism, Atmosphere, Foreshadowing,

Imagery, Inference, Metaphor,
Parallelism, Simile, Symbol

Keller, Holly. *That's Mine, Horace.* New York: Greenwillow Books (HarperCollins), 2000.
Irony, Parallelism, Serendipity

Kimmel, Eric A. *Grizz!* Illus. by Andrew Glass. New York: Holiday House, 2000.
Atmosphere, Hyperbole, Inference, Motif, Poetic Justice, Simile, Understatement

Kirkpatrick, Katherine. *Redcoats and Petticoats.* Illus. by Ronald Himler. New York: Holiday House, 1999.
Foreshadowing, Inference

Kitamura, Satoshi. *Me and My Cat?* New York: Farrar Straus Giroux, 2000.
Antithesis, Inference, Irony, Parallelism, Point of View, Understatement

Krensky, Stephen. *The Youngest Fairy Godmother Ever.* Illus. by Diana Cain Bluthenthal. New York: Simon & Schuster Books for Young Readers, 2000.
Allusion, Irony, Understatement

Krudop, Walter Lyon. *The Man Who Caught Fish.* New York: Farrar Straus Giroux, 2000.
Foreshadowing, Poetic Justice, Theme

Krudop, Walter Lyon. *Something Is Growing.* New York: Atheneum Books for Young Readers (Simon & Schuster), 1995.
Foreshadowing, Satire

Kurtz, Jane. *Faraway Home.* Illus. by E.B. Lewis. New York: Gulliver Books (Harcourt), 2000.
Foreshadowing, Imagery, Metaphor, Simile

Kurtz, Jane. *River Friendly, River Wild.* Illus. by Neil Brennan. New York: Simon & Schuster Books for Young Readers, 2000.

Antithesis, Aphorism, Atmosphere, Imagery, Metaphor, Onomatopoeia, Simile

Laden, Nina. *Roberto the Insect Architect.* San Francisco: Chronicle Books, 2000.
Alliteration, Allusion, Antithesis, Cliché, Parallelism, Pun

Lamstein, Sarah Marwil. *I Like Your Buttons!* Illus. by Nancy Cote. Morton Grove, IL: Albert Whitman, 1999.
Irony, Serendipity, Theme

Lawson, Julie. *Emma and the Silk Train.* Illus. by Paul Mombourquette. Buffalo, NY: Kids Can Press, 1997.
Ambiguity, Foreshadowing, Imagery, Inference, Parallelism, Simile

Littlesugar, Amy. *Tree of Hope.* Illus. by Floyd Cooper. New York: Philomel (Penguin Putnam), 1999.
Cliché, Flashback, Foreshadowing, Inference, Paradox, Serendipity, Simile, Stereotype/Reverse Stereotype, Symbol

Lorbiecki, Marybeth. *Just One Flick of a Finger.* Illus. by David Diaz. New York: Dial (Penguin Putnam), 1996.
Antithesis, Foreshadowing, Inference, Internal Rhyme, Metaphor, Pun, Simile, Theme

Lowell, Susan. *Cindy Ellen: A Wild Western Cinderella.* Illus. by Jane Manning. New York: Joanna Cotler Books (HarperCollins), 2000.
Alliteration, Aphorism, Foreshadowing, Internal Rhyme, Parallelism, Parody, Simile, Tone

Lowell, Susan. *Little Red Cowboy Hat.* Illus. by Randy Cecil. New York: Henry Holt & Co., 1997.
Aphorism, Atmosphere, Caricature, Hyperbole, Inference, Onomatopoeia, Parody, Simile, Stereotype/ Reverse Stereotype, Tone

Lum, Kate. *What! Cried Granny: An Almost Bedtime Story*. Illus. By Adrian Johnson. New York: Dial (Penguin Putnam), 1998.
Hyperbole, Inference

Lyon, George Ella. *One Lucky Girl*. Illus. by Irene Trivas. New York: DK Pub., 2000.
Ambiguity, Antithesis, Foreshadowing, Imagery, Inference, Metaphor, Parallelism, Simile

McKissack, Patricia. *The Honest to Goodness Truth*. Illus. by Giselle Potter. New York: Atheneum Books for Young Readers (Simon & Schuster), 2000.
Ambiguity, Antithesis, Aphorism, Foreshadowing, Paradox, Simile, Understatement

McNaughton, Colin. *Yum!* New York: Harcourt Brace, 1998.
Allusion, Ambiguity, Pun, Satire, Tone, Understatement

Mahy, Margaret. *Simply Delicious*. Illus. by Jonathan Allen. New York: Orchard Books, 1999.
Alliteration, Foreshadowing, Hyperbole, Internal Rhyme, Poetic Justice, Simile, Understatement

*Mamet, David. *Henrietta*. Illus. by Elizabeth Dahlie. Boston: Houghton Mifflin, 1999.
Inference, Irony, Personification, Pun, Satire, Serendipity, Tone

Martin, Bill. *Chicken Chuck*. Illus. by Steven Salerno. New York: Winslow Press, 2000.
Satire, Symbol

Martin, Jacqueline Briggs. *Snowflake Bentley*. Illus. by Mary Azarian. Boston: Houghton Mifflin, 1998 (Caldecott—1999).
Antithesis, Imagery, Parallelism, Simile

*Martin, Nora. *The Stone Dancers*. Illus. by Jill Kastner. New York: Atheneum Books for Young Readers (Simon & Schuster), 1995.
Aphorism, Imagery, Inference, Irony, Metaphor, Parallel Story, Simile

*Meddaugh, Susan. *Hog-Eye*. New York: Walter Lorraine Books (Houghton Mifflin), 1995.
Allusion, Antithesis, Flashback, Foreshadowing, Hyperbole, Inference, Irony, Understatement

Meggs, Libby Phillips. *Go Home! The True Story of James the Cat*. Morton Grove, IL: Albert Whitman, 2000.
Ambiguity, Antithesis, Connotation, Inference, Metaphor, Point of View, Simile

Miller, William. *The Piano*. Illus. by Susan Keeter. New York: Lee & Low Books, 2000.
Inference, Theme

Mitchell, Adrian. *Nobody Rides the Unicorn*. Illus. by Stephen Lambert. New York: Arthur A. Levine Books (Scholastic), 1999.
Poetic Justice, Pun, Simile

Mochizuki, Ken. *Passage to Freedom: The Sugihara Story*. Illus. by Dom Lee. Afterward by Hiroki Sugihara. New York: Lee & Low, 1997.
Antithesis, Aphorism, Foreshadowing, Point of View, Theme

Modarressi, Mitra. *Yard Sale*. New York: DK Pub., 2000.
Allusion, Antithesis, Connotation, Hyperbole, Inference, Paradox, Serendipity, Understatement

Morimoto, Junko. *The Two Bullies*. Trans. by Isao Morimoto. New York: Crown (Random House), 1997.
Irony, Serendipity

*Morrison, Toni with Slade Morrison. *The Big Box*. Illus. by Giselle Potter. New York: Hyperion, 1999.
Antithesis, Inference, Internal Rhyme, Irony, Oxymoron, Satire, Theme

*Myers, Christopher. *Black Cat*. New York: Scholastic Press, 1999.
Alliteration, Imagery, Internal Rhyme, Metaphor, Simile

*Myers, Tim. *Basho and the Fox*. Illus. by Oki S. Han. New York: Marshall Cavendish, 2000.
Ambiguity, Antithesis, Aphorism, Imagery, Irony, Motif, Parallelism, Theme

Nickle, John. *The Ant Bully*. New York: Scholastic Press, 1999.
Antihero, Antithesis, Foreshadowing, Inference, Personification, Poetic Justice, Point of View

*Nolen, Jerdine. *Big Jabe*. Illus. by Kadir Nelson. New York: Lothrop, Lee & Shepard, 2000.
Allusion, Anachronism, Antithesis, Flashback, Flash-forward, Foreshadowing, Hyperbole, Imagery, Inference, Parallelism, Simile, Symbol, Understatement

O'Malley, Kevin. *Bud*. New York: Walker & Company, 2000.
Antithesis, Aphorism, Foreshadowing, Inference, Irony, Pun, Theme, Understatement

Osborne, Mary Pope. *Kate and the Beanstalk*. Illus. by Giselle Potter. New York: Atheneum Books for Young Readers (Simon & Schuster), 2000.
Hyperbole, Inference, Motif, Poetic Justice, Simile, Stereotype/Reverse Stereotype

*Pacilio, V.J. *Ling Cho and His Three Friends*. Illus. by Scott Cook. New York: Farrar Straus Giroux, 2000.
Alliteration, Aphorism, Irony, Paradox, Poetic Justice, Theme

Pawagi, Manjusha. *The Girl Who Hated Books*. Illus. by Leanne Franson. Hillsboro, OR: Beyond Words, 1998.
Alliteration, Allusion, Antithesis, Foreshadowing, Hyperbole, Inference, Internal Rhyme, Pun, Tone

Preston, Tim. *The Lonely Scarecrow*. Illus. by Maggie Kneen. New York: Dutton Children's Books (Penguin Books), 1999.
Imagery, Inference, Metaphor, Paradox, Parallelism, Theme

Ruurs, Margriet. *Emma and the Coyote*. Illus. by Barbara Spurll. New York: Stoddart Kids, 1999.
Alliteration, Foreshadowing, Imagery, Inference, Irony, Motif, Parallelism, Serendipity, Simile

*Say, Allen. *The Sign Painter*. Boston: Walter Lorraine Books (Houghton Mifflin), 2000.
Ambiguity, Antithesis, Imagery, Inference, Point of View, Theme, Tone

Scamell, Ragnhild. *Toby's Doll's House*. Illus. by Adrian Reynolds. London: Levinson Books, 1998.
Paradox, Serendipity, Stereotype/Reverse Stereotype

Sierra, Judy. *The Gift of the Crocodile: A Cinderella Story*. Illus. by Reynold Ruffins. New York: Simon and Schuster Books for Young Readers, 2000.
Foreshadowing, Irony, Motif, Poetic Justice, Pun

Souhami, Jessica. *No Dinner! The Story of the Old Woman and the Pumpkin*. New York: Marshall Cavendish, 1999.
Motif, Onomatopoeia

Steig, William. *Wizzil.* Illus. by Quentin
Blake. New York: Farrar Straus
Giroux, 2000.
*Alliteration, Ambiguity, Connotation,
Foreshadowing, Internal Rhyme,
Irony, Serendipity, Tone*

*St. George, Judith. *So You Want to Be
President?* Illus. by David Small. New
York: Philomel (Penguin Putnam
Books for Young Readers), 2000.
(Caldecott-2000)
*Antithesis, Atmosphere, Caricature,
Parallelism, Tone*

Strete, Craig Kee. *The Lost Boy and the
Monster.* Illus. by Steve Johnson and
Lou Fancher. New York: G.P.
Putnam's Sons (Penguin Books for
Young Readers), 1999.
*Ambiguity, Connotation, Internal
Rhyme, Motif, Poetic Justice,
Simile, Theme, Tone*

Turner, Ann. *Drummer Boy: Marching to
the Civil War.* Illus. by Mark Hess.
New York: HarperCollins, 1998.
*Atmosphere, Imagery, Point of View,
Simile*

*Turner, Ann. *Red Flower Goes West.* Illus.
by Dennis Nolan. New York:
Hyperion Books for Children, 1999.
*Connotation, Inference, Metaphor,
Parallelism, Simile, Symbol*

Turner, Ann. *Secrets from the Dollhouse.*
Illus. by Raúl Colón. New York:
HarperCollins, 2000.
*Foreshadowing, Imagery, Metaphor,
Personification, Point of View,
Simile*

*Van Allsburg, Chris. *The Sweetest Fig.*
Boston: Houghton Mifflin, 1993.
Inference, Irony, Poetic Justice

Waite, Judy. *Mouse, Look Out!* Illus. by
Norma Burgin. New York: Dutton
Children's Books (Penguin Putnam),
1998.

*Alliteration, Atmosphere, Internal
Rhyme, Metaphor, Poetic Justice,
Simile*

Wallace, Karen. *Scarlette Beane.* Illus. by Jon
Berkeley. New York: Dial Books for
Young Readers (Penguin Putnam),
2000.
*Foreshadowing, Hyperbole, Pun,
Simile*

White, Linda Arms. *Comes a Wind.* Illus.
by Tom Curry. New York: DK Pub.,
2000.
*Atmosphere, Foreshadowing,
Hyperbole, Inference, Parallelism,
Simile*

*Wilkon, Piotr. *Rosie the Cool Cat.* Illus.
by Jozef Wilkon. New York: Viking
(Penguin Books), 1989.
*Antithesis, Foreshadowing, Inference,
Irony, Poetic Justice, Satire,
Stereotype/Reverse Stereotype,
Symbol*

*Wisniewski, David. *Golem.* New York:
Clarion Books (Houghton Mifflin),
1996 (Caldecott—1997).
*Analogy, Atmosphere,
Foreshadowing, Imagery,
Inference, Irony, Motif, Paradox,
Simile*

*Wisniewski, David. *Tough Cookie.* New
York: Lothrop, Lee & Shepard
(William Morrow), 1999.
*Analogy, Parody, Pun, Satire, Simile,
Stereotype/Reverese Stereotype,
Theme*

*Yaccarino, Dan. *Deep in the Jungle.* New
York: Anne Schwartz Books
Atheneum Books for Young Readers
(Simon & Schuster), 2000.
*Anachronism, Antihero, Antithesis,
Black Humor, Foreshadowing,
Irony, Motif, Parallelism, Poetic
Justice, Pun, Tone*

Zagwÿn, Deborah. *Apple Batter*. Berkeley,
CA: Tricycle Press, 1999.
*Alliteration, Analogy, Antithesis,
Foreshadowing, Inference, Irony,
Parallelism, Pun, Simile*

APPENDIX 2:
RESOURCES LISTED
BY TITLE

◆◆◆◆◆◆◆◆◆◆◆◆

Alice Nizzy Nazzy, the Witch of Santa Fe. Johnston, Tony. G.P. Putnam's Sons, 1995.
Alliteration, Connotation, Foreshadowing, Hyperbole, Internal Rhyme, Motif, Poetic Justice, Simile

Amelia's Road. Altman, Linda Jacobs. Lee & Low, 1993.
Alliteration, Antithesis, Connotation, Serendipity, Simile, Symbol

The Ant Bully. Nickle, John. Scholastic Press, 1999.
Antihero, Antithesis, Foreshadowing, Inference, Personification, Poetic Justice, Point of View

Apple Batter. Zagwÿn, Deborah. Tricycle Press, 1999.
Alliteration, Analogy, Antithesis, Foreshadowing, Inference, Irony, Parallelism, Pun, Simile

The Art Lesson. DePaola, Tomie. G.P. Putnam's Sons, 1989.
Atmosphere, Flash-Forward, Inference, Irony, Parallelism, Serendipity, Theme

A Band of Angels: A Story Inspired by the Jubilee Singers. Hopkinson, Deborah. Atheneum (Simon & Schuster), 1999.
Antithesis, Foreshadowing, Irony, Simile

*Basho and the Fox. Myers, Tim. Marshall Cavendish, 2000.
Ambiguity, Antithesis, Aphorism, Imagery, Irony, Motif, Parallelism, Theme

Bearhide and Crow. Johnson, Paul Brett. Holiday House, 2000.
Atmosphere, Poetic Justice, Serendipity

Bewildered for Three Days: As to Why Daniel Boone Never Wore His Coonskin Cap. Glass, Andrew. Holiday House, 2000.
Atmosphere, Flashback, Foreshadowing, Motif, Point of View, Tone, Understatement

*The Big Box. Morrison, Toni, with Slade Morrison. Hyperion, 1999.

Antithesis, Inference, Internal Rhyme,
     Irony, Oxymoron, Satire, Theme
*Big Jabe. Nolen, Jerdine. Lothrop, Lee
     & Shepard, 2000.
     Allusion, Anachronism, Antithesis,
          Flashback, Flash-Forward,
          Foreshadowing, Hyperbole,
          Imagery, Inference, Parallelism,
          Simile, Symbol, Understatement
Big Old Bones. Carrick, Carol. Clarion,
     1989.
     Irony, Understatement
*Black Cat. Myers, Christopher.
     Scholastic Press, 1999.
     Alliteration, Imagery, Internal
          Rhyme, Metaphor, Simile
Bud. O'Malley, Kevin. Walker &
     Company, 2000.
     Antithesis, Aphorism, Foreshadowing,
          Inference, Irony, Pun, Theme,
          Understatement
*Buttons. Cole, Brock. Farrar Straus
     Giroux, 2000.
     Aphorism, Inference, Irony, Pun,
          Tone
Can You Do This, Old Badger? Bunting,
     Eve. Harcourt, 1999.
     Ambiguity, Foreshadowing, Theme
Chicken Chuck. Martin, Bill. Winslow
     Press, 2000.
     Satire, Symbol
Cindy Ellen: A Wild Western Cinderella.
     Lowell, Susan. HarperCollins, 2000.
     Alliteration, Aphorism,
          Foreshadowing, Internal Rhyme,
          Parallelism, Parody, Simile, Tone
*Click, Clack, Moo Cows That Type.
     Cronin, Doreen. Simon & Schuster,
     2000.
     Inference, Irony, Symbol
Come On, Rain! Hesse, Karen. Scholastic
     Press, 1999.

Alliteration, Foreshadowing,
     Hyperbole, Imagery, Metaphor,
     Paradox, Simile
Comes a Wind. White, Linda Arms. DK
     Pub., 2000.
     Atmosphere, Foreshadowing,
          Hyperbole, Inference, Parallelism,
          Simile
*Deep in the Jungle. Yaccarino, Dan. Anne
     Schwartz/Athneneum (Simon &
     Schuster), 2000.
     Anachronism, Antihero, Antithesis,
          Black Humor, Foreshadowing,
          Irony, Motif, Parallelism, Poetic
          Justice, Pun, Tone
Dinner at Magritte's. Garland, Michael.
     Dutton (Penguin), 1995.
     Cliché, Foreshadowing, Inference
Down the Winding Road. Johnson, Angela.
     DK Ink, 2000.
     Anachronism, Atmosphere, Inference,
          Irony
Dragon Scales and Willow Leaves. Givens,
     Terryl. G.P. Putnam's Sons, 1997.
     Alliteration, Antithesis, Imagery,
          Metaphor, Point of View, Simile
Drummer Boy: Marching to the Civil War.
     Turner, Ann. HarperCollins, 1998.
     Atmosphere, Imagery, Point of View,
          Simile
*Edna. Burleigh, Robert. Orchard Books,
     2000.
     Atmosphere, Foreshadowing, Imagery,
          Parallelism, Simile
Emma and the Coyote. Ruurs, Margriet.
     Stoddart Kids, 1999.
     Alliteration, Foreshadowing, Imagery,
          Inference, Irony, Motif,
          Parallelism, Serendipity, Simile
Emma and the Silk Train. Lawson, Julie.
     Kids Can Press, 1997.
     Ambiguity, Foreshadowing, Imagery,
          Inference, Parallelism, Simile

Faraway Home. Kurtz, Jane. Harcourt, 2000.
Foreshadowing, Imagery, Metaphor, Simile

Fiddlin' Sam. Dengler, Marianna. Rising Moon (Northland), 1999.
Antithesis, Atmosphere, Foreshadowing, Inference, Internal Rhyme, Parallelism, Serendipity

*Fly, Eagle, Fly! Gregorowski, Christopher. McElderry (Simon & Schuster), 2000.
Analogy, Antithesis, Foreshadowing, Imagery, Motif, Parallelism

Friend Frog. Ada, Alma Flor. Gulliver Books (Harcourt), 2000.
Paradox

The Full Belly Bowl. Aylesworth, Jim. Atheneum (Simon & Schuster), 1999.
Foreshadowing, Irony

The Gift of the Crocodile: A Cinderella Story. Sierra, Judy. Simon & Schuster Books for Young Readers, 2000.
Foreshadowing, Irony, Motif, Poetic Justice, Pun

The Girl Who Hated Books. Pawagi, Manjusha. Beyond Words, 1998.
Alliteration, Allusion, Antithesis, Foreshadowing, Hyperbole, Inference, Internal Rhyme, Pun, Tone

Go Home! The True Story of James the Cat. Meggs, Libby Phillips. Albert Whitman, 2000.
Ambiguity, Antithesis, Connotation, Inference, Metaphor, Point of View, Simile

Goldilocks Returns. Ernst, Lisa Campbell. Simon & Schuster, 2000.
Allusion, Antihero, Connotation, Flash-forward, Inference, Irony, Parallelism, Tone, Understatement

*Golem. Wisniewski, David. Clarion Books (Houghton Mifflin), 1996 (Caldecott—1997).
Analogy, Atmosphere, Foreshadowing, Imagery, Inference, Irony, Motif, Paradox, Simile

Goodbye, Geese. Carlstrom, Nancy. Philomel (Putnam Books), 1991.
Metaphor, Simile

Grizz! Kimmel, Eric A. Holiday House, 2000.
Atmosphere, Hyperbole, Inference, Motif, Poetic Justice, Simile, Understatement

Harriet, You'll Drive Me Wild. Fox, Mem. Harcourt, 2000.
Foreshadowing, Inference, Understatement

*Henrietta. Mamet, David. Houghton Mifflin, 1999.
Inference, Irony, Personification, Pun, Satire, Serendipity, Tone

*Henry Hikes to Fitchburg. Johnson, D.B. Houghton Mifflin, 2000.
Allusion, Irony, Paradox, Theme, Understatement

The Hidden Forest. Baker, Jeannie. Greenwillow Books (HarperCollins), 2000.
Connotation, Imagery, Inference, Simile

*Hog-Eye. Meddaugh, Susan. Walter Lorraine Books (Houghton Mifflin), 1995.
Allusion, Antithesis, Flashback, Foreshadowing, Hyperbole, Inference, Irony, Understatement

*Hogula, Dread Pig of Night. Gralley, Jean. Henry Holt, 1999.
Alliteration, Allusion, Antihero, Aphorism, Cliché, Foreshadowing, Inference, Irony, Poetic Justice,

Pun, Simile, Stereotype/Reverse
Stereotype, Understatement

The Honest to Goodness Truth. McKissack,
Patricia. Atheneum (Simon &
Schuster), 2000.
Ambiguity, Antithesis, Aphorism,
Foreshadowing, Paradox, Simile,
Understatement

Horace and Morris but Mostly Dolores.
Howe, James. Atheneum (Simon &
Schuster), 1999.
Allusion, Internal Rhyme,
Parallelism, Pun, Stereotype/
Reverse Stereotype, Theme

The House Gobbaleen. Alexander, Lloyd.
Dutton Children's Books (Penguin
Books), 1995.
Ambiguity, Foreshadowing,
Hyperbole, Inference, Irony,
Simile, Theme, Tone,
Understatement

I Like Your Buttons! Lamstein, Sarah
Marwil. Albert Whitman, 1999.
Irony, Serendipity, Theme

Just One Flick of a Finger. Lorbiecki,
Marybeth. Dial (Penguin Putnam),
1996.
Antithesis, Foreshadowing, Inference,
Internal Rhyme, Metaphor, Pun,
Simile, Theme

Kate and the Beanstalk. Osborne, Mary
Pope. Atheneum (Simon &
Schuster), 2000.
Hyperbole, Inference, Motif, Poetic
Justice, Simile, Stereotype/Reverse
Stereotype

*Ling Cho and His Three Friends. Pacilio,
V.J. Farrar Straus Giroux, 2000.
Alliteration, Aphorism, Irony,
Paradox, Poetic Justice, Theme

Little Red Cowboy Hat. Lowell, Susan.
Henry Holt, 1997.
Aphorism, Atmosphere, Caricature,
Hyperbole, Inference,

Onomatopoeia, Parody, Simile,
Stereotype/Reverse Stereotype,
Tone

Lizzy and Skunk. Fitzpatrick, Marie
Louise. DK Ink, 2000.
Irony, Parallelism, Personification

The Lonely Scarecrow. Preston, Tim.
Dutton (Penguin Books), 1999.
Imagery, Inference, Metaphor,
Paradox, Parallelism, Theme

The Lost Boy and the Monster. Strete,
Craig Kee. G.P. Putnam's Sons
(Penguin Books for Young Readers),
1999.
Ambiguity, Connotations, Internal
Rhymes, Motif, Poetic Justice,
Simile, Theme, Tone

Lottie's Princess Dress. Dórrie, Doris. Dial
(Penguin Putnam), 1998.
Antithesis, Paradox, Theme,
Understatement

Mabel Dancing. Hest, Amy. Candlewick
Press, 2000.
Atmosphere, Foreshadowing, Imagery,
Parallelism

Mama and Me and the Model T. Gibbons,
Faye. Morrow, 1999.
Foreshadowing, Hyperbole, Imagery,
Inference, Onomatopoeia,
Parallelism, Stereotype/Reverse
Stereotype, Understatement

The Man Who Caught Fish. Krudop,
Walter Lyon. Farrar Straus Giroux,
2000.
Foreshadowing, Poetic Justice, Theme

Me and My Cat? Kitamura, Satoshi.
Farrar Straus Giroux, 2000.
Antithesis, Inference, Irony,
Parallelism, Point of View,
Understatement

*The Memory String. Bunting, Eve.
Clarion Books (Houghton Mifflin),
2000.

Ambiguity, Antithesis, Aphorism,
    Foreshadowing, Imagery,
    Inference, Parallelism, Simile
Mouse, Look Out! Waite, Judy. Dutton
    (Penguin Putnam), 1998.
    Alliteration, Atmosphere, Internal
    Rhyme, Metaphor, Poetic Justice,
    Simile
Mr. Wolf's Pancakes. Fearnley, Jan. Little
    Tiger Press, 1999.
    Allusion, Antihero, Black Humor,
    Irony, Poetic Justice, Stereotype/
    Reverse Stereotype
The Music in Derrick's Heart. Battle-
    Lavert, Gwendolyn. Holiday House,
    2000.
    Aphorism, Atmosphere, Inference,
    Simile, Tone
No Dinner! The Story of the Old Woman
    and the Pumpkin. Souhami, Jessica.
    Marshall Cavendish, 1999.
    Motif, Onomatopoeia
Nobody Rides the Unicorn. Mitchell,
    Adrian. Arthur A. Levine books
    (Scholastic), 1999.
    Poetic Justice, Pun, Simile
Old Dry Frye: A Deliciously Funny Tall Tale.
    Johnson, Paul Brett. Scholastic
    Press, 1999.
    Black Humor, Cliché, Hyperbole,
    Inference, Poetic Justice,
    Serendipity, Tone, Understatement
One Duck. Hutchins, Hazel. Annick
    (Firefly Books), 1999.
    Antithesis, Atmosphere, Imagery,
    Inference, Onomatopoeia,
    Parallelism, Tone
One Lucky Girl. Lyon, George Ella. DK
    Pub., 2000.
    Ambiguity, Antithesis,
    Foreshadowing, Imagery,
    Inference, Metaphor, Parallelism,
    Simile

Passage to Freedom. Mochizuki, Ken. Lee
    & Low, 1997.
    Antithesis, Aphorism, Foreshadowing,
    Point of View, Theme
*Peace Crane. Hamanaka, Sheila. Morrow
    Junior Books, 1995.
    Allusion, Antithesis, Flash-forward,
    Imagery, Simile, Symbol
The Piano. Miller, William. Lee & Low
    Books, 2000.
    Inference, Theme
*Pierre's Dream. Armstrong, Jennifer. Dial
    (Penguin Putnam), 1999.
    Antihero, Foreshadowing, Inference,
    Irony, Theme
Pig and Crow. Chorao, Kay. Henry Holt,
    2000.
    Paradox
*Red Flower Goes West. Turner, Ann.
    Hyperion, 1999.
    Connotation, Inference, Metaphor,
    Parallelism, Simile, Symbol
Redcoats and Petticoats. Kirkpatrick,
    Katherine. Holiday House, 1999.
    Foreshadowing, Inference
River Friendly, River Wild. Kurtz, Jane.
    Simon & Schuster, 2000.
    Antithesis, Aphorism, Atmosphere,
    Imagery, Metaphor,
    Onomatopoeia, Simile
Roberto the Insect Architect. Laden, Nina.
    Chronicle Books, 2000.
    Alliteration, Allusion, Antithesis,
    Cliché, Parallelism, Pun
*Rosie the Cool Cat. Wilkon, Piotr. Viking
    (Penguin Books), 1989.
    Antithesis, Foreshadowing, Inference,
    Irony, Poetic Justice, Satire,
    Stereotype/Reverse Stereotype,
    Symbol
Scarlette Beane. Wallace, Karen. Dial
    (Penguin Putnam), 2000.
    Foreshadowing, Hyperbole, Pun,
    Simile

Secrets from the Dollhouse. Turner, Ann. HarperCollins, 2000.
   Foreshadowing, Imagery, Metaphor, Personification, Point of View, Simile

The Sign Painter. Say, Allen. Walter Lorraine Books (Houghton Mifflin), 2000.
   Ambiguity, Antithesis, Imagery, Inference, Point of View, Theme, Tone

Simply Delicious. Mahy, Margaret. Orchard Books, 1999.
   Alliteration, Foreshadowing, Hyperbole, Internal Rhyme, Poetic Justice, Simile, Understatement

Sister Yessa's Story. Greenfield, Karen. HarperCollins, 1992.
   Inference, Parallel Story

Snowflake Bentley. Martin, Jacqueline Briggs. Houghton Mifflin, 1998 (Caldecott—1999).
   Antithesis, Imagery, Parallelism, Simile

So You Want to Be President? St. George, Judith. New York: Philomel (Penguin Putnam Books for Young Readers), 2000. (Caldecott—2000)
   Antithesis, Atmosphere, Caricature, Parallelism, Tone

Something Is Growing. Krudop, Walter Lyon. Atheneum (Simon & Schuster), 1995.
   Foreshadowing, Satire

The Spirit of the Maasai Man. Berkeley, Laura. Barefoot Books, 2000.
   Imagery, Symbol, Theme, Tone

A Spoon for Every Bite. Hayes, Joe. Orchard Books, 1996.
   Ambiguity, Antihero, Antithesis, Foreshadowing, Hyperbole, Motif, Poetic Justice

Squiggle's Tale. Dahn, André. Chronicle, 2000.
   Ambiguity, Understatement

The Stone Dancers. Martin, Nora. Atheneum (Simon & Schuster), 1995.
   Aphorism, Imagery, Inference, Irony, Metaphor, Parallel Story, Simile

Swan in Love. Bunting, Eve. Atheneum (Simon & Schuster), 2000.
   Antithesis, Aphorism, Foreshadowing, Imagery, Inference, Simile, Theme

The Sweetest Fig. Van Allsburg, Chris. Houghton Mifflin, 1993.
   Inference, Irony, Poetic Justice

Switch on the Night. Bradbury, Ray. Alfred A. Knopf, 1983.
   Alliteration, Antithesis, Internal Rhyme, Irony, Metaphor, Motif, Paradox, Simile, Symbol

The Table Where Rich People Sit. Baylor, Byrd. Charles Scribner's Sons, 1994.
   Antihero, Aphorism, Foreshadowing, Irony, Paradox

The Tale of the Turnip. Alderson, Brian. Candlewick Press, 1999.
   Connotation, Hyperbole, Motif, Poetic Justice, Satire, Tone

Tambourine Moon. Jones, Joy. Simon & Schuster, 1999.
   Antithesis, Hyperbole, Imagery, Personification, Simile

That's Mine, Horace. Keller, Holly. Greenwillow Books (HarperCollins), 2000.
   Irony, Parallelism, Serendipity

The Three Little Dinosaurs. Harris, Jim. Pelican Publishing, 1999.
   Antithesis, Foreshadowing, Inference, Parody, Poetic Justice, Tone

Toby's Doll's House. Scamell, Ragnhild. Levinson Books, 1998.
   Paradox, Serendipity, Stereotype/ Reverse Stereotype

Tough Cookie. Wisniewski, David. Lothrop, Lee & Shepard (William Morrow), 1999.

Analogy, Parody, Pun, Satire, Simile,
Stereotype/Reverse Stereotype,
Theme

Tree of Hope. Littlesugar, Amy. Philomel
(Penguin Putnam), 1999.
Cliché, Flashback, Foreshadowing,
Inference, Paradox, Serendipity,
Simile, Stereotype/Reverse
Stereotype, Symbol

Trouble on Thunder Mountain. Hoban,
Russell. Orchard Books (Grolier),
2000.
Aphorism, Connotation,
Foreshadowing, Hyperbole, Irony,
Poetic Justice, Satire,
Understatement

The Two Bullies. Morimoto, Junko.
Crown (Random House), 1997.
Irony, Serendipity

The Video Shop Sparrow. Cowley, Joy.
Boyds Mills Press, 1999.
Inference, Satire, Theme, Tone

*Voices in the Park. Browne, Anthony. DK
Pub., 1998.
Connotation, Foreshadowing,
Inference, Point of View

*Waiting to Sing. Kaplan, Howard. DK
Ink, 2000.
Allusion, Antithesis, Aphorism,
Atmosphere, Foreshadowing,
Imagery, Inference, Metaphor,
Parallelism, Simile, Symbol

Wemberly Worried. Henkes, Kevin.
Greenwillow Books (HarperCollins),
2000.
Antithesis, Cliché, Irony, Parallelism

*What! Cried Granny: An Almost Bedtime
Story.* Lum, Kate. Dial (Penguin
Putnam), 1998.
Hyperbole, Inference

Why? Camp, Lindsay. G.P. Putnam's
Sons, (Penguin Putnam), 1998.
Inference, Irony, Paradox, Serendipity,
Understatement

Wizzil. Steig, William. Farrar Straus
Giroux, 2000.
Alliteration, Ambiguity, Connotation,
Foreshadowing, Internal Rhyme,
Irony, Serendipity, Tone

*The Worry Stone. Dengler, Marianna.
Rising Moon (Northland), 1996.
Antithesis, Flashback,
Foreshadowing, Inference, Parallel
Story, Parallelism

Yard Sale. Modarressi, Mitra. DK Pub.,
2000.
Allusion, Antithesis, Connotation,
Hyperbole, Inference, Paradox,
Serendipity, Understatement

**The Yellow Star: The Legend of King
Christian X of Denmark.* Deedy,
Carmen Agra. Peachtree, 2000.
Antithesis, Aphorism, Atmosphere,
Foreshadowing, Inference, Irony,
Paradox, Parallelism, Pun, Simile,
Symbol, Theme

Yoshi's Feast. Kajikawa, Kimiko. DK Ink,
2000.
Antithesis, Aphorism, Foreshadowing,
Inference, Onomatopoeia,
Parallelism, Poetic Justice

The Youngest Fairy Godmother Ever.
Krensky, Stephen. Simon &
Schuster, 2000.
Allusion, Irony, Understatement

Yum! McNaughton, Colin. Harcourt
Brace, 1998.
Allusion, Ambiguity, Pun, Satire,
Tone, Understatement

APPENDIX 3:
RESOURCES GROUPED
BY ART STYLE

❖❖❖❖❖❖❖❖❖❖❖

CARTOON

Alice Nizzy Nazzy, the Witch of Santa Fe. Johnston, Tony. G.P. Putnam's Sons, 1995.
(*also* Folk)

The Ant Bully. Nickle, John. Scholastic Press, 1999.
(*also* Expressionism)

Apple Batter. Zagwÿn, Deborah. Tricycle Press, 1999.
(*also* Expressionism)

The Art Lesson. DePaola, Tomie. G.P. Putnam's Sons, 1989.

Bearhide and Crow. Johnson, Paul Brett. Holiday House, 2000.

Big Old Bones. Carrick, Carol. Clarion Books, 1989.

Bud. O'Malley, Kevin. Walker & Company, 2000.

*Buttons. Cole, Brock. Farrar Straus Giroux, 2000.

Cindy Ellen: A Wild Western Cinderella. Lowell, Susan. HarperCollins, 2000.
(*also* Expressionism)

*Click, Clack, Moo Cows That Type. Cronin, Doreen. Simon & Schuster, 2000

*Deep in the Jungle. Yaccarino, Dan. Anne Schwartz Atheneum (Simon & Schuster), 2000.
(*also* Naïve)

The Full Belly Bowl. Aylesworth, Jim. Atheneum (Simon & Schuster), 1999.

The Girl Who Hated Books. Pawagi, Manjusha. Beyond Words, 1998.
(*also* Expressionism)

Goldilocks Returns. Ernst, Lisa Campbell. Simon & Schuster, 2000.

Grizz! Kimmel, Eric A. Holiday House, 2000.
(*also* Expressionism)

Harriet, You'll Drive Me Wild. Fox, Mem. Harcourt, 2000.

*Henrietta. Mamet, David. Houghton Mifflin, 1999.
(*also* Impressionism)

Hog-Eye. Meddaugh, Susan. Walter Lorraine Books (Houghton Mifflin), 1995.

Hogula, Dread Pig of Night. Gralley, Jean. Henry Holt, 1999.
(*also* Expressionism)

Horace and Morris but Mostly Dolores. Howe, James. Atheneum (Simon & Schuster), 1999.
(*also* Collage)

The House Gobbaleen. Alexander, Lloyd. Dutton Children's Books (Penguin Books), 1995.

I Like Your Buttons! Lamstein, Sarah Marwil. Albert Whitman, 1999.

Little Red Cowboy Hat. Lowell, Susan. Henry Holt, 1997.
(*also* Expressionism, Naïve)

Lizzy and Skunk. Fitzpatrick, Marie-Louise. DK Ink, 2000

The Lonely Scarecrow. Preston, Tim. Dutton (Penguin Books), 1999.

Me and My Cat? Kitamura, Satoshi. Farrar Straus Giroux, 2000.

Mr. Wolf's Pancakes. Fearnley, Jan. Little Tiger Press, 1999.

Old Dry Frye. Johnson, Paul Brett. Scholastic Press, 1999.

Pig and Crow. Chorao, Kay. Henry Holt, 2000.

Rosie the Cool Cat. Wilkon, Piotr. Viking (Penguin Books), 1989.
(*also* Expressionism)

Simply Delicious. Mahy, Margaret. Orchard Books, 1999.

So You Want to Be President? St. George, Judith. Philomel (Penguin Putnam Books for Young Readers), 2000 (Caldecott—2000)

The Tale of the Turnip. Alderson, Brian. Candlewick Press, 1999.

That's Mine, Horace. Keller, Holly. Greenwillow Books (HarperCollins), 2000.

Toby's Doll's House. Scamell, Ragnhild. Levinson Books, 1998.

Trouble on Thunder Mountain. Hoban, Russell. Orchard Books (Grolier), 2000.

The Two Bullies. Morimoto, Junko. Crown (Random House), 1997.
(*also* Expressionism)

The Video Shop Sparrow. Cowley, Joy. Boyds Mills Press, 1999.

Wemberly Worried. Henkes, Kevin. Greenwillow Books (HarperCollins), 2000.

What! Cried Granny. Lum, Kate. Dial (Penguin Putnam), 1998.
(*also* Expressionism)

Why? Camp, Lindsay. G.P. Putnam's Sons (Penguin Putnam Books for Young Readers), 1998.

Wizzil. Steig, William. Farrar Straus Giroux, 2000.

The Youngest Fairy Godmother Ever. Krensky, Stephen. Simon & Schuster, 2000.

Yum! McNaughton, Colin. Harcourt Brace, 1998.

COLLAGE

Black Cat. Myers, Christopher. Scholastic Press, 1999.

Chicken Chuck. Martin, Bill. Winslow Press, 2000.

Golem. Wisniewski, David. Clarion Books (Houghton Mifflin), 1996 (Caldecott—1997)
(*also* Expressionism)

The Hidden Forest. Baker, Jeannie. Greenwillow Books (Harper Collins), 2000.

Horace and Morris but Mostly Dolores. Howe, James. Atheneum (Simon & Schuster), 1999.
(*also* Cartoon)

Roberto the Insect Architect. Laden, Nina. Chronicle Books, 2000.

*Tough Cookie. Wisniewski, David. Lothrop, Lee & Shepard (William Morrow), 1999.
(*also* Expressionism)

Yoshi's Feast. Kajikawa, Kimiko. DK Ink, 2000.
(*also* Expressionism, Folk)

EXPRESSIONISM

The Ant Bully. Nickle, John. Scholastic Press, 1999.
(*also* Cartoon)

Apple Batter. Zagwÿn, Deborah. Tricycle Press, 1999.
(*also* Cartoon)

A Band of Angels. Hopkinson, Deborah. Atheneum (Simon & Schuster), 1999.

*Big Jabe. Nolen, Jerdine. Lothrop, Lee & Shepard, 2000

Can You Do This, Old Badger? Bunting, Eve. Harcourt, 1999.

Cindy Ellen: A Wild Western Cinderella. Lowell, Susan. HarperCollins, 2000.
(*also* Cartoon)

Come On, Rain! Hesse, Karen. Scholastic Press, 1999.

Comes a Wind. White, Linda Arms. Dorling Kindersley, 2000.
(*also* Naïve)

Down the Winding Road. Johnson, Angela. DK Ink, 2000.

Dragon Scales and Willow Leaves. Givens, Terryl. G.P. Putnam's Sons, 1997.
(*also* Impressionism)

*Edna. Burleigh, Robert. Orchard Books, 2000.

Emma and the Coyote. Ruurs, Margriet. Stoddart Kids, 1999.

Faraway Home. Kurtz, Jane. Gulliver Books (Harcourt), 2000.

Fiddlin' Sam. Dengler, Marianna. Rising Moon (Northland), 1999.
(*also* Realism)

*Fly, Eagle, Fly! Gregorowski, Christopher. McElderry (Simon & Schuster), 2000.

Friend Frog. Ada, Alma Flor. Gulliver Books (Harcourt & Co.), 2000.
(*also* Realism)

The Girl Who Hated Books. Pawagi, Manjusha. Beyond Words, 1998.
(*also* Cartoon)

*Golem. Wisniewski, David. Clarion Books (Houghton Mifflin), 1996. (Caldecott—1997)
(*also* Collage)

Goodbye, Geese. Carlstrom, Nancy. Philomel (Putnam Books), 1991.

Grizz! Kimmel, Eric A. Holiday House, 2000.
(*also* Cartoon)

*Henry Hikes to Fitchburg. Johnson, D.B. Houghton Mifflin, 2000.

*Hogula, Dread Pig of Night. Gralley, Jean. Henry Holt, 1999.
(*also* Cartoon)

The Honest to Goodness Truth. McKissack, Patricia. Atheneum (Simon & Schuster), 2000.
(*also* Naïve)

Just One Flick of a Finger. Lorbiecki, Marybeth. Dial (Penguin Putnam), 1996.

Kate and the Beanstalk. Osborne, Mary Pope. Atheneum (Simon & Schuster), 2000.
(*also* Naïve)

Little Red Cowboy Hat. Lowell, Susan. Henry Holt, 1997.
(*also* Cartoon, Naïve)

The Lost Boy and the Monster. Strete, Craig Kee. G.P. Putnam's Sons (Penguin Books for Young Readers), 1999.

Lottie's Princess Dress. Dórrie, Doris. Dial (Penguin Putnam), 1998.
(*also* Naïve}

Mabel Dancing. Hest, Amy. Candlewick Press, 2000.

Mama and Me and the Model T. Gibbons, Faye. Morrow, 1999.

The Music in Derrick's Heart. Battle-Lavert, Gwendolyn. Holiday House, 2000.

One Duck. Hutchins, Hazel. Annick (Firefly Books), 1999.

Passage to Freedom. Mochizuki, Ken. Lee & Low, 1997.

*Peace Crane. Hamanaka, Sheila. Morrow Junior Books, 1995.

The Piano. Miller, William. Lee & Low Books, 2000.

*Pierre's Dream. Armstrong, Jennifer. Dial (Penguin Putnam), 1999.

*Rosie the Cool Cat. Wilkon, Piotr. Viking (Penguin Books), 1989.
(*also* Cartoon)

Scarlette Beane. Wallace, Karen. Dial (Penguin Putnam), 2000.

Sister Yessa's Story. Greenfield, Karen. Geringer (HarperCollins), 1992.

*The Spirit of the Maasai Man. Berkeley, Laura. Barefoot Books, 2000.
(*also* Realism)

*Swan in Love. Bunting, Eve. Athenum (Simon & Schuster), 2000.

*The Table Where Rich People Sit. Baylor, Byrd. Charles Scribner's Sons, 1994.

Tambourine Moon. Jones, Joy. Simon & Schuster, 1999.

The Three Little Dinosaurs. Harris, Jim. Pelican Publishing, 1999.

*Tough Cookie. Wisniewski, David. Lothrop, Lee & Shepard (William Morrow), 1999.
(*also* Collage)

The Two Bullies. Morimoto, Junko. Crown (Random House), 1997.
(*also* Cartoon)

*Waiting to Sing. Kaplan, Howard. DK Ink, 2000.

What! Cried Granny. Lum, Kate. Dial (Penguin Putnam), 1998.
(*also* Cartoon)

*The Worry Stone. Dengler, Mariana. Rising Moon (Northland), 1996.
(*also* Realism)

Yoshi's Feast. Kajikawa, Kimiko. DK Ink, 2000.
(*also* Collage, Folk)

FOLK

Alice Nizzy Nazzy, the Witch of Santa Fe. Johnston, Tony. G.P. Putnam's sons, 1995.
(*also* Cartoon)

Amelia's Road. Altman, Linda Jacobs. Lee & Low, 1993.

*Basho and the Fox. Myers, Tim. Marshall Cavendish, 2000.

The Gift of the Crocodile: A Cinderella Story. Sierra, Judy. Simon & Schuster, 2000.

*Ling Cho and His Three Friends. Pacilio, V.J. Farrar Straus Giroux, 2000.
(*also* Impressionism)

The Lost Boy and the Monster. Strete, Craig Kee. G.P. Putnam's Sons (Penguin Books for Young Readers), 1999.

The Man Who Caught Fish. Krudop, Walter Lyon. Farrar Straus Giroux, 2000.
(*also* Impressionism)

No Dinner! The Story of the Old Woman and the Pumpkin. Souhami, Jessica. Marshall Cavendish, 1999.

Secrets from the Dollhouse. Turner, Ann. HarperCollins, 2000.

Snowflake Bentley. Martin, Jacqueline Briggs. Houghton Mifflin, 1998 (Caldecott—1999)

Yoshi's Feast. Kajikawa, Kimiko. DK Ink, 2000.
(also Collage, Expressionism)

IMPRESSIONISM

Bewildered for Three Days: As to Why Daniel Boone Never Wore His Coonskin Cap. Glass, Andrew. Holiday House, 2000.

Dragon Scales and Willow Leaves. Givens, Terryl. G.P. Putnam's Sons, 1997.
(also Expressionism)

Emma and the Silk Train. Lawson, Julie. Kids Can Press, 1997.

*Henrietta. Mamet, David. Houghton Mifflin, 1999.
(also Cartoon)

*Ling Cho and His Three Friends. Pacilio, V.J. Farrar Straus Giroux, 2000.
(also Folk)

The Man Who Caught Fish. Krudop, Walter Lyon. Farrar Straus Giroux, 2000.
(also Folk)

*The Memory String. Bunting, Eve. Clarion Books (Houghton Mifflin), 2000.

One Lucky Girl. Lyon, George Ella. DK Pub., 2000.

Redcoats and Petticoats. Kirkpatrick, Katherine. Holiday House, 1999.

River Friendly, River Wild. Kurtz, Jane. Simon & Schuster, 2000.

Something Is Growing. Krudop, Walter Lyon. Atheneum (Simon & Schuster), 1995.

Squiggle's Tale. Dahn, André. Chronicle, 2000.

*The Stone Dancers. Martin, Nora. Atheneum (Simon & Schuster), 1995.

Tree of Hope. Littlesugar, Amy. Philomel (Penguin Putnam), 1999.

*The Yellow Star: The Legend of King Christian X of Denmark. Deedy, Carmen Agra. Peachtree, 2000

NAÏVE

*The Big Box. Morrison, Toni, with Slade Morrison. Hyperion, 1999.

Comes a Wind. White, Linda Arms. DK Pub., 2000.
(also Expressionism)

*Deep in the Jungle. Yaccarino, Dan. Anne Schwartz/Atheneum (Simon & Schuster), 2000.
(also Cartoon)

The Honest to Goodness Truth. McKissack, Patricia. Atheneum (Simon & Schuster), 2000.
(also Expressionism)

Kate and the Beanstalk. Osborne, Mary Pope. Atheneum (Simon & Schuster), 2000.
(also Expressionism)

Little Red Cowboy Hat. Lowell, Susan. Henry Holt, 1997.
(also Cartoon, Expressionism)

Lottie's Princess Dress. Dórrie, Doris. Dial (Penguin Putnam), 1998.
(also Expressionism)

Nobody Rides the Unicorn. Mitchell, Adrian. Arthur A. Levine Books (Scholastic), 1999.

Yard Sale. Modarressi, Mitra. DK Pub., 2000.

REALISM

Drummer Boy: Marching to the Civil War. Turner, Ann. HarperCollins, 1998.

Fiddlin' Sam. Dengler, Marianna. Rising Moon (Northland), 1999.
(*also* Expressionism)

Friend Frog. Ada, Alma Flor. Gulliver Books (Harcourt), 2000.
(*also* Expressionism)

Go Home! Meggs, Libby Phillips. Albert Whitman, 2000.

Mouse, Look Out! Waite, Judy. Dutton (Penguin Putnam), 1998.

*Red Flower Goes West. Turner, Ann. Hyperion Books for Children, 1999.

*The Sign Painter. Say, Allen. Walter Lorraine Books (Houghton Mifflin), 2000.

*The Spirit of the Maasai Man. Berkeley, Laura. Barefoot Books, 2000.
(*also* Expressionism)

*A Spoon for Every Bite. Hayes, Joe. Orchard Books, 1996.

*The Sweetest Fig. Van Allsburg, Chris. Houghton Mifflin, 1993.

*The Worry Stone. Dengler, Marianna. Rising Moon (Northland), 1996.
(*also* Expressionism)

SURREALISM

Dinner at Magritte's. Garland, Michael. Dutton (Penguin), 1995.

Switch on the Night. Bradbury, Ray. Alfred A. Knopf, 1983.

*Voices in the Park. Browne, Anthony. DK Pub., 1998.

APPENDIX 4:
RESOURCES GROUPED
BY CURRICULUM TIE-IN

❖❖❖❖❖❖❖❖❖❖❖

ART

American Indian

The Lost Boy and the Monster. Strete, Craig Kee. G.P. Putnam's sons (Penguin Books for Young Readers), 1999. *Also* Folktales (American Indian)

Biography

Dinner at Magritte's. Garland, Michael. Dutton (Penguin Putnam), 1995.

Medium and Technique

*Black Cat. Myers, Christopher. Scholastic Press, 1999.

ATHLETICS

Baseball

Apple Batter. Zagwÿn, Deborah. Tricycle Press, 1999. *Also* Science (Apple Production)

ECONOMICS

Unions

*Click, Clack, Moo Cows That Type. Cronin, Doreen. Simon & Schuster, 2000.

GEOGRAPHY

American Southwest

*The Table Where Rich People Sit. Baylor, Byrd. Charles Scribner's Sons, 1994. *Also* Literature (Parables)

Animal Habitats

*The Spirit of the Maasai Man. Berkeley, Laura. Barefoot Books, 2000. *Also* Science (Zoos)

Ethiopia

Faraway Home. Kurtz, Jane. Gulliver Books (Harcourt), 2000. *Also* Social Science (Immigration—Ethiopia)

Flood—Grand Forks, North Dakota

River Friendly, River Wild. Kurtz, Jane. Simon & Schuster, 2000.

New Mexico

Alice Nizzy Nazzy, the Witch of Santa Fe. Johnston, Tony. G.P. Putnam's Sons, 1995.
Also Literature (Fairy Tales— America), Social Science (Values)

HISTORY

American Presidents

*So You Want to Be President? St. George, Judith. Philomel (Penguin Putnam Books for Young Readers), 2000 (Caldecott—2000).

American Southwest

*A Spoon for Every Bite. Hayes, Joe. Orchard Books, 1996.
Also Literature (Folktales— Hispanic), Social Science (Values)

Biography—Daniel Boone

Bewildered for Three Days: As to Why Daniel Boone Never Wore His Coonskin Cap. Glass, Andrew. Holiday House, 2000.

Black Culture

A Band of Angels. Hopkinson, Deborah. Atheneum (Simon & Schuster), 1999.

Black Culture—Depression

Tree of Hope. Littlesugar, Amy. Philomel (Penguin Putnam), 1999.

Chumash Indians

*The Worry Stone. Dengler, Marianna. Rising Moon (Northland), 1996.
Also Social Science (Grandparents, Intergenerational Relationships)

Civil War

Drummer Boy: Marching to the Civil War. Turner, Ann. HarperCollins, 1998.

Japan

*Basho and the Fox. Myers, Tim. Marshall Cavendish, 2000.
Also Social Science (Self-esteem)

Nineteenth-Century England

The Tale of the Turnip. Alderson, Brian. Candlewick Press, 1999.

Nineteenth-Century France

*The Stone Dancers. Martin, Nora. Atheneum (Simon & Schuster), 1995.
Also Literature (Legends), Social Science (Values)

Railroads—Silk

Emma and the Silk Train. Lawson, Julie. Kids Can Press, 1997.

Revolutionary War

Redcoats and Petticoats. Kirkpatrick, Katherine. Holiday House, 1999.

Slavery—America

*Big Jabe. Nolen, Jerdine. Lothrop, Lee & Shepard, 2000.
Also Literature (Tall Tales)

Thailand

The Man Who Caught Fish. Krudop, Walter Lyon. Farrar Straus Giroux, 2000.
Also Literature (Folktales—Thailand)

War and Peace—Japan and America

*Peace Crane. Hamanaka, Sheila. Morrow Junior Books, 1995.

Westward Expansion

*Red Flower Goes West. Turner, Ann. Hyperion Books for Children, 1999.

World War II

Passage to Freedom. Mochizuki, Ken. Lee & Low, 1997.

World War II—Nazi Occupation—Denmark

*The Yellow Star: The Legend of King Christian X of Denmark. Deedy, Carmen Agra. Peachtree, 2000.
Also Literature (Legends), Social Science (Values)

LITERATURE

Biography—Poets

*Edna. Burleigh, Robert. Orchard Books, 2000.

Cumulative Tales

No Dinner! The Story of the Old Woman and the Pumpkin. Souhami, Jessica. Marshall Cavendish, 1999.
Also Literature (Folktales—India)

Simply Delicious. Mahy, Margaret. Orchard Books, 1999.

Fable

*Henrietta. Mamet, David. Houghton Mifflin, 1999.
Also Social Science (Diversity)

Fairy Tales—America

Alice Nizzy Nazzy, the Witch of Santa Fe. Johnston, Tony. G.P. Putnam's Sons, 1995.
Also Geography (New Mexico)

*Buttons. Cole, Brock. Farrar Straus Giroux, 2000.

Grizz! Kimmel, Eric A. Holiday House, 2000.

Folktales—American Indian

The Lost Boy and the Monster. Strete, Craig Kee. G.P. Putnam's Sons (Penguin Books for Young Readers), 1999.
Also Art (American Indian)

Folktales—England

The Tale of the Turnip. Alderson, Brian. Candlewick Press, 1999.

Folktales—Hispanic

*A Spoon for Every Bite. Hayes, Joe. Orchard Books, 1996.
Also History (American Southwest), Social Science (Values)

Folktales—India

No Dinner! The Story of the Old Woman and the Pumpkin. Souhami, Jessica. Marshall Cavendish, 1999.
Also Literature (Cumulative Tales)

Folktales—Indonesia

The Gift of the Crocodile: A Cinderella Story. Sierra, Judy. Simon and Schuster Books for Young Readers, 2000.

Folktales—Japan

The Two Bullies. Morimoto, Junko. Crown (Random House), 1997.

Yoshi's Feast. Kajikawa, Kimiko. DK Ink, 2000.

Folktales—Modern

The House Gobbaleen. Alexander, Lloyd. Dutton Children's Books (Penguin Books), 1995.
Also Social Science (Values)

Kate and the Beanstalk. Osborne, Mary Pope. Atheneum (Simon & Schuster), 2000.
Also Social Science (Values)

Folktales—Thailand

The Man Who Caught Fish. Krudop, Walter Lyon. Farrar Straus Giroux, 2000.
Also History (Thailand)

Henry David Thoreau

Henry Hikes to Fitchburg. Johnson, D.B. Houghton Mifflin, 2000.
Also Philosophy (Quality of Life)

Legends

Golem. Wisniewski, David. Clarion Books (Houghton Mifflin), 1996 (Caldecott—1997).
Also Social Science (Values)

Sister Yessa's Story. Greenfield, Karen. Geringer (HarperCollins), 1992.

The Stone Dancers. Martin, Nora. Atheneum (Simon & Schuster), 1995.
Also History (Nineteenth-Century France)

The Yellow Star: The Legend of King Christian X of Denmark. Deedy, Carmen Agra. Peachtree, 2000.
Also History (World War II—Nazi Occupation—Denmark), Social Science (Values)

Parables

Deep in the Jungle. Yaccarino, Dan. Anne Schwartz/Atheneum (Simon & Schuster), 2000.

Fly, Eagle, Fly! Gregorowski, Christopher. McElderry (Simon & Schuster), 2000.

The Table Where Rich People Sit. Baylor, Byrd. Charles Scribner's Sons, 1994.
Also Geography (American Southwest)

Tall Tales

Bewildered for Three Days: As to Why Daniel Boone Never Wore His Coonskin Cap. Glass, Andrew. Holiday House, 2000.

Big Jabe. Nolen, Jerdine. Lothrop, Lee & Shepard, 2000.
Also History (Slavery—America)

Hog-Eye. Meddaugh, Susan. Walter Lorraine Books (Houghton Mifflin), 1995.

Comes a Wind. White, Linda Arms. DK Pub., 2000.

Old Dry Frye. Johnson, Paul Brett. Scholastic Press, 1999.

Scarlette Beane. Wallace, Karen. Dial (Penguin Putnam), 2000.

MUSIC

Piano

Waiting to Sing. Kaplan, Howard. DK Ink, 2000.
Also Social Science (Death, Family Relationships)

PHILOSOPHY

Quality of Life

Henry Hikes to Fitchburg. Johnson, D.B. Houghton Mifflin, 2000.
Also Literature (Henry David Thoreau)

The Sign Painter. Say, Allen. Walter Lorraine Books (Houghton Mifflin), 2000.

SCIENCE

Agriculture)

One Duck. Hutchins, Hazel. Annick (Firefly Books), 1999.

Animal Behavior

Friend Frog. Ada, Alma Flor. Gulliver Books (Harcourt), 2000.

One Duck. Hutchins, Hazel. Annick (Firefly Books), 1999.
Also Agriculture

Apple Production

Apple Butter. Zagwÿn, Deborah. Tricycle Press, 1999.
Also Athletics (Baseball)

Astronomy

Switch on the Night. Bradbury, Ray. Alfred A. Knopf, 1983.
Also Social Science (Fears)

Ecology

Something Is Growing. Krudop, Walter Lyon. Atheneum (Simon & Schuster), 1995.

Trouble on Thunder Mountain. Hoban, Russell. Orchard Books (Grolier), 2000.

Gardening

Bud. O'Malley, Kevin. New York: Walker & Company, 2000.
Also Social Science (Family Relationships, Values)

Meteorology

Come On, Rain! Hesse, Karen. Scholastic Press, 1999.

Snowflake Bentley. Martin, Jacqueline Briggs. Houghton Mifflin, 1998 (Caldecott—1999).
Also Science (Photography)

Ocean Ecology

The Hidden Forest. Baker, Jeannie. Greenwillow Books (HarperCollins), 2000.

Paleontology

Big Old Bones. Carrick, Carol. Clarion Books, 1989.

Photography

Snowflake Bentley. Martin, Jacqueline Briggs. Houghton Mifflin, 1998 (Caldecott—1999).
Also Science (Meterology)

Seasons

Goodbye, Geese. Carlstrom, Nancy. Philomel (Putnam Books), 1991.

The Lonely Scarecrow. Preston, Tim. Dutton (Penguin Books), 1999.
Also Social Science (Friendship)

Tornadoes

One Lucky Girl. Lyon, George Ella. DK Pub., 2000.
Also Social Science (Family Relationships)

Zoos

*The Spirit of the Maasai Man. Berkeley, Laura. Barefoot Books, 2000.
Also Geography (Animal Habitats)

SOCIAL SCIENCE

Animal Companions

Go Home! Meggs, Libby Phillips. Albert Whitman, 2000.

Me and My Cat? Kitamura, Satoshi. Farrar Straus Giroux, 2000.
Also Social Science (Values)

Appalachian Culture

Old Dry Frye. Johnson, Paul Brett. Scholastic Press, 1999.

Bullies

The Ant Bully. Nickle, John. Scholastic Press, 1999.
Also Social Science (Values)

Just One Flick of a Finger. Lorbiecki, Marybeth. Dial (Penguin Putnam), 1996.

The Two Bullies. Morimoto, Junko. Crown (Random House), 1997.
Also Literature (Folktales—Japan)

Conduct & Behavior

Mr. Wolf's Pancakes. Fearnley, Jan. Little Tiger Press, 1999.

Conflict Resolution

Lottie's Princess Dress. Dórrie, Doris. Dial (Penguin Putnam), 1998.

Death

*Waiting to Sing. Kaplan, Howard. DK Ink, 2000.
Also Music (Piano), Social Science (Family Relationships, Feelings)

Diversity

*Henrietta. Mamet, David. Houghton Mifflin, 1999.
Also Literature (Fables)

Ethnicity—African American

The Music in Derrick's Heart. Battle-Lavert, Gwendolyn. Holiday House, 2000.

Tambourine Moon. Jones, Joy. Simon & Schuster Books for Young Readers, 1999.
Also Social Science (Grandparents)

Family Relationships

Bud. O'Malley, Kevin. Walker & Company, 2000.
Also Science (Gardening), Social Science (Values)

Down the Winding Road. Johnson, Angela. DK Ink, 2000.

Harriet, You'll Drive Me Wild. Fox, Mem. Harcourt, 2000.

Mabel Dancing. Hest, Amy. Candlewick Press, 2000.
Also Social Science (Values)

Mama and Me and the Model T. Gibbons, Faye. Morrow, 1999.

*The Memory String. Bunting, Eve. Clarion Books (Houghton Mifflin), 2000.

One Lucky Girl. Lyon, George Ella. Dorling Kindersley, 2000.
Also Science (Tornadoes)

*Rosie the Cool Cat. Wilkon, Piotr. Viking (Penguin Books), 1989.
Also Social Science (Individuality, Values)

Toby's Doll's House. Scamell, Ragnhild. Levinson Books, 1998.

*Waiting to Sing. Kaplan, Howard. DK Ink, 2000.
Also Music (Piano), Social Science (Death, Feelings)

Why? Camp, Lindsay. G.P. Putnam's Sons (Penguin Putnam Books for Young Readers), 1998.

Fears

Lizzy and Skunk. Fitzpatrick, Marie-Louise. DK Ink, 2000.
Also Social Science (Self-esteem)

Switch on the Night. Bradbury, Ray. Alfred A. Knopf, 1983.
Also Science (Astronomy)

Wemberly Worried. Henkes, Kevin. Greenwillow Books (HarperCollins), 2000.

Feelings

Voices in the Park. Browne, Anthony. DK Pub., 1998.

Waiting to Sing. Kaplan, Howard. DK Ink, 2000.
Also Music (Piano), Social Science (Death, Family Relationships)

Friendship

Hogula, Dread Pig of Night. Gralley, Jean. Henry Holt, 1999.

Ling Cho and His Three Friends. Pacilio, V.J. Farrar Straus Giroux, 2000.
Also Social Science (Values)

The Lonely Scarecrow. Preston, Tim. Dutton (Penguin Books), 1999.
Also Science (Seasons)

Pig and Crow. Chorao, Kay. Henry Holt, 2000.
Also Social Science (Values)

Tough Cookie. Wisniewski, David. Lothrop, Lee & Shepard (William Morrow), 1999.

Gender Equality

Horace and Morris but Mostly Dolores. Howe, James. Atheneum (Simon & Schuster), 1999.

Grandparents

Tambourine Moon. Jones, Joy. Simon & Schuster Books for Young Readers, 1999.
Also Social Science (Ethnicity—African-American)

What! Cried Granny: An Almost Bedtime Story. Lum, Kate. Dial (Penguin Putnam), 1998.

The Worry Stone. Dengler, Marianna. Rising Moon (Northland), 1996.
Also History (Chumash Indians), Social Science (Intergeneration-al Relationships)

Grief

The Memory String. Bunting, Eve. Clarion Books (Houghton Mifflin), 2000.

Immigration-Ethiopia

Faraway Home. Kurtz, Jane. Gulliver Books (Harcourt), 2000.
Also Geography (Ethiopia)

Individuality

The Art Lesson. DePaola, Tomie. G.P. Putnam's Sons, 1989.

Dragon Scales and Willow Leaves. Givens, Terryl. G.P. Putnam's Sons, 1997.

Rosie the Cool Cat. Wilkon, Piotr. Viking (Penguin Books), 1989.
Also Social Science (Family Relationships)

Intergenerational Relationships

Can You Do This, Old Badger? Bunting, Eve. Harcourt, 1999.

The Worry Stone. Dengler, Marianna. Rising Moon (Northland), 1996
Also History (Chumash Indians), Social Science (Grandparents)

Love

Swan in Love. Bunting, Eve. Atheneum (Simon & Schuster), 2000.

Wizzil. Steig, William. Farrar Straus Giroux, 2000

Migrant Workers

Amelia's Road. Altman, Linda Jacobs. Lee & Low, 1993.

Missouri Ozarks

Fiddlin' Sam. Dengler, Marianna. Rising Moon (Northland), 1999.

Self-esteem

Basho and the Fox. Myers, Tim. Marshall Cavendish, 2000.
Also History (Japan)

Cindy Ellen: A Wild Western Cinderella. Lowell, Susan. Cotler (HarperCollins), 2000.

Emma and the Coyote. Ruurs, Margriet. Stoddart Kids, 1999.

Lizzy and Skunk. Fitzpatrick, Marie-Louise. DK Ink, 2000.
Also Social Science (Fears)

Values

Alice Nizzy Nazzy, the Witch of Santa Fe. Johnston, Tony. G.P. Putnam's Sons, 1995.
Also Geography (New Mexico), Literature (Fairy Tales—America)

The Ant Bully. Nickle, John. Scholastic Press, 1999.
Also Social Science (Bullies)

The Big Box. Morrison, Toni. Hyperion, 1999.

Bud. O'Malley, Kevin. Walker & Company, 2000.
Also Science (Gardening), Social Science (Family Relationships)

Chicken Chuck. Martin, Bill. Winslow Press, 2000.

Deep in the Jungle. Yaccarino, Dan. Anne Schwartz/Atheneum (Simon & Schuster), 2000.

The Full Belly Bowl. Aylesworth, Jim. Atheneum (Simon & Schuster), 1999.

Golem. Wisniewski, David. Clarion Books (Houghton Mifflin), 1996 (Caldecott—1997).
Also Literature (Legends)

The Honest to Goodness Truth. McKissack, Patricia. Atheneum (Simon & Schuster, 2000).

The House Gobbaleen. Alexander, Lloyd. Dutton Children's Books (Penguin Books), 1995.
Also Literature (Folktales—Modern)

I Like Your Buttons! Lamstein, Sarah Marwil. Albert Whitman, 1999.

Kate and the Beanstalk. Osborne, Mary Pope. Atheneum (Simon & Schuster), 2000.
Also Literature (Folktales—Modern)

Ling Cho and His Three Friends. Pacilio, V.J. Farrar Straus Giroux, 2000.
Also Social Science (Friendship)

Mabel Dancing. Hest, Amy. Candlewick Press, 2000.
Also Social Science (Family Relationships)

Me and My Cat? Kitamura, Satoshi. Farrar Straus Giroux, 2000.
Also Social Science (Animal Companions)

Nobody Rides the Unicorn. Mitchell, Adrian. Arthur A. Levine Books (Scholastic), 1999.

The Piano. Miller, William. Lee & Low Books, 2000.

Pierre's Dream. Armstrong, Jennifer. Dial (Penguin Putnam), 1999.

Pig and Crow. Chorao, Kay. Henry Holt, 2000.
Also Social Science (Friendship)

Roberto the Insect Architect. Laden, Nina. Chronicle Books, 2000.

Rosie the Cool Cat. Wilkon, Piotr. Viking (Penguin Books), 1989.
Also Social Science (Family Relationships)

*A *Spoon for Every Bite.* Hayes, Joe. Orchard Books, 1996.

Also History (American Southwest), Literature (Folktales—Hispanic)

The Stone Dancers. Martin, Nora. Atheneum (Simon & Schuster), 1995.

Also History (Nineteenth-Century France), Literature (Legends)

That's Mine, Horace. Keller, Holly. Greenwillow Books (HarperCollins), 2000.

The Video Shop Sparrow. Cowley, Joy. Boyds Mills Press, 1999.

The Yellow Star: The Legend of King Christian X of Denmark. Deedy, Carmen Agra. Peachtree, 2000.

Also History (World War II—Nazi Occupation—Denmark), Literature (Legends)

The Youngest Fairy Godmother Ever. Krensky, Stephen. Simon & Schuster, 2000.

Yum! McNaughton, Colin. Harcourt Brace, 1998.

APPENDIX 5:
ALL–AGES RESOURCES

❖❖❖❖❖❖❖❖❖❖❖

Basho and the Fox. Myers, Tim. Marshall Cavendish, 2000.
> *Ambiguity, Antithesis, Aphorism, Imagery, Irony, Motif, Parallelism, Theme*

The Big Box. Morrison, Toni, with Slade Morrison. Hyperion, 1999.
> *Inference, Internal Rhyme, Irony, Oxymoron, Satire, Theme*

Big Jabe. Nolen, Jerdine. Lothrop, Lee & Shepard, 2000.
> *Allusion, Anachronism, Antithesis, Flashback, Flash-forward, Foreshadowing, Hyperbole, Imagery, Inference, Parallelism, Simile, Symbol, Understatement*

Black Cat. Myers, Christopher. Scholastic Press, 1999.
> *Alliteration, Imagery, Internal Rhyme, Metaphor, Simile*

Buttons. Cole, Brock. Farrar Straus Giroux, 2000.
> *Aphorism, Inference, Irony, Pun, Tone*

Click, Clack, Moo Cows That Type. Cronin, Doreen. Simon & Schuster. 2000.
> *Inference, Irony, Symbol*

Deep in the Jungle. Yaccarino, Dan. Anne Schwartz/Atheneum (Simon & Schuster), 2000.
> *Anachronism, Antihero, Antithesis, Black Humor, Foreshadowing, Irony, Motif, Parallelism, Poetic Justice, Pun, Tone*

Edna. Burleigh, Robert. Orchard Books, 2000.
> *Atmosphere, Foreshadowing, Imagery, Parallelism, Simile*

Fly, Eagle, Fly! Gregorowski, Christopher. McElderry (Simon & Schuster), 2000.
> *Analogy, Antithesis, Foreshadowing, Imagery, Motif, Parallelism*

Golem. Wisniewski, David. Clarion Books (Houghton Mifflin), 1996 (Caldecott—1997).
> *Analogy, Atmosphere,*

Foreshadowing, Imagery,
Inference, Irony, Motif, Paradox,
Simile

Henrietta. Mamet, David. Houghton
Mifflin, 1999.
Inference, Irony, Personification, Pun,
Satire, Serendipity, Tone

Henry Hikes to Fitchburg. Johnson, D.B.
Houghton Mifflin, 2000.
Allusion, Irony, Paradox, Theme,
Understatement

Hog-Eye. Meddaugh, Susan. Walter
Lorraine Books (Houghton Mifflin),
1995.
Allusion, Antithesis, Flashback,
Foreshadowing, Hyperbole,
Inference, Irony, Understatement

Hogula, Dread Pig of Night. Gralley, Jean.
Henry Holt, 1999.
Alliteration, Allusion, Antihero,
Aphorism, Cliché, Foreshadowing,
Inference, Irony, Poetic Justice,
Pun, Simile, Stereotype/Reverse
Stereotype, Understatement

Ling Cho and His Three Friends. Pacilio,
V.J. Farrar Straus Giroux, 2000.
Alliteration, Aphorism, Irony,
Paradox, Poetic Justice, Theme

The Memory String. Bunting, Eve. Clarion
Books (Houghton Mifflin), 2000.
Ambiguity, Antithesis, Aphorism,
Foreshadowing, Imagery,
Inference, Parallelism, Simile

Peace Crane. Hamanaka, Sheila. Morrow
Junior Books, 1995.
Allusion, Antithesis, Flash-Forward,
Imagery, Simile, Symbol

Pierre's Dream. Armstrong, Jennifer. Dial
(Penguin Putnam), 1999.
Antihero, Foreshadowing, Inference,
Irony, Theme

Red Flower Goes West. Turner, Ann.
Hyperion Books for Children, 1999.

Connotation, Inference, Metaphor,
Parallelism, Simile, Symbol

Rosie the Cool Cat. Wilkon, Piotr. Viking
(Penguin Books), 1989.
Antithesis, Foreshadowing, Inference,
Irony, Poetic Justice, Satire,
Stereotype/Reverse Stereotype,
Symbol

The Sign Painter. Say, Allen. Walter
Lorraine Books (Houghton Mifflin),
2000.
Ambiguity, Antithesis, Imagery,
Inference, Point of View, Theme,
Tone

So You Want to Be President? St. George,
Judith. Philomel (Penguin Putnam
Books for Young Readers), 2000
(Caldecott—2000).
Antithesis, Atmosphere, Caricature,
Parallelism, Tone

The Spirit of the Maasai Man. Berkeley,
Laura. Barefoot Books, 2000.
Imagery, Symbol, Theme, Tone

A Spoon for Every Bite. Hayes, Joe.
Orchard Books, 1996.
Ambiguity, Antihero, Antithesis,
Foreshadowing, Hyperbole, Motif,
Poetic Justice

The Stone Dancers. Martin, Nora.
Atheneum (Simon & Schuster), 1995.
Aphorism, Imagery, Inference, Irony,
Metaphor, Parallel Story, Simile

Swan in Love. Bunting, Eve. Atheneum
(Simon & Schuster), 2000.
Antithesis, Aphorism, Foreshadowing,
Imagery, Inference, Simile, Theme

The Sweetest Fig. Van Allsburg, Chris.
Houghton Mifflin, 1993.
Inference, Irony, Poetic Justice

The Table Where Rich People Sit. Baylor,
Byrd. Charles Scribner's Sons,
1994.
Antihero, Aphorism, Foreshadowing,
Irony, Paradox

Tough Cookie. Wisniewski, David. Lothrop, Lee & Shepard (William Morrow), 1999.
   Analogy, Parody, Pun, Satire, Simile, Stereotype/Reverse Stereotype, Theme

Voices in the Park. Browne, Anthony. DK Pub., 1998.
   Connotation, Foreshadowing, Inference, Point of View

Waiting to Sing. Kaplan, Howard. DK Ink, 2000.
   Allusion, Antithesis, Aphorism, Atmosphere, Foreshadowing,
   Imagery, Inference, Metaphor, Parallelism, Simile, Symbol

The Worry Stone. Dengler, Marianna. Rising Moon (Northland), 1996
   Antithesis, Flashback, Foreshadowing, Inference, Parallel Story, Parallelism

The Yellow Star: The Legend of King Christian X of Denmark. Deedy, Carmen Agra. Peachtree, 2000.
   Antithesis, Aphorism, Atmosphere, Foreshadowing, Inference, Irony, Paradox, Parallelism, Pun, Simile, Symbol, Theme

INDEX

❖❖❖❖❖❖❖❖❖❖❖

About the Author

SUSAN HALL is a journalist and government reporter in Tipton, Iowa. Previously, she was a school and public librarian working for 12 years primarily with grades K–8. Ms. Hall is now writing picture books, building from her experience with reference and resource works. She is also the author of volumes one and two of *Using Picture Storybooks to Teach Literary Devices* and *Using Picture Storybooks to Teach Character Education.*